Luther and His Opponents **ink** Against the Devil

Luther and His Opponents

ink

Against the Devil

Harry Loewen

WLU PRESS
WILFRID LAURIER
UNIVERSITY PRESS

Wilfrid Laurier University Press acknowledges the support of the Canada Council for the Arts for our publishing program. We acknowledge the financial support of the Government of Canada through the Canada Book Fund for our publishing activities.

 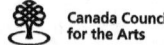

Library and Archives Canada Cataloguing in Publication

Loewen, Harry, 1930–, author
    Ink against the devil : Luther and his opponents / Harry Loewen.

Includes bibliographical references and index.
Issued in print and electronic formats.
ISBN 978-1-77112-135-4 (bound).—ISBN 978-1-77112-136-1 (pbk.).—
ISBN 978-1-77112-081-4 (pdf).—ISBN 978-1-77112-082-1 (epub)

    1. Luther, Martin, 1483–1546—Adversaries. 2. Reformation. I. Title.

BR334.2.L57 2015   270.6   C2015-900229-X
                                                                         C2015-900230-3

Cover design by Blakeley Words+Pictures. Front-cover image: *Portrait of Martin Luther* (1528), by Lucas Cranach the Elder (1472–1553). Text design by Lime Design Inc.

© 2015 Wilfrid Laurier University Press
Waterloo, Ontario, Canada
www.wlupress.wlu.ca

This book is printed on FSC® certified paper and is certified Ecologo. It contains post-consumer fibre, is processed chlorine free, and is manufactured using biogas energy.

Printed in Canada

Every reasonable effort has been made to acquire permission for copyright material used in this text, and to acknowledge all such indebtedness accurately. Any errors and omissions called to the publisher's attention will be corrected in future printings.

No part of this publication may be reproduced, stored in a retrieval system, or transmitted, in any form or by any means, without the prior written consent of the publisher or a licence from the Canadian Copyright Licensing Agency (Access Copyright). For an Access Copyright licence, visit http://www.accesscopyright.ca or call toll free to 1-800-893-5777.

This book is dedicated to **James Urry –** exemplary scholar, esteemed colleague, and close friend. Without his initial encouragement this book would never have been written.

And to son **Jeffery Francis Loewen –** whose literary and linguistic knowledge and skills helped to bring this book to a successful conclusion.

Contents

Foreword by Walter Klaassen xi

Preface xiii
My Earlier Luther Book † The Title † My Target Audience
A Word of Thanks

List of Abbreviations xix

i In Search of a Gracious God 1
Luther Not the First Reformer † To Find a Gracious God †
God's Grace Found † Luther's Theology

ii Luther's Early Red-Hot Pen 11
The Ninety-Five Theses † Major Reformation Writings †
The War of Pamphlets † Birth of Religious Fundamentalism

iii Dissenting Groups and Why They Opposed Luther 23
Great Variety of Radicals † Origins of the Radical Reformers †
Why They Left Luther

iv   **The Enemies Within:**
Luther and the Wittenberg Radicals 33
Karlstadt and Luther † The Zwickau Prophets †
The Augustinian Monks † Return from the Wartburg †
Order Restored † The Presence of Christ in Holy
Communion † Final Encounter with Karlstadt

v   **"The Soft-Living Flesh of Wittenberg":**
Luther's Struggle and the Revolutionaries 53
Luther on Authority Prior to 1525 † The Common Man
and Authority † Thomas Müntzer † Differences Between
Müntzer and Luther † Müntzer's Radicalism

vi   **"I Commanded Them to be Killed":**
Luther and the Peasants 71
Luther's Responsibility for the Peasants' War † The Twelve
Articles † Luther Against the Peasants † Concerning the
Harsh Booklet † Concluding Comments † Revolution of
the Common Man † Non-Peasant Participants † A Note
on Luther and Capitalism

vii   **Two Riders of the Human Will:**
Luther Opposes Erasmus and Humanism 89
Humanists and the Reformation † Luther and Erasmus †
Erasmus and Pope Adrian VI † Erasmus on Free Will †
Luther on the Bondage of the Will † A Bitter Erasmus †
Stalemate? † A Note on Anabaptists and Free Will

viii   **Luther Knew and Opposed the Evangelical Anabaptists** 113
Origin and Spread of Anabaptism † Müntzer and the
Swiss Brethren † Doctrine or Ethics? † Conclusion

ix **"I Told You So":**
Luther and the Anabaptist Kingdom in Münster 149
"I told you so!" † Kingdom of Münster Begins †
The Prophets Arrive † Jan van Leyden and Polygamy †
Luther and the Münsterites † Was Luther Correct? †
Anabaptism and Münsterism † Menno Simons and Münster

x **Much Ado about Spirit and Matter:**
Luther and the Spiritualists 165
Inner and Outer Word † Hans Denck † Luther on Hans
Denck † Caspar von Schwenckfeld † Much Ado about
Spirit and Matter † Luther and the Word of God †
Schwenckfeld and the Word of God † Concluding
Comments

xi **Three in One or One in Three?**
Luther Opposes the Rationalists 185
The Spirits Luther Had Called Up † Law and Gospel †
Concerning the Trinity † Anti-Trinitarians †
Michael Servetus

xii **To Believe What You Like?**
Luther and His Opponents on Tolerance and Religious Liberty 201
Luther's Early Views on Tolerance † Ecclesiastical Visitations †
What to Do with Heretics † Sedition and Blasphemy †
Luther's Changed View † Anabaptists on Tolerance †
Tolerance Problematical during the Reformation † Tolerance
among Some Spiritualists † A Note on Persecution †
Conclusion

xiii "Drive Them Out of the Land!"
Luther on the Jews 225
A Personal Experience † The Judensau of Wittenberg †

xiv **The Cross and the Crescent: Luther Opposes the Turks and Islam** 243
The Turkish Threat † Wars Against the Turks † How to Wage War Against the Turks † Mohammedan Beliefs † The Emperor Must Lead the War † Süleyman the Magnificent † War Sermon Against the Turks † Concluding Observations

xv "An Institution of the Devil!"
Luther's Last Battle Against the Papacy 261
Against Hanswurst † The Politics of Hanswurst † Background for *Against the Papacy* † Content of *Against the Papacy* † Three Questions about the Papacy † A Note on Catholic Writers Against Luther

xvi **Conclusion and Evaluation** 279
Radical Reformers Vindicated † The Other Side † Luther's Tragedy † Rights and Wrongs † Other Opponents

Epilogue 293
Selected Bibliography 299
Index 317

Foreword

Forty years ago I wrote the foreword to the original edition of this book. I never dreamed that I would be asked to do it also for this second edition. I do it again with pleasure because the author is a long-time friend and also because, in some important respects, this is a new book.

This version is almost triple the size of the original; a lot has been added to the story and its interpretation. Books are normally revised to strengthen the author's thesis by presenting new supportive research. Although it could have been, this was not Professor Loewen's intention. He presents us with an enlargement of his original work, not based on the extensive research of forty years done by others on all of the dramatis personae of the Reformation era, but rather by adding more actors to the plot. Martin Luther threw ink pots not only at Anabaptists, peasant revolutionaries, and unaffiliated spiritualists. The author now gives quite as much attention to Luther's other targets, to the prince of humanists, Erasmus, who could not abide Luther's predestinarian theology, to the Jews by whom he felt betrayed, to the Muslim Turks who militarily threatened Europe, and to the papal church, always Luther's number one nemesis, and chief threat to his theology of salvation by grace through faith. The new title of this book includes all of them, and considerably enlarges the context and engagement of Martin Luther with his critical contemporaries. For, of course, we meet not only the great reformer and his assessment of his opponents, but also the measured judgment of Professor Loewen as he gives the reader access to them from their own recorded responses.

One of the salient features of this edition is the author's skilful and extensive summary of Luther's writings against Erasmus and the papal church. They illuminate the main pillars of Luther's theology and its consistency throughout as he responded to and attacked his opponents. The author's dismay at the vulgar viciousness of Luther's attacks on the Jews echoes that of the translators of his works. The author portrays an old man no longer physically well, and feeling betrayed not only by the Jews and others of his opponents, but perhaps also by his early confidence that his principle of *sola scriptura*, coupled with the light of the one Holy Spirit, would lead to a truly unified church.

Professor Loewen's passion for greater mutual understanding among Christians is evident throughout. This is a book for the church. He tells us that its aim is to contribute to the need for "better ecumenicity and Christian charity." The book will be especially useful for discerning Christian readers and for students in Christian schools and colleges who will learn here about the causes of the Christian divisions imposed on them by past controversies. They will also be drawn into the author's own urging toward a Christian and human community united by its shared commitment to Christ, the Head of the Church.

Walter Klaassen

‖ Preface

MY EARLIER LUTHER BOOK

This book is an expanded version of my earlier book, *Luther and the Radicals: Another Look at Some Aspects of the Struggle Between Luther and the Radical Reformers* (WLU Press, 1974). The book was originally my MA thesis, completed and accepted in 1961 by the Department of History of the University of Manitoba under the guidance of the late Professor T. Oleson. As a Mennonite, it was my pleasure to work with Professor Oleson, who had converted from Lutheranism to Roman Catholicism. While deeply committed to the Catholic faith, he remained sympathetically critical of both traditions. From him, among others, I learned to view all religions, including the Catholic, Lutheran, Mennonite, and others, both sympathetically and critically.

Reviews of my book from non-Mennonite critics at the time were more positive than from Mennonite reviewers. When I first approached the subject in the early 1960s, I felt that much of the literature coming from Mennonite academics was critical toward the magisterial reformers, with good reason. The sixteenth-century reformers, including Luther, not only damned the so-called "left wing of the Reformation," but also agreed with, and often encouraged, the persecution of the dissident groups. I felt, however, that as scholars we needed to be fair in understanding the positions of both Luther and those who dissented from him. At the time I increasingly felt that the differences between the two positions were often more differences in *emphasis* rather than *substance*. In time, however, especially as I taught Reformation issues at the University of Winnipeg, I saw more and more that from the standpoint of the two groups at the time, the struggle between them was over what they believed to be fundamental beliefs rather than mere emphases in doctrine and practice. How else are we to understand Luther's eventual persecution of the dissident groups on the one hand, and the radical groups' acceptance of suffering and even death for what they believed, on the other? The present book reflects my modified understanding of Luther and his opponents.

This expanded version includes many of the Luther and Reformation studies published after my first book appeared. I have added several new chapters in which I deal with additional opponents of Luther, not just the reformer's struggle with the radicals, as in my earlier book. I have also chosen a different title, making this publication virtually a new book. What is entirely new are chapters on Luther and Erasmus, Luther and the Jews, Luther's writings against the Turks, and a chapter on Luther's final condemnation of the papacy.

THE TITLE

A word about the title, *Luther and His Opponents: Ink Against the Devil*, is no doubt in order. For Luther and his adversaries, religious beliefs were of the utmost importance, so much so that believers were often willing to fight and die for them. Some people in the twenty-first century might ask what the fuss was all about. But as this book assumes, the religious issues of the Reformation period were not only important to many people in those "dark ages," they continue to be of importance to many people today, especially religious believers.

At the centre of this clash stands Martin Luther who, as legend has it, threw an inkwell at the devil when this adversary sought to hinder Luther in his work. That story is, of course, a myth, but the stories about Luther's struggle with his opponents were all too real. These conflicts were fought with spoken and written words by the combatants, hence *Ink Against the Devil* seems appropriate. After Gutenberg's invention of printing with movable type half a century earlier, the pen truly became mightier than the sword. And Luther was a master with the pen, his writing metaphorically killing his many opponents with ink. Many against whom Luther used his pen had to die for what they believed. Luther's opponents in turn defended themselves against the reformer, but only with ink, not with lethal weapons.

Among Luther's first opponents were, of course, the Roman Catholic Church in general and the popes in particular. Against these opponents the reformer struggled from the time he left the monastery until the end of his life. Catholicism and the papacy appear in every chapter of this book, but there is a chapter at the end that deals with the old and angry Luther hurling invective specifically at his old foes. Among Luther's Protestant opponents were radicals who dissented from the reformer, especially Karlstadt, Müntzer, and others who were attracted to Wittenberg, the centre of the Reformation. Then there were the revolutionary and peaceful Anabaptists, some spiritualists, rationalists, nominalists, anti-Trinitarians, and Renaissance humanists like Erasmus. Non-Christians, such as the Jews and Turks, Luther also opposed and fought because he considered them dangerous to Christianity in general and the Reformation in paticular.

Because the general reader may not know the content of Luther's writings against his non-Christian opponents well, I provide summaries of the texts of these writings, followed by brief analyses. The so-called magisterial or mainline reformers such as Zwingli, Calvin, the Reformed and later the Anglicans, are not treated as Luther's opponents in this book. Although they and Luther profoundly disagreed on some theological issues, they saw each other as fellow reformers. Luther eventually toned down his rhetoric toward the radical reformers, but his writings against the papacy culminated in *Against the Roman Papacy, an Institution of the Devil* (1545) just a year before the reformer's death.

MY TARGET AUDIENCE

❛ **In my years of teaching** in colleges and universities and working in the Mennonite churches, I found that many students and members of the church were woefully ignorant of church history, including the Reformation period. I thus wrote this book primarily for interested general readers and students who still take their religious faith and theology seriously, but who at the same time do not know much about them. It is my hope that the issues that were raised in the sixteenth century might contribute not only to a better understanding of them, but also to a renewed interest in, acceptance of, and tolerance toward different beliefs and religious practices. After all, many faith issues that were stumbling blocks in the sixteenth century are no longer so in today's society. As the epilogue shows, Lutherans and the descendants of former opponents are beginning to come together to repent for what they did to each other centuries ago and to ask for forgiveness. Lutherans are also acknowledging that the reformer was wrong and sinned grievously in writing against the Jews, thus contributing to the anti-Semitism of later centuries and to the Holocaust during the Second World War. It is my hope that this book will contribute to readers' greater interest in Reformation issues and a need for better ecumenism and Christian charity.

A WORD OF THANKS

I take pleasure in acknowledging several colleagues who encouraged and helped me as this book progressed. It was my friend and colleague James Urry of New Zealand, an anthropologist and historian of Mennonite studies, who first strongly suggested that my earlier book *Luther and the Radicals* should be revised. James also kept sending me valuable source materials for the new project. I am thus honoured to dedicate this book to him.

In October of 2011 my wife and I travelled again to Germany, and it was there that I finally decided to tackle the new project. While in Germany I read as much as I possibly could of the new materials dealing with Luther and Reformation issues. I also visited Lutherstadt-Wittenberg again and saw how the city was beginning to prepare for the 500th anniversary of the Protestant Reformation (1517–2017). A year before, in 2010, Lutherans and Mennonites had met formally in Stuttgart, Germany, agreeing to forgive each other and become reconciled for the pain the two bodies had inflicted on each other centuries earlier. All this made me feel more and more positive about revising and expanding my earlier book, believing that there might now be more interest by both Lutherans and Mennonites, among others, in the subject. While travelling to Germany repeatedly, my wife and I always found comfortable accommodation in the residences of the University of Mannheim. The staff of the public library of Mannheim, where I spent much time doing my research and reading, did all they could to assist me.

My colleague and friend for many years, Walter Klaassen, now living in active retirememt in Saskatoon, Saskatchewan, felt that the new book should not be primarily for Reformation scholars, but for "people in the church," as he put it. After I had completed the first draft, Professor Klaassen read it and then wrote: "It is impressive in its breadth. It is the only work I know that deals with Luther and most of his [opponents] and the specific issues with each one of them." Professor James M. Stayer of Queen's University at Kingston, Ontario, also read the first draft and offered valuable suggestions. While I have gained much from my colleagues' insights, including those of the anonymous readers for Wilfrid Laurier University Press, I am wholly responsible for the book's content, interpretation, and writing style – and of course the mistakes readers will no doubt discover.

Members of my family and many of my personal friends have also been most encouraging in my work. They often had to listen to me talk, at times endlessly, about the issues I was working on. They also supplied me with reading materials they thought I should know about. Sons Harry, Charles, and Jeffrey and their families gave me much moral and practical support during the last stages of my working on the book. Their support was especially appreciated during my months-long convalescence in hospital and at home. They also kept me informed about new books and trends in literature and philosophy. It was through Harry and Jeffrey that I got to know the Marxist philosopher Slavoj Žižek, who, though an atheist, writes about religious issues, including Luther and his influence on modern thinking. And my wife, Gertrude, who often had to listen patiently to my Reformation stories, was my first sounding board about what I was thinking, reading, and writing. Without her constant support and encouragement this book would not have seen the light of day. John Braun of Kelowna, British Columbia, a Christian layman and friend, gave me as a gift his ten-volume edition of *Luthers Werke* (Berlin 1905). This Luther edition was a constant companion on my desk.

Finally, I am most grateful to Wilfrid Laurier University Press and its anonymous readers for accepting my manuscript for publication. I am especially grateful to Lisa Quinn, the Press's acquisitions editor, who ably guided the manuscript through its many stages to its eventual publication. To all I express my heartfelt thanks.

I use the following tools of the trade: as a concession to the general reader I have dispensed with content footnotes or endnotes. The short reference notes are included within the text in brackets. My references to writers are indicated by the sources in which I found them, including their translations into English, except when, on occasion, I have translated them myself. Contrary to the practice of offsetting longer quotations, I have kept all quotations within quotation marks within the text. This retains the flow of the story, making the reader less tempted to skip longer quotations. It is my hope that interested readers will benefit from the extensive bibliography of primary and secondary sources at the end of the book.

Harry Loewen

List of Abbreviations

CE	*The Catholic Encyclopedia.* Ed. by Charles G. Herbermann et al. 15 vols. New York, 1907–1912.
CCL	*The Cambridge Companion to Martin Luther.* Edited by Donald K. McKim. Cambridge University Press, 2003.
CS	*Corpus Schwenckfeldianorum.* 19 vols. Leipzig and Pennsburg, PA, 1907–1961.
EA	*Martin Luthers Sämmtliche Werke.* 65 vols. Erlangen und Frankfurt a.M., 1826–1855.
JMS	*Journal of Mennonite Studies.* Published by the Chair in Mennonite Studies, Winnipeg, Canada 1983–.
LH	*Luther Handbuch.* Albrecht Beutel (Hg.). 2. Auflage. Tübingen: Mohr Siebeck, 2010.
Werke	*Luthers Werke.* 10 Bände. Berlin 1905. (C.A. Schwetschke und Sohn, dritte Auflage. Auslieferung für Amerika: Wartburg Pub. House, Chicago).
LW	*Luther's Works.* Published by Concordia Publishing House and Fortress Press, 1956–.

ME	*The Mennonite Encyclopedia.* 5 vols. Scottdale, PA: Mennonite Publishing House, 1955, 1990.
MQR	*Mennonite Quarterly Review.* Goshen, Indiana.
SLA	*Martin Luthers Sämmtliche Schriften.* 23 vols. St. Louis, MO, 1880–1910.
WA	*Martin Luthers Werke.* Kritische Gesammtausgabe. Weimar, 1883–1948.
WA, Br.	*Martin Luthers Werke.* Briefwechsel. Weimar, 1930–1948.
WA, DB	*Martin Luthers Werke.* Die Deutsche Bibel. Weimar, 1906–1961.
WA, Tr.	*Martin Luthers Werke.* Tischreden. Weimar, 1912–1921.

In Search of a Gracious God

LUTHER NOT THE FIRST REFORMER

When Martin Luther (1483–1546) decided to abandon his legal studies at the University of Erfurt in 1505 and instead become a monk against the wishes of his father, he became, without intending it, the father of the Protestant Reformation. His experience of the grace of God led him to a distinct theology all his own, namely that of justification by faith and the grace of God alone. His conversion and resulting theology ultimately took him out of the Roman Catholic Church. Moreover, Luther's new insights soon led him to his early writings, which profoundly influenced other individuals and groups, who also experienced a need for a deeper spirituality and a reformation of the old church. Ironically, the individuals who were at first drawn to the reformer and became his close supporters and, in some cases, associates, soon not only dissented from the Catholic Church, but also from Luther. Remaining true to his newly experienced theology, Luther found it necessary, rightly or wrongly, to oppose those who dissented from him and in time came to oppose him. The issues between

Luther and his opponents often caused them to be locked in a bitter struggle. It has only been recently, as late as the twentieth and twenty-first centuries, that the bitter struggle between Luther and his opponents has seen some healing and reconciliation among their descendants.

There is still the question of whether Luther's break with the Roman Church and the innovations and changes in church and society that followed should be seen as a "reformation" or a "revolution." Protestants generally call it a "reformation," and it was that. For Catholics, however, the breakup of the centuries-old church was both violent and revolutionary. There seems little doubt that after 1500 the old European institutions, especially the social and religious institutions, were changing, often radically, heralding the end of the medieval age and the beginning of modern times. In the end, many aspects of the old church were both reformed and transformed, but the way the changes were brought about was radical and revolutionary. And, as happens in most revolutions, there was widespread destruction, even bloodshed. Luther's radical break with Rome, the radical reformers' separating of church and state, Thomas Müntzer's revolutionary program, the peasants' demands and their revolts against the feudal system, and the Anabaptists' establishment of a kingdom in Münster, however short-lived – all this was most radical and revolutionary. Between 1500 and 1648, with the Peace of Westphalia which ended the Thirty Years' War, Europe in general and Germany in particular became a divided and torn world.

Luther may have been the occasion or the fuse that ignited this revolution in sixteenth-century Germany, but he was not the one who caused it. We need not go into detail about the efforts at reform in earlier centuries. Suffice it to say that reformers and reform movements existed long before Luther. The Waldensians in twelfth-century France were among the first to demand reform in the doctrines and life of Roman Catholicism. They came close to believing and practising what later Anabaptists believed. In England John Wycliffe (ca. 1328–ca.1384), a severe critic of the church's dogma and practices was dismissed from the University of Oxford in 1381 because of his criticism, but his followers, the so-called Lollards, continued with their demands for reform. The Brothers of the Common Life, a religious community in the Netherlands, was established in the late fourteenth century to teach and model Christian living. As a young student, Luther studied with this community. Jan Hus (ca. 1370–1415), a follower of Wycliffe's ideas and concerns, was a priest and professor at the

University of Prague in what is now the Czech Republic. He was pronounced a heretic at the Council of Constance and burned at the stake in 1415. When Martin Luther discovered his writings, he recognized Hus as a fellow reformer a hundred years before him. In fact, Catholic critics were quick to connect Luther's name with that of Hus, even suggesting that he should share the fate of the Czech reformer. Luther thus stood in a long tradition of individuals and groups that saw a need for a thorough reformation of the Roman Catholic Church "in head and members," that is, from top to bottom.

TO FIND A GRACIOUS GOD

Some details of the story of how Luther decided to enter a monastery may be legendary, but the core of the story is true. On July 2, 1505, while on his way back home from the University of Erfurt, where he had recently completed a master's degree and started his law studies, Luther was caught in a violent thunderstorm and thrown to the ground by the air pressure it created. Terrified, Luther cried out "Saint Anne help! I will become a monk!" Luther's decision to abandon his law studies and become a monk was no doubt earth-shattering for the young student. While those who knew him, including his father, found his decision to enter a monastery sudden and unexpected Luther would have been thinking about it for some time before this experience. As his early life in the monastery was to show, the young man was primarily concerned not about the moral or theological state of his church – which came later – but about his soul (Kittelson 261).

Many men before Luther had entered the monastery to make satisfaction for sin, to fulfill a vow, or to dedicate themselves to the love and service of God. Many monks and nuns before Luther had struggled through the agonies of the soul, but through the media of prayer, the sacraments, or even mysticism, they had been able to resolve their spiritual problems. Luther, for some reason, failed to find peace. As Heinrich Boehmer states: "The one thing ... that distinguishes Luther from the great mass of ascetics is simply the fact, that all the means of quieting such doubts provided for by the old monastic teachers not only failed but rather had a completely opposite effect; that is, they merely increased his inner distress and anxiety" (Boehmer 87).

In his commentary on Galatians in 1531, Luther reflected on his years in the monastery. While devoting himself to fasting, vigils, prayers, attending masses, and other disciplines, he constantly inspired mistrust, doubt, fear, and hatred. For Luther, Christ was not the gracious and forgiving Saviour as experienced by many other seekers, but a fearful judge, seen as sitting on a rainbow (as Christ was often pictured) ready to execute judgment upon the wicked. Luther tells us he feared him more than the devil. He could not call upon his name, he wrote in 1537, nor could he even bear to hear his name mentioned (WA 40, 275).

What might have caused Luther's fear and sense of unworthiness? The Brothers of the Common Life, with whom Luther had studied in Magdeburg (1497–98), might have intensified his belief in the sinfulness of human nature; St. Augustine's doctrine of human nature and predestination may have added to his feelings of despondency; and his unsuccessful attempts to find peace of soul may have confirmed his belief in the bondage of the will, namely, that he could do absolutely nothing to attain salvation and receive forgiveness of his sins (Mueller 156–7). Some have also suggested that the plague that raged in Erfurt around 1505 may have instilled the fear of death in the young Luther (Marius 44).

Luther's deep depression in the monastery and in his first years in Wittenberg was also connected with his long struggle to find faith and a gracious God, a struggle that included a profound sense of sinfulness and fear of God's wrath (Steinmetz 7–11). The German word *Anfechtungen* (severe inner conflict) was used by Luther to describe his sense of spiritual attacks and trials, despair, terror, and religious crisis that he continued to experience not only in the monastery, but also periodically throughout his life. Sometimes when he was thinking about Christ the judge, or when he first performed the Mass and thus came into the direct presence of Christ, or even when he viewed a crucifix – on many such occasions he would sometimes recoil in terror, for at such times he saw and heard an angry judge (LW 54, 19–20).

Another important cause, perhaps *the* cause, of Luther's *Anfechtungen*, was his meditations on God's eternal election. With St. Augustine he came to believe that God predestines some for salvation and some for damnation, but humans do not know what they have been predestined for because that lies in God's hidden will. "The *Anfechtungen* of being abandoned by God," as Martin Brecht comments, "was fundamentally the problem of God's election or reprobation" (Brecht 1, 80). Brecht further states that Luther's *Anfechtungen* "was not a psychic affliction, but the living God confronting him. A medical diagnosis cannot explain all this, for it is evident that, despite all these trials, Luther continued to work steadfastly." Indeed, Luther's capacity for work and the output of pamphlets and volume after volume throughout his life is amazing, to say the least.

GOD'S GRACE FOUND

It was Luther's spiritual superior and confessor, the mystically inclined Vicar-General Johann von Staupitz (ca. 1460–1524) who pointed the struggling young man to the love of God in Christ. Later in life Luther gave Staupitz the credit for helping him through his trying years in the monastery. Staupitz not only pulled Luther away from his preoccupation with an angry and judging Christ, but also showed him how to overcome his terrors over predestination. In addition, Staupitz pointed the struggling Luther to the suffering and forsaken Christ on the cross, and even suggested that his *Anfechtungen* was God's way of preparing him for great and important work for the church. Thus Luther's experience of separation from God, like Christ's on the cross, was actually evidence, according to Staupitz, that he was especially near to God and destined to accomplish much good in God's kingdom (Brecht 1, 80).

Luther's breakthrough and his new understanding and experience of the grace of God occurred during his so-called "tower experience" when he lectured at the University of Wittenberg on the books of the Bible. But this breakthrough came only gradually. The idea of God's righteousness and human sinfulness continued to cause Luther much anxiety; in view of God's holiness and his own sinfulness Luther continued to feel condemned by a righteous God – until he was struck by such biblical passages as Romans 1:17 and Habakkuk 2:4, where he read that "the just shall live by his faith" and not by pleasing God by performing good works. He had read these passages before, but now they took on a new meaning for him. He concluded from these biblical verses that grace and forgiveness are only to be derived from faith. All human attempts to find peace of mind and soul are thus in vain. It is God alone who attributes divine righteousness to sinful men and women without any human participation, and does so only on account of Christ's suffering and death for humankind. For the first time in his life this devout monk saw God and himself in a new light and with new eyes. He had in fact become a "new creation" as the New Testament (2 Cor. 5:17) puts it.

It would be incorrect to say that with his experience in the monastery Luther had discovered the concept of grace as opposed to the "law" of the Roman Church. Luther's experience was not altogether new, or something that Catholicism did not know. In fact, the Catholic Church had a highly developed doctrine of grace, but the difference between Catholicism and Luther's experience was that while the Church had the power to bring down the grace of God through the channels of the sacraments, the reformer experienced God's grace directly, without, as he put it, "the works of man." It is thus a Christ-centred experience that lies at the basis of Luther's theology of the cross and God's working in human hearts. In obtaining grace and forgiveness, Luther's experience excluded all human effort, or "good works," as he put it. Luther's later struggle with the various radicals, the papacy, the Anabaptists, Erasmus, and other opponents, all of whom allowed at least some measure of human participation in human redemption, must be understood from Luther's intense experience and his resulting theology.

Luther's sense of having grasped the full truth about the redemption of human beings by God's grace alone was so strong that there was no doubt in his mind that it was not only biblical, but that it was the heart of the gospel. Whoever did not accept this doctrine of "justification by faith alone" could not be saved. In a letter of December 21, 1525, to the Catholic Duke George of Saxony, Luther wrote that no one, including the hostile duke, would succeed in quenching *his*, Luther's, gospel. His gospel would accomplish its divine work in the hearts of men and women, for the gospel was not his own but God's. In 1530 Luther wrote to Chancellor Gregory Brück of the Electorate of Saxony that his cause was God's cause, and that God could never forget those who had made God's cause their own. In view of Luther's experience of *sola fide* (by faith alone) it is thus not surprising that he would never tolerate any person or group that deviated from his central theology.

Luther's dramatic conversion not only emphasized the biblical doctrine of justification by faith alone, it was also coupled with another principle, namely that of *sola scriptura* (by Scriptures only). Since Luther had found the answer to his spiritual anguish in the Bible, it followed that the Scriptures became his absolute authority in matters of faith and morals. In interpreting the Bible Luther's experience of justification by faith held a central position. In essence this meant that a Christian had the right to interpret the Word of God according to his or her personal understanding of it. For Luther the individual conscience, enlightened by the Holy Spirit, thus became, in addition to the Bible, a Christian's highest court of appeal. In 1521, for example, Luther pronounced at the Diet of Worms that to act against conscience is not allowed. According to him, neither bishop nor pope, nor anyone else, had the right to prescribe or impose a single syllable to any Christian. For Luther, conscience was freed from obedience to anyone or anything that was contrary to God's Word.

It is important to stress, however, that for Luther only a conscience held captive and enlightened by God's Word can be an infallible guide in the life of a believer. The alternative to the conscience being "imprisoned by God's Word," is, as Heiko Oberman writes, the conscience "imprisoned by the Devil." And if it is the devil that is in possession of one's conscience, this enemy of the soul accuses and plagues the Christian through his conscience and leaves him no peace. According to Luther, the devil is thus a *Magister conscientiae,* the master of conscience. As Oberman puts it, quoting Luther, "conscience is the natural kingdom of the Devil. He attacks us ceaselessly, not only from without [by our external enemies] but also from within – via the conscience" (Oberman, *The Reformation* 65).

In emphasizing the importance of conscience Luther of course lay himself open to the charge that he and his followers interpreted the Bible subjectively, that is, according to personal experiences and individuals' points of view. Luther, however, was convinced that he interpreted Scripture by the Holy Spirit and according to the plain sense of the Word of God. He emphasized time and again that he had no wish to be known as a man more learned or pious than others. He wished Scriptures to be sovereign and not interpreted according to his own mind or the mind of another, but by itself and its own spirit (Zeeden 5). Luther's quarrel with the Catholic Church was that it did not interpret the Bible according to what its plain sense was; and the plain sense of Scriptures, according to Luther, was its teaching about the inadequacy of human beings before a sovereign God and their salvation through the sacrificial suffering and death of Christ for humankind. This right of interpretation of Scriptures Luther granted at first to all other Christian believers as well, because he believed that all Christians of good will would of necessity arrive at his own interpretation of the Bible. In this belief, as time would tell, Luther was mistaken. And this mistake would lead to much misunderstanding and strife in the Lutheran camp and beyond.

LUTHER'S THEOLOGY

⁋ **Luther's principles** of *sola fide* and *sola scriptura* led without any premeditation on the reformer's part to all his subsequent activity as a churchman and reformer. Whoever – be they individuals, authorities, or groups – contradicted his theological principles, Luther did not doubt for a moment that he was right and that all his opponents were wrong. For him the doctrine of justification by faith alone (*Rechtfertigung durch den Glauben*) was, to the end of his life, the sum total and substance of the gospel, the heart of Christian theology, the central truth of the Christian faith, and the article of the standing or falling church. For Luther, only those who understood and taught the article of justification by faith alone correctly were considered true theologians. In his lectures on Galatians in 1531, Luther pointed out that if the article of justification is lost all Christian doctrine is lost at the same time. Those who do not hold to this important theological article are, according to Luther, Jews, Turks, papists, or heretics. Before his table guests Luther said: "Dear gentlemen, let us hold fast to and love the article concerning justification and salvation, for if we lose it, we cannot win the battle and be victorious." According to Luther, the *Schwaermer*, as he called some of his enthusiastic opponents, had totally missed this article of faith (Werke 8, 307).

Luther had not learned or grasped his theology all at once, he tells us, but had searched for it in the Bible over time through hard work and most painful *Anfechtungen* (inner trials) in the monastery. Like St. Paul who had a "thorn in his flesh" (2. Cor. 12:7) and whom the devil beat with fists, so Luther too "had the pope, the universities, and many learned men through whom the devil hung around his neck and plagued him." This drove Luther to study the Bible intensely and thus he came to understand it. "If we do not have such a devil," Luther said, "we are just speculative theologians" who try to understand with our reason only. Scriptures must be read and reflected upon with prayer and struggle, and then acted upon (Werke 8, 203). Luther tells us that he knew many monks who never read the Bible. Even his colleague Karlstadt, Luther said in his Table Talks, became a doctor "without ever having seen a Bible," and the Archbishop of Mainz at the Diet of Augsburg, 1530, was seen looking into the Bible, upon which he was asked what he was doing "with that book." He answered, "I don't know what kind of a book this is, because everything in it is against us!" (Werke, 208, 112–13, 235). Such stories must have amused Luther's table companions.

Luther's sense of having grasped the heart of biblical theology was so strong that this doctrine became the standard by which he evaluated and judged all the biblical books and epistles. Some critics have charged that Luther, with some justification, deliberately carried a "protestant" spirit into his German translation of the Bible. For example, Luther inserted the word *allein* (alone or only) in Romans 3:28 in spite of all the objections by his learned colleagues. He did not regard as fully inspired those books of the New Testament that seemed to contradict or weaken the doctrine of justification by faith alone. The epistles of Hebrews, James, Jude, and Revelation belonged to this group. The Epistle of James, which seemed to stress the greater importance of "works" over "faith," was a particular stumbling block for the reformer. He called it "an epistle of straw" (WA, DB, 6, 10), meaning that it was worthless; he even wished to exclude it from the New Testament canon. He went so far as to say, perhaps in jest, that some day he would use the Epistle of James to heat his stove! In his "Preface to the Epistle of James" Luther gives reasons for not wishing to include this book in the biblical canon: it directs opposition to St. Paul and all the other books of the New Testament; and it declares that Abraham was justified by his works when he offered up his son (LW, 35, 395–7). Not once, Luther states, does James give Christians any instruction or reminder about the passion of Christ, the resurrection, or the spirit of Christ. For Luther it was impossible to reconcile St. Paul (who emphasizes the doctrine of faith) with St. James, who advocates works in addition to faith. If someone could reconcile the two for him, Luther stated before his table companions, the reformer would consent to being called a fool (Werke 8, 193). Ironically, it was Luther's senior colleague and one of the first supporters of his reformation, Andreas Bodenstein von Karlstadt, who was strongly attracted to the ethics of the epistle of St. James. Karlstadt loved the

Epistle of James because it combined faith and works – something that would later contribute to his falling out with the reformer.

Luther's spiritual difficulties, his *Anfechtungen*, did not end with his "tower experience" at the university, but continued throughout his life, especially at times when he was ill. He often saw his *Anfechtungen* as trials and temptations that came from the devil. In his Table Talks he often spoke about his doubts regarding his work as a reformer (Werke 8, 260–9). He often asked himself: What if my teaching and preaching were all a mistake and I through my work have destroyed so much and that I am the one who is responsible for the damnation of countless souls? To counter such trials and doubts, Luther convinced himself, often with the help of friends, that God had especially called him to his reformation work, that he was the only one equipped to carry it through, and that his doubts came from the devil, who did not want the reformation to succeed. And, Luther told his table guests, often a good meal and a strong drink before bedtime also helped to drive away the devil and the *Anfechtungen*!

According to Luther, the reality and power of the devil must not be underestimated. It may well be, according to Oberman, that it was Luther who actually "discovered" Satan in the real sense of the word. When the reformer was plagued by thoughts of inadequacy, failure, sinfulness, and profound doubts about a loving God, he assumed that the devil was behind it and used his conscience to torment himself. Ironically, this knowledge of the devil's presence assured Luther that he was loved and forgiven by God, for the devil never torments the godless who belong to him already, but only those who have faith in God and seek to do his will (Oberman, *The Reformation* 65–6).

Luther's Early Red-Hot Pen

THE NINETY-FIVE THESES

In popular **Protestant thinking,** October 31, 1517, is considered the date when the Augustinian monk Luther posted or nailed his *Ninety-Five Theses* or propositions to the door of the Castle Church in Wittenberg, thus giving expression to his spiritual concerns and his new-found theology (Werke 1, 97–108). Luther himself never mentioned that he *nailed* the *Ninety-Five Theses* on this date to the Castle Church. It was one hundred years later, in 1617, that Protestants wished to demonstrate to the world the dramatic and symbolic significance of Luther's heroic act by showing his anger against the church's preaching of indulgences. October 31, 1517, thus became the official beginning of the Protestant Reformation. In writing his *Theses* and sending the Archbishop of Mainz a copy, Luther did not see himself as a reformer of the church, but simply as a concerned churchman and theologian. It is significant that the *Theses* were written in Latin. They were not intended for the general public but for theological colleagues for debate and discussion.

The occasion for Luther's concerned and angry pen, giving vent to what was on his heart and mind, was the sale of indulgences authorized by Pope Leo X and the Archbishop Albert of Mainz to raise funds for the building of St. Peter's Basilica in Rome and other expenses. An indulgence, according to Catholic teaching, was the full or partial remission of temporal punishment, "due for sins which have already been forgiven." An indulgence was granted after the sinner had confessed his or her sins and received absolution. The Catholic Church believed that indulgences draw on the "Treasury of Merit" accumulated by Christ's meritorious sacrifice on the cross and the many meritorious works of the saints. A sinner thus draws on and benefits from the merits of Christ and the good works of saints. For Luther the sale of indulgences was open to greed and other abuses, and, more important, they substituted "good works" and other human efforts for the grace of God through Christ's death on the cross.

What was generally not known at the time of Luther's publication of his *Theses* was that a portion of the funds from the sale of indulgences was assigned to the very young Archbishop of Mainz (only 17 years old) to repay the money he had borrowed from the Fugger bankers in Augsburg to procure the lucrative archbishopric. Luther's prince, the Elector Frederick the Wise (1463–1525), did not allow Johannes Tetzel, the highly successful preacher of indulgences, to come into his territory, but people from around Wittenberg went across the nearby border to purchase indulgences, returning with the satisfaction that their sins and those of their loved ones had been forgiven and that now they did not need to repent or give any other satisfaction for their sins.

Luther, who was not only concerned about the salvation of his own soul but also for the souls of his church members, could not sit idly by without protesting against such blatant abuse. He wrote a letter of concern to the Archbishop of Mainz and included a copy of his *Ninety-Five Theses*. While at first Luther had no intention of attacking the church, the tone of his writing contained an undercurrent of angry challenge in several of the propositions. Thesis 86, for example, asks: "Why does the pope, whose wealth today is greater than the wealth of the richest money princes, not build the basilica of Saint Peter with his own money instead of with the money of poor believers?" (Werke 1, 107–8). Luther also objected to a statement attributed to Johann Tetzel, the zealous indulgence salesman: "As soon as the coin in the coffer rings, the soul from purgatory springs." Luther, on the other hand, insisted that since forgiveness was

God's alone to grant, those who claimed that indulgences released the buyers from all punishment and granted them salvation were wrong.

Luther speaks of *Busse* and *Reue* (remorse, penitence, repentance) in at least fifteen of the *Ninety-Five Theses*, suggesting that only remorse and repentance before God, not payment of money, can absolve a sinner from all penalties. In fact, as the first Thesis has it, all of a believer's life must be one of repentance (*dass alles Leben der Gläubigen Busse sein soll*) (100). Christians should not be lulled to sleep by being promised false security, that there is no danger, as the indulgence preachers say, but be told that people need to follow Christ through much suffering, death, and hell, and to enter the kingdom of heaven though much suffering.

It has been suggested, that while the "*Ninety-Five Theses* burst onto the European scene like wildfire, they were … not all that original or inflammatory" (Whitford 181). Pope Leo X, in fact, dismissed them as the rantings of another "drunk monk." Also, when the *Theses* appeared, there were no reactions or responses from any theologians or from the academic community around Wittenberg. But, as Whitford continues, "Where Leo saw a drunken monk, pamphleteers saw gold. They recognized early that Luther's *Theses* touched a raw nerve. The extent to which Luther gave voice to popular discontent surprised (even scared) Luther" (182). Eager publishers translated and turned out copies of the *Theses* at an extraordinary rate, bringing Luther early fame and influence. This sudden focus on Luther's activity would both help and hurt the reformer in the near future.

While Luther at this time did not see himself as a reformer of the church, but only as a concerned pastor, there is little doubt that he intended his "discovered" gospel to spread widely to the nobility as well as to the common people. He also must have known that the substance of his proposed disputation would become public knowledge. That Luther must have had these thoughts in mind seems to be borne out by the fact that on the afternoon of October 31, he preached in the city church of Wittenberg on the substance of his contention, namely "Indulgences and Grace." Then also, once his *Theses* had become a public issue, Luther threw himself with zeal and vigour into the battle, without tiring of writing, teaching, preaching, and disputing on the issues close to his heart. He soon kept three printing presses entirely occupied. By 1521, Luther had progressed to such an extent in his opposition to Rome that his earlier humble submission to the pope had given way to outright rebellion against the church.

MAJOR REFORMATION WRITINGS

Sermon Concerning Good Works

❧ In 1520 Luther published four major booklets that were to become fundamental in his reformation work, destructive to the established authority of the Catholic Church, and influential in the formation of various religious and social groups. The first of these booklets Luther calls *A Sermon Concerning Good Works* (Werke 1, 1–96). He dedicated this writing to Duke Johann of Saxony, brother to the Elector Frederick the Wise, Luther's sovereign.

What began as a "sermon" developed under Luther's pen into a meditation and instruction on the place good works occupy in a Christian's life. Luther, who just a few years earlier had gone throught the agony of finding a gracious God through doing good works but failed, here instructs his readers that works acceptable to God are deeds that result from faith. "The first and highest, and most noble good work," Luther states, "is faith in Christ." And good works are not only those activities that relate to services in the church, as the church teaches, but also such ordinary things as "occupational work, walking, standing, eating, drinking, sleeping, and other works that have to do with human activity" – provided they are done in faith (Werke, 6–7). Whatever is not done in faith, even when one obeys all of God's commandments, is not a good work but actually a sinful act in the eyes of God.

Luther then interprets the Ten Commandments, applying them to various aspects in a Christian's life. Showing that faith is the greatest good work a Christian can perform, Luther gives numerous examples of how the Ten Commandments must be followed, not as demands from God but as a result of God's love for the redeemed sinner. Faith and good works belong together like two people in a marriage relationship. A man and a woman who love one another will freely perform good works for each other, not because they have to but because they love each other (9). So it is with the Ten Commandments. They are not performed because of divine compulsion, but because God loves us and we in turn love him.

What is most provocative in this work is Luther's interpretation and application of the fourth commandment, which deals with honouring and obeying one's parents. Parents must train their children in godliness and the children in turn must obey their parents in all things, except when the parents are irrational or evil (67). Similarly, the church, the spiritual mother, should be loved and obeyed, except when she is wrong and evil. And Luther assumes that the papal church is wrong. Applying this commandment to temporal authorities, Luther states that subjects must obey them even when they do wrong. However, when a government is obviously evil and intent on committing some wrong, subjects need not obey, but at the same time they must accept the consequences of their disobedience.

What is even more radical in this writing is Luther urging the temporal governments to punish the spiritual powers, because the church councils in the past had not succeeded in reforming the church (74). "For this reason we must resist the spiritual powers, because they do wrong, and not oppose the temporal powers even though they do wrong" (76).

As a reformation writing, this booklet achieved several things. It spelled out in clear and simple German how a Christian coming out of the old church must see the law and good works in relation to faith and the Christian life. Christians are free in Christ to live their life, not in fear of and in bondage to church rules, but in faith in whatever they do. For Christians the distinction between their religious and so-called secular life is removed. All their life must be and can be a life of faith and thus acceptable to God. For Luther's readers the implications of this *Sermon* were quite radical. It turned the monastic ideal of doing good works upside down, making faith more important than good works.

To the Christian Nobility of the German Nation (Werke 1, 197–290).

This booklet was completed in July 1520. Before August more than 4,000 copies – an enormous number for that time – had been printed and a new edition was called for. Luther begins by stating that since the Catholic clergy cannot bring about the much needed reform of the church, the German nobles should be moved to action to help reform come about. He then destroys what he calls the three walls behind which the papacy is hiding, namely, that the spiritual power is above secular authority, that the pope alone has the authority to correctly interpret the text of the Bible, and that the pope alone may call a general council for the reformation of the church. The "first wall" Luther attacks and destroys by stating that all Christians, whether they are clergy or laypersons, are equal in the sight of God, for they are all spiritual, they have all been baptized, and they have all received the gospel of Christ. The only difference between the laity and the clergy is that of function. Since God has ordained that the secular powers punish the wicked and reward the good subjects, Luther argues, it is the princes' right and obligation to discipline the wicked popes as well.

Luther attacks the "second wall" of the papacy, that the pope alone can correctly interpret the Bible, by asserting that all Christians have the right to read and interpret Scriptures, for the Spirit of God resides in all those who belong to Christ. The "third wall," that only the pope has the authority to call a general council, collapses automatically with the first two. Since all baptized Christians are in truth priests and bishops (the priesthood of all believers principle), and all have the right to interpret Scriptues, the pope, it logically follows, cannot hold a special position above all others. If the pope is evil – and Luther assumes that he is – the magistrates have the right, and, Luther implies, it is their duty to call a general council to discuss and then act to bring about the needed reformation of the church.

There are other statements in this tract that became dynamite in the hands of various social and religious groups. If we fight the Turks, Luther argues, and thieves and murderers are being hanged, why then should we tolerate the wickedness and robbery of the popes? Are they not criminals who need to be punished? God has made us free from all human laws that contradict God's law and imperil our soul's salvation; in spiritual matters Christians need not recognize any authority above the Word of God. The clergy should have the freedom to marry, for to prohibit marriage is contrary to human nature and all natural law; all pilgrimages to Rome ought to discontinue; private masses, the interdict used to punish Christians in some territories, and all festivals, except Sunday as a day of rest, should be abolished. The Word of God must be taught to all people. Universities, according to Luther, are gates of hell if they do not train young people in Holy Scriptures and godliness.

Other passages in the booklet, which were later to encourage the formation of sectarian groups, pertained to the autonomy of local churches. If a little group of Christians, Luther explains, were taken into exile where there is no ordained priest, and if they were to elect one from among them, married or unmarried, they could confer on him the authority to baptize, to say Mass, to absolve from penalties, and to preach, and he would be as true a priest as if he had been ordained by a bishop or by the pope. Ironically, this argument, which Luther no doubt applied primarily to himself and his followers who with him rebelled against Rome, was later taken up by the many dissenting groups and applied to their own situation in their struggle against the reformer.

To the Christian Nobility was a firebrand. Some feared that the pamphlet might lead to a religious war. Some of Luther's friends, especially his fellow friar Johannes Lang, were fearful of the consequences and warned Luther not to publish the booklet. Luther's first major book on reforming the church did not cause a war at the time, but its influence on the public was great. The destruction of the "three walls" of the papacy and Luther's ideas of the "priesthood of all believers" led in time to the emancipation of the laity from churchly control and to their direct involvement in the affairs of the church. The first evidence of this was seen in the attempted reforms in Wittenberg during Luther's absence while hiding at the Wartburg castle. Later this lay movement found expression in the formation of radical groups in central and southern Germany and in Switzerland. Luther's boldness in announcing his program of reform inspired many younger and older readers and hearers of the reformer to participate in practical ways. Anticlericalism which had been simmering below the surface for a long time would now soon break open, resulting in concrete action, be it in demonstrations against the church or in destruction of images and church property. People began to feel free to express their dissatisfaction in various ways with the late medieval church in general and those who had governed it for many centuries. Luther concluded *To the Christian Nobility* with the announcement that he had "another song" to sing against Rome, by which he meant that another booklet against the Roman Church was to follow.

In October Luther published *The Babylonian Captivity of the Church* (Werke 2, 375–511), written in Latin and geared toward a more theologically educated reading audience. It was mostly this booklet that initiated the so-called sacramental controversy, the controversy that erupted about the number and validity of the seven sacraments. The following seven church functions were and are considered sacraments in the Roman Catholic Church: baptism, the Eucharist (Holy Communion), penance or reconciliation, confirmation, marriage, holy orders or ordination, and the last rite or anointing the sick and dying.

Luther begins by denying that there are seven sacraments as the Roman Church had them, stating that there should possibly be just three sacraments, namely baptism, repentance, and the Eucharist. He wonders aloud, however, whether according to the usage of Scripture there should be more than just one, namely the Eucharist or the Lord's Supper, with the other two, baptism and penance, being reduced to what he calls "sacramental signs." In the end, however, Luther comes to the conclusion that only baptism and the Lord's Supper are biblical sacraments. The other five Catholic sacraments Luther eliminates altogether. Moreover, Luther continues, the Catholic Mass ought to be abolished because it has become a "good work" and another sacrifice, thereby eliminating the sacrifice Christ accomplished for humankind once and for all on the cross. Also, external things in the worship service, such as vestments and ornaments, should be done away with because they detract from the essence of worshipping God. Religious orders are unscriptural, according to Luther, and show contempt for the common things of life. Luther also insists that the cup must not be withheld from the lay communicants, as is the practice under Catholicism. Luther's writing against these old practices would soon lead to radical innovations in Wittenberg, with Karlstadt being the first of Luther's colleagues to celebrate communion in both kinds, that is, the communicant receiving both the bread *and* the wine.

Luther's thinking on baptism seems somewhat confused and confusing. In the later emergence of the Anabaptists, Luther's views on baptism gave rise to as much controversy as his view on the Lord's Supper. Luther here seems to recognize baptismal regeneration (the belief that a person's conversion takes place in baptism), but he also speaks of baptism as a "symbol" of a person's death and resurrection in Christ. Luther also adds that if baptism is to be valid, a baptized person must continue to believe in Christ's merits for sinners. In connection with infant baptism, however, he states that infants are aided by the faith of others, namely the faith of their parents or sponsors. This confusion in Luther's thinking was soon to become evident in others. Both the Anabaptists, who demanded personal faith *before* baptism, and the believers in infant baptism, later appealed to Luther's teaching. However, Luther's belief in infant baptism hardened after 1525 when the Anabaptists appeared and insisted on believers,' or adult, baptism only. But the views of the Anabaptists also hardened, because they saw the two sacraments, baptism and the Lord's Supper, as symbols only, not true sacraments.

The book had an immediate impact on Luther's followers who, during the reformer's time hiding at the Wartburg castle, sought to advance the reformation in Wittenberg. Men such as Philip Melanchthon and Andreas von Karlstadt attempted to modernize the Mass by abolishing the clergy's vestments and by administering Holy Communion in both kinds. But for many people in Wittenberg the changes went too far and too fast. It would soon become evident that Luther's colleagues and followers had either misunderstood the way reformation was to proceed or that Luther had changed his mind on the speed of reform when he saw the violent changes, such as image breaking, taking place while he was away from Wittenberg. He soon resolved to preach moderation for the sake of the "weak consciences," as he put it; ordinary people were not ready to proceed that fast.

There was another booklet of great importance that Luther published in 1520, *The Freedom of a Christian* (Werke 1, 197–290). In a letter to Pope Leo X Luther wrote that it would be good for him to read this piece, for the booklet was a complete summary of how a Christian ought to live. Luther writes that humans are unable to fulfill the demands of the Old Testament law. Faith in Christ releases Christians from the old law and thus makes them free in Christ. It is faith alone and not human deeds that justify an individual before God. Human good works or deeds are then the *result* of having been made just by God and an expression of gratitude to God. Good works in themselves do not make one good, but an individual of faith will perform good deeds because he or she has been saved by the grace of God. Luther thus rejects good works as a means of salvation, but he does *not* say that good works are not necessary. As far as a Christian's relationship to God is concerned only faith matters. But as far as a Christian's relationship to other people goes, faith must express itself in love, that is, in good deeds toward others.

The freedom in Christ is a freedom from sin and from the demands of the Old Testament law; it is not freedom from Christian responsibility and morality. In fact, an important point in *The Freedom of a Christian* is Luther's teaching about the priesthood of all believers, dispelling all notions about possible license in a Christian's lifestyle. The Christian is both king and priest before God, positions that carry dignity and a high degree of moral responsibility.

Luther's emphasis on the importance of humans' justification by faith and not by works, and his teaching on the freedom of Christians, led some individuals within the Lutheran camp to live without any ethical restraints, as Luther himself later admitted. The result was the so-called antinomian controversy (the question of whether grace releases Christians from obeying moral laws), which led Luther to modify some of his earlier pronouncements on the relationship between law and freedom.

The implications and effects of Luther's conversion experience and his early writings must be kept in mind if one is to understand the individuals and groups who at first were attracted to Luther but later turned away from him as a person and from some of his teachings. Luther's radical break with the medieval church and his reformation principles had a powerful influence on both the clergy and laypersons. His example and writings had awakened in laypersons an entirely new conception of their obligations to the existing order. As members of the new priesthood, laypersons could not sit idly by while the church was held in doctrinal and institutional bondage. Both nobles and laypersons felt they needed to act to correct the abuses in church and society.

Luther's treatment of the biblical canon, questioning some books and assigning greater value to others, created doubt in some people's minds about whether the Scriptures were inspired by God, and contributed to the later spread of rationalism. Moreover, Luther's writings of 1520 had some influence on the Zwickau prophets and Thomas Müntzer. Although a theologian in his own right, Müntzer nevertheless at first hailed Luther as a fellow reformer, but later went his own way and became a leader in the struggle for social justice and the Peasants' War of 1525. When Luther encountered what he called the "enthusiasts" and "false brethren," he had to modify some of his earlier ideas about the universal priesthood of all believers, or at least differentiate more clearly between those who were truly believers and those who were Christians in name only.

THE WAR OF PAMPHLETS

⁋ **In view of Luther's prodigious output of writings** before and after his appearance at the Diet of Worms, an explanation of our subtitle, *Ink Against the Devil,* seems in order. Writers have shown that the quantity and popularity of Luther's writings eclipsed all others at the time. Had it not been for the new printing press with movable type, thanks to Gutenberg – comparable to the computer technology of today – Luther's rebellion against Rome might have been a flash in the pan, and the rebel would have ended up a martyr. As it was, however, the rebel and reformer became popular almost overnight and a bestseller at that. Thomas Brady observes, "The unchallenged star of this drama of the printed word was Martin Luther. During the quarter-century of his public life, German presses may have produced some 3.1 million copies of his writings, not counting whole and partial editions of his German translation of the Bible" (Brady, 164–5). This "tsunami" of Luther's print was soon joined by other evangelical writers, bringing "the total volume of evangelical comment, instruction, and agitation in print to 6.3 million items produced, sold, and read" (165).

The word from the pulpit did not lag behind the printed word. The new Lutheran congregations in the towns and villages required pastors and ministers to explain the new message of the reformer. While few ministers were able to match the powerful preaching of Luther, the congregations in urban centres listened attentively to their Lutheran preachers, as there was so much instruction necessary to guide them in the many changes of their lives and worship. Nor was the preaching dull, for Luther's pamphlets explained the reformer's message with the help of printed cartoons ridiculing and maligning the papal opponents. They even imitated the "Jewish sow" motif by showing cartoons of the pope riding a pig. Luther's messages were also acted out. The poets Hans Sachs (1494–1576) of Nürnberg, and especially Niklas Manuel (1484–1530) of Bern, Switzerland, were very effective at dramatizing important reformation issues. Catholic writers responded, of course, in kind. The Franciscan friar Thomas Murner (1475–1537), for example, portrayed the reformer in a satire as a seven-headed monster, calling him, among other things, "heresiarch" and "antichrist" (168–73).

BIRTH OF RELIGIOUS FUNDAMENTALISM

⟪ **To conclude this chapter,** Luther's intense religious experience and convictions in the monastery and subsequently as a young theology professor at the University of Wittenberg, coupled with various social and political circumstances, made it impossible for him to tolerate not only the papacy and all that it stood for, but also those who dissented from him and even opposed him. Luther's theology, derived from the agony of his search for salvation, and his early reformation writings, explain to a large extent his inability or unwillingness to tolerate his Catholic, radical, and Renaissance humanist opponents. To these must be added Luther's non-Christian opponents, the Jews and the Turks, to be discussed later in this book. Luther's experience of God's grace and his conviction of what the truth was, led to something Luther could not have foreseen in the sixteenth century: what Robert Glenn Howart has recently called Christian "fundamentalism," the view that anyone who experiences the grace of God individually, as Luther did, who claims to *know the truth* for certain, does not from henceforth need to submit to any other authority, be it religious or secular. This led to much religious strife and even wars among European states. In time a kind of "pluralism" needed to be devised by the secular states, so as to allow their subjects and citizens to live in peace side by side, even though they did not necessarily believe the same thing in matters of religious faith and moral conduct (Howart). This pluralism and its resulting tolerance is of course taken for granted today.

Dissenting Groups and Why They Opposed Luther

GREAT VARIETY OF RADICALS

The different groups that dissented from Martin Luther were all lumped together by the reformer, who called them such names as *rebels, enthusiasts, fanatics, visionaries, baptists,* or, most commonly, *Wiedertäufer* (Anabaptists, re-baptizers). The diversity of these groups makes it difficult to decide which group or individuals might be included in a study of the so-called radical reformers movement. However, to lump them all together is not only inaccurate, but also highly unfair to those who in their own way sincerely sought to carry out the teachings of the gospels and of the great reformer who became an example for many of them.

Most of the radicals did not wish to be called the names Luther applied to them; they certainly did not want to be known as Anabaptists, for they did not regard infant baptism as a true baptism. Moreover, although most radical groups opposed infant baptism, not all accepted adult baptism; each group had a different understanding of baptism. For some groups, baptism was merely an expression of their concept of the church, which according to them consisted of baptized believers only. For others, baptism was an act of initiation whereby new members were received into the community. For still others, the Mennonites, for example, baptism was a symbol of an inner transformation and dedication to Christ. However apparent some of their differences may have been, in one respect the various groups were all alike: they were all *radical* in their theology and in how they approached their work of reform. Compromise, moderation, and consideration of other institutions and views were largely foreign to them. They sought to reform, some by violent means, all existing orders, be they social, economic, political, or religious. In their quest for new churches or other institutions, many of them disregarded all tradition and past historical development.

Some groups attempted to re-establish the primitive or early church, whereas others felt called to inaugurate the kingdom of God as if it had never existed before. The designation *radical reformers* has thus been applied to all individuals and groups that dissented from the leading or magisterial reformers like Luther, Zwingli, and Calvin, and at the same time opposed Roman Catholicism. Because of their diversity it is thus difficult to classify them. Even their contemporaries found it almost impossible to differentiate between the groups. The great German spiritualist chronicler Sebastian Franck (1499–1543), for example, wrote with perhaps some exaggeration but generally accurately: "There are many more sects and opinions, which I do not all know and cannot describe, but it seems to me that there are not two to be found who agree with each other on all points" (Bax, *Rise and Fall* 51).

Some historians have attempted to classify the dissidents according to their conception of the church. There were those who believed in a restored and gathered community of baptized believers under strict ethical discipline and separation from the world and the secular state. Generally, the Swiss, the South German, and Mennonite Anabaptists belonged to this group. Then there were the Hutterites or Hutterian Brethren, as they called themselves, who believed in a church-community in which all material things were held in common and members lived together in closed communities.

The Münsterites, that is, the Anabaptists, who in 1534–35 tried to establish by force an earthly kingdom in the city of Münster in Westphalia, believed in a church-kingdom on earth as the ideal church. Then there were also men like Sebastian Franck, Caspar Schwenckfeld, and Hans Denck, among others, who held to an inward, invisible, spiritual, and universal church. The more rationally inclined radicals, like the Polish Faustus Socinus (1539–1604) and the Spaniard Michael Servetus (1511–1553), who denied the Trinity, were generally called anti-Trinitarians, the spiritual ancestors of today's Unitarians. Luther looked upon this confusion and division among the radical reformers as a clear sign of their ungodliness, and he condemned them all throughout his life as non-Christians, even devil-inspired people.

Historians of Anabaptism generally agree on a threefold division within the radical movement, differentiating between spiritualists, Anabaptists, and rationalists. According to Mennonite historians, there was a pronounced difference between spiritualists like Caspar Schwenckfeld and Anabaptists like Michael Sattler. Anabaptists looked to the past, seeking to recreate or restore Christianity along New Testament lines. Spiritualists, on the other hand, sought to look more inward and to the future in an attempt to create a new church. The rationalists were greatly influenced by Renaissance humanism, seeking to explain the mysteries of religion according to reason and common sense. The so-called antinomians and anti-Trinitarians were part of this group. Later in his life Luther dealt with these groups as well.

In view of this great variety of the radical reformers, it has been asked whether Luther was justified in lumping them all together and fighting them indiscriminately. Perhaps Luther should have taken the time to study the various groups more thoroughly before passing judgment on them, but as far as he was concerned all dissident groups had certain important traits and ideas in common. All shared their opposition to Luther and Catholicism, but there were other important issues and doctrinal beliefs that separated them from the reformer. Most of them in varying degrees rejected the reformer's main reformation principles, particularly his doctrine of justification by faith alone. Most of the radicals emphasized in one way or another the principle of communalism, a point that may account for the popularity of the Anabaptist message among the rural and urban lower classes. Most groups opposed Luther's teaching on the enslaved or un-free will, believing in at least a limited freedom of the will, especially when it came to salvation. Luther, on the other hand, felt with some justification that their emphasis on what he called "works" would lead to legalism. That is, an excessive adherence to laws and rules, as opposed to full freedom in Christ. Most radicals, except for the spiritualists, sought to establish a visible church of believers, whereas Luther leaned more toward an "invisible church" consisting of all Christians past, present, and future. A visible church, the Anabaptists held, must consist only of voluntary believers. This caused them to reject infant baptism, something that Luther defended to the very end.

Almost all radicals regarded the centuries between Constantine the Great in the fourth century and the sixteenth century as a period of spiritual decline and apostasy. Thomas Müntzer went so far as to claim that the true church had disappeared immediately after the last apostles in the first century. Most important for Luther, all the radicals repudiated the "real presence," that is, the belief that Christ was really and physically present in the Eucharist. For Luther this was the most damnable characteristic of most dissidents, for in denying the real presence of Christ in the bread and wine they rejected Christ altogether, hence they could not be considered Christians at all.

ORIGINS OF THE RADICAL REFORMERS

❰❰ **Since about the middle of the twentieth century** scholars of Anabaptism have sought to determine more precisely the geographical and ideological origins of the Anabaptist movement. Some have argued that a Zurich group, the so-called Swiss Brethren, was the real beginning of the Anabaptist movement, which spread northward from Switzerland to Germany along the Rhine regions and on to the Netherlands. Harold S. Bender (1897–1962) and some of his colleagues at Goshen College in Indiana held this view. They believed that the Swiss Conrad Grebel, Feliz Manz, and George Blaurock, all young men who had at first followed Ulrich Zwingli and who in January 1525 performed the first adult baptism on each other, were the "true" evangelical Anabaptists who contributed to the rise and development of Anabaptism in other places. According to this view, radicals like Thomas Müntzer and the Münsterite Anabaptists did not really belong to Anabaptism. For some of these scholars, not even Balthasar Hubmaier in southern Germany (because he was not totally committed to pacifism) and the gentle and spiritualistically inclined Hans Denck of Nürnberg, should be included with the Anabaptists. Only the Swiss Brethren and their brand of Anabaptism was considered true evangelical Anabaptism.

Other scholars have argued that the Anabaptist movement had not just one geographical beginning, but arose in several places independent of other groups. The Swiss Brethren may have been the first to baptize adults, but other groups in southern and northern Germany and in the Netherlands established Anabaptist communities independent of the Swiss Anabaptists. In this view the evangelistic work of men such as Hubmaier, Hans Hut, Pilgram Marpeck, and Jacob Hutter, among others, in the south, and Melchior Hoffman (1495–1544) and Menno Simons and his colleagues in the Netherlands and northern Germany, are given credit for the establishment of Anabaptism independent of the Swiss Brethren. The controversy about *monogenesis* (one geographical origin) and *polygenesis* (multiple origins) resulted in an article entitled "From Monogenesis to Polygenesis" in a 1975 issue of MQR. That Anabaptism originated in several locations in Europe, not just in one, and that it was much more varied than previously held, is the view generally accepted by historians today.

It is still not clear whether the sixteenth-century radicals owe their origin to some medieval heretical groups or just to the Reformation of the sixteenth century or to both. Some earlier historians have insisted on their medieval origin, connecting them with reformers such as Wycliffe in England, the Waldensians in southern France, and Jan Hus in Bohemia. Ronald A. Knox, for example, pointed to the following similarities of beliefs between these medieval groups and the radicals: Both groups held that the church was for serious Christians only; both believed that the iniquity in the world must be actively opposed; and both felt called to correct the abusive and sinful deeds of the churches of their time. Other characteristics, such as opposition to warfare and serving in the military, the taking of oaths, and participation and service as magistrates in the state were part of both the medieval heretics and the later Anabaptists (Knox 126–7).

Others connect the radicals historically with the medieval mystics such as Tauler, Eckhard, Suso, and the Brothers of the Common Life, under whose influence some of the dissidents had come (Huch 240–1). Some writers have pointed out that the *Devotio Moderna* (Modern Devotion), a fourteenth-century religious movement in the Netherlands, formed the basis for the piety of the Anabaptists, giving them the idea of a conventicle-like separation from the world (Stupperich 14). Some Anabaptists themselves believed that they were the spiritual descendants of Waldensian groups in southern France (Zieglschmid 39–40). Historian Thomas Lindsay some time ago simply stated: "[T]he whole Anabaptist movement was medieval to the core" (Lindsay 441). Although no direct historical links between the Anabaptists and the medieval groups have been established, Anabaptism particularly flourished in areas where the Waldensians had existed in large numbers in the fourteenth and fifteenth centuries. It may well be that these followers of Peter Waldo, the so-called "poor men of Lyons," had prepared the ground long before the Anabaptists emerged in the Reformation era.

There is also the question of whether Renaissance humanism may have been responsible for the rise of some of the radicals. Johan Huizinga held with Walter Köhler that Erasmus was the father of Anabaptism. Robert Kreider, in a study of the lives of the leading evangelical Anabaptists, concluded that most of them had studied under humanist teachers. According to Kreider, the theological emphases of the Anabaptists, such as the freedom of the will, non-resistance (in the case of the peaceful groups), the separation of church and state, and the stress on ethics rather than dogma, were similar to the principles advocated by the Christian humanists. Kreider insists, however, that Anabaptism went beyond humanism in that it fixed its eye not upon human accomplishments but on God and salvation in Christ (Kreider 123–41).

More recently, historian Abraham Friesen has demonstrated that Erasmus of Rotterdam contributed significantly to the rise and beliefs of the peaceful Anabaptists (Friesen, *Erasmus*). How much of an influence humanism in general had on the rise of Anabaptism is still a question, but there seems little doubt that rationalists such as the anti-Trinitarians belonged within Renaissance humanism. They not only emphasized human things and achievements, they also applied both reason and faith to their theology and way of life. Yet even the religious rationalists, including the Socinians and other anti-Trinitarians, may never have come out into the open had they not been stimulated or given courage by the Reformation in general and Luther in particular.

Although the origin of the radical groups needs to be further studied, the view that most of them were actually "children" or "stepchildren" of the Reformation seems to correspond with some important facts. Many of the dissidents, such as Karlstadt, Müntzer, Melchior Hoffman, Hans Denck, Balthasar Hubmaier, Bernt Rothman, Menno Simons and others, were former admirers of Luther, and some of them had been followers and close associates of the reformer. Some of them had been Lutheran ministers for some time, and most of them had at one time or another taken courage from Luther's teaching and writings. While the radicals deviated from Luther in many points, many of them adhered to at least some of the principles he enunciated. Like Luther, they rejected the authority of the Catholic Church in favour of the principles of *sola fide* and *sola scriptura*, however they interpreted these principles. Like Luther, they stressed the importance of the Holy Spirit in the life of believers, and like Luther they believed in personal faith, in freedom of conscience, in the priesthood of all believers, and in the active involvement of Christians in the concerns of the church.

The difference between Luther and the dissident groups was often a difference in interpretation and emphasis of Reformation principles, rather than a difference in essential beliefs. However, both Luther and the radicals themselves saw their differences in terms of essential core beliefs and values. Today it is easy to belittle these differences, but during the Reformation the differences often resulted in intolerance, persecution, and even martyrdom. Many of the radicals had been close to what the reformer had believed and taught so that when they were rejected and persecuted by Luther and other magisterial reformers, not only were they disappointed and hurt they also felt betrayed. The oppressed peasants and urban workers especially, as we shall see, at first believed that Luther was on their side; but when he condemned them when they rebelled against their overlords and employers, they felt bitterly betrayed.

Whatever the connection between the radical reformers and Luther may have been, it was Luther who caused them, directly or indirectly, to come boldly into the open and encouraged their views and work by his own example of rebellion and his provocative early writings. Whether the various radical groups would have appeared without the work of the magisterial reformers, especially Luther, cannot be answered; that the radicals appealed to Luther's works, teaching, and example is a fact. Ernst Troeltsch concludes, "Although greatly assisted by some lingering traces of the influence of the Waldensians and other sects ... at bottom ... the whole [radical] movement belonged to the Reformation. It was caused by the Reformation; it appealed to its principles and ideals, and it remained in closest touch with it" (Troeltsch 699; see also Zschäbitz 122–40).

WHY THEY LEFT LUTHER

❡ **In the documents of the Anabaptists in particular** there appears, as Franklin Littell states, a tone of disappointment and sadness about Luther: "In their records they refer to Luther half in praise and half in sorrow, as a leader whom they first followed but who did not carry them through to as thorough a reformation as they had anticipated" (Littell, *The Anabaptist View* 4). Similarly, an unknown Anabaptist expressed himself in 1538 as follows: "While still in the national church, we obtained much instruction from the writings of Luther [about the mass and other papal ceremonies, regarding repentance, conversion, and the true Christian life]. But I could not close my eyes to the fact that the doctrine which was preached ... was not carried out" (Bender, "Anabaptist Vision" 76). And Menno Simons, leader of the Dutch and North German Anabaptists, writes in his *The True Christian Faith* (1541) that the Lutherans emphasize the doctrine of justification by faith to the point that anyone who also preaches the necessity of good works is considered a heretic" (Simons 334). With reference to infant baptism, Menno Simons writes, "[A]lthough they [Lutherans] have in the past condemned unto hell all the institutions and commands of men, and have written one volume after another against them, yet they, alas, altogether continue to cling to this rude abomination, because they do not want to assume the cross, nor the reproach of the world" (Simons 712). A similar view is expressed in an anonymous booklet, written between 1525 and 1535. The writer admits his debt to the "evangelical preachers" for pointing him to the divine truths, but then goes on to accuse them of speaking "the truth of Christ partly" and of not wanting "to pass through the narrow gate" of suffering and consistent Christian living (Hillerbrand, "An Early Anabaptist" 334).

The writer of *Die älteste Chronik der Hutterischen Brüder* (1943) is very hard on Luther and other evangelical preachers. He accuses Luther and other leading reformers of having succeeded in breaking down wicked Roman Catholicism, but failing to build a better church. Also, the evangelicals have attached themselves to magistrates and princes, trusting in human power rather than in God. Moreover, they have retained infant baptism; they are defending their doctrines with the sword; and they live worldly lives. Their greatest merit, the writer concludes sarcastically, is to eat meat, take women to wives, scold the popes, monks, and clerics, and to live as they please (Zieglschmid 42–4).

While such sweeping criticism may be an oversimplification of Luther's teaching concerning the Christian life, the reformer did in fact teach that good works do not make a person good, and he certainly de-emphasized the necessity of good works, especially regarding salvation. Time and again Luther stressed that a person must be good before he or she can perform good works. Where justification is concerned, works are altogether out of place. There faith alone reigns, according to Luther. As will be seen in the chapter on Luther and Erasmus in their debate about free or un-free will, Luther was not altogether indifferent to good works, but he did question human freedom and rejected the necessity of good works for salvation.

Some radicals dissented from Luther for social, economic, or political reasons. Thomas Müntzer's religious and political ideas, for example, were radical and seen as destructive of many established institutions; he believed that they needed to be destroyed before the kingdom of God could arrive. For Luther such views were unacceptable. The peasants and the "common man" in southern Germany, wanting to be free of feudal oppression and unjust restrictions, often resorted to violence in the name of Luther's early writings. Even the more peaceful Anabaptists held views on economic practices, such as tithes and the community of goods, that ran counter to tradition and accepted customs at the time (Crous 42–4).

From where Luther and other magisterial reformers stood, these issues were seen as radical, both religiously and socially, adding convincing reasons for opposing them. Add to this the splintering nature of Protestant belief caused by the principles of *sola scriptura* and the priesthood of all believers, and the right of each individual to interpret the Bible according to one's understanding, and it becomes clear that Luther and the dissident groups were on a collision course.

The Enemies Within
Luther and the Wittenberg Radicals

In April 1521 Luther appeared before the high religious and imperial dignitaries at the Diet of Worms in Germany to defend his writings. Asked to recant the errors found in his published books and pamphlets that lay spread out on a table, he stated courageously that he would not retract anything he had written, for to go against one's conscience was wrong. The Catholic party at the gathering and Emperor Charles V sought to silence Luther and make him incapable of agitating any further against the pope and the church, and if possible even to kill him. But on his way back to Wittenberg, Luther was "kidnapped" by some horsemen appointed by the Elector of Saxony, Frederick the Wise, and taken secretly into solitary confinement at the Wartburg castle for his protection. Luther used his time in the Wartburg to translate the New Testament into German. But while Luther was away from the capital of the Reformation, the spirits he had called up would not go away or lie idle. Men such as Gabriel Zwilling, Justus Jonas, Andreas von Karlstadt, and Philip Melanchthon, threw themselves into the work of reform according to what they thought was in agreement with Luther's ideas and wishes. But, as they would discover, while Luther was initially in agreement with what they were doing, he soon saw the danger of their radical actions and sought to put a stop to them.

KARLSTADT AND LUTHER

❦ **Andreas Bodenstein von Karlstadt (1481–1541)** has been held most responsible for the initial innovations and at times violent outbreaks at Wittenberg in the winter of 1521–22. Karlstadt was born in Bavaria in southern Germany. In 1499 he enrolled at the University of Erfurt where he studied until 1504, the year in which he came to the newly established University of Wittenberg, where he became famous as a teacher of philosophy. Other than Luther, Karlstadt clung at first to the old scholasticism, believing in the supreme authority of St. Thomas Aquinas (1225–1274) and other medieval theologians. By 1510 Karlstadt had acquired all the higher academic degrees, and in that year he also became archdeacon at a church in Wittenberg. As archdeacon he was required to preach, say Mass once a week, and to lecture at the university. In 1511 he became chancellor at Wittenberg University, and in 1512 he awarded Luther the doctorate degree in theology. From 1515 to 1516 Karlstadt studied in Rome, where he obtained the double degree in canon and civil law, hoping to become the dean of the Castle Church in Wittenberg. To his disappointment, however, when he returned to Wittenberg he did not get the hoped for position.

It was Luther who acquainted Karlstadt with the church father St. Augustine (354–430), whose writings he then began to read with great interest. He soon broke with scholasticism (the medieval way of reasoning) and adopted Luther's critical view of the medieval schoolmen. Karlstadt's beliefs were further challenged during his stay in Rome where he saw first-hand large-scale corruption in the Roman Catholic Church. In 1516 he published 151 theses that contained the fundamental traits of his later theology. In these theses he criticized the Greek philosopher Aristotle and the medieval scholastics and pondered the question, no doubt stimulated by Luther, whether the human will was free and capable of attaining to God. Karlstadt soon shared the reformer's hostility toward Roman Catholicism, but apparently there never existed a personal friendship or close relationship between him and Luther.

The widening gap between the two men soon became apparent. After his disputation with the Catholic Dr. Johann Eck in June and July 1518, Karlstadt began to emphasize Luther's new doctrine of justification by faith and grace, writing tracts against indulgences and justification through good works. But Luther, who was particularly sensitive on these points, soon detected some theological flaws in the writings of his senior colleague. Whereas Luther strongly emphasized justification by faith alone, Karlstadt believed and taught that justification was only the beginning of a Christian's life and that sanctification, that is, truly Christian living, had to follow. Luther believed that it was unnecessary to emphasize right living since it would follow once a sinner was forgiven, redeemed, and justified by God.

Karlstadt's lectures on justification and holy living were well attended. But when Karlstadt did not agree with Luther about the book of St. James, but instead was attracted by the strict discipline and emphasis on holiness in St. James, Luther began to suspect the soundness of his colleague's theology. Detecting what he thought was a dangerous legalism in Karlstadt's teaching, Luther, according to Hermann Barge, sought to disuade students from attending Karlstadt's lectures (Barge I, 196–200). Then when King Christian II of Denmark asked Wittenberg for assistance with the Protestant Reformation in his country, there is reason to believe that both Luther and Frederick the Wise recommended Karlstadt in order to be rid of him in Saxony. Karlstadt was happy to go to Denmark early in 1521, but after only six weeks of apparently fruitless activity there, the combined resistance of the Danish clergy and nobility forced him to leave the country. Apparently, to the dismay of both Luther and the Elector, Karlstadt returned to Wittenberg to continue his reform work there.

On December 17, 1521, the congregation of Wittenberg submitted six articles demanding reform to the city council. They included the demand that the Last Supper be administered in both kinds, that relics in the churches be abolished, that compulsory masses be ended, that beer parlours and houses of ill repute be closed, and that the Word of God be allowed to be preached freely. Karlstadt was pleased that the council was well disposed toward these reform measures; for him this was a clear sign that God's favour rested upon his undertaking. In the absence of Luther, who was still at the Wartburg in hiding, Karlstadt confidently assumed the spiritual leadership in Wittenberg.

On Christmas Day 1521, approximately 2,000 people celebrated Mass in the Castle Church, with Karlstadt officiating, not in priestly garments but in plain clothes. The Mass was recited partly in Latin and partly in German in an abbreviated form, omitting all passages that referred to the Mass as a sacrifice of Christ. With the permission of the city council and the support of the university faculty, Karlstadt distributed the Eucharist in both kinds, even permitting laypersons to take the bread in their hands. This radical way of celebrating the Mass seemed to break the dams in Wittenberg. Priests, monks, and nuns left their posts and began to marry, and the tonsured friars let their hair grow; from now on priests wore plain clothes while saying Mass; the divine services were more and more recited in the German language; masses for the dead were no longer conducted; here and there religious images were broken by zealous young men; and to the elector's chagrin, attendance at the university began to decline. On January 19, 1522, Karlstadt himself married a young girl. When Luther heard of Karlstadt's marriage, he seemed happy about it. "I am very pleased over Karlstadt's marriage," he wrote, "I know the girl" (Bainton, *Here I Stand* 155). Perhaps Luther did not realize that about three years later he too would become a married man.

THE ZWICKAU PROPHETS

During the turmoil in Wittenberg there appeared on December 27, 1521, certain laymen from Zwickau, a town near the Bohemian border, whence they had been expelled for holding unorthodox views and advocating radical measures of reform (Werke 8, 181). Nickolaus Storch and Markus Stübner were the most outstanding among these "enthusiasts," as Luther called them; they claimed to be prophets and relied on the Holy Spirit rather than on the written word of the Bible. Although they had not been re-baptized as adults, they were against infant baptism and advocated the establishment of the kingdom of God on earth. Stübner, a former student at Wittenberg, was quite well versed in the text of the Bible. Melanchthon, while much attracted to the Zwickau prophets, was at the same time disturbed at not being able to refute their talk about the Holy Spirit and visions. While uneasy about the prophets, he felt that their arguments were actually based on Scriptures. On the day of the prophets' arrival in Wittenberg, Melanchthon wrote to the elector: "They say wonderful things of themselves: that they have been commissioned to teach by a clear voice from God; that they are able to see into the future; briefly, that they are prophetic and apostolic men. I can hardly say how much they affect me.... It is evident from many reasons that there are spirits in them, but no one save Martin [Luther] can judge of them" (Vedder 183).

Why had these prophets come to Wittenberg? Did they expect to find a spiritual home there, or did they believe they had something to offer, such as doctrines perhaps that Luther had neglected to include in his teaching? The latter seems to be the case, for early in 1522 the prophets met with Luther and conferred with him. When the reformer questioned them about their authority and credentials, Markus Stübner replied that in about seven years, he, Luther, would see a miracle that would substantiate their divine mission. However, sensing the danger from the prophets' subjectivism Luther had dismissed them without further arguing with them. As far as he was concerned, the Zwickau prophets were dangerous servants of the devil.

There is little evidence to suggest that Karlstadt had all that much in common with the new prophets. The prophets were highly mystical, believing in a passive resignation to God, while at the same time advocating the use of the sword against the wicked. According to Stübner, the ungodly would be destroyed in about six or seven years. Then at last there would be just one way, one baptism, and one faith. Karlstadt, on the other hand, was far from advocating the killing of the wicked. He also wrote to Thomas Müntzer that he too should abstain from all violent and revolutionary notions. Moreover, the prophets rejected on the whole the written word of the Bible and relied on visions and dreams, while Karlstadt, like Luther, believed in a personal experience of salvation and based his faith on written Scriptures. Yet, like Melanchthon, Karlstadt was impressed by the prophets and was inspired and influenced by them in his own reform efforts. Karlstadt began to stress the Old Testament prophets in his preaching, particularly the books of Malachi and Zachariah, and he wrote enthusiastically to Müntzer that he had talked more about visions and dreams than anybody else on the faculty at the university (Bainton, *Luther Today*, 118).

Although Luther was concerned about the possible influence of the Zwickau prophets on his colleagues and the populace of Wittenberg, he did not think it necessary to return just yet to Wittenberg because of them. In letters, however, he warned the Wittenbergers against the teachings of the eloquent enthusiasts. "When these men talk of sweetness and of being transported to the third heaven," he wrote, "do not believe them. Divine Majesty does not speak directly to men. God is a consuming fire, and the dreams and visions of the saints are terrible.... Prove the spirits; and if you are not able to do so, then take the advice of Gamaliel and wait" (Bainton, *Here I Stand*, 161). In another letter Luther expressed the fear that Frederick, the Elector, might use force to check the influence of the prophets. "I am sure," he wrote, "we can restrain these fire brands without the sword. I hope the prince will not imbrue his hands in their blood. I see no reason why on their account I should come home" at this time (161–2).

On January 24, 1522, the Council of Wittenberg published its first ordinance of the Reformation, sanctioning most innovations in the city. The communicant was allowed to touch the bread in the Last Supper; images were to be abolished; the Mass was to be conducted in Karlstadt's fashion; Luther's ideas on social reform, such as the prohibition of begging, were to be carried out; and prostitution and all manner of immorality were to be banned from the city. Karlstadt was overjoyed. God, according to him, had softened the hearts of the magistrates who now assisted with his reforms. However, the excesses that accompanied these changes concerned Frederick the Wise, especially after Duke George, a Catholic prince across the borders of electoral Saxony, began to complain about the radicalism in Wittenberg and accused Frederick of condoning the disorder.

There were good reasons for such concerns. Some princes ordered their students to leave the University of Wittenberg and the city and return home. Many people in Wittenberg were confused, especially about how the Mass was celebrated, the wearing or not wearing of vestments during the worship service, and other ecclesiastical changes. At last, on February 13 the elector intervened, ordering that no further images were to be broken, that no essential parts of the Mass were to be omitted, and, most important, that Karlstadt was not to preach anymore. While he was sympathetic to some of the many needed reforms, the elector felt that the haste and speed with which the changes took place was detrimental to the "weak" Christians, that is, those who were not ready for such drastic changes. Melanchthon was happy to submit to Frederick's orders, but Karlstadt intended to continue with the reforms until he had reached his objectives. He was not alone in being eager to make changes as soon as possible. The Augustinian monks, Luther's former monastic brothers, were also on his side.

THE AUGUSTINIAN MONKS

❰ **As early as October 1521,** the Augustinian monks of Wittenberg, under the fiery leadership of Gabriel Zwilling, began to advocate abolishing private masses. Even Karlstadt, in a dispute with the zealous monks, advocated caution so as not to give their enemies occasion for criticism. Melanchthon supported Zwilling on the ground that he had the Word of God and the example of the apostles on his side but everyone knew that the Mass could only be abolished with the approval of Frederick the Wise. The Elector was concerned and counselled moderation, ordering the university to set up a commission to investigate the disturbances and then report to him. This was done, and a letter expressing the more moderate views of Karlstadt was sent to the elector.

At first Luther's sympathies seemed to be on the side of the enthusiastic Wittenbergers who advocated innovative reform measures. Viewing the situation from the Wartburg, Luther hoped that the reformation would be both thorough and speedy (Bainton, *Here I Stand* 157–8). However, when he learned about the radical intentions of the Augustinian monks, Luther decided to write several pamphlets, including *On Monastic Vows*, *A Blast Against the Archbishop of Mainz*, and *Concerning the Abuse of the Mass*. These tracts were sent to George Spalatin, chancellor of Saxony, instructing him to have them published immediately. When Spalatin hesitated, Luther became quite impatient. The pamphlet on *Concerning the Abuse of the Mass*, written in November 1521, in both Latin and German, skilfully steers between Spalatin's fearful conservatism on the one hand and the Wittenbergers' radicalism on the other (Werke 2, 175–288).

Luther dedicated *Concerning the Abuse of the Mass* to his "dear brothers, the Augustinians at Wittenberg," the monks with whom he had shared his earlier life. He begins by expressing his joy at the monks' zeal in reforming the Mass at their monastery, but he also wonders whether all of them act from motives of pure love and faith. Luther than strikes a more radical note, evidently aimed at people like Chancellor Spalatin who were afraid of measures that might get out of hand. Luther states that he is writing this pamphlet because his earlier writings on the subject had not stirred the people to more concrete action. He is not concerned about what tradition, the saints, the church fathers, or the Parisian theologians have taught and done; if a certain religious practice does not agree with Holy Scripture, it must be abandoned. Not even St. Paul or an angel from heaven may impose doctrines contrary to God's Word. And as far as the sacrifice of the Catholic Mass is concerned, it is definitely from the devil and hence it must be abolished.

Luther's attack upon the "papists" about the sacrificial aspect of the Mass is most extreme, encouraging his followers to proceed with their reform measures in spite of the "howls and objections of their enemies." Fearing, however, that Karlstadt and the people of Wittenberg might easily misinterpret him and resort to unwarranted violence, Luther counsels that in all reform efforts the "weak brethren" should be considered and that faith and love should be applied at all times. And to Spalatin Luther wrote that he approved of the proposal to abolish the masses in Wittenberg.

When rumours of the disturbances continued to reach him at the Wartburg, Luther became especially uneasy about reports of increasing radicalism and violence. On December 4, 1521, he decided to visit Wittenberg to see the situation for himself. He appeared secretly on the streets of the city and was generally well pleased with what he saw. The day before, however, there had been violence; students and some townsfolk had invaded a parish church and had molested the worshippers before the Virgin Mary there. On his way back to the Wartburg, Luther also sensed a spirit of rebellion in the air. Yet on December 5 he still wrote to Chancellor Spalatin that all he saw and heard pleased him well, but added that he was concerned about the radicalism of some and that he would write them and counsel moderation.

Back at the Wartburg, Luther must have thought more seriously about the disturbances in Wittenberg, feeling that the situation might get out of hand and thereby jeopardize all genuine efforts of reform and undo what had been accomplished thus far. He decided to write the Wittenbergers and tell them not to proceed too hastily, warning them that such haste came from the devil. He was not against innovations, Luther continued, but reforms must be the result of the preaching of the Word of God, for there are many brothers and sisters in places like Leipzig, Meissen, and elsewhere who also need to be taken to heaven.

The letter was followed by another pamphlet, *A True Admonition to all Christians to Keep from Uproar and Sedition* (Werke 7, 203–22), which he had promised Spalatin at the end of 1521 that he would write. In this tract Luther argues that only properly constituted secular authorities may bring about needed changes by force and thereby destroy the power of the papacy; since it is the secular authorities' sacred duty to punish wickedness, their punitive action could not be considered rebellious. In the end, however, it is God who must step in to destroy the wickedness of the papacy, even through the sword of the princes if need be. The common people, on the other hand, should obey the magistrates. The papists charge us with rebellion and sedition, Luther continues, but this is a lie, for we preach obedience to the secular powers that have been instituted by God. "Those who have read my teaching correctly, will not rebel," Luther insists, "they have not learned it from me."

In this tract Luther steers carefully between his hatred of the papal system and what it does to true faith, and his concern about the Wittenbergers taking matters into their own hands and using violence to end that system. He calls upon his followers to "teach, preach, speak, and write" that all man-made papal laws are nothing, and that they should not give any money for bulls, candles, bells, tablets, and churches. They would thus work legitimately and with the support of God's Word against that system and not by force. And if force is to be used, only the magistrates can use it. Luther then strikes an optimistic note: the preaching of the Word of God will soon destroy the papal system; and after two years there will be no pope, cardinals, or monks, and no masses, rules, or statutes. However, Christians may not use violence and they must always have consideration for those Christians who are weak in their faith.

In analyzing Luther's attempt to steer between Spalatin's timidity and the Augustinian monks' radicalism, some writers have been severe in their criticism of the reformer. Vedder, for example, states, "[Luther] had uttered sweeping opinions in favor of freedom of conscience, liberty of private judgment, the authority of Scripture, and the priesthood of all believers – opinions that contained logical implications of which he was at the time unconscious, and that he rejected as soon as others, more logical than he, attempted to realize them" (Vedder, *The Reformation* 194). Perhaps, but there was more to this, as the following events will show.

RETURN FROM THE WARTBURG

⟪ Watching the events and developments from his hideout at the Wartburg with increasing concern, Luther decided that the time had come for him to return to Wittenberg. In letters to Chancellor Spalatin and Frederick the Wise he expressed concern about the breaking of images, the enthusiasm of the Zwickau prophets, and the evident intentions of the devil in Wittenberg. But in view of the political situation in Germany, and that ever since the Diet of Worms there had been a price on Luther's head, the Elector was against Luther leaving his hiding place. Luther replied that he was not afraid of Duke George or anyone else, and that he was not in need of the Elector's protection, for God was with him. The gospel of Christ had suffered violence in Wittenberg. This was reason enough for his immediate return.

Luther, in fact, stated three reasons for wishing to return to Wittenberg: First, the church at Wittenberg and the council had invited him to return; second, during his absence the devil had intruded into his fold; third, since many people, particularly the common people, had misapplied and perverted the gospel, there was great danger that people might even rebel against all legitimate authorities. In a letter to Spalatin Luther wrote that he too was in favour of the reforms in Wittenberg, but *he* intended to bring about changes by preaching only the Word of God and not by force. On March 6, 1522, the reformer arrived in Wittenberg, thus making good his earlier intention of not staying any longer than Easter at the Wartburg.

To restore order in the city Luther preached eight consecutive sermons from March 9 to 17 (Werke 1, 320–2). The sermons were directed against the enthusiastic reformers, especially Karlstadt, but Luther refrained from mentioning anyone by name. Luther first of all accuses the Wittenbergers of having disregarded those weak in faith and of having acted without faith and love in their zeal to bring about changes. "I want to tell you plainly," he states in his seventh sermon, "if you will not act in love among yourselves, God will send a plague" to punish you. Reform is good in itself, but the haste with which it has been done is clearly against God. Some preachers in Wittenberg, he continues, have not been called to preach. He, Luther, is their minister called by God and they should have listened to him and asked him first before doing anything drastic. This might have seemed hypocritical or at least questionable to some of his hearers, for Luther had actually approved much of what the Wittenbergers had been doing while he was away.

Some things, Luther continues, are commanded in Scriptures and others are not. There is no biblical support for breaking images. St. Paul knew very well that images were of no use, yet he was not called upon to destroy them. Nor has he, Luther, ever done anything by brute force. For while he slept, Luther adds, perhaps humorously, God's Word accomplished more than what mere force could have done. Moreover, Moses does not speak against the keeping of images but only against worshipping them. After all, only the legal, that is, the secular authorities, have the right to abolish ecclesiastical abuses using force. On the question of laymen touching the sacrament, Luther agrees that Christ and the apostles took the bread in their hands, but these minor things are irrelevant and should not be made into law. Above all else, Luther concludes, a Christian's freedom in Christ must be preserved at all times and a middle course must be followed between certain practices of the past and the innovations in question.

Luther's way of preaching had a calming effect on his audience. It was not only *what* he said and advised about what to do and what not to do, but also his *manner* of preaching, which was persuasive. Albert Burer, a student at the University of Wittenberg, has portrayed Luther as a preacher in the pulpit most positively: "His facial expression is kind, mild, and good-natured. His voice is pleasant and sonorous, and one must marvel at his winsome gift of speech. What he says, teaches and does is quite pious, even though his godless opponents claim the opposite. Whoever has heard him once – unless he is a stone – would gladly hear him again and again, for he drives home his points, like nails, into the minds of his hearers. In short, in him nothing is lacking that belongs to the perfected piety of the Christian religion" (Brecht 2, 57).

After preaching his eight sermons, Luther wrote a pamphlet to repeat and further clarify the issues touched upon in his sermons. His tract *Concerning the Sacrament and Other Innovations* (LW 51, 233–67), is typical of how Luther approached reforms. Regarding external things in the church service, such as the wearing of vestments, the touching of the sacramental bread, Luther advises that Christians must follow their conscience and inner conviction; if one is convinced that the Word of God demands certain practical changes, then one ought to do them. Extremes and radicalism, on the other hand, must always be avoided. There was a time, the reformer laments, when the devil sought to make people "too popish," but now the devil wants to make them "too evangelical." Such practices as auricular confession and celibacy, for example, may all be contrary to God's Word, but one should never forget that a new wine might be too strong for the old wineskins. Haste in these things, he concludes, is always dangerous.

Why did Luther move so decisively against the hasty reforms in Wittenberg, and particularly against his colleague Karlstadt? Some have suggested that Luther became jealous of Karlstadt's popularity and success (CE 9, 449). Letters have been cited in which Luther speaks of Karlstadt's ambition and his attempt to establish his rule and system on the ruin of the reformer's authority (Vedder 191; Littell, *The Anabaptist View* 7). And in Luther's *Table Talks* there are references to Karlstadt's jealousy of the reformer and to Luther's feeling that he, Luther, was more learned than all others, including Karlstadt, which suggests that there may have been personal or professional rivalry between the two colleagues (EA 61, 4).

While it may be true that the very human Luther was not able to tolerate a person who acted without consulting him first and who even threatened to challenge his leadership, the reasons for Luther's caution about the Reformation must be sought deeper than in the mere personality clashes of the two men. Luther's apparent change of attitude and action toward how the Reformation was to proceed stemmed, according to Walter Nigg, from the circumstances in which Luther suddenly found himself, as well as from the double nature of Luther's character. According to Nigg, Luther was one of the greatest revolutionaries ever, yet in his soul he was the most conservative person that ever was. "This mighty revolutionary, who brought the world to the point of explosion, was at the same time a born conservative who drew back in dread from violence and unrest." Luther thus showed the other, more conservative, side in his dispute with Karlstadt and the Wittenberg "enthusiasts" (Nigg 305).

While Nigg's view of Luther's double nature is correct, it must also be acknowledged that Luther was and remained a realist; he knew almost intuitively when to change and act according to the circumstances, but especially when it came to the practical requirements of reform. Luther was certainly practical enough to know than an alliance with certain of his followers, however sincere, could very well jeopardize his cause. Whether his followers had misunderstood what he had taught about Christian freedom, as Luther claimed, is debatable. Luther should have known what effect his writings would have. In retrospect the events in Wittenberg following the disorders and Luther's subsequent preaching and writings bear out the point that Luther was primarily concerned about the success of the Reformation. To achieve his overall objectives, Luther was also prepared to ally himself with the magistrates and princes, "the secular bishops," who were also, according to the reformer, responsible for the success of the Reformation.

ORDER RESTORED

⁋ **Luther's appearance in Wittenberg,** his sermons, and his writings dealing with the events produced the desired effects. As early as March 9, only three days after the reformer's return, Hieronymous Schurf, a councillor in Wittenberg, wrote to the elector that with Luther now at home all would be well and that his sermons would make an end to all that the devil and his followers had done. Karlstadt was pushed aside and forbidden to preach, although he was permitted to remain on the university's faculty. The Lord's Supper *sub una specie* (the bread only for the laity) and the raising of the host (the bread) during communion were restored. All except Karlstadt repented of their rashness and radicalism. For the repentant Gabriel Zwilling Luther was happy to find a pastoral position in the nearby town of Altenburg. In a letter to the former Augustinian monk, Luther advises him to behave in an orderly manner and wear a priest's dress, and to remember that he is sent to those who are weak in the faith and "must still be fed with milk" (Luther, *Letters* 105). Melanchthon too was in full harmony with Luther again. On March 15, Councillor Schurf reported to the elector that Luther had managed to bring the Wittenbergers back to the truth, that the educated and the uneducated were once again full of joy, and that Karlstadt, although still dissatisfied, would be unable to do any harm (WA, Br 2, 472–3).

With regard to Karlstadt, Luther wrote toward the end of March: "I have offended Karlstadt ... although I do not condemn his doctrine, except that he has busied himself in merely external things, to the neglect of true Christian doctrine, that is, faith and charity. For his unwise way of teaching has led the people to feel that the only thing they have to do to be Christians is to communicate [the Last Supper] in both kinds, take the bread and cup in their hands, neglect confession and break images" (Vedder, *The Reformation* 191). Karlstadt continued to smart under Luther's humiliation and appeared to wait for an opportunity for revenge. But when he attempted to publish an article against Luther, the plot was discovered and foiled by the city council. As time went on Karlstadt became more inclined toward mysticism, began to despise the pastoral ministry, and went to live for some time as a peasant in Segrena near Wittenberg, calling himself a "new layman." While he was absent from Wittenberg he continued to collect his university salary. In 1524 he accepted a call to the congregation of Orlamünde which was most happy to receive such a learned professor as pastor who was willing to lead the church members in their crusade against images, infant baptism, and the mass.

Away from Wittenberg, Karlstadt was now free to write against Luther, attacking the reformer's "forbearance for weak Christians," especially criticizing him for his view of justification by faith alone. Luther was of course annoyed. Early in 1524 he informed Chancellor George Brück of Karlstadt's printing press in Jena and advised him to censor his writings. "Although this cannot do much injury to our ministry," Luther wrote, "still it is apt to bring dishonor to our Prince and University, as both have promised that nothing should be published without censorship by proper parties" (Luther, *Letters* 119–20). The authorities took the necessary steps to silence Karlstadt. Luther must have known that in silencing his former colleague he was not consistent with his earlier views on the censorship of his own writings.

Less than a year before the Peasants' War, Luther made a tour through the country, preaching against the "spirit of Alstedt," by which he meant the influence and activities of Thomas Müntzer of Alstedt and of Karlstadt. On August 22 he was in Jena where he preached against the breaking of images, the wrong teaching about the sacraments, and radicalism in general. Karlstadt was in the audience. After the sermon Luther and Karlstadt met at an inn, where Karlstadt sought to justify himself by pointing out that holding different views about the Last Supper and other practices had nothing to do with the "spirit of Alstedt." He further accused Luther of stabbing him in the back instead of admonishing him like a Christian brother, of censoring his writings, and of forbidding him to preach freely. After accusing each other of jealousy and vanity, the interview ended with Luther giving Karlstadt the freedom to write and publish against him as much as he wished, tossing a coin to him as a token of this freedom (EA 64, 384–95).

After this comical event between the two clergymen, the town council and congregation of Orlamünde wrote a letter to Luther, accusing him of identifying them with the "spirit of Alstedt." When the reformer passed through the town some time later, he discussed their letter with the council point by point, showing that there were theological errors in it. The Orlamünders insisted, however, that they were also true Christians, arguing with Luther that on the basis of the Old Testament it was wrong to "worship of images." They also pointed out that according to Luther's earlier writings as well as according to Scriptures, they had the right to call and maintain their own pastor. Luther tried to reason with them, but the resentment and hostility against him were obvious. Fearing for his life, Luther was forced to leave the town. In September 1524 the Saxon authorities, with Luther's support, demanded that Karlstadt, the "restless spirit," be banished. The congregation interceded in vain on behalf of their pastor and his pregnant wife and child. In his farewell address to the people of Orlamünde, Karlstadt closed with the words: "Andreas Bodenstein, expelled by Luther, unheard and unconvinced." A month later Luther wrote what appears to be an uneasy confession, namely that he who at first was to become a martyr, had now caused others to become martyrs (WA, Br. 3, 361). Indeed!

After Karlstadt was driven from Saxony he went to Strasbourg, Basel, Zurich, and other places, all the while writing against Luther and his theology, particularly against the reformer's keeping of the "real presence" in the Eucharist. Karlstadt, no doubt, must be held responsible for initiating the "sacramental controversy" that caused so much strife among the Protestant groups.

THE PRESENCE OF CHRIST IN HOLY COMMUNION

❲❲ **According to Roman Catholic teaching** the Mass is a commemoration of Christ's death on the cross and a repeated sacrifice of Christ every time it is celebrated. The presence of Christ in the Mass is not just a figure or symbol of his presence, but a real presence materially and physically. As the Council of Trent later stated: "If any man deny that in the sacrament of the Holy Eucharist are contained truly, really and substantially, the body and blood, together with the soul and divinity of our Lord Jesus Christ, and consequently the Whole Christ, but says that He is there only as a sign, figure, or power, let him be anathema" (O'Rafferty 94). The real presence of Christ in the Mass was known as transubstantiation. According to Catholic teaching, when the host and the chalice are elevated during the celebration of the Mass, these earthly elements are miraculously transubstantiated (transformed) into the real body and blood of Christ.

Luther first expressed his views about the Mass in his pamphlet *On the Babylonian Captivity of the Church* (1520). In this writing he attacked Holy Communion in one kind, the doctrine of transubstantiation, and the sacrificial nature of the Mass. He rejected transubstantiation because he felt that the doctrine minimized the importance of material or earthly substances. He always remained suspicious of views that underestimated the physical or the material, the real, in favour of the "purely spiritual" aspects of life (Kramm 53).

Luther never used the term "consubstantiation," but it came from how he explained the joining of the spiritual and material in communion: just as in a red-hot bar the fire and the metal do not lose their separate identities, so is Christ in, with, and under the elements of the Eucharist. Or, just as God and the human became one in Christ's incarnation, so too do the elements of bread and wine and Christ's body become one, both retaining, however, their distinct substances (EA 29, 265–6).

In this view Luther believed he was following the church fathers, especially St. Augustine. When Tertullian called the Last Supper a *figura* (figure) of Christ, he did not, according to Luther, mean just a figure or symbol, as Karlstradt, Zwingli, and most Anabaptists believed, but a material form (*Gestalt*), something tangible and substantial (EA 30, 108–10). Luther thus continued to believe, with the Catholic Church, in the "real presence" of Christ in Holy Communion.

Luther's main objection to the Catholic Mass was that the old church continued to believe that in the Eucharist Christ was repeatedly sacrificed. This view struck at the very heart of Luther's experience of salvation and his subsequent theology. Christ had died once and for all time on the cross; to call the Mass a sacrifice implied that Christ needed to be sacrificed again for the benefit of sinful humanity. If St. Augustine called the Mass a sacrifice, he simply meant, according to Luther, that it reminds us of Christ's sacrifice in the past (EA 30, 144–5). Luther also denied the human role in the transaction of the Eucharist altogether, for humans are completely passive in the presence of God, receiving what Christ's grace freely offers. Thus Luther's retention of the real presence and his rejection of the sacrificial nature of the Mass were, according to Bornkamm, the result of the reformer's "yearning for a reality of grace not less real than his sins.... His doctrine of Holy Communion is an expression of his faith in this reality of God in the midst of the world's reality and the reality of man's *Anfechtung*; it is the ultimate deduction of his belief in the reality of forgiveness" (Bornkamm, *Luther's World* 112). Similarly, Martin Brecht observes that in the Eucharist Luther experienced his unworthiness and nothingness before a holy God, but at the same time found in the reality of Christ's presence a gracious and forgiving God (Brecht 1, 79–82).

Of the radicals, Karlstadt was the first to be at variance with Luther on the issue of the real presence; Zwingli and the Anabaptists were to follow Karlstadt. Karlstadt insisted that Christ's body and blood were not really, certainly not bodily or physically, present in the Last Supper, but that the elements of bread and wine simply *represented* Christ and that in partaking of them the believers remembered or commemorated his death on the cross, or at best experienced the *spiritual presence* of Christ. When Christ said, "This is my body," Karlstadt explained, he pointed to himself, not to the bread and wine. In a letter to Chancellor Brück, Karlstadt emphatically stated that Christ's words of institution were most clear on this point and that they were not to be understood literally. But Luther, according to Karlstadt, perverted the clear meaning of Scriptures (Enders VI, 339ff.).

Luther was not slow to accept the challenge of the real presence. In the winter of 1524–25 he wrote a most biting booklet, *Against the Celestial Prophets – Concerning Images and the Sacrament* (LW 40, 73–223), in which he attacked the Zwickau prophets, Thomas Müntzer, and, above all, Karlstadt. With this booklet Luther sets out to answer all of Karlstadt's writings against the reformer. He begins by pointing out that in dissenting from the true teaching on communion, Karlstadt has become an apostate from the faith and an enemy of Christ. Luther then turns to Karlstadt's criticism that the Lutherans call the Last Supper a Mass, which implies that it is thought of as a sacrifice. Luther replies that there is nothing in the name as long as the Mass is not regarded as a sacrificial offering in the Roman Catholic sense.

Christ's words of institution, Luther argues, must be taken literally. In fact, the text of the Bible must be taken literally whenever possible, unless it demands a symbolic or any other interpretation. In reading the Bible, common sense and faith must decide whether Scripture is to be understood literally or symbolically. About Holy Communion, our faith clearly teaches that Christ's body is literally in the elements of the bread and the wine. How the two elements contain Christ is a divine mystery; but it is a truth, for the Word of God cannot lie. To rationalize about this mystery, as Karlstadt does, is from the devil. There is nothing automatic in partaking of the Lord's Supper, as Karlstadt interprets Luther's conception of the real presence; the recipient must have faith in Christ before he or she can benefit spiritually from Holy Communion. When the bread and wine are taken in true faith, there is forgiveness and spiritual power in the sacrament; without faith there is damnation, for the partaker is unworthy to receive the elements in which Christ resides. Luther concludes his *Against the Celestial Prophets* by pointing out that the enthusiasts have completely misunderstood the great truth of the Eucharist, because they have not experienced the forgiveness of God.

There are few theologians today who would consider the Eucharistic controversy as seriously as it was felt and fought in Luther's time. But the issue was very important during the Reformation. What was begun with the Wittenberg radicals like Karlstadt was soon to be continued with Zwingli, the spiritualist Caspar Schwenckfeld, and the Anabaptists. But as Steinmetz has argued, Luther's defence of the real presence of Christ in the Eucharist not only had relevance for the reformer and his immediate followers, but also for Protestant theology today. Among other things, according to Steinmetz, "The eucharist is important as a place where God has attached the promise of his saving and accessible presence. Wherever I turn, God is there; bu he is only there for me where he has bound himself to accessibility by his promise" (Steinmetz, *Luther*, 82–3).

FINAL ENCOUNTER WITH KARLSTADT

Luther's final encounter with Karlstadt came after the Peasants' War in 1525. When the war broke out, Karlstadt was active as a minister in the region of Rothenburg ob der Tauber (on the Tauber River). When he went to pacify the peasants in the region, counselling moderation and peace, he made himself unpopular with them. Karlstadt had rejected Müntzer's more radical views, but since Luther's writings against the militant radicals had also included Luther's former colleague, Karlstadt was seen as a radical as well. Hence he was now pursued, like other revolutionaries, by the authorities. On June 12, Karlstadt wrote to Luther from Frankfurt on the Main, asking him to forgive him for writing against him. In the letter he points out that he has decided not to write nor preach anymore, and he humbly asks his erstwhile colleague and friend to speak for him and his family to the Saxon authorities so that he and his family may be permitted to return to their homeland. Karlstadt is most willing to give full satisfaction to Luther for all that he has done to him (Enders 5, 193–4). In addition, Karlstadt wrote a tract in which he justified himself against his alleged participation in the Peasants' War, asking Luther to publish the letter in order to vindicate his name.

Luther was gracious. In a pamphlet addressed "to all Christians" (EA 64, 404–8), Luther states that although Karlstadt is his foe on account of his doctrine on the Last Supper, it is a Christian's duty to give aid even to an enemy. Luther expresses the hope that Karlstadt will soon come to accept the correct interpretation of the Eucharist. Moreover, according to Luther, the Peasants' War was not so much the result of the activities of the fanatical preachers as the fault of the princes and bishops, who had driven the poor peasants to such extremities that they were forced to resort to violence. Luther thus asks all princes to accept Karlstadt's apology and believe him for the sake of Christ.

Upon Luther's request, Karlstadt wrote a partial recantation of his Eucharistic views, for which Luther supplied a preface (EA 64, 408–10). In it Luther writes that he is happy to accept Karlstadt's explanation that he is still seeking the truth about the Lord's Supper; he also recalls that all the titles of Karlstadt's previous writings were usually in the form of questions rather than dogmatic statements. Although, Luther writes, it is dangerous to waver in one's faith as Karlstadt does, it is still our Christian duty to assist the erring one in brotherly love.

Luther apparently failed to speak to the elector on behalf of Karlstadt, but he invited his former colleague to come and live in his house. Karlstadt accepted the invitation, but the newly established relationship between the two men did not last for long. Karlstadt retracted his recantation, and he and his family were again compelled to leave Saxony. His wayward life ended when he found an open door with the Swiss reformers, who supported Karlstadt, especially when Luther renewed his attack on him. In 1534 Karlstadt was called to Basel as preacher and professor there, a position he held until 1541, when he died during a plague. Luther was convinced that Karlstadt would suffer penalties in hell for his heretical views on the Lord's Supper.

Luther was unable to forget his senior colleague. In his *Table Talks* he spoke about him repeatedly (Werke 8, 186–7). Karlstadt, according to Luther, was ambitious, vain, impudent, and jealous of his younger colleague. He wanted to be more learned than anyone else, and Luther would gladly have yielded this honour to him "had it not been against God," for he, Luther, was more learned than "all sophists and theologians." When Karlstadt returned from Rome in 1515, Luther mocks, he was well dressed, but later, "from pure envy" (*aus lauter Neid*), he became a peasant (*Bauer*), walked about without a hat and did not want to be called doctor but simply "neigbour Andrew" because Christ had forbidden his followers to use titles like "rabbi" (teacher). Karlstadt also condemned academic promotions, but when he officiated at academic functions he still accepted the customary fee of two gulden, which he did not consider hypocritical. Whether completely true or not, Luther's portrait of Karlstadt in the *Table Talks* must have been a subject of great merriment around the table.

{v}

"The Soft-Living Flesh of Wittenberg"
Luther's Struggle and the Revolutionaries

Luther's struggle with the Wittenberg radicals had not yet ended when there arose on the southern horizon a most formidable foe, not only to Lutheranism but also, as far as Luther was concerned, to the social and political structures of German society. Thomas Müntzer (ca. 1489–1525), the Lutheran pastor at Zwickau, whence in 1521 the Zwickau prophets had come to Wittenberg, dissented from the reformer and contributed to the spreading of discontent among the peasants of central and southern Germany. Unlike Karlstadt, Müntzer was not content with just opposing the existing order with his pen; in his writings and sermons he advocated the destruction of the godless to make room for the reign of the kingdom of God. The vehemence, logic, and persuasion with which his ideas were proclaimed, fanned the spreading flames of the Peasants' War. Müntzer was not the only leader in the struggle, but for centuries to come he was seen through the eyes of Luther and his followers as the main villain in the Peasants' War. However, Müntzer has gradually emerged in the historiography of the Reformation, particularly among historians on the ideological left, as a significant thinker, theologian, and social reformer.

There is no doubt that Luther's writings prior to 1525 had confused men's thinking about a Christian's relationship to church and state. Luther's writings about a Christian's freedom, the oppressive and corrupt church, and the responsibility of the princes to do something about the social and political conditions, struck a positive chord among many groups in society, including the common people, who agreed that action was necessary to correct the existing state of affairs. Luther himself saw that the "common man" suffered under the unfair rule of the nobles and princes. But when the reformer realized how his writings and his own example of rebellion were interpreted and applied to what he considered purely worldly conditions, he was not slow to turn against the rebels. As will also become evident, the vehemence with which Luther turned against Müntzer and the peasants may have been partly due to his feeling of being personally responsible for the rebellion and bloodshed. Others certainly saw him as having substantially contributed to the Peasant's War.

LUTHER ON AUTHORITY PRIOR TO 1525

⟪ Luther's views on the subjects and the state remained fairly consistent to the end. In his earliest writings he emphasized that the "common man" had to submit to the magistrates at all times. Rebellion, according to Romans 13, Luther's classic passage on the subject, was against the will of God, and rebels against the state were to be punished severely. In some instances, however, Luther qualified his general position in favour of insubordination to the state, especially when it came to spiritual or church matters. As will be seen, in spiritual matters the state had no business interfering in the lives of individuals or the church. But the people of the time, who experienced the church and state as one overall oppressive authority, did not distinguish between the two realms as distinctly as Luther did.

In the early sixteenth century rebellion was everywhere in the air. Belfort Bax was correct when he wrote, "The Lutheran Reformation, from its inception in 1517 down to the Peasants' War of 1525, at once absorbed, and was absorbed by all the revolutionary elements of the time. Up to the last-mentioned date it gathered revolutionary force year by year" (Bax 27–8). Similarly, Hans-Juergen Goertz argues that "the entire Reformation was radical – in its confrontation of power with saving truth, in its zeal for root and branch reform, and in the way its discourse moved into 'spontaneous socialization'" (Matheson 104). As we have seen earlier, what is commonly called a reformation was actually a revolution, with all the characteristics that go with that concept.

Luther, however, differentiated clearly between the two powers: the spiritual and the temporal. To rebel against the spiritual authorities when they are in the wrong is permissible and sometimes necessary, whereas to rebel against the magistrates, the temporal authorities, is not allowed. In his interpretation of the fourth commandment in his treatise on good works (1520) Luther stated, "one must resist the spiritual power when it does not do right and not resist the temporal power even though it does wrong" (Werke I, 81–3). Time and again, however, Luther explained that if the temporal powers and authorities should urge a subject to act contrary to the commandments of God, or prevent a Christian from living according to biblical principles, obedience to them was to be withdrawn, for one ought to obey God rather than men.

Luther's language against the spiritual powers was especially harsh. To John Lang he wrote on August 18, 1520, that he was convinced that the papacy was the seat of the true and real Antichrist. As far as Luther was concerned, he owed the pope no other obedience than that which he owed the very Antichrist (WA, Br. 2, 167). Elsewhere he stated that it would be far better to kill all the bishops and destroy all monasteries and other churchly institutions than to allow one single soul, not to mention all souls, to perish on account of them (Ritter 136–7). In a letter to the artist Lucas Cranach in April 28, 1521, Luther recalls his humiliating treatment at the Diet of Worms, where he had been asked to recant his writings without even being refuted by learned theologians. "Oh, we blind Germans," he wrote, "how childish we act to allow the Romanists to make fools of us in this miserable manner" (Werke 8, 357–8). His early reformation writings, especially the booklet *To the Christian Nobility*, were filled with statements that were bound to incite rebellious feelings and actions against the spiritual oppressors.

The censorship of the New Testament in Bavaria gave Luther an occasion to treat the question of a Christian's obedience to secular rulers more fully. In January 1523 he published his carefully worked-out booklet *Secular Authority: To What Extent it Should be Obeyed* (Werke 7, 223–73). There are two kingdoms, Luther begins, the kingdom of God and the kingdom of this world. The children of God, who belong to God's kingdom, need no human laws, but the wicked people, who are the vast majority, cannot be held in check without laws and the use of force. Since Christians are ruled by the Spirit of God they need not subject themselves to the magistrates and their laws, but for the sake of order in society and as an example for the wicked, Christians subject themselves freely to human government, pay all required taxes, and generally seek the good of their fellow human beings.

To the question of whether Christians may bear arms, the reformer replies that as Christians they have no need of the sword, and as far as their *private* life is concerned they would rather suffer pain and injustice than use force against another human being. Since Christians, however, must also seek the welfare of their neighbours as well as that of the state, they gladly bear arms for their government, for to refuse to do so would imperil the safety of society. All saints in the Old Testament, Luther states, used the sword, and although the Mosaic law need not be binding in the new dispensation, Christians are obliged to follow the example of God's people, for right will always remain right.

Having said this much in favour of obedience to secular governments, Luther goes on to define the limits of temporal powers in spiritual issues. First, the secular princes have no jurisdiction over the souls of their subjects. No prince, bishop, or any other ruler can make laws about their subjects' beliefs, and no power may compel subjects to believe this or that. Secular rulers have power in strictly temporal matters. They have no right, for example, to interfere with the publication and distribution of Christian literature, for to do so means interfering in the strictly spiritual realm. Even heresy should be of no concern to the temporal rulers, for heresy belongs to the jurisdiction of the bishops and pastors. Heretical teachings must deal with the Word of God only. Since heresy is of a spiritual nature, iron, fire, and water cannot prevail against it.

Second, in a lord–vassal relationship the vassal must be careful to observe his obedience to the master. Vassals may never attack their lord; all they can do is to implore their overlord to do what is right and to refrain from committing evil. A prince, however, may attack and punish his own subjects who rebel, provided of course that all offers of peace have been rejected. On the other hand, if a lord or the government should plan to do evil, a subject need not obey. If a subject, however, is in doubt or ignorant about what the lord or government is about to do, he should obey his lord or government with a clear conscience. This would also apply to just and unjust wars. If a subject is not sure whether the war is just or unjust, the ruler or the government should be given the benefit of the doubt and the subject should go to war and serve with a clear conscience (Werke 7, 269–73). In Luther's reasoning about church–state relations and a subject's part in it, he simply followed medieval feudal theory.

In the same year, 1523, Luther published another pamphlet that had far-reaching consequences. In *That a Christian Congregation has the Right and Power to Judge All Doctrine* (Werke 7, 140–50), he argues that bishops have no right to teach falsely, for false doctrines endanger the spiritual life of their flocks. It is the duty of the Christian congregation to determine whether the doctrines taught are according to God's Word. In taking over judgment in matters of faith and doctrine, bishops and councils act against the express command of Christ. Spiritual tyrants who rule over people contrary to the will of God are to be driven out of Christendom like wolves and thieves. The strong and provocative language of this pamphlet was taken to heart by the peasants and encouraged them to later demand in their Twelve Articles reasonable changes to their situations.

THE COMMOM MAN AND AUTHORITY

In these two different approaches to the two kingdoms, Luther remained consistent to the end. While his statements and the vehemence with which he at times uttered them could be applied to *any* oppressive authority, whether spiritual or temporal, it is wrong to accuse Luther of knowingly or intentionally inciting individuals and groups to rebel against temporal governments. For Luther, whether a temporal government was good or bad, it was divinely established for the punishment of the wicked and for the protection of the innocent. At the same time Luther cannot be absolved entirely from the responsibility of contributing to peoples' longing and desire for, and expectation of a better life. The peasants, the "common man," may have been misguided in applying Luther's principles to their specific economic, religious, and social situations, and they may also have misunderstood his pronouncements about freedom and opposition to Rome. At the same time, they did not distinguish the boundary between Luther's spiritual and temporal realms too carefully.

They knew that they were treated unjustly by both their spiritual and secular rulers and suffered the effects of this injustice. And when they saw that their Christian overlords did not rule according to their professed Christian faith, they saw no other alternative but to rebel, often in the name of Luther himself. But in turning against them, Luther disappointed them and they felt betrayed.

Thus, when a theologically educated and gifted Christian leader like Thomas Müntzer eloquently articulated the plight of the downtrodden and called for action, many peasants and artisans accepted his leadership in the hope that he would lead them to a more tolerable life, especially to a more just existence. They rallied around him and were even willing to die in their attempt to achieve justice.

THOMAS MÜNTZER

⟪ **Thomas Müntzer (ca. 1490–1525)** was born in Stollberg in the Harz Mountains of Saxony. Not much is known about his life. What is known is that he received a good education at the University of Leipzig and Frankfurt on the Oder. He knew the Bible and the medieval mystics well, and was acquainted with Plato, St. Augustine, and most of the classical Christian writers. At some unknown date, perhaps 1513, he became a priest, and in 1516 he became provost at a nunnery at Frohse. Müntzer was a fluent and powerful preacher, and soon had a reputation as a theologian. In 1519 he became assistant and supply preacher to Franz Günther of Nordhausen, a devoted Martinian, as Luther's followers were sometimes called. Although Müntzer did not belong to the circle of "Wittenberg men," it was on Luther's recommendation that in 1520 he received his most prominent appointment to date, that of supply preacher at Our Lady's Church in Zwickau.

The preacher at Zwickau, Sylvius Egranus, an Erasmian humanist, had taken a long leave to visit the famous Erasmus and other scholars in the Rhineland area and in southwest Germany. Upon Egranus' return, Müntzer became preacher in the Church of St. Catherine, which was attended mostly by weavers and generally by the poorly paid proletariat. Influenced by the Zwickau prophets, especially Nickolaus Storch, Müntzer soon began to quarrel with the monks in the town, creating a general disturbance among the already restless citizens of Zwickau. When Luther was informed about Müntzer's activity in Zwickau, he more or less approved of his zeal for the evangelical cause. But in April 1521 Müntzer had to leave the town.

Until February 1522 we find Müntzer in Prague where he drew up his now famous "Prague Manifesto," which became the program for his later activities. The Manifesto was a visionary document, proposing a new church of the spirit, which was not to depend on the letter of the Bible only, but also on direct communications from God. According to the Manifesto, the God who had inscribed the tablets of the law at Sinai inscribes with his finger his will and eternal wisdom in the hearts of men and women. "The script not being written with ink, no man can read it ... unless God himself opens up the human mind. This he does in his elect from the very beginning, so that they are no longer uncertain but have invincible testimony from the Holy Spirit who bears witness, with our witness, that we are children of God, Rom. 8" (Gritsch 56).

The pure church of Christ, according to Müntzer, became prostituted shortly after the death of the apostles and the early followers of Christ due to the scholars, who always wanted to be on top. God permitted this to happen so that the work of men might be exposed for all people to see. According to Müntzer, "monkish clergy shall never represent the true church. Instead, the elect friends of God's word will be instructed in prophesy, just as St. Paul was, so that they might really experience how amiably God speaks with his elect." "I will, for the sake of God," Müntzer stated, "sacrifice my life in order to reveal this truth" (57).

Müntzer then called upon the people of Bohemia to help him in the work of true reformation, and promised the punishment of God's judgment for those who will refuse: "God will perform marvelous feats with his elect, especially in this land; for here shall begin a new church, and this nation will become a mirror to the entire world. I therefore call on everyone to assist in defending the word of God.... If you refuse, God will have you slain by the Turks when they come next year" (58). Referring to his own mission, Müntzer stated, "The time of harvest is at hand. That is why God himself has hired me to labor in his harvest. I have sharpened my sickle; my mind is honed for truth.... Christ will give his kingdom to the elect in a little while."

Müntzer wrote at least several versions of the Manifesto, including one in German, one in Latin, and one in Czechoslovakian (Rupp 174–81). The German version primarily addressed the plight of the common people in Bohemia, emphasizing especially the principle of the priesthood of all believers; the Latin version, in more polished rhetoric, sought the support of influential noblemen and scholars. "I have entered your famous land, my most esteemed Bohemian brethren," Müntzer wrote, "desiring nothing but to strengthen the living Word of God so that it might not be returned empty" (Gritsch 49).

Müntzer's vision somehow failed to impress the people in the land of Jan Hus. Markus Stübner, who had accompanied Müntzer to Prague, was stoned and barely escaped with his life, and Müntzer was put in jail. It is hard to say whether this treatment of the two men also shows popular disapproval of Müntzer's vision and activity. In December 1521, Stübner and his fellow prophets from Zwickau turned up in Wittenberg where Karlstadt, as we have seen, had begun to head his radical reformation. It is likely that Müntzer also came to Wittenberg in the winter of 1521–22 (Rupp 181–2), and thereafter moved from town to town, disappointed at not finding sufficiently open minds and hearts for his gospel und program.

Müntzer's first real success came when in the spring of 1523 he was appointed minister of Allstedt, a small town in the Harz region inhabited by poor and restless ore miners who looked for changes that would at last make their existence easier to bear. Although the town itself had only a few hundred people, Müntzer's sermons, in which he expounded in consecutive order the books of the Bible, attracted thousands of listeners. According to Müntzer, "the poor thirsty folk did so yearn for the truth that all the streets were full of people come to hear it." Müntzer conducted the worship services in German, distributed the Last Supper in both kinds, and wrote several tracts about the Mass and against infant baptism. It was also at this time that Müntzer, like Karlstadt before him, married a former nun, as Luther would do two years later.

As late as July 9, 1523, Müntzer had still not broken with Luther, for on that date he wrote a conciliatory letter to the reformer in Wittenberg. In this letter he suggested, however, that the difference between him and Luther was their different views about the Spirit of God and divine visions and revelations. During the following winter Müntzer founded the Allstedt League, a society that was to carry out by all possible means, including violence if necessary, the Prague program. It was at this time that a nearby Catholic chapel went up in flames. The League may have been responsible for it, although Allstedt was known for its acts of destruction before Müntzer's arrival. In any case, after the formation of the Allstedt League the differences between Luther and Müntzer became more apparent.

DIFFERENCES BETWEEN MÜNTZER AND LUTHER

❰❰ Thomas Müntzer was well grounded in Luther's doctrines of salvation and the priesthood of all believers. He was, however, even more deeply steeped in the literature of the German mystics and held radical views similar to those of the Bohemian Taborites of the fifteenth century. He believed that personal salvation enabled a Christian to communicate with God directly through the Spirit. From the fourteenth-century mystic Johannes Tauler, Münzer had borrowed the idea of Christian suffering, a necessary part in the life of each follower of Christ. Müntzer's doctrine concerning the "bitter Christ," as opposed to what he called Luther's "sweet Christ," grew directly out of this theology of the cross. He believed that Luther made the way to salvation too easy, telling people simply to believe, thus making a "doll out of God" to be played with at will. The godless people who seek to avoid all suffering and the cross, he said, like the idea of someone suffering for them. Suffering, according to Müntzer's theology, is necessary in order to prepare the heart for the Spirit to enter it in all his glory.

Müntzer had written to Luther: "A man cannot know Christ's doctrines unless he has suffered the waves and billows of great waters which overwhelm the Elect … so that a man hopes beyond hope and seeks the one will of God in the Day of Visitation, beyond all expectations" (Rupp 188). And again in this letter, written in Latin, "No mortal understands Christ and his teaching, what is true and what is false, if he has not conformed his will to the cross" (Gritsch 79). Luther might have agreed with Müntzer's theology of suffering, for inner agony and the way of the cross were part of the reformer's life and teaching; but by now Luther had become suspicious of Müntzer's activities in Zwickau, Prague, and Allstedt, and his mystical experience of the "bitter Christ" was foreign to Luther's view of his own understanding of the work of Christ.

Luther and Müntzer were diametrically opposed in their understanding of the authority of the *written* Word of God. For Luther, as we have seen, the Bible was the revealed will of God for the believer, and the written Word the highest court of appeal in spiritual matters. For Müntzer, on the other hand, this adherence to the biblical text, the letter of the Bible, was nothing but "bibliolatry," the worship of external letters. The Bible was a record of God's revelation to individuals in biblical times and a *testimony* to that which Christians felt and experienced in their hearts (Gerdes 89). Adherence to the mere letter of the Bible, according to Müntzer, leads to spiritual death rather than to life. Moreover, he believed the biblical text was inadequate without a divinely inspired interpreter, that is, a person of God inspired by the Spirit of God. Müntzer stated that anyone who had not received "the living testimony of God, Rom. 8, knows nothing significant to say concerning God, even though he had eaten a hundred thousand Bibles." Unless Christians are instructed by the Holy Spirit they cannot understand the Bible, they deceive themselves, and Christ becomes for them a "wooden Christ" ("dichtet sich einen hölzernen Christus") (Meusel 285). Without this heavenly interpreter, according to Müntzer, the Bible remains a book sealed with seven seals, that is, mysterious, hidden, and incomprehensible.

Müntzer, according to Luther, had advocated the observance of several stages before God could reveal himself directly to the individual believer. First, man has to get rid of all coarseness and sin (*Entgröbung*); second, he has to meditate and think on the new life in Christ and eternity (*Studierung*); third, he has to contemplate the sinfulness of sin and God's grace to man; fourth, he has to feel sorrow and repent genuinely of his former sinful life (*Langeweile*); last, he must attain to a state of perfect resignation before God (*tiefe Gelassenheit*), at which point the voice of God will be heard (EA 61, 64).

Here we see Müntzer's indebtedness to the German mystics; the language is Tauler's. Even though Luther too was inclined to a measure of mysticism (Leppin LH 57–61), Müntzer's experience was too subjective; it placed man rather than God in the centre. Luther needed the external Word of God and the visible sacraments to assure him of God's grace and favour. It is interesting, however, that Luther never talked of his assurance of salvation; he left the matter wholly to God, stating that one must believe in the grace of God, but remain uncertain concerning one's own election and that of others (Thiel 445). For Müntzer, on the other hand, there was no question about his election, for the indwelling Holy Spirit was a sure sign of his salvation.

Toward the end of 1523 Luther wrote to Spalatin that he had begged the officials of Allstedt to beware of Müntzer. According to Luther, Müntzer was dangerous, undermining wherever possible the work of the Reformation (Luther, *Letters* 117). And Müntzer felt the same about the reformer at Wittenberg, looking upon him as the self-appointed pope of the new movement.

The battle lines were thus drawn between the two men, and on the question of church and state they collided head-on.

MÜNTZER'S RADICALISM

❮ **Luther believed** that the temporal powers existed as a result of sin and that the magistrates and princes were tools in the hands of God to keep order and wickedness in check. On numerous occasions Luther condemned the abuses of secular power, but he never preached or advocated insubordination to, or abolition of, temporal governments. Thomas Müntzer, on the other hand, was convinced that the time had come for God to eradicate godless and evil governments through the action of his followers. To understand Müntzer's reasoning in this regard, it is important that we consider his view of history, which is best expressed in his *Fürstenpredigt* ("Princes Sermon"), preached on July 13, 1524, before Duke John and his son as they passed through Allstedt (Meusel 278–93). In this sermon, Müntzer sought to persuade them to begin a "revolution from above," but when he failed to convince the princes to act he appealed a few months later to the peasants and artisans to do God's work (Goertz, *Deutschland* 34).

The sermon was based on the prophet Daniel, chapter 2; it had as its object the sympathies of the Saxon authorities for Müntzer's cause. In Daniel 2, Müntzer explains, King Nebuchadnezzar has a dream that his magicians and sorcerers are unable to interpret. When Daniel is brought before the king and told about the dream, the king has forgotten what it was. Daniel not only tells the king what the dream actually was but also interprets its meaning. The king, according to Daniel, saw a great image or statue whose head was of gold, its breast and arms of silver, its belly and thighs of bronze, its legs of iron, and its feet partly of iron and partly of clay. As the king beheld the image, "a stone was cut out by no human hand, and it smote the image on its feet of iron and clay, and broke them in pieces, and became the chaff of the threshing floors.... But the stone that struck the image became a great mountain and filled the whole earth" (Daniel 2:31–5). Daniel then proceeds to interpret the king's dream, telling the king that he is the head of gold and that the kingdoms after him will be of decreasing value, until in the end God will set up his kingdom, which will destroy all the kingdoms represented by the image.

Following the medieval interpretation of Nebuchadnezzar's statue, Müntzer explains that the golden head represents Babylon, the breast and arms represent the kingdom of the Medes and Persians, the belly and thighs the government of Greece, the legs of iron represent tyrannous Rome, and the feet of iron and clay represent the secular and spiritual governments of Münzer's time. When Christ came, he wanted to establish his kingdom on earth, according to Müntzer; but shortly after the death of the apostles the Christian church was prostituted by godless men and false teachers, and throughout the ages the church became a mixture of iron and clay, a union, or combination, of the sacred and profane. To make his point about this union as graphically vivid as possible, Müntzer uses the image of eels and serpents sexually intertwined in one big lump. The clergy are the serpents, according to Müntzer, and the temporal rulers are the eels, and both are obviously both shameless and godless (Meusel 288–9).

Continuing his sermon, Müntzer explains that through all types of acts, ceremonies, and man-made ways of salvation, people have been led astray from the path of truth. But the "little stone," God's Kingdom, will soon fill the whole earth and it is Christians' duty to assist God in his gigantic work. The wicked ones must be destroyed in the fear of the Lord, for they only hinder the progress of God's cause on earth. Becoming more eloquent, Müntzer urges the Saxon princes to wield the sword against all those who oppose the truth and hinder the gospel. If the princes fail in their God-given task, the peasants, who often perceive the truth more clearly than their temporal rulers, will take the matter into their own hands and do what is needed. The evildoers should not be allowed to live any longer, according to Müntzer, for the godless have no right to live when they are in the way of the pious (Goertz, *Deutschland* 25–8).

Some may object, Müntzer interjects, that the apostles did not use force or violence, but it must be remembered that Peter was a timid man of whom even Christ said that he feared death. Moreover, had it been in the power of St. Paul to push his teaching to its conclusion among the Athenians, who worshipped idols (Acts 17:16–34), he would have broken their idols as Moses had commanded and as it was later practised. The godless have two alternatives: they can either deny their faith in Christ, or they can do away with their idols. According to Romans 13, Müntzer insists, it is the duty of the temporal powers to wield the sword against the wicked. If the Christian princes do not act according to God's Word, the sword will be taken from them, for they confess Christ with their mouth only and deny him with their actions. The death of the godless is the only way to bring the church back to its original purity. The godless have no right to live, Müntzer concludes, except as the elect believers wish to grant it to them. Müntzer then exclaims triumphantly: "Rejoice, you true friends of God, that for the enemies of the cross their heart has fallen into their breaches."

Besides advocating violence against godless rulers and false teachers, other points in Müntzer's sermon ran contrary to Luther's teachings. Basing his view on Daniel's insight into divine will, Müntzer stresses God's immediate revelations to the saints. In this the times have not changed, says Müntzer, for God still reveals his secrets to his friends. But teachers who teach otherwise (and here Müntzer no doubt had Luther in mind) are completely wrong. The Spirit of God reveals himself to those who listen to him and who are receptive to his promptings. Müntzer certainly believes that God has revealed the future to him, and the dukes of Saxony need a Daniel so that the truth might also be revealed to them. Müntzer is doubtless suggesting here that he, not Luther, should be the spiritual guide of the princes (Hinrichs 43–4). Just as King Nebuchadnezzar honoured and listened to Daniel, so should the temporal princes now heed Müntzer's words. Attacking Luther's teaching about the two kingdoms, without mentioning the reformer by name, Müntzer points out that the princes have been fooled into believing that their only duty is to look after law and order in their realm, not to concern themselves with spiritual matters. According to Müntzer, the princes have a responsibility in spiritual matters as well. This is of course what Luther also believed, but each interpreted their view of the princes' responsibility to their own advantage.

After Müntzer's sermon, the Saxon princes were thoroughly confused and asked Luther for advice as to what to do. When the reformer heard about the "Princes Sermon," he was aghast at what he saw as the audacity of his former follower. As far as Luther was concerned, it was not the duty of the state to set up utopia on earth but to prevent earth from becoming chaotic. In *A Letter to the Princes of Saxony Concerning the Seditious Spirit* (LW 40, 45–59), Luther warned the magistrates against the "spirit of Allstedt" and advised them to be on guard against prophets who claim to hear voices and have visions. Why is Müntzer afraid to answer for his views to him, Luther? Although he, Luther, had no voices from heaven, he had not been afraid to appear at Leipzig, Augsburg, and Worms when he was asked by his enemies to do so. Luther then laments that it was he who won the victory over the pope and that now his deserters exploit this victory for their own cause and advantage. His advice to the princes is to let these prophets preach and teach, as long as they do not take up arms against the government. But as soon as they draw the sword they must be banished at once from the land. The spirits must fight it out between themselves, Luther writes, for he is quite confident that the true doctrine will prevail in the end. It is interesting to note that at this time Luther still did not advocate force, persecution, or the death penalty for his opponents.

When Müntzer continued to encourage his followers to resist and even go to war against the authorities, the Elector of Saxony summoned Müntzer to appear in Weimar in August 1524 to give an account of his activities and views. The commission to examine Müntzer consisted of Duke John, who had heard the "Princes Sermon," Chancellor Brück, and three professors from Wittenberg, all sympathetic to Luther. Müntzer was accused of inciting people to riot, counselling peasants to withhold their taxes, and of despising and resisting governments. After the hearing, Müntzer was informed that after due deliberation with the Elector about his case, he would soon be notified about the outcome of the proceedings, but in the meantime he was to conduct himself "peacefully" (Meusel 52–3).

Müntzer did not wait to learn what the Saxon authorities would decide in his case. Fearing the worst, he left Allstedt and fled to nearby Mühlhausen, Thuringia, where he wrote an angry pamphlet against Luther with the title, *Thomas Müntzer's Answer to the Spiritless, Soft-Living Flesh at Wittenberg* (Meusel 294–308). Müntzer calls Luther, among other things, "Brother softlife," "Doctor liar," "Father soft-step," "Pope of Wittenberg," "Virgin Martin," "Educated rascal," "Leader of the blind," "Arch-devil," and "Arch-heathen." Müntzer compares himself to Christ, who was also persecuted by the Jews and the Pharisees. Luther, the Pharisee and servant of princes, knows what is good for him and thus refuses to speak out against the tyranny of the nobles, which, according to Müntzer, is the cause of the rebellious attitude among the peasants and craftsworkers. Müntzer is not impressed with Luther's supposed courage at Leipzig, Augsburg, and Worms. When Luther appeared before his enemies, he had powerful friends at his side; in fact, Müntzer claims, had he faltered and yielded before the emperor at Worms, the nobles would likely have stabbed him to death.

In a letter of August 14, 1524, Luther warned the Council of Mühlhausen not to receive Müntzer, for his activities in Zwickau and Allstedt had shown that he was a murderer. Müntzer, suggested Luther, should be asked who had called and sent him to preach. If he insisted that it was the Spirit of God, he should be required to do miracles, for God always attests extraordinary activities with signs and wonders (EA 58, 253–5). But the letter came too late. Müntzer had arrived in Mühlhausen a few days earlier and had been welcomed by the town. With the help of other radicals, notably Heinrich Pfeifer, among other social revolutionaries, the town council was overthrown and radical reforms were introduced (Goertz, *Deutschland* 126ff). However, after only two months of restless activity, Müntzer was compelled to leave Mühlhausen and flee to Nürnberg where he exerted some influence on Hans Denck, who later became one of the leaders of the peaceful Anabaptists (Friedmann, "Thomas Müntzer's Relation" 78). In November and December of 1524 Müntzer wandered throughout southern Germany, preaching his revolutionary gospel. But his work at rousing the masses did not have much success. Apparently Müntzer was more popular in Mühlhausen, but not all of Thuringia was open to his ideas, and Franconia rejected him outright (Bax 33–4). It has also been shown that Müntzer cannot be held responsible for the revolt in the Upper Rhine regions (Schiff 89–90). If Müntzer was successful in arousing the peasants to action, his success was a limited one at best. As will be seen, after the defeat of the peasants Müntzer held them at least partly responsible for their defeat.

In February 1525, Müntzer was back in Mühlhausen, where Heinrich Pfeifer had also returned by the end of 1524. In the hope of at last rousing the discontented groups among the peasants and workers to concrete action, Müntzer wrote an explosive letter, addressed to the miners of Mansfeld. "Dear brothers, how long will you sleep?" Müntzer urges his readers. "How often have I told you as to how it is to be done! God can no longer reveal himself [to you] you must act.... Get to it. It is time! The wicked despair like dogs.... You must strike now while the fire is hot! Don't let the swords cool from the blood of the princes.... It is impossible to have peace and be free while the wicked rule over you.... It is God's war and he will fight for you." Müntzer signed his call to arms: "Thomas Müntzer, a servant of God against the godless" (Meusel 273–4).

Similarly, in a letter to Duke Ernest of Mansfeld, written on May 12, Münzer warns "Brother Ernest" not to oppress and persecute the Christians in his domain, for God will not permit such cruelty to go unpunished. "The eternal living God has commanded that you be deprived of your power by force, which has been granted us. You are of no use to Christendom; you are harmful to the friends of God.... We demand an answer at once, or else we shall move against you in the name of the hosts of God." Again Müntzer signed his name, but now added, "with the sword of Gideon" (273–6).

As Hans-Juergen Goertz observes, Müntzer hoped to achieve a reformation that would extend, theologically and geographically, beyond Mühlhausen and the surrounding areas; Müntzer worked toward the establishment of God's reign on earth that would bring freedom to all and where God would rule over all things (Goertz, *Deutschland* 128–9). But tragically for the visionary, on May 15, 1525, the sword struck at last in the battle near Frankenhausen, between the nobles and the peasants, but not to the advantage of Müntzer and the commoners. The battle ended in defeat for both Müntzer and the peasant groups he led. Five thousand commoners lay slaughtered. Only six of the nobles' forces were killed. The difference in the number of dead on both sides showed that the peasants were the victims, not the attackers (Schilling 311). On May 27, Müntzer and fifty-three of his followers were captured, tortured, and beheaded in Mühlhausen.

Before he died, Müntzer apparently recanted his radicalism and then received the Mass according to the Catholic rite, although his recantation has been questioned. Even as he faced death, this radical reformer urgently entreated the princes and nobles to deal more mercifully and justly with their subjects and govern them according to God's Word. As to the failure of his movement, Manfred Bensing suggests that since Müntzer was mainly concerned with the religious and ethical training of the peasants and other working people, his ideas and visions for them demanded too much for their comprehension. But Müntzer also saw God's judgment in the failure. "The collapse of the revolt seemed to him to be the judgment of God on the as yet unpurified people, but not synonymous with the defeat of his idea of a new society" (Bensing, "Müntzer, Thomas" 620).

Müntzer's ideas and visions of a just society did not die with their author. The sources generally indicate that this rebel was highly esteemed by many common people until the late 1530s and after. Not without reason did Luther continue to warn people against the "spirit of Allstedt." Shortly after Müntzer's death,

Luther published his *A Terrible Story and Judgment of God Upon Thomas Müntzer* (WA 18, 362–74), addressed to his "beloved Germans." Luther states that he writes this story to show how God judges so righteously, "to warn, to terrify, and to admonish" those who are still contemplating rebellion, and to comfort and strengthen those who suffer on account of the rebels. After commenting on some of Müntzer's radical pamphlets, which are shown to be "diabolical" in spirit, Luther concludes his *Terrible Story* by elaborating on the false hopes and confidence the peasants had placed in their leader. Müntzer had promised that one peasant would be able to kill a thousand enemies, Luther wrote, and that the prophet himself would divert the bullets into his sleeves. Instead, said Luther, 5,000 disillusioned peasants lay brutally murdered near Frankenhausen. Luther expresses sorrow about the fate of the peasants, but he regards it as God's judgment upon them and he will continue to pray for the ultimate victory of the princes. Similarly, Luther wrote to John Rühel, his brother-in-law, that he was glad that Müntzer was now dead: "It is the judgment of God. He who takes the sword shall perish by the sword" (Luther, *Letters* 139). Even years later the memory of Thomas Müntzer continued to haunt Luther. On several occasions Luther told stories about his former foe, and from time to time he referred to Müntzer's death as God's punishment for rebellion, blasphemy, and unbelief. Luther never changed his mind about Müntzer. "Whoever has seen Müntzer, may say he has seen the bodily devil." And Luther never regretted, as he put it, killing Müntzer. "I have killed Müntzer. His death is on my conscience, but I have done it because he wanted to kill my Christ" (Schilling 317).

Luther may have sincerely believed that Thomas Müntzer was evil, and justly punished by God, but after Müntzer's death and in the following decades religious groups such as the Hutterian Brethren continued to think and speak well of this "Mystic with the Hammer." It is also significant that among Mennonite historians today Müntzer is not seen as the evil revolutionary Luther and other magisterian reformers had portrayed him as, but as a religious thinker and pious activist, however misguided he may have been in his view of lethal force. After all, this radical reformer had the good of the poor and downtrodden masses at heart. From Conrad Grebel's letter to Müntzer in 1524 to present-day historiography, this prophet of the "common man" finds sympathy and admiration from the descendants of those who experienced persecution through the ages (Friesen, *Thomas Müntzer*).

The view that Müntzer was a sincere religious believer and theologian, however, is contrary to the view of Marxist historians, who see Müntzer as a proto-Communist revolutionary. Müntzer's Christian language in his appeals to the rulers and peasants, according to some Marxist writers, was simply his way of reaching the peasants and proletarians' ears and hearts. Some of them have even suggested that he was an atheist. However, such views of Müntzer may not only be anachronistic, projecting much later ideas onto an earlier time, but also miss the mark in understanding the man, his theology, and his main concerns. Münzer was an apocalyptic mystic and visionary, awaiting the coming of God's kingdom on earth, and at the same time a revolutionary who sought to bring God's kingdom about with the help of the common people, but in the end tragically failed.

{vi}

"I Commanded Them to be Killed"
Luther and the Peasants

LUTHER'S RESPONSIBILITY FOR THE PEASANTS' WAR

Neither Luther nor the Wittenberg radicals, including Thomas Müntzer, can be held directly responsible for the Peasants' War that broke out in 1525 with such unprecedented fury. The war was a repetition on a larger scale of many similar attempts in the past, and the interests underlying all of them were not primarily religious – although religious considerations played an important part – but political, social, and economic. There had been peasants' revolts in many countries in late medieval Europe, among others, Bulgaria in 1277–80; Flanders in 1323–28; England in 1381; and the so-called "Poor Conrad" rebellion in Würtemberg in 1514, just three years before Luther's revolt in 1517. All these rebellions were expressions of peasants' discontent and cries for economic and social justice. The Peasants' War in 1525 was thus a rebellion in line with a long history of peasants' revolts throughout Europe.

In this book we are not delving much into the background or the progress of the 1524–25 conflagration, but are primarily interested in Luther's part in the rebellion and his attitude toward the rebellious peasants as expressed in his writings. As we shall see, the relationship between Luther and the peasants had far-reaching consequences, not only for the peasants and common people in general, but also for the radical reformation and the rise and development of Anabaptism. It may seem ironic that Luther, who often spoke of his humble and peasant-like beginnings, did not concern himself much with the peasants and their lot prior to 1525. From the beginning of his reformation work, his concern was the nobles to whom he appealed for support, not the peasants or artisans. It was, however, during and after the Peasants' War that Luther increasingly turned his attention to the peasants and artisans, the "common man" (*der gemeine Mann*), that is, the lower classes in society. It must also be stated at the outset that Luther never intended to use the plight and the poor conditions of the common people in the cause of his reformation work. In fact, as we shall see, his attitude and actions during the Peasant' War harmed the cause of the Reformation considerably (Kohnle, LH 134–9).

While Luther should not be accused of having caused the Peasants' War, as some have done, it was no doubt due to the reformer's influence that this war in its magnitude and ferocity surpassed any seen in Germany before. The conviction, and at times violent language, with which Luther expressed his views in his early writings, left their mark on all strata of German society, including the peasants and urban workers. Luther's statements with regard to Christian freedom, social justice, and the limits of papal and temporal powers, became especially dangerous weapons in the hands of the victims of the dying feudal order. For many peasants, the reformer became the central figure of the revolutionary movement, political and social no less than religious. Luther's attacks upon many features of the existing order, his criticism of the increasing luxury of the prosperous classes, his denunciation of the greed of great commercial magnates, his condemnation of the tyranny and corruption of civil rulers as well as ecclesiastical leaders – all this tended to inflame the populace and spread impatience and discontent among them (Bax).

Luther's contemporaries, both friends and foes, were fully aware of the reformer's indirect contribution to the social discontent among the peasants.

The humanist Ulrich Zasius wrote, "Luther has plunged Germany into such a state of frenzy that one must perforce regard as peace and safety the mere hope of not being knocked on the head" (Brentano 197). In his *Hyperaspistes* Erasmus wrote: "We have the fruit of your spirit – you cannot make men believe that the occasion of these tumults was not furnished by your pamphlets, especially those in German. But, O Luther, I do not yet think so ill of you as to suppose that you intended this" (Vedder 253). Erasmus again: "You Luther refuse to acknowledge the insurgents, but they acknowledge you, and the instigators of this war claim the Gospel as their guide" (Brentano 197).

Some Catholic opponents were especially critical of Luther's alleged wilful contribution to the outbreak of the Peasants' War. Jerome Emser (1477–1527) and Johann Cochlaeus (1479–1552), both fierce opponents of the reformer, wrote vicious pamphlets against Luther, arguing that his writings on freedom from all laws and on the priesthood of all believers encouraged people to throw off both their spiritual and temporal yokes and take matters into their own hands. But these opponents of Luther either failed or did not want to understand Luther's teaching about the two realms. Luther had always taught obedience and submission to temporal governments (Edwards, *Printing* 149–62).

It is certainly true, as Erasmus put it, that Luther had not intended the rebellion. Luther's own example of rebellion against Rome and his writings were revolutionary in nature, to be sure, but from Luther's point of view, as Edwards has argued, his work and writings were misunderstood, misinterpreted, and often misapplied by the common people. Some of his tracts, such as *The Freedom of a Christian*, were written for the instruction and encouragement of laypersons, but the peasants and other rebels used them for their own ends. Other writings, such as *To the Christian Nobility*, were meant only for the nobility, but the commoners thought they were an appeal to them to fight against all oppression and a special assignment for them to bring about a reformation of the old order. Luther's gospel of Christian liberty was sometimes changed from the reformer's meaning of an inner, spiritual, freedom of the spiritually reborn individual, to mean freedom from social injustice and from the economic bondage of feudalism (Kohnle, LH 135).

THE TWELVE ARTICLES

☾ In March 1525 the peasants of southwesternern Germany drew up twelve articles, asking certain concessions and alleviations of the feudal lords. The articles "are without doubt the most influential statements of the resisting commoners" as James Stayer writes (*The German Peasants' War* 49). While the names of the authors or compilers of the *Twelve Articles* are not known, it is believed that a priest and a local furrier at Memmingen in Upper Swabia were behind them (Brady 186). The articles were addressed "To the Christian Reader" and were highly religious in tone and content, each article supported with ample passages from Scripture, similar to Luther using Scripture in his writings to support his assertions. The demands included the following points: that the Christian congregation have the freedom to elect their own priest and that the priest be supported by the tithes of the community; that the status of servitude to the feudal lords be abolished; that there be freedom of hunting and that the woods be accessible to all; that the services due to the lords be diminished; and that the princes and nobles no longer oppress the peasants. Article 3 especially emphasizes freedom for all: "It has until now been the custom for the lords to own us as their property. This is deplorable, for Christ redeemed and bought us all with His precious blood, the lowliest shepherd as well as the greatest lord, with no exceptions ... the Bible proves that we are free and [we] want to be free." The authors of the *Twelve Articles,* according to Thomas Brady, did not want freedom only for themselves, but for all people, regardless of rank or station in life (Brady 187). In the twelfth article the peasants agreed to delete any point that the princes might object to, provided it could be proved that the objectionable article was contrary to the Word of God and reason. This was certainly in keeping with the standard of judgment that Luther himself applied in acting against his opponents.

Some feel that the attitude of most German peasants in 1525 is not to be sought in the extreme radicalism of a Thomas Müntzer but in the nature and tone of the *Twelve Articles*. Interestingly, in 1525 some rebels' armies even invited the lords to join them as brothers (Brady 187). The articles were no doubt reasonable demands and seemed to express a truly Christian spirit. The peasants themselves certainly believed that their demands were also in line with the Wittenberg theologians. They even suggested at times that Luther and Melanchthon be the referees in the disputes between them and the nobles (Kohnle, LH 135).

Luther at first also believed that the articles were an expression of just grievances on the part of the peasants. But when the disturbances began to increase in the south, Luther wrote his *Warning Toward Peace Based on the Twelve Articles* (Werke 7, 303–40; LW 46, 3–43), in which he addressed both the nobles and the peasants. Luther begins the first part of the pamphlet, directed at the princes, by citing Psalm 7:16: "His mischief returns upon his head, and on his own pate his violence descends." Luther then accuses the princes and bishops of opposing the gospel and of oppressing the peasants, warning them that judgment is certain to come upon them, for it is not the peasants but God himself who is against them. The princes are fully responsible for spreading social and political unrest. Luther agrees that the demands of the *Twelve Articles* are reasonable and that they show a great deal of restraint on the part of the peasants; the princes should yield and accept them, for he, Luther, would have demanded much more. Concluding the first part, the reformer scolds the nobles for making his doctrines responsible for the disturbances; the peasants will teach the princes a lesson for such blasphemy.

In the second part of the pamphlet Luther turns to the peasants, his "beloved friends" and "brothers," as he calls them, admonishing them not to heed the fanatical preaching of the "enthusiasts" who incite them to godless action. It is against all natural law and against the Word of God to oppose the temporal rulers, no matter how evil they may be. If the peasants cannot endure it in one place, Luther advises, they should seek refuge elsewhere, and God will deliver his children from all troubles. The peasants should not rebel against the authorities, for rebellion will retard the progress of the gospel and play into the hands of the devil.

In reviewing the articles one by one, Luther states that the first, the one about choosing a pastor, is in agreement with the Word of God. The second, which deals with the abolition of tithes, is outright robbery, for tithes rightfully belong to the government. The third article, about the abolition of servitude, is quite repulsive because it degrades the spiritual freedom in Christ to a carnal level. After all, did not Abraham and the other patriarchs own slaves? The remaining articles Luther leaves to the judgment of lawyers, for as a minister of God he cannot advise in such mundane matters as forest laws and hunting regulations. As a minister of the gospel, his duty is to instruct consciences only. In conclusion, Luther tries to pacify both sides, stating that a good conscience must be maintained at all times.

Luther's intentions in writing the tract were both sincere and well meant, but his exhortations were imprudently expressed. The fact that Luther addressed both sides in the same pamphlet may have doomed any possibility of it being successful in stemming the tide of insurrection. The ambiguous tone of the tract was interpreted by the peasants to their own advantage and served to stimulate rather than to pacify the insurgents. In fact, the document strikes one as more favourable to the rebels than to their opponents. However, Luther's train of reasoning did not convince the peasants. As far as they were concerned, Luther at first seemed to state that their case was reasonable and then decided to withdraw.

On the other hand, as far as the nobles were concerned, the tract seemed to strengthen their position considerably by admitting their right to rule over their subjects, however oppressively. Thus on the one hand Luther merely threatened the princes with the judgment of God, which was not taken too seriously by the nobles, and on the other counselled the peasants to be patient in the face of oppression. While the peasants were confused, the nobles saw clearly what they had to do to suppress the uprising, something they were already doing successfully everywhere.

LUTHER AGAINST THE PEASANTS

❪ **The disturbances** continued to spring up in various localities. When Luther learned that he was being quoted in support of lawlessness and violence, he felt compelled to act more decisively. In April 1525 he visited Eisleben, his birthplace, and received much first-hand information concerning acts of violence committed by the rebels. He toured the region, risking his life in an effort to calm the people and if possible to restore peace. The situation, however, seemed to be out of hand. Luther's preaching to the peasants fell on deaf ears. In May he wrote from Seeburg to John Rühel in Mansfeld, urging him to use the sword against the rebellious peasants, quoting Scriptures, "For those who take the sword must perish by the sword" (WA, Br. 3, 479–82). Frederick the Wise, who was on his deathbed as the revolt gathered momentum, was of a different opinion, advising his brother who was to succeed him to do all he could to pacify the insurgents and to attack them only as a last resort (WA Br. 3, 508). Returning to Wittenberg, Luther was now determined to write a pamphlet against the disturbances. On May 6 he wrote his tract, *Against the Murderous and Plundering Bands Among the Peasants* (Werke 7, 342–52; LW 46, 49–55), for which he has been severely criticized to this day.

In his *Against the Peasants* Luther indicts the rebels on three charges, for which they need to be severely punished: first, the peasants have broken their oath to their legitimate government, hence they are subject to arrest and trial; second, they have robbed and murdered, for which they have surely deserved death both in body and soul; and, third, they have covered their sins in the name of Christian brotherhood, thereby blaspheming God and disgracing his holy name. Luther compares the rebels to a mad dog that must be quickly destroyed lest it contaminate a whole community. He calls upon all people to flee from the peasants as from the very devil and urges the rulers to put away all scruples about inflicting the death penalty upon the rebels. In his previous pamphlet the princes were a set of scoundrels for the most part, responsible for the uprising; now they are God's ministers called upon to restore order.

For Luther, the peasants' quoting of Scriptures in support of their rights, and contending that as baptized Christians they can demand what they need from the Christian nobles, is nothing but greed and blasphemy. They want to have all things that do not belong to them in common, and at the same time keep their own things for themselves. "These are fine Christians!" Luther mocks. "I think that there is not a single devil left in hell, for they have all entered the peasants" (Werke 7, 348–9). The nobles are told that if they fall in this war they will be true martyrs, for they will die in the service of love for their neighbour, whereas whoever is killed on the peasants' side will suffer forever in hell. In the end Luther calls upon all nobles who can to stab, beat, and strangle the peasants (*steche, schlage, würge hier, wer da kann*), for such strange times have come that a prince can more easily earn heaven through bloodshed than another through prayer (Werke 7, 351).

In the last paragraph Luther is certain that his advice to kill the peasants and to flee from them is right: "Here every pious Christian say Amen. For this prayer is right and good and pleases God, this I know. But if someone thinks this is too hard, one should know that rebellion is unbearable [*unerträglich*] and that the destruction of the world is to be expected" (353). In other words, according to Luther, the rebellion and war of the peasants is in its seriousness comparable to and indicative of the apocalypse.

Considering the circumstances in which the reformer suddenly found himself and what a successful rebellion would have meant to his cause, his attitude toward the rebellious peasants is understandable. But, as a Christian pastor, the sharp language he used cannot be excused, and the wisdom of writing the tract may seriously be questioned. Luther must have known when he wrote it that the princes were winning everywhere and that the commoners were fighting with very primitive weapons, spades and hoes, against overwhelming odds. The burgo-master of Zwickau, for example, expressed the thought that the princes would have punished the rebellious peasants severely enough, thus there was no need for Luther to encourage them to do what they were doing so well already (355).

Luther, however, had his reasons for writing so harshly against the rebels. Karlstadt, Müntzer, and their followers, with their radical gospel about the overthrow of the godless and the establishment of God's rule on earth, were not to be trusted. Luther sincerely believed, wrongly or rightly, that the radicals' destructive opinions were not only contrary to Scripture, but also opposed to the traditional and accepted feudal system of the time. For Luther, the threat that the peasants' rebellion posed to the existing order was comparable to the threat that the Ottoman Turks posed to the existence of Christian Europe, a threat Christendom was very conscious of at the time.

It must also be remembered that Luther suffered greatly from the accusations of his enemies that he was responsible for the Peasants' War, an accusation from which he wished to clear himself. It has also been suggested that Luther was fearful that in view of his earlier tract, in which he had called the peasants his friends and brothers, the nobles might withdraw their support from him and his reform efforts (Smithson 177–8). Whether this thought entered his mind cannot be established, but there is some evidence to suggest that Luther was not so certain that the rebels would be defeated in the end. In his *Against the Murderous Peasants* Luther wrote that if the peasants should win the war – "God forbid" he added – the nobles would have nevertheless fought and died in a good cause and with a good conscience (Werke 7, 351).

Those who insist that the intent and purpose of most of Luther's writings ws primarily religious and theological are only partly correct. It must be remembered that theological and practical considerations for Luther were all more or less one when it came to Reformation issues. This was especially so when he dealt with practical issues like rebellion and war. Thus his tract against the peasants addressed both theological and political issues, and in doing so combined religious, social, and economic concerns, all closely related to Luther's work. Above all, however, for Luther the theologian, it was St. Paul's teaching about the functions of secular governments, as expressed in Romans 13, which gave him the assurance that it was a serious offence against God and the divinely instituted social and political order for subjects to rebel against legitimate temporal governments.

CONCERNING THE HARSH BOOKLET

❰ Luther's treatment of the rebellious commoners had serious consequences for both him as a person and the future of the Reformation. Not only did the peasants and the enemies of the Reformation accuse Luther of flattering and supporting the nobles against the rebels, but some friends also found it difficult to understand the reformer. Had he not, they asked, dismissed all kindness and mercy, and encouraged the bloodthirsty princes in their cruel slaughter? Had he not, by advocating gruesome and bloody deeds and saying that they merited heaven, betrayed his principle of justification by faith alone? Had he not betrayed those who quoted him in support of their actions? The answers to these questions were affirmative as far as the peasants and Luther's opponents were concerned.

In July of that fateful year, after pressure from his friends, Luther decided to explain and justify what he had written against the peasants. In a tract, entitled *An Open Letter Concerning the Harsh Booklet Against the Peasants* (Werke 7, 355–82; LW 46, 59–85), dedicated to his friend Caspar Müller of Mansfeld, Luther goes into great detail to justify his tract against the peasants. In this tract he even threatens those who criticize him, for they thus show that they are on the peasants' side and may be rebels themselves who deserve punishment (Werke 7, 360). He addresses three groups of his critics: those smart know-it-alls who now condemn him because of his tract; the "blood-hounds" who are on the peasants' side and now demand mercy for them; and those well-meaning people who cannot differentiate between God's kingdom and the worldly kingdom, a subject, Luther says, he has written about so often.

Luther emphatically states that he will not retract anything in his harsh booklet, and that it matters little whether it displeases anyone or not, as long as it pleases God. Whether one should be merciful or not is of little concern to him when the Word of God on these issues is plain. One cannot persuade a rebel with reason, for he will not listen to sense; these peasants must be answered with the fist until the blood gushes forth from their noses (*dass der Schweiss [blood] zur Nase ausgehe*). Luther adds, "Mercy here, mercy there. We now speak about God's Word, which states that the king must be honoured and that the rebels must be destroyed" (361). Luther then again summarizes his teaching on the spiritual and secular kingdoms and what their functions are. And the function of the secular kingdom is to punish the rebels and to protect the innocent.

That the nobles abused their power in punishing the rebels is none of his concern, for they have not learned such cruelty from him, and what is more, they too will have to answer for their wickedness. He is far from flattering the princes, he writes; in the near future he will write against them as well. Had the temporal authorities listened to his persistent warnings against the fanatical preachers before the war, all this misery, cruelty, and bloodshed could have been prevented. Rebellion against the temporal powers is a worse crime than murder, Luther argues, for a murderer just kills ordinary or common persons, but a rebel who strikes at governments, as the peasants did, strikes at the heads of legitimate institutions, thus destroying the entire temporal order, which was instituted by God (376–7). To illustrate his point more dramatically, Luther says that even if he were the servant of a Turkish master, it would be his duty to protect his Turkish overlord to the point of his own life.

Luther then speaks of what he wrote about earning heaven throught bloodshed and that such cruel deeds were better than prayer. According to Luther, his critics had completely misunderstood him. In his harsh booklet, Luther writes, he did not speak of salvation and good works, but about the duties of Christian princes, whose responsibility it is to quell insurrection and restore order, and that in doing so princes perform a good work and please God. According to Luther, the princes would even become martyrs if they should die in doing God's will. But those who on the princes' side committed atrocities and cruelty to the innocent or fleeing peasants will have to answer to God for their sins.

As an example of such brutality and misdeeds, Luther speaks of what he had heard about Thomas Müntzer's pregnant widow who, according to the story, was sexually abused by an immoral man on the princes' side. "Scriptures calls such men who molest a poor, forsaken and pregnant little woman not human beings but beasts, so I too will not call them human beings," Luther writes (381). Luther writes in conclusion that with this *Open Letter* he has answered all, both the peasants and the nobles, and that both must remain in their God-given calling and live and act as Christians where God has placed them.

CONCLUDING COMMENTS

⁌ **Before the end of 1525** the main revolt was brutally crushed. Luther himself assumed that a word from him would have gone far to turn the tide in favour of the rebels. In one of his *Table Talks* Luther said boastfully: "Preachers are the biggest killers, because they admonish the governments to punish the bad boys [*böse Buben*]. I, M. Luther, have killed all the peasants, for I ordered them to be slaughtered; all their blood is on my head. But I put this to the account of our Lord God, for he commanded me to speak that way" (Werke 8, 189). In May 1525 he wrote to John Rühel, who was moved with compassion for the poor suffering people, not to take it too hard, for had God not judged the rebels, Satan would have done even more harm (WA Br. 3, 507). In another letter, Luther again assured Rühel that God knows who among the peasants is guilty or who is innocent. If there are innocent people among the insurgents, he writes, God will save and protect them. Most of them, however, are without any sense and therefore had to be punished. If one wished to pray for the peasants, one should pray that they might become more submissive to the temporal authorities. If they refuse to obey, no mercy should be shown them (WA Br. 3, 515).

There were others among Luther's supporters who continued to feel ill at ease about the heavy lot of the common people. When the nobleman Heinrich von Einsiedel was troubled in his conscience about the heavy dues the peasants continued to pay, he asked Luther for advice in the matter. The reformer replied that the "common man" ought to have burdens imposed upon him, for otherwise he would become overbearing. And commenting in one of his sermons about slavery in Abraham's time, Luther stated, "It were even a good thing were it still so. For else no man may compel nor tame the servile folk" (Bax 352–3). In his booklet *On Whether Soldiers Can be Saved* (Werke 7, 383–432), Luther wrote in 1526 that he was inclined to "boast" that ever since the time of the apostles the temporal powers and governments had never been so clearly described or so highly praised as by him, as even his enemies had to admit! But the sincere gratitude that he should have earned as a reward never came from the princes. Instead, Luther laments, his doctrine is reviled and condemned as seditious and as striking at the government. The irony here is obvious.

The suppression of the Peasants' War had negative effects on the entire Lutheran reform movement. By taking his stand against the common people, Luther kept the support of many princes and nobles and thus assured the continued success of the magisterial reformation. But the commoners' hopes that Lutheranism would become the means of effecting a political and social reformation as well were shattered. As a result of the defeat of the peasants the Reformation ceased to be a popular movement. Peasants, artisans, commoners, and others who sympathized with the lot of the oppressed and disadvantaged, were bitterly disillusioned and hopelessly alienated from all that Luther stood for. In southern Germany where the war raged most, the population generally remained faithful to Roman Catholicism or else converted to Anabaptism, which after 1525 appeared to be spreading more rapidly. There is some evidence that Anabaptist preachers used the peasants' defeat as propaganda for the promotion of their type of Christianity. There seems to be no doubt that the failure of the peasants' movement in 1525 drove some simple folk into the arms of Anabaptism.

REVOLUTION OF THE COMMON MAN

What in 1524 began as sporadic disturbances, revolts, and rebellions by the common people in southern and southwestern Germany against their overlords developed by April 1525 into a full-scale war, hence the label Peasants' War, not just revolt, is appropriate as of that date. The number of combatants in this armed conflict and the resulting dead, especially on the side of the commoners, certainly warrants this label. The combined and well-armed forces of the princes and their mercenaries fought against poorly equipped and badly organized bands of some 300,000 peasants and other commoners with an unprecedented fury. In the end there was a veritable rout, with the princes pursuing the fleeing peasants and killing them mercilessly.

The commoners' movement that resulted in the revolts must be seen as part of the Reformation. Most of the common people sincerely believed that it was appropriate to apply the gospel to social, economic, and political issues, as Luther did to religious issues. Thomas Müntzer, it must be remembered, was a Christian theologian. His social program was inspired by Christian ideals, mysticism, and the inner Word of God. His belief in the destruction of the godless was derived from the Old Testament prophets and the belief that the present age was coming to an end and that the ultimate reign of God was about to begin. Müntzer's belief in violence was of a more defensive, not so much aggressive nature; it was the enemies of God, according to him, who had initiated the oppression, and the rebels thus needed to respond to their aggression and violence to defend themselves (Goertz, MQR 106).

At the end of the war some of its leaders, including Thomas Müntzer, as we have seen in the previous chapter, were punished with the death penalty. The princes, with Luther's wholehearted endorsement, were elated about their victory. But the belief in justice and equity based on the gospel survived among many of the peasants and other common folk. After 1525 some groups of Anabaptists sought to withdraw from the political, economic, and religious entanglements of society, and established communities in which they either, based on Acts 2 and 4, "held all things in common," like the Hutterian Brethren or generously shared their earthly possessions with their co-religionists. Thus the Peasants' War, as James Stayer has claimed, was an essentially formative experience for early Anabaptist leaders, with lasting results (*The German Peasants' War*). Among the results was also the emerging belief among some groups, especially the peaceful Anabaptists, that violence was not the ultimate answer to settling disputes and differences, be they of a religious, economic, or political nature, but that more peaceful means needed to be devised. There are some historians who argue that those who were defeated in 1525 learned valuable lessons for the future from their defeat (Schorlemmer, *Selig sind die Verlierer*), and that eventually their ideas would prevail. Thomas Müntzer, fighting against overwhelming odds and defeated in 1525, believed that in the end the oppressed people "will be free, and God alone will be their lord" (Stayer, *The German*

Peasants' War 109). This was certainly true of Anabaptism. While Anabaptists were implicated in the Peasants' War and were severely persecuted, they developed peaceful communities and churches, and into the free church movement of modern times. But for all these "loosers" the road toward such goals remained a long and arduous one.

NON-PEASANT PARTICIPANTS

☾ **The Peasants' War** was by no means only a war of commoners. Many different non-peasant agitators actively participated in the rebellion, and many more in the towns and countyside sympathized with the plight of the common people. In fact, one might rightly speak of an urban revolution, for most of the writers for reform came from the towns and cities. Some of the towns even opened their gates to the approaching rebels. What is perhaps not as well known is that even some aristocratic individuals and groups participated in the revolt. One Goetz von Berlichingen (ca. 1480–1562), a Franconian knight and fighter, for example, was persuaded by the Odenwald rebels to join them. Unfortunately for the rebels, however, when the Swabian League's army advanced near Würzburg in 1525, Goetz deserted the peasants and left them to their fate (Brady 188). Another Franconian nobleman, Florian Geyer (ca. 1490–1525) was, like many other German knights, at first attracted to Luther, but later became disillusioned and supported the rebel armies. Like Thomas Müntzer he became a hero among the peasants. Among other city people who were sympathetic toward the peasants' cause were Hans Hergot and his wife Kunegunde, printers and publishers of politically and theologically subversive writings in Nürnberg. Even the famous Nürnberg artist Albrecht Dürer (1471–1528), an admirer of Luther, had supporters of the peasants among his apprentices, and the artist himself was sympathetic toward the suffering peasants. His *Design for a Dead Peasant* (1525), in which a peasant sits on farming implements with a sword thrust through his back, suggests not that the artist ridiculed the peasants, as some have suggested, but that he was sympathetic toward the suffering common people (cf. Mittig) and wanted to express their lot in a monument. Helmut Böhme, in an interesting article about a dream Dürer had in 1525, shows that the artist had a bad conscience about not supporting the peasants and their leader Thomas Müntzer

(Böhme) more fully. All this non-peasant involvement suggests that the Peasants' War involved more participants than just the common people.

A NOTE ON LUTHER AND CAPITALISM

Luther's harsh attitude and writings against the peasants in 1525 leave the impression that the reformer was not only heartless toward the common people, but that he also had little understanding about and interest in the economic conditions of his time. The fact is, however, that sermons and pamphlets exist showing that Luther was both sympathetic toward the poor and the common people on the one hand, and knowledgeable about the emerging capitalist class on the other. Throughout his career he castigated rich and avaricious business people in no uncertain terms. As early as 1519 Luther preached *A Brief Sermon on Usury* and in 1524 he published a longer tract, *Concerning Business and Usury* (Werke 7, 107–37). In 1540 he wrote an *Admonition to the Clergy to Preach Against Usury*. In his 1541 *Admonition to Pray Against the Turks*, Luther critically summarizes the economic conditions in Germany: he writes that times have changed, from a land-based economy to commerce, finance, and credit, and that with this change comes the god mammon or greed taking hold of farmers, craftsmen, nobles, and princes. The merchants raise prices, charge exorbitant interests on loans, and deprive the poor and needy of their livelihood. Usury has become a god and no one can oppose this evil deity.

Luther uses very harsh words against usury (*Wucher*, profiteering) and usurers (those who make excessive and unfair profit):

> The heathen [of old] were able, by the light of reason, to conclude that a usurer is a double-eyed thief and murderer. We Christians, however, hold them in such honour, that we fairly worship them for the sake of their money.... Meanwhile we hang the small thieves.... Little thieves are put in the stocks, great thieves go flaunting in gold and silk.... Therefore is there, on this earth, no greater enemy of man (after the devil) than a gripe-money, and usurer, for he wants to be God over all men ... a usurer and money-glutton ... would have the whole world perish of hunger and thirst, misery and want ... so that he may have all

to himself, and everyone may receive from him as from a God, and be his serf for ever more.... And since we break on the wheel, and behead, highwaymen, murderers, and housebreakers, how much more ought we to break on the wheel and kill ... hunt down, curse and behead all usurers." (Nitsch 33)

Luther mocks the usurers who think the reformer is naive about economic matters and conditions. They say that he, Luther, may well know his Psalms and Matthew, but that he knows little about money and that he had better stay in his calling as a preacher and not meddle in economic affairs. Luther replies that as a minister of the gospel it is his calling and right to oppose the "damned usurers." He has no doubt that the Turks or some other calamity will soon teach the usurers a lesson, namely "that Luther has understood well what usury is." Luther adds that he knows well the usurers in Leipzig, Augsburg, Frankfurt and other places, the people who oppress the poor and the small business people with their greedy practices (Werke 7, 494–5).

According to S. Eck, one of the editors of the *Luthers Werke* edition of 1905, the rise of capitalism was not the result of the Reformation, but was a "poisonous plant" that grew up in the soil of Renaissance humanism. The sources of capitalism, according to Eck, were to be found in Florence, Venice, and Genoa whence the spirit of capitalism moved north across the Alps and into Germany. Luther actually tried to stem the tide of advancing capitalism, preaching and writing against it. Moreover, Luther seemed to be prophetic about what capitalism would do and knew intuitively that as a force it was not only secular and anti-religious, but also sinful and evil in that it disregarded human values and oppressed the poor (Werke 7, 512). According to Carter Lindberg, "Luther found the calculating entrepreneur distasteful. He was convinced that the capitalist spirit divorced money from use for human needs and necessitated an economy of acquisition" (Lindberg 172).

Luther not only *wrote* against what Max Weber has termed the "spirit of capitalism," but also sought to provide in a practical way for the needy and economically disadvantaged in the Protestant territories. On Luther's initiative, as early as 1520/1521 the city council of Wittenberg established a "common chest" (*Gemeinen Kasten*) for the benefit of the poor and needy who were unable to provide for themselves and their dependants. Before the Reformation, monasteries provided such services, but after monasticism and begging were abolished in Protestant territories new ways had to be found to assist the needy. After Luther, charity such as almsgiving and other "good works" was no longer considered spiritually meritorious. In medieval times both the rich and the poor benefited from poverty. Poverty was seen as a meritorious virtue by which heaven could be gained, and for the rich, helping the poor was a meritorious good work as well. Luther's new teaching of justification by faith alone and not by good works did not do away with good works, but the good works were now to be the *result* of faith and expressions of love for one's neighbour.

With the abolition of monasticism, and monks and nuns leaving their former life, poverty was now often seen as the result of wilful idleness. The emphasis was now on the necessity of labour according to St. Paul's words in 2 Thess. 3:10: "If anyone will not work, neither shall he eat." Luther, the ex-monk, who rejected all good works as a means of salvation, showed by his own example that former monks and nuns had to enter the work force and live "ordinary" lives, lives that in turn were now seen as holy in the sight of God. But there were still poor and unemployed people who through no fault of their own were poor and needed financial help. This is where the common chests in Protestant areas came in, which in time were not administered by the churches but by the civic governments.

The idea of the sacred nature of *all* work, no matter how high or lowly, had its beginnings with Luther. The German word *Beruf* (calling), as Max Weber suggests, comes from the reformer and means that whatever station in life or occupation the individual is in comes from God. In Luther's translation of the Apocryphal book Jesus Sirach, chapter 12:20–1, the word *Beruf* occurs twice: "[R]emain in your calling; trust God and remain in your calling" (my translation) ("behare in deinem Beruf; vertraue du Gott und bleibe in deinem Beruf"). But Luther, as Max Weber observes, cannot be held responsible for the rise of the spirit of capitalism, for that distinction belongs to Calvinism (Weber, chapter 3), but his emphasis on the necessity and sanctity of manual and mental labour contributed to professional and commercial activity. Luther was not against trade and commerce as such, but only against what he considered usury and the exploitative nature of the market.

Luther was medieval in his thinking about credit, interest, and capital in general. With Aristotle, he, like the medieval schoolmen at the time, believed that hard cash or money, unlike productive soil and manual and mental work, is sterile and unproductive; hence to take high interest for a loan that a person of means is able to provide is usury and sin. Some merchants and bankers at the time demanded and got up to fifty percent; according to Luther this was outright robbery. If a person of means has money to lend, he or she should do it out of a heart of generosity and love. In the end Luther agreed that four or at the most five percent interest on a loan was acceptable. In the meantime, Luther continued to lobby the civic powers to halt the steady advance of capitalistic enterprise, but with little support from the authorities. As Lindberg comments, "Luther discovered it was easier to motivate assistance to the poor than to curb the economic structures and practices that created and fostered the conditions of poverty" (Lindberg 172). As late as 1546, while in Eisleben, Luther spoke of having resisted and wanting to destroy avarice and profiteering (*wehren und gar ausrotten*), but being unable to do so, just as he had been unable to resist and destroy such sins as stealing, adultery, and whoring with his many sermons (Werke 8, 278ff.)

{vii}

Two Riders of the Human Will
Luther Opposes Erasmus and Humanism

HUMANISTS AND THE REFORMATION

Some writers have noted a large gap between Renaissance humanism and the Reformation of the sixteenth century, but such differences as existed must not be overemphasized. For the purposes of this chapter, we shall focus on Erasmus as representing humanism and on Luther as representative of the Reformation, culminating in their clash on the question of free will.

Luther has sometimes been seen as more medieval in his thinking than Erasmus, but it must not be forgotten that the reformer was also a product of Christian humanism, which inspired him, and was shaped by it. Humanism's call of "back to the sources" was also heard by Luther, and in studying the classical writers, the church fathers like St. Augustine, and the ancient languages, Luther can be considered part of the humanistic movement. As a student at the University of Erfurt, the centre of German university humanism, the young Luther moved in humanistic circles, heard lectures by humanists, and had friends among them. These connections were not discontinued after he entered the Augustinian order of monks in 1505. And in his reformation activity he benefited greatly from the work of one of the greatest northern humanists, Erasmus, whose 1516 translation of the Greek New Testament Luther used at the Wartburg castle in translating his September New Testament of 1521/1522 (Leppin, LH, 68–9).

Both the humanists (especially the North European humanists) and the reformers knew that there was much wrong with the papal church and thus demanded reform. Some humanists, such as Jacob Wimphling, Beatus Rhenanus, Thomas Murner, Sebastian Brant, author of *The Ship of Fools,* and above all Erasmus of Rotterdam, were critical of the church and were at first favourably inclined toward Luther's work. In the end, however, they shied away from a radical solution to the church's problems because as humanists and individuals more rationally inclined than Luther, they did not want a complete break with the old church. They wanted to see the church reformed but not destroyed. The humanists often admired Luther's bold actions and writings, but the provocative and often abusive language Luther used against high-ranking church officials in the end turned them away from the reformer.

Johannes Cochlaeus (1479–1552), for example, was at first on Luther's side, but he turned against him in 1522 and wrote him a letter of reproach: "Do you suppose that we wish to excuse or defend the sins and wickedness of the clergy? God save us! We would far rather help you to root them out, as far as it can be done legitimately.... But Christ does not teach such methods as you are carrying on so offensively with 'Antichrist,' 'brothels,' 'Devil's nests,' 'cesspools,' and other unheard-of terms of abuse, not to speak of your threatenings of sword, bloodshed, and murder. O Luther, you were never taught this method of working by Christ!" (Durant 426).

But Luther's language and style in attacking the church was only one part of the humanists' quarrel with the reformer. Like Luther they also noted a deterioration of morals and ethics in Germany, but they ascribed this decline in spiritual life to the disruption of churchly authority, especially to the reformer's rejection of "good works" as meritorious. But there was more that the humanists objected to in Luther. Some felt that Luther seemed to downgrade and disapprove of secular learning, even criticizing universities that did not teach the Word of God and godliness, as he had written in 1520 in his *Babylonian Captivity of the Church*. The humanists also lamented the fact that serious classical scholarship was declining in some instances, and that printing presses like Froben in Basel suffered financially because the learned works they were producing at great cost were finding fewer purchasers than before. But pamphlets and cartoons on both sides of the religious battle increased, to the dismay of some humanists, especially after Luther's posting of the *Ninety-Five Theses* in 1517. None of this heated and acrimonious writing contributed positively to humanistic discourse (427).

It is of course true that Luther turned away from the paganism of the classical writers and instead emphasized the teaching of Scriptures and Christian values. In his *To the Christian Nobility* (1520) Luther addressed the need for reform in higher education. For example, the great regard that the monastic schools held for Aristotle and other pagan writers needed to change. "It hurts me," Luther wrote, "that the damned, proud and roguish pagan [Aristotle] with his false and deceitful words has led astray and fooled so many of the best Christians" (Werke 1, 274). But Luther did not wish to entirely throw out the Greek philosopher held in such high regard by the medieval schoolmen. He certainly wished to keep Aristotle's books on logic, rhetoric, and poetry, which were good to read and for learning how to speak and preach well (275).

Luther's concern for a well-rounded Christian education can also be seen in his 1524 missive *To the Councilmen in Germany that they Establish and Maintain Christian Schools* (Werke 3, 6–34). This interesting document impresses even the modern reader with the reformer's humanistic concerns and insight into the educational needs of his time. According to Luther, both boys and girls in Germany ought to receive a basic education. He advises placing copies of good books in schools and libraries, including the Bible in several languages, biblical commentaries, some Greek and Latin poets and speakers, books in the liberal arts, books on law and medicine, and especially chronicles and historical works, for these works, according to Luther, are the most useful to learn about nature, the world, and God's work in creation. But most important for Luther is the study of languages, especially Hebrew and Greek, for the Bible was given in these languages. To have the Bible in German is of course very important, but in order to delve deeper into God's Word, Hebrew and Greek are necessary.

Luther also addresses other aspects of education, such as the value of physical training and the teaching and practising of the arts, such as singing and music. Luther himself wrote and composed many hymns and music. Singing and music were for Luther both expressions of beautiful art and means of worshipping God. He often advised that singing could dispel moods of depression in times of melancholy and sadness. Luther was not even averse to dancing at weddings and attending theatrical performances such as comedies, as long as they did not lead to frivolity and sin. But the beauties of nature and the many works of God in creation filled Luther with awe and sensual and spiritual delight. For example, he often spoke in his *Table Talks* about God's wonders in the animal and plant world (Werke 8, 253–60). He once complained that the humanist Erasmus had no eye for the works of nature, saying, that he, Erasmus, looked at works of nature like a cow looked at a new gate (Weydmann 127–32).

According to Luther, it is largely towns and cities' responsibility to provide a general public education, for the following reasons: First, parents do not have the means, skills, or the time for educating their children and young people. Second, princes are not much interested in public education, so the towns must look after schooling. For Luther, public education is not just for preparing young people for work in the church, but also for practical and useful occupations and trades in the temporal realm. It is especially in regard to Luther's emphasis on "calling" (*Beruf*), seeing the equal importance of all occupations under God, that Luther seeks to engage city and town councils for education. He expresses the hope that all regions in Germany will eventually heed his call to do something for German boys and girls in this regard (Werke 3, 34).

While both the humanists and the reformers welcomed the revival of learning and scholarship, especially in languages, the two groups were far apart when it came to the religious and spiritual longings of people in church and society. The humanists were all in favour of correcting the abuses in church and society and in promoting humanistic values, but they were not as much concerned about the existential questions of the heart, the *Sitz im Leben* (focus in life), as it were. This is where a reformer like Luther, who had deeply experienced the longings of the human heart and had wrestled with sin, guilt, and *Anfechtung*, was able to help many religiously inclined men and women. In the sixteenth century there were many people who still thought more in religious terms than secular terms. As a reformer and humanist, Luther combined both aspects within his person. But Luther's deep faith and religious thinking was more or less foreign to many of the more rationally and secularly inclined Renaissance humanists like Erasmus. The conflict that developed between the humanist Erasmus and the theologian Luther must be seen against this background of two contrasting personalities.

LUTHER AND ERASMUS

⟪ **Desiderius Erasmus of Rotterdam (1466–1536)** was a Dutch Renaissance humanist, Catholic priest, and theologian, and one of the most influential thinkers and writers of his time. Like Luther, Erasmus was critical of the corruption of the Roman papacy, especially of its sale of indulgences which he lampooned in his *Praise of Folly* (1511). Luther was thus initially drawn to this prince of humanists, respecting his learning and reputation and benefiting from his scholarship. The two men never met in person, but they did exchange cordial letters from time to time. Luther hoped that Erasmus would join him in his reform efforts, a hope that was not without some basis. When Luther in 1517 posted his *Ninety-Five Theses* for debate, Erasmus applauded them. In March 1518 he sent copies of the *Theses* to John Colet and Thomas More, his friends and fellow scholars in England. To Colet he wrote: "The Roman Curia has cast aside all shame. What is more impudent than these indulgences?" A few months later he wrote to another of his friends about how much the *Theses* were accepted by the people: "I hear that Luther is approved by all good men, but it is said that [not all his writings are of equal quality]." Erasmus then adds: "I think his Theses will please all, except a few about purgatory, which they who make their living from it [by selling indulgences] don't want taken from them" (Durand 428).

As Luther passed from criticism of indulgences to outright rebellion and rejection of the papacy, the gentler and more conciliatory humanist Erasmus began to waver in his enthusiasm for the reformer. He believed that church reform could be advanced better by appealing to the good will of the humanist pope, Leo X, and other concerned princes of the church, rather than through such radical action. Like Luther, Erasmus used his pen in the cause of reform and enlightenment, but his writings, while very critical of the church, included both educational material and satires like *In Praise of Folly*, rather then frontal attacks on the church, like Luther's tract *The Babylonian Captivity of the Church*. Erasmus believed that peace could still be restored between Luther and the church if both sides would lower their voices. In February 1519 Erasmus advised the Basel publisher Froben not to publish any more of Luther's writings because they were too inflammatory. In April of that year, however, he still advised the Elector Frederick the Wise to continue protecting Luther.

In May 1519 Erasmus wrote Luther a long letter from the University of Louvain, expressing his concern about what people in his circles thought about his, Erasmus's, connection with Luther: "Dear brother in Christ," the humanist wrote, "your epistle, showing the keenness of your mind and breathing a Christian spirit, was most pleasant to me. I cannot tell you what a commotion your books are raising here. These men cannot by any means be disabused of the suspicion that your works are written by my aid, and that I am, as they call it, the standard-bearer of your party.... I have testified to them that you are entirely unknowm to me, that I have not read your books, and neither approve nor disapprove of your writings, but that *they* should read them before they speak so loudly." Erasmus then advises Luther not to spread his opinions with such vehemence from the pulpits, as they inflame the crowds to excitement and rash action.

Erasmus then comes to the main issue of the letter: "For yourself you have good friends in England, even among the greatest persons there. You have friends here too – me in particular. As for me, my business is with literature. I confine myself to it as far as I can, and keep aloof from other quarrels; but generally I think courtesy to opponents is more effective than violence.... It might be wiser of you to denounce those who misuse the Pope's authority than to censure the Pope himself. So also with kings and princes."

Erasmus sounds like a teacher giving one of his younger students some praise, but also blame: "Old institutions cannot be rooted up in an instant. Quiet argument may do more than wholesale condemnation. Avoid all appearance of sedition. Keep cool. Do not get angry. Do not hate anybody. Do not be excited over the noise you have made." Erasmus closes his letter: "I have looked into your *Commentary on the Psalms,* and am much pleased with it.... Christ give you His spirit, for his own glory and the world's good" (Durant 430; cf. Rummel 196–7).

That Erasmus considered Luther a humanist as well as a reformer at this time is seen from a letter of October 19, 1519, also from Louvain, to the Archbishop of Mainz (Rummel 198–205). He writes about the theologians at the university and elsewhere who attack scholars like Luther, Reuchlin, and himself, without having read them. These critics, according to Erasmus, are not interested in humanistic learning but only in their own prestige and position. "I cannot refrain from letting you into one secret," Erasmus writes, "that those people have very different objects in view from those that their words profess. They have long resented the new blossoming of the humanities." According to Erasmus, the critics charge Luther with heresy without having proven that he is actually a heretic. They certainly cannot charge him with loose living or seeking high places or money, so the Dominicans among them, Erasmus regrets to say, "are even more criminal than they are ignorant" (203).

In this letter to the archbishop, Erasmus states that Luther has written things that are not so much irreligious as ill advised. He has hurt the feelings of the theologians, and, worst of all, Luther does not attach much importance to Thomas Aquinas and other schoolmen. Also, he reduces the profit to be made from indulgences and he does not respect the orders of the mendicants or the decision and practices of the Catholic Church. However, he pays the gospels the highest respect and opposes the church against the gospels. But can these things be called heresies, for which a person is to be punished? In the old days a heretic was one who dissented from Scriptures, but nowadays anyone who disagrees with Aquinas is called a heretic. Whatever the theologians do not like or understand they call heresy. It is a serious crime to violate the faith, to be sure, but not all things should be forced into a question of faith or doctrine (204).

In this letter Erasmus asks the archbishop to do two things: first to protect humanistic studies against the old school, the scholastics, as much as he can, and second, not to listen to Luther's many enemies. Erasmus asserts that he has not read much of Luther and that he will never leave the old church. He believes, however, that Luther's concerns need to be taken more seriously before he is condemned.

Catholic theologians at the University of Louvain, however, continued to attack Erasmus as the "fountainhead of the Lutheran flood." In October 1520 the Catholic Hieronimous Aleander (1480–1542) posted the papal bull *Exsurge Domine*, threatening Luther with excommunication if he persisted in his heresy. Aleander at this time also accused Erasmus of being a secret fomenter of the revolt. Erasmus was consequently expelled from Louvain, after which he moved to Cologne where he defended Luther in a conference with the Elector of Saxony. When Frederick the Wise asked Erasmus why Luther had been condemned, Erasmus gave the now famous answer: "Luther had sinned gravely, he had struck out against the bellies of the monks and the crown of the pope" (Augustijn 124). In a statement known as *Axiomata Erasmi* of December 1520, Erasmus suggested to the elector that Luther's request to be tried by impartial judges was reasonable, for the cause Luther fought for was just and evangelical. Erasmus then, together with the Dominican theologian Johann Faber, wrote to the young Emperor Charles V, recommending that he, the emperor, Henry VIII of England, Louis II of Hungary, and he, Erasmus, appoint an impartial tribunal to examine Luther's case before anything against him was undertaken.

Moreover, in a letter to Cardinal Lorenzo Campeggio, Erasmus urged justice for Luther. "No one has yet answered him or pointed out his faults," Erasmus writes. "How, while there are persons calling themselves bishops, whose moral character is abominable, can it be right to persecute [Luther] a man of unblemished life, in whose writings distinquished and excellent persons have found so mucht to admire? The object has been simply to destroy him and his books out of mind and memory, and it can only be done when he is proved wrong." If we want truth, Erasmus continues, a person ought to be free to say what he thinks without fear. "Nothing could have been more ridiculous or unwise than the Pope's bull. It was unlike Leo X, and those who were sent to publish it only made things worse" (Durant 431).

After the Diet of Worms in the spring of 1521, on May 10 of that year Erasmus wrote a long letter to Justus Jonas, professor at the University of Erfurt and a close supporter of Luther. In this letter Erasmus expresses his disappointment about Luther's unyielding attitude and rebellion against Rome. Luther claims to be a Christian but he certainly has not learned any gentleness from Christ, St. Paul, St. Augustine, and other saints in the church. Erasmus had expected Luther to be more gentleman-like in his criticism of the abuses in the church, but instead Luther and his followers' tracts and pamphlets have inflamed the populace toward strife and warfare. "I do not of course deny that sometimes God uses war, pestilence, and distress to correct his flock; but religious men have no call to introduce war or suffering contrary to their religion" (Rummel 209). Luther, according to Erasmus, "might have done wonders for Christ's flock by teaching the *philosophy of the Gospel* [my emphasis]; he might have done great services to the world by publishing books, had he refrained from things that could not fail to end in strife." Erasmus adds sadly, "My own work has lost a great part of the good effect I hoped for, thanks to him" (213).

Erasmus concludes his letter to Justus Jonas by assuring him that his attitude toward Luther has not changed: "I have always wished that some things could be altered which I never liked and that he could then devote himself entirely to the *gospel philosophy* [my emphasis] from which the standards of our generation have so lamentably fallen away. I have always wanted to see him put right rather than put down. I used to wish that he would treat Christ's business in such a way that leaders of the church might approve, or at least not disapprove. I wanted Luther to be loved in such a way that it might be safe to love him openly" (214–15).

This letter to one of Luther's friends is most revealing about the essential difference between the representative of the best in Christian humanism and the representative of a thorough reformation of the church in "head and members." Erasmus the humanist certainly approved of Luther's exposing of the corruption in the church and hoped that corrective changes would come from such criticism. But he thought that these changes could be brought about by an appeal to the best intellects and good will in the church and society. Luther's "philosophy of the Gospel," that is gentleness, love, non-violence, and patience, would do more good than the opposite. Luther the reformer, on the other hand, knowing the deep-seated sinfulness of the human heart, believed that only a "thunderbolt" from above, God himself, could bring about the necessary changes.

ERASMUS AND POPE ADRIAN VI

❰ **The relationship between Erasmus and the papal court** at this time is most revealing about the humanist's struggle with church reform and his inability to do much to bring Luther back to the fold. In December 1522 the new pope, Adrian VI, wrote to Erasmus, suggesting that he could help to recover the ground lost through Luther. The pope, Erasmus's countryman and a friend since their school days in the Netherlands, invited the now famous humanist to come to Rome to do his work there and stay with him. "Come to me in Rome," the pope writes, "You will find here the books which you will need [presumably to prepare for work against Luther]. You will have myself and other learned men to consult with; and if you will do what I ask you will have no cause for regret" (Durant 433).

Opening his heart to the pope in a letter of February 1523, Erasmus answered that he would accept the invitation to come to Rome with pleasure if his health allowed. But as to writing against Luther, Erasmus states: "I have not learning enough [!]. You think my words will have authority. Alas, my popularity, such as I had, is turned to hatred. Once I was Prince of Letters, Star of Germany ... High Priest of Learning, champion of a purer theology." Things have changed. Erasmus then suggests what might be done about the problem of Luther. The pope might apply gentle measures against Luther, for force, as some suggest, will not do and in the end will result in bloodshed. Don't ask about what heresy deserves, but ask how to deal with heresy wisely. I would suggest, Erasmus writes, that you discover the roots of the moral disease and deal with them, but punish no one. What has taken place should be regarded as a punishment sent by God. Erasmus, however, suggests that if possible there should be a check on the printing presses and that the pope should let the world know and see that he means in earnest to reform the abuses in the church. "If your Holiness desires to know what are [the abuses] to which I refer, send persons whom you can trust to every part of Latin Christendom. Let them consult the wisest men they can find in the different countries; and you will soon know."

The well-intentioned Pope Adrian died in the year that Erasmus wrote this most revealing letter. Pope Clement VII (1523–1534), who succeeded him, also urged Erasmus to enter more openly the ranks of those who opposed the reformer. According to Luther, Pope Clement VII was the worst rogue (*Schalk*) on earth (Werke 8, 147). Thus with pressure from many Catholic theologians and humanists mounting, Erasmus at last decided to write against some issues in Luther's theology, not to attack Luther nor to negate the Reformation – with which he was in general agreement – but to ask the reformer to moderate his tone.

But there was also a more personal reason for his decision to write against Luther. Erasmus had heard that Luther had given him credit for much of the good work he had done, but concluded that, like Moses in the desert, he [Erasmus] had failed to enter the Holy Land (Kaufmann, LH 147). In fact, on June 20, 1523, Luther had written to Oecolompadius in Basel: "He [Erasmus] has done what he was ordained to do: he has introduced the ancient languages ... [but] he will probably die like Moses in the land of Moab. He does not lead to better studies that teach piety. I would rather he would entirely abstain from explaining and paraphrasing the Scriptures, for he is not up to this work.... He has done enough to uncover the evil; but to reveal the good and to lead into the land of promise, is not his business, in my opinion" (P. Schaff 429).

Luther also wrote Erasmus privately in April 1524, first to thank him for his valuable work in literature and textual research, but also to advise him to leave theology to others: "[We] have chosen to put up with your weakness and thank God for the gifts he has given you," Luther wrote, "[but] you have neither the aptitude nor the courage to be a Reformer, so please stand aside" (cited in Thompson 343). The caustic remark must have been the last straw for the great humanist; in fact, he took it as a declaration of war and now went on the attack against the reformer.

ERASMUS ON FREE WILL

❰ **Duke George of Saxony,** the English king Henry VIII, and other oponents of Luther continued to urge Erasmus to write against the heretic (Kaufmann, LH 147). When Luther published his *Babylonian Captivity of the Church* (1520) in which he reduced the seven Catholic sacraments to just two, Henry VIII, in 1521, published his *Assertio septem sacramentorum adversus Martinuum Lutherum* in which he defended the seven Catholic sacraments and papal authority in teaching the Catholic faith. In gratitude for his support, Pope Leo X awarded the king the title *Defensor fidei*, defender of the faith. In writing his tract against Luther, the English king was assisted by John Fisher, bishop of Rochester, and the philosopher and politician Thomas More, who also wrote against Luther. In 1522, Hieronymus Emser, Luther's opponent, translated King Henry's piece into German, whereupon Luther answered the English king in both Latin and German with his book *Contra Henricum regem Angliae* (Against Henry the English king). Luther does not spare his royal opponent, calling him repeatedly "the lying king [*Lügenkönig*] of England," and "you are a coarse Heinz [*grober heyntz*, meaning a boor] and you will remain a Heinz." Luther does not take the king's argument too seriously because the king does not deal with biblical theology and just repeats what the church has always taught about the seven sacraments.

After some reluctance to write against Luther, in the end Erasmus chose the age-old question of whether the human will was free, particularly with regard to salvation, or whether the will played a minor role in receiving the grace of God. As he had worked on the question of free will before, it did not take him long to compose his treatise against Luther. In fact, Erasmus had already sent King Henry VIII and some friends in Basel copies of his work before Luther even saw it.

The theological issue of free will goes back to St. Augustine and the British monk Pelagius in the fifth century. St. Augustine taught that in the salvation of humankind it is all God's work, whereas Pelagius held that humans cooperated with God in receiving redeeming grace. Erasmus knew that the question of free will lay at the heart of Luther's theology and his work as a reformer. Thus, in August or September 1524, Erasmus published his *De libero arbitrio diatribe sive collatio* or *On Free Will*, arguing that there is *limited* freedom of the human will in receiving divine grace, and especially in Christians' performing good works. Without at least some human freedom, which, according to Erasmus, Scripture teaches, all positive human achievements and good works are pointless and worthless.

Erasmus admits that he does not understand the mystery of moral freedom, nor can he reconcile it with God's omniscience and omnipotence. But as a humanist, as a thinking human being, he cannot accept the doctrine of predestination and determinism without giving up his human dignity, values, and life itself. His study of Scriptures and of the church fathers, Erasmus states, does not require such sacrifice of him. The liberal popular historian Will Durant, commenting on Erasmus's *On Free Will*, states: "To Erasmus it seemed obvious that a God who punished sins that His creature has made by Him could not help committing [*sic*], was an immoral monster unworthy of worship or praise; and to ascribe such conduct to Christ's 'Father in heaven' would be the direst blasphemy" (Durant 434). This is no doubt an oversimplification of Luther's teaching, but this is how many liberal humanists saw and still see Luther's theological position on predestination.

Erasmus believed that weighty theological issues in Christian theology such as free will in the act of salvation, over which there had been debates for a long time, needed to be discussed rationally among theologians and other scholars and possibly compromises made. As far as he was concerned, all humans possessed at least a limited measure of free will, and the doctrine of predestination, as Luther taught it, did not agree with Holy Scriptures or with Renaissance humanist thinking. In his treatise Erasmus argues that God's foreknowledge of events was not the cause of events, and that repentance, conversion, and baptism depended on humans' free will. For Erasmus, God's foreknowledge is not determinative; God simply knows what human beings will choose. Men and women need to accept God's grace freely. Grace, according to Erasmus, is certainly necessary for salvation, but the human individual needed at least a measure of free will to accept or reject the grace God offered. Also, in the daily life of a believer, free will is necessary to strive for goodness and to live ethically. All this had been taught by the Catholic Church for centuries. In denying free will Luther not only goes against traditional Catholic teaching, Erasmus writes, but also comes close to being a heretic.

Erasmus, the experienced debater, argued not only from Scriptures but also from the church fathers, that while grace and salvation come from God, the individual must agree to accept God's grace, thus there is free will. Justin Martyr believed that unless humans have the power to choose, they cannot be held accountable for what they do; he held that punishment and reward depended on the choices human beings make. Irenaeus also believed that human beings are endowed with reason and can choose to live for God or against God's will. Clement of Alexandria also held that Christians are saved by their voluntary choice to accept God's grace. Tertullian believed that human beings were created with a free will by God and were free to either obey God or to resist him. Erasmus was confident that he had made a good case for at least a limited measure of free will in human salvation.

Pope Clement VII was pleased to receive a copy of Erasmus' treatise, but most Catholics were disappointed by its conciliatory tone and philosophical arguments. They had hoped that the book would have shown more clearly where Erasmus stood. Some even believed that Erasmus was still a secret admirer of Luther. Melanchthon, however, was favourably impressed with the treatise. Whereas he had earlier expressed predestinarian views in his *Loci communes*, he omitted the doctrine of predestination in later editions. Like Erasmus, Melanchthon also still hoped for peace between Luther and his Catholic opponents. For Luther, however, there could be no compromise or peace on the issue of free will between Pelagian humanists and Roman Catholics on the one hand, and the Word of God and the cause of the Reformation on the other. In fact, Luther had expressed his view about human freedom quite bluntly before, saying that after sin had come into the world there is free will in name only, and if free will does what its nature is, it only commits mortal sins (Kaufmann, LH 147). With Luther's unyielding position, the controversy between the humanist and the reformer was sealed.

LUTHER ON THE BONDAGE OF THE WILL

⁋ **Due to distracting circumstances** in Luther's life and work, he was unable to respond to Erasmus's treatise immediately. The year 1525 was a momentous and difficult period for Luther and all those who were close to him. Among the distractions were the social unrest that led to the Peasants' War and Luther's writings about these issues, especially his harsh booklets against the peasants and the emotional fallout that came from them. On a more personal level, the ex-monk had decided to marry an ex-nun, Catherine von Bora, "to confound the pope, the devil and the peasants," as he put it. It is thus surprising that at this time in his life Luther was able to write a fairly involved academic work on the question of free will at all, still less as an answer to one of the great Christian humanists and thinkers of the time.

By December 1525 Luther had completed his book *De Servo Arbitrio* (literally *On Un-free Will*) or simply *On the Bondage of the Will* (Werke Ergänzungsband II 203–521). Luther valued this writing of his highly, claiming later that this book and his *Catechism* were the best things he had ever written. Reading Luther's argument about the un-free will one can see why the reformer thought this book so important. In it Luther expressed at length what the Reformation was all about, namely that human beings born in sin needed to be redeemed and that only God in Christ could redeem them by his grace and faith *alone*, without any help from either the church, its institutions, or by any part, however small, of the human will. Luther would not even agree with Erasmus that before God's grace could enter the human heart, the individual had to will or at least agree to what God was doing. Salvation was all God's doing while the human individual remained completely passive – and God remained God and absolutely sovereign. In other words, in redemption God was all and the human individual was nothing.

To be fair to the arguments of Erasmus, it bears repeating that he also believed that in salvation human beings are redeemed by grace. He stated it all along and with many biblical passages to back up his argument. However, according to Erasmus, an individual, confronted with God's grace, needed to agree to accept salvation, and this is where the human will comes in. Luther in response, however, argued that human beings, because of their fall into sin (*Erbsünde*, original sin), are incapable of even responding positively to the grace of God. And that is because sin has so corrupted humans, and the flesh, that there is nothing in the human being that can will what God wills. Carnal human beings can only will what is evil. Even the human spirit agrees with what the sinful flesh is inclined to do: The same human being, the same soul, the same human spirit, as Luther argues, are intermixed and corrupted (*vermischt und verdorben*) by the sinful desires of the flesh (*Begehren des Fleisches*), hence human "free will" can do nothing except sin (Stockhausen 19). The will is bound by sin and the devil, and it is only God who can defeat sin and the devil by his power and become the master in a person's life. But once the individual is redeemed, a Christian has free will to do what is good and pleasing to God. To put Luther's view in its simplest form: The human will is like a beast of burden. If God rides it, it wishes and goes as God wills; if, however, the devil rides it, it wishes and goes as the devil wills. Nor can the will choose its rider. The two riders thus fight for the will's possession, but God foresees, foreordains, and accomplishes all things by his eternal and unchanging will. Luther states triumphantly that by this thunderbolt "free will sinks shattered in the dust."

The humanists and all rationalists in the sixteenth century, including Erasmus, could not accept the view of an enslaved human will nor a God who acted arbitrarily, seemingly against all common sense and reason. But for Luther, whether humanists, rationalists, or Pelagians liked it or not, in the act of salvation it is all God and the human individual is nothing. What was and is most difficult for rationalists of all types to accept was Luther's view of God's "hidden will" by which God not only foresees or foreknows all things but also foreordains all things, including a person's salvation or damnation. Known as divine determinism or predestination, this doctrine which went back in its earliest form to St. Augustine, was eventually accepted by most magisterial reformers, including Calvin, who today is known especially for his teaching of predestination. The Catholic view was and still is somewhere in between St. Augustine and Pelagius, calling for a certain cooperation between God and the human individual in salvation. Also, most Anabaptists, as we shall see, believed that while God redeems humans by his grace through faith, human beings not only need to respond willingly to God but also be capable of responding redemptively to the offered grace of God.

Roland H. Bainton expressed his own and many subsequent thinkers' difficulty with Luther's view of a sovereign God and the depravity of human nature upon which the reformer based his theology of the un-free or enslaved will. The passage from Bainton, quoting Luther, deserves to be cited in full: "Common sense and natural reason are highly offended that God by His mere will deserts, hardens, and damns, as if He delighted in sin and in such eternal torments, He Who is said to be of such mercy and goodness. Such a concept of God seems wicked, cruel, and intolerable, and by it many men have been revolted in all ages. I myself was once offended to the very depth of the abyss of desperation, so that I wished that I had never been created."

Bainton was apparently willing to accept this harsh doctrine, at least not questioning it much, and quotes Luther further: "There is no use trying to get away from this [doctrine] by ingenious distinctions. Natural reason, however much it is offended, must admit the consequences of the omniscience and omnipotence of God.... If it is difficult to believe in God's mercy and goodness when He damns those who do not deserve it, we must recall that if God's justice could be recognized as just by human comprehension, it would not be divine" (Bainton, *Here I Stand* 196–7). Erasmus, the Renaissance humanist, however, would not capitulate to a doctrine that seemed so unreasonable and ran contrary to his theology and the tradition of the church.

Luther knew that his book would hurt Erasmus and he was sorry about that. Toward the end of it, he writes that if he was too sharp (*zu scharf*) against Erasmus's book on free will, he asks for forgiveness, for he did not write with malice. However, he was angry (*es erregte mich*) that Erasmus, with his great reputation, suppressed (*gewaltig bedrücktest*) the cause of Jesus Christ. But then, Luther adds humorously, even if one is a master of his pen, it can occasionally become too hot and hurtful. But Erasmus too, who strives for moderation and is almost frosty in his book on free will, Luther writes, nevertheless shoots wounding and poisonous darts at him. "But that does not matter," Luther adds, "we need to forgive each other, for we are all human beings in whom there is nothing that is not human" (Werke Ergänzungsband II 463–4).

In the last few pages of his book, Luther gives Erasmus some credit for choosing a subject for the debate that was central to the Reformation and that lay at the heart of Luther's theology. Luther is glad that Erasmus did not deal with such paltry things as the papacy, purgatory, indulgences, and other such farcical matters. Erasmus was the only one, Luther states, who had seen the kernel of the matter and who then "set the knife to the throat," meaning that he went straight to the heart of the isssue. Had Luther's other opponents, those enthusiasts who prided themselves on their new spirits and visions, done the same thing, there would now be fewer rebellions and sects and more peace and unity (520).

But then Luther himself "sets the knife" at the throat of his humanist opponent, saying that if Erasmus cannot treat the matter of free will better than he has done in his *Diatribe*, it would have been better if he had just stayed with his great talents, namely his specialty in the literary sciences and languages, for it is here that Erasmus has made a name for himself and from which he, Luther, has learned and benefited greatly. But in the matter of his theology, in this case the subject of free will, Erasmus, according to Luther, simply does not measure up. In fact, the humanist does not even know all that much about it. Luther also chides Erasmus for stating that his views are opinions only and not assertions, and that opinions can be discussed and argued. Luther states, on the contrary, that he himself has expressed *assertions* in his book, that is, his firm convictions, and suggests that they be accepted in obedience to the Word of God. Luther concludes, "May the Lord, whose matter this is, enlighten you [Erasmus] and make you a vessel to his honour and glory. Amen" (520–1).

As a scholar and theologian Luther was a master not only of arguing his case skilfully and powerfully, but also of connecting with his readers, who, no matter how scholarly the subject, found the issues under discussion interesting and important. It is thus not surprising that Luther's belief in the complete depravity of human nature and the bondage of the human will, including that the individual cannot even cooperate, even a little, in salvation, was in the end accepted by his followers, including the scholarly Protestant reformers. As noted above, in Luther Calvin found his doctrine of predestination, election, and reprobation and transmitted this doctrine to France, Holland, Scotland, England, and even America. Catholics and most of the radical reformers, on the other hand, generally sided with Erasmus.

A BITTER ERASMUS

❰ **Erasmus was obviously disappointed** in Luther's *On the Bondage of the Will*, not so much because the reformer did not agree with him, but because Luther attacked him and his arguments so bluntly and in a language that demeaned him and his understanding of Scriptures and the church fathers. Luther knew that he had hurt Erasmus and so he wrote him a letter of appeasement, but the letter came too late, after a hurt and bitter Erasmus had already written *Hyperaspistes* ("The Defender"), his angry answer to Luther's *De Servo Arbitrio*. On April 11, 1526, Erasmus wrote Luther from Basel: "Your letter has been delivered too late; but had it arrived in the best of time, it would not have moved me one whit. I am not so simple as to be appeased by one or two pleasantries or soothed by flattery after receiving so many more than mortal wounds" (Huizinga 240–1). Erasmus tells Luther that all know that he writes abusively against his opponents, but never has he "written against anyone so frenziedly, nay, what is more abominable, so maliciously" (241). "And what has all this to do with the subject," Erasmus asks, "all this facetious abuse, these slanderous lies, charging me with atheism, Epicureanism, skepticism … blasphemy, and what not."

Erasmus charges Luther with not properly expounding Scriptures on the issue of free will, but simply claiming that his opinion *is* the Word of God. Moreover, Erasmus writes, all who disagree with Luther are judged by him as not having the Holy Spirit. Even within his own camp, Erasmus writes, Luther had some disagreeable people like Karlstadt thrown out of Wittenberg. Erasmus states that he reveres the word of God with his whole heart, but he does not believe that whatever Luther asserts is necessarily the word of God. Luther has the Bible say what he wants it to say and what fits his own teachings.

Erasmus further states that Luther's book on the enslaved will has finally convinced him that he must and will remain with his church rather than follow Luther in his break with Catholicism. He will never withdraw from his church nor commit his faith and salvation to Luther's faith. Erasmus adds a satirical note about the reformer's arrogance, as he calls it, in claiming that at last he has discovered the correct gospel after a long tradition of what the church believed; Luther wants people to believe that the gospel was hidden for centuries by Satan and that it has now been unveiled by him, and that there is no better interpretation of the Bible anywhere but in Wittenberg.

The Erasmus–Luther controversy was never resolved and the relationship between the two men deteriorated. Erasmus's *Hyperaspistes*, according to Philip Schaff, made Luther's predestinarian views responsible for "fatalistic and immoral consequences" in sixteenth-century society. The outrages of the Peasants' War of 1525, for example, confirmed Erasmus in his views. Also, the humanist continued to speak of the Reformation as a tragedy, "or rather a comedy." As a Renaissance humanist, he regarded the Reformation as a public calamity, which brought ruin to the arts and letters, and anarchy to the church. Erasmus drew a deplorable picture of Luther's reformation, which Capito, Bucer, and other preachers in Strasbourg tried to refute in 1530. But Erasmus also continued to complain about the great luxury in evangelical circles, that adulteries were more frequent than before, and other complaints (P. Schaff, 433).

Emperor Charles V subsequently asked Erasmus to be a counsellor at the Diet of Augsburg in 1531, but the humanist declined because he was not well and knew that he would not please either side. Nevertheless, Erasmus continued his efforts for peace between the reformers and Catholics, and recommended tolerance and courtesy toward the Protestant rebels. But he also continued to believe that the old church needed to be reformed, for example, to allow for clerical marriages and for the Lord's Supper to be administered in both kinds. He also felt that the church should yield some of its immense land holdings to secular states and for public uses. Moreover, such thorny and divisive issues as free will, the real presence in the Last Supper, and predestination should be left undefined and open to different interpretations.

This generally tolerant but now sad prince of the humanists, however, would remain true to the beleaguered Roman Church. Addressing Luther in his *Hyperaspistes* Erasmus says "I have never been an apostate from the Catholic Church. I know that in this Church, which you call the Papist Church, there are many who displease me, but such I also see in your Church. One bears more easily the evils to which one is accustomed. Therefore I bear with this Church, until I shall see a better.... And he does not sail badly who steers a middle course between two several evils" (Huizinga 165).

But was it really possible for Erasmus to steer a middle course? As time went on, people on both sides turned away from the humanist. As Erasmus observed about the great height from which he had fallen: "I who, formerly, in countless letters was addressed as thrice great hero, Prince of letters, Sun of studies, maintainer of true theology, am now ignored, or represented in quite different colours" (166). Neverthelss, the great humanist would continue to use his busy pen to address and influence scholars, church dignitaries, nobles, students, and magistrates, and all those who would listen to his counsel of moderation and reason.

STALEMATE?

❰ **Luther,** for his part, felt so strongly about the issue of free versus enslaved human will not only because he had experienced the unmerited grace of God so profoundly after a long struggle for salvation, but also because he believed that God's majesty, inscrutable knowledge, action, and divine will demanded that God be God and that the sinful human individual remain totally powerless – until redeemed by the grace of God. For Luther this view of God was not merely a theological opinion, as humanists like Erasmus thought, but a truth on which his own faith and the Reformation would depend. Almost from the beginning Luther felt instinctively that there existed between him and Erasmus an unbridgeable gulf and that no intimate working relationship between the two intellectual giants would ever be possible. At first he hoped that Erasmus might be drawn in to the cause of the Reformation, but eventually he realized that the intellectual, the scholar, the literary critic – and the cynic – was unwilling or perhaps unable to make a commitment to a deeper Christian faith. In Luther's many references to Erasmus in his *Table Talks,* the humanist was increasingly seen more negatively than positively and as a religiously indifferent career-building intellectual. When Erasmus died in Protestant Basel as a Catholic in 1536 and even refused the presence of a priest at his bedside, Luther's doubts about Erasmus's professed Christianity were reconfirmed (Kaufmann, LH 151).

The year 1525 marks the great divide between Renaissance humanism and the Reformation. In Luther's view, humanism, with its stress on human creativity, cultural and artistic progress, and achievement rather than God, diminished God in his majesty, glory, and sovereignty. According to Luther, the humanists did not take sin and the depravity of human nature seriously. When Luther, in his book *De Servo Arbitrio*, dramatically announced that his writing against free will knocks his opponents to the ground and dashes them to pieces, it was not just hyperbole; it was a serious truth he believed in. Significantly, after this controversy humanism and the Reformation were more clearly defined. They were both antagonistic and complementary opposites. Both Erasmus and Luther came to see this clearly. The Catholic Church then and now sought to combine the two more closely, insisting that human freedom, however limited, is needed for the divine and the human to interact to achieve religious and cultural progress. Also, as will be seen in the next section, many of the radical reformers, such as the Anabaptists, while accepting justification by faith, believed that denying free will and Christians' striving to live by both faith and practice would make much of the Scriptures meaningless.

It seems significant that Lutherans after Luther seemed to move away from the reformer's extreme position on the bondage of the will. The Lutheran confessions of faith are much more cautious in their answers to what constitutes Luther's position. In his 1535 edition of *Loci communes*, Melanchthon sided with Erasmus in several respects, as he had done when the humanist's book first appeared in 1524. Melanchthon's position was later sharply attacked in the Lutheran Church. However, "the extreme acute formulation of Luther's position was adopted by Calvin rather than by Luther's own pupils. In fact, by rejecting [perhaps modifying?] Calvin's doctrine of predestination, they indirectly attacked Luther himself" (Augustijn 145).

A NOTE ON ANABAPTISTS AND FREE WILL

⟪ **While there were some minor differences** among the radical reformers on free will, generally they more or less steered a middle course between Luther and Erasmus. Like Luther, most Anabaptists believed that the individual is redeemed by the grace of God by faith, but they stressed that a sanctified life must follow justification as evidence of salvation. However, like Erasmus, Anabaptists believed that the individual is free to accept or reject God's offer of grace, and like the humanists they had many biblical passages to back up their belief in limited free will. Luther called this view semi-Pelagian because it diminished the absolute sovereignty of God in salvation and gave too much credit to human initiative.

Among the Anabaptists were at least two men of note who wrote well-argued treatises on the question of free will: Hans Denck of Augsburg and Balthasar Hubmaier of Nikolsburg. As we are mostly concerned with Luther and Erasmus's positions in this chapter, the Anabaptist position will be sketched only briefly. There is no doubt, however, that the Anabaptists were well aware of the debate between the two Renaissance and Reformation giants.

Hans Denck's fairly philosophical–theological tract *Whether God Is the Cause of Evil* (Williams and Mergal 86–111), appeared in 1526, a year after Luther's book on the subject. Denck believed that through Adam and Eve's disobedience all humans had inherited original sinfulness, but "that only the flesh was corrupted by Adam's fall and that the spirit was made the prisoner of the flesh" (ME II, 387). With reference to Luther, whom Denck calls a "rogue" in connection with the reformer's "hidden" will of God, Denck implies that it is absurd to delve into something we know nothing about. Denck speaks of God's foreknowledge in human redemption and asks why we should concern ourselves about God's *hidden* will when we know what God's *revealed* will for all of us is, namely to obey his well-known commandments (Williams and Mergal 104). We know that God does not desire the death of sinners but that they should come to him, repent of their sins and then live by God's grace. But they have to accept God's grace, and that is where human freedom comes in (109).

With reference to the logic that some are predestined to be damned and cannot do anything to be saved, Denck writes: "Is it not ... malicious when our divines [including Luther] say that he bids someone be invited to the Supper but that it is not his will that this person come? Surely he does not give someone grace and secretly wish to withdraw it again. God does not work up repentance in us for our sins and secretly adjudge us guilty of hell" (109–10). While Denck's thinking is not all that clearly expressed, there is no doubt about what he wishes to convey, namely that humans know what God has in mind for them, that they have freedom to respond positively to God's offer of salvation, and that they need not worry about God's so-called hidden will.

Balthasar Hubmaier's treatise *On Free Will* (Williams and Mergal 112–35), which appeared in 1527, is more lucid than Denck's tract. Similar to Luther, Hubmaier clearly differentiated between God's secret or "repelling will" and God's "revealed will." According to God's revealed will, God's grace is available to all who wish to accept it. But according to God's "repelling will," God will judge and punish those who are wilfully blind and hard of heart and who refuse to accept God's "attracting" grace. According to the anthropology of the time, Hubmaier divided the human being into three parts, body, soul, and spirit. Before Adam's transgression, according to Hubmaier, all three parts were good. But after his fall into sin Adam lost his freedom, for himself and for all his descendants. The flesh or the body was now corrupted and had to die. "But the spirit of man," Hubmaier states, "has remained utterly upright and intact before, during and after the Fall, for it took part, neither by counsel nor by action, yea, it did not in any way consent to or approve of the eating of the forbidden fruit by the flesh." Hubmaier adds, "But it was forced, against its will, as a prisoner in the body, to participate in the eating" (120).

As to the soul, according to Hubmaier, "through the disobedience of Adam [it] was so maimed in will and wounded even unto death that it can of itself not even choose good or reject evil, for it has lost the knowledge of good and evil, and nothing is left to it but to sin and to die" (120–1). But the third part of the human individual, the spirit, has preserved its integrity even after the fall and is capable of turning to God. As Hubmaier puts it, "If I will, I can be saved, by the grace of God. If I will not, I shall be damned – and that by my own fault, from obstinacy and self-will" (127). Hubmaier is quite impatient with Luther and others who deny the freedom of the will, saying, "[I]t is clear and evident what rubbish all they have introduced into Christendom who deny the freedom of will in man, saying that this freedom is a vain and empty designation and nothing in itself" (131).

With regard to predestination, Hubmaier is similar to Denck, but his logic is clearer and more interesting. Referring to Romans 9:18, where the Scriptures speak of God showing mercy to some and hardening the hearts of others, Hubmaier says: "That is a reference to the omnipotent and hidden will of God, who owes nothing to anyone. Therefore he [God] may, without injustice, have mercy on whom he will, or harden the same, save or damn him." But Scriptures also speak of a revealed will of God "by which he [God] makes all men to be saved, and to come to the knowledge of truth." All who receive God's grace in Christ receive the power to become children of God. "Hence we can easily infer," Hubmaier states, "that God according to his preached and revealed Word absolutely does not want to harden, to blind, to damn anyone, save those who of their own evil and by their own choice wish to be hardened, blinded, and damned" (132). As humans we need not be too concerned about knowing or understanding God's hidden will. "But let us take hold of his revealed will and divide it, according to the ordinance of Scripture, into an *attracting* and a *repelling* [my emphasis] … will" (134). According to God's attracting will, God wills that all humans be saved. But God turns away from those who do not receive but reject him, and lets them go their own way. They thus experience God's repelling will. "Nor can anyone ask Him (Rom. 9:20)," Hubmaier concludes, "Why dost thou thus? His attracting will is the will of his mercy. His repelling will is the will of his justice and punishment. We – not God – we, with our sins, are guilty before it" (135).

The South German Anabaptist leader Pilgram Marpeck, unlike Denck and Hubmaier, accepted the total depravity of human beings. He thus stressed Christ's atonement to a greater extent than Hubmaier. However, he accepted Hubmaier's distinction between God's attracting and repelling will. Other Anabaptist leaders, such as Peter Riedemann of the Hutterian Brethren and the Dutch religious leader Menno Simons, generally believed the same thing as Hubmaier but stressed to a greater extent the practical and ethical aspects of a Christian's life. They all agreed with Luther in justification by the grace of God but at the same time stressed strongly that after their salvation Christians must give practical evidence of their justification. As F.J. Wray puts it: "In general, Anabaptist concern with the problem of free will appears to have been motivated by three considerations. In the first place, God is righteous; therefore, He can in no way be responsible for evil. Secondly, without free will there can be no real repentance, which for Anabaptists was an indispensable element in entering the Christian life. Thirdly, without free will there can be no real commitment to discipleship," that is, to following Christ in life, as Hans Denck put it (ME II, 388–9).

Luther Knew and Opposed the Evangelical Anabaptists

Today some **Anabaptist scholars** tend to steer clear of the designation "evangelical" in Anabaptism, but I use the term advisedly to differentiate between the peaceful groups, including the Mennonites, on the one hand, and the more revolutionary and Münsterite Anabaptists, on the other.

Luther did not have as much to do with the so-called evangelical or peaceful Anabaptists as with the other radical groups, but he did speak from time to time about them and seemed to know a great deal about what they believed and practised and even wrote a treatise about them when asked for advice by "two pastors." These Anabaptists acknowledged Luther as an important leader in the Reformation, and that it was he who had first shown them the way out of Roman Catholicism. In fact, it can be argued, as this book does, that had it not been for Luther's role in the Reformation, in all likelihood the Anabaptist movement would not have emerged, certainly not in the form that it did. The Anabaptists were thus, if not Luther's spiritual children, certainly, as Leonard Verduin has called them his spiritual stepchildren (Verduin).

ORIGIN AND SPREAD OF ANABAPTISM

⟪ **There are at least three main views** about the origins of sixteenth-century Anabaptism. The oldest view stems from Karl Holl (1866–1926), historian at Tübingen and Berlin, who believed that Anabaptism originated with the Zwickau prophets and Thomas Müntzer. Luther may have in part been responsible for this view, for he lumped all radicals together, calling them, among other names, *Wiedertäufer* (re-baptizers or Anabaptists). This view is no longer accepted by most historians, for while the Zwickau prophets and Müntzer questioned and in some cases even advocated the abolition of infant baptism, there is no evidence that they were re-baptized and actually re-baptized as believing adults (Bender, "Zwickauer Propheten" 266ff.).

Another view holds that Zurich, Switzerland, was the cradle of the Anabaptist movement, at least of *evangelical* Anabaptism. Historically it has been established that the first adult, or believer's baptism, was performed in Zurich in January 1525 in the house of Felix Manz when, after a group Bible study, one George Blaurock asked Conrad Grebel to baptize him with what he called the true Christian baptism. Grebel, who was not an ordained minister, performed the rite. Blaurock in turn baptized Grebel, Felix Manz, and others. On the same night, the first Anabaptists were banished from Zurich for the offence of re-baptism.

A third, more recent, view sees the beginning of Anabaptism in both Switzerland and in various places in German-speaking areas. This view of Anabaptist origins has been called the "polygenesis theory," meaning that the Anabaptists began not just in one geographical area or place like Zurich, but in several places around the same time. While the Swiss Anabaptists, also known as Swiss Brethren, were more inclined to quietism and a more pious lifestyle than the South German Anabaptists, who tended to be more radical and varied in their theological beliefs and practices, both groups generally belonged to the same movement.

In 1526, Bathasar Hubmaier, a former Catholic German who had become an Anabaptist and was in close contact with the Swiss Brethren, baptized Hans Denck of Nürnberg; in the same year Denck baptized his friend Hans Hut, who had been influenced by Thomas Müntzer's apocalyptic views. In the fall of 1526, representatives of both Anabaptist wings gathered for a conference in

Strasbourg where their differences became apparent. Denck, a follower of the *German Theology*, emphasized faith and love in contrast to the Swiss baptists' stress on the literal biblical texts and such rites as baptism and the Last Supper. The two Anabaptist wings did not believe in the "real presence" in communion, which made them suspect to Luther. The Swiss *Schleitheim Confession* of 1527, named after the town of Schleitheim on the border between Germany and Switzerland, distanced the Swiss from the South German groups because they inclined more to mysticism and stressed the inner Word. Thus the two wings of Anabaptism, despite having had considerable contact with one another, sprang up and followed their courses independent of each other.

Another important independent Anabaptist group was in northwestern Germany and the Netherlands, which eventually became known as the Mennonites, with Menno Simons (1496–1561) as its leader. Menno, as he is generally known, was a follower of Melchior Hoffman (ca. 1495–1543), but in 1536, after the collapse of the revolutionary Anabaptists in Münster, Menno gathered the scattered remnants of the Anabaptists there, and helped to organize them into peaceful congregations in the Netherlands and northwestern Germany. Since the name "Anabaptist" was associated with the Münsterite rebellion and violence, even the Swiss and South German Anabaptists eventually adopted the name "Mennonite" after the more peaceful Dutch leader. Today the name Mennonite still stands, except, ironically, among the Dutch, Menno's home, who continue to call themselves "Doopsgezinden" ("baptism-minded ones").

◇◇◇◇◇◇◇◇◇◇◇

Great Variety

Luther has been criticized for not distinguishing more clearly between the more militant radicals and the more peaceful Swiss Brethren and South German Anabaptists. But the Anabaptists themselves did not differentiate very much among the various factions either, and there was considerable contact between the different groups, making it difficult for reformers like Luther to see their differences. Sixteenth-century writers do not present a uniform picture of the origin and variety of Anabaptists, thus leaving it to individual observers to decide who and what the Anabaptists were and where they came from. Both leaders and laypersons belonging to one or the other religious persuasion, judged the various groups on the basis of their experiences or contacts with them. Since there was no one outstanding leader among them like Luther, Zwingli, and Calvin among the magisterial reformers, it was difficult for contemporary observers to know exactly what the Anabaptists believed or practised.

Sebastian Franck (1499–ca. 1543), for example, mentioned none of the Swiss Brethren leaders by name; as far as he was concerned, such South German Anabaptists as Balthasar Hubmaier, Hans Denck, and Hans Hut were the leading men of the movement. Urbanus Rhegius (1484–1541), one of the Protestant reformers, however, named Hans Denck only as a distinguished Anabaptist leader. Luther and Melanchthon apparently did not know much about the Swiss Anabaptists and thought of the movement as having sprung from the Zwickau prophets, Karlstadt, and Thomas Müntzer. In this chapter we are primarily interested in the relationship between Luther and the more peaceful Swiss and some South German, Dutch, and North German Anabaptists, the so-called evangelical wing of Anabaptism.

The Swiss Brethren

It is not within the scope of this book to deal in detail with the break between Ulrich Zwingli (1484–1531), the Swiss reformer, and the Swiss Brethren who dissented from Zwingli. On the surface it seems that the schism was caused by details, such as Conrad Grebel's opposition to usury and tithes, the use of leavened bread in communion, the mixing of wine with water, and others, all of which Zwingli regarded as unimportant matters. Conrad Grebel and his group looked upon Zwingli's indifference to such details as a "false forbearance" toward Catholic practices. From their reading of the Bible the Swiss Brethren had come to believe that more radicalism in these matters was needed. Zwingli, like Luther before him, considered it wise and prudent to move more slowly for the sake of the "weak" in the faith. Grebel and his group, on the other hand, looked upon this hesitation "as a spiritless slipping along, as a compromising yielding which was bound to result in serious danger to the cause of the Gospel" (Bender, *Conrad Grebel* 173). But the fundamental issue in the dispute between the Swiss Anabaptists and the reformers was the issue of a voluntary church composed only of adult believers, which the Anabaptists advocated and the magisterial reformers rejected. Coupled with this was the conviction among the Anabaptists that the church was to be free and independent of the state, a principle that today has found wide acceptance. As will be shown, these principles had wide ramifications. They involved such issues as individualism, religious tolerance, separation of church and state, military service, and church discipline.

Social Strata of Anabaptists

Until recently it was held that the Anabaptists had come mostly from the lower strata of society. This view is no doubt correct as far as the Anabaptists' later history is concerned, but in the early stages of their development this was not so. In tracing the social background of the Swiss Brethren it has been found that many of them came from the cities and that the leaders included leading humanists (Conrad Grebel), priests (Menno Simons), monks (Michael Sattler), evangelical preachers (Michael Wüst), scholars (Felix Manz), and even a few noblemen. Also, some South German Anabaptist leaders were university-trained. Balthasar Hubmaier had been a professor at the University of Ingolstadt and Hans Denck was a humanist scholar (Peachey 91–4).

Apparently, economic considerations did not play an appreciable part in the early rise of evangelical Anabaptism; in its inception and early stages the movement was largely religious. Even the first peasants, who were baptized by Anabaptist leaders, were more concerned about their relationship to God than about earthly goods (Blanke, "Zollikon 1525," 262). This is seen from their powerfully emotional conversion experience which resembled Luther's, and which was the direct result of the evangelistic preaching of the first Anabaptists (Zieglschmid 46–7). As a result of persecution, however, the movement was soon deprived of its spiritual and intellectual leadership, thus leaving the radical reformers with largely uneducated lay preachers who, although sincere in their attempts to propagate the gospel, were unable to cope with the various complicated issues affecting sixteenth-century Anabaptism. Furthermore, after the defeat of the peasants in

1525, many among the disillusioned masses listened eagerly to any preacher who promised them a better life in this world. There is thus little doubt that in time the passionate preaching of these simple "hedgepreachers" (literally preachers hiding behind hedges), as Luther called those who were not properly "called" to be preachers, resulted in congregations of common people. These commoners were often anti-clerical in that they hated the educated clergy, the nobility, the rulers, and magistrates, and the "learned ones" among the Catholics and the Reformed (Zschäbitsch 49–50). Among the lower classes the learning of the clergy and university-trained leaders was often seen as dangerous to their simple faith.

Rapid Spread

Several forces caused the Anabaptists to spread rapidly in many directions, especially between 1525 and 1530. Persecution and socio-economic factors have been alluded to. Also, like Luther, Anabaptists were convinced that they had found the truth and that they were inwardly compelled to share their faith with others, which made them into zealous evangelists in their communities and beyond. This in turn caused the authorities to drive them out of their homes and countries. Felix Manz (ca. 1498–1527), a co-founder of the original Grebel group in Zurich, was the first to be drowned by order of the Zurich authorities and with the approval of Zwingli. The rest of the early Swiss Brethren were able to escape by fleeing. Wherever they went they propagated their gospel. In spite of persecution, suffering, and often death, they felt God's call to convey their understanding of the Bible and faith to others.

Luther himself had encouraged his followers to suffer and if necessary die for the sake of the Christian truth. Having been close to death himself after the Diet of Worms, Luther wrote in 1522 that the greatest work that follows from faith is that one must confess Christ, sealing that confession with one's blood if necessary. Luther spoke of his own willingness to die if necessary for his faith, but no doubt he thought of his followers as well (WA 12, 228). In 1523 he had stated that if there were not enough ministers to preach the gospel, lay Christians would be required to assume this task, for obedience to the Word of God was important. When God calls, he stated, a Christian must be willing to forsake father, mother, relatives, the government, and even the church in serving the church (WA 28, 24–5).

When the radicals, and later the Anabaptists in particular, followed Luther's teaching to the letter in this regard, the reformer opposed them on the basis that the great mission of Christ to go into all the world to preach the gospel applied to apostolic times only; at present, all Christians ought to remain in their particular calling or position. He was convinced that some men were called by God to the ministry of the church, while others, the lay members in the church, were to testify privately about God's grace in whatever occupation they were in. Without a special calling from God and the church no one could be recognized as a preacher.

But the success of the "hedgepreachers" was phenomenal. As early as 1531 Sebastian Franck wrote: "The Anabaptists spread so rapidly that their teaching soon covered the land as it were. They soon gained a large following, and baptized thousands, drawing to themselves many sincere souls for God.... They increased so rapidly that the world feared an uprising by them" (Bender, "Anabaptist Vision" 69). While Franck may have exaggerated for effect, the Anabaptists did spread eastward along the Danube River, giving rise to the Hutterian Brethren, and northward along the Rhine River, establishing Anabaptist communities wherever they went.

However, the Swiss and South German Anabaptists appear to have had little or no direct influence on the rise of Anabaptism in the Netherlands, where Menno Simons came from. It was Melchior Hoffman (ca. 1495–1544) from Schwäbisch-Hall in Swabia in southern Germany and a former follower of Luther, who conducted his missionary activity in northwestern Germany and the Netherlands. He can be considered the father of Melchiorite and Mennonite Anabaptism in those parts. Thus, while there were no direct connections between the southern and northern Anabaptists, the similarities of their beliefs and practices were considerable, which was no doubt due to their social and economic circumstances, especially the common source of their faith, namely the Bible (Hershberger 71).

Luther's Contact with the Swiss

As late as 1528 Luther stated that he knew little about the Anabaptists and their teachings. In response to the question of what he thought about re-baptism, Luther wrote an open missive, *Concerning Rebaptism, A Letter to Two Pastors* (LW 40, 229–62). In this pamphlet Luther states that electoral Saxony is still free of such ministers as Balthasar Hubmaier, who teach false doctrines, and that until now he has had little occasion to think seriously about the matter of baptism. Since the Anabaptists confined their missionary activity to Hesse, where Duke Philip tolerated them, Luther's knowledge of them was secondhand, derived largely from such prejudiced persons as Melanchthon, Urbanus Rhegius, and certain students who came to study at the University of Wittenberg. Luther's admission that he did not know the Anabaptists well shows that he did differentiate to a certain extent between the Anabaptists on the one hand and the Wittenberg radicals, with whom he was acquainted all too well, on the other. Luther believed with Melanchthon, however, that the Zwickau prophets, Karlstadt, and Müntzer were largely responsible for the rise of the Anabaptists.

There is some evidence that Conrad Grebel, of the Swiss Brethren, wrote Luther a letter in September 1524. The letter has been lost, but Grebel announced his intention of writing Luther to his brother-in-law Joachim Vadian (1484–1551), stating that he had found the courage to admonish Luther for his leniency toward certain religious practices (Bender, *Conrad Grebel* 119). Grebel no doubt learned about Luther's attitude toward the Wittenberg radicals from one of Karlstadt's friends, Gerhard Westerburg, whom Karlstadt had sent to the Grebel group to announce his coming to Zurich. It is known that the Swiss Brethren resented Luther's treatment of Karlstadt (Barge 207–8).

In a letter to Thomas Müntzer, dated September 5, 1524, Grebel briefly summarizes the content of his letter to Luther: "I, C. Grebel, desired to write to Luther in the name of all of us to admonish him to desist from his forbearance which he is practicing without the support of Scripture, and which he is promoting in the world and in which others are following him.... So I wrote in my name and of the other brethren to Luther and admonished him to desist from the false forbearance of the weak, which weak ones they themselves are" (Williams and Mergal 83).

It must have taken some courage for the young Grebel to "admonish" the famous, and older, German reformer. It is known that Luther actually received the letter from the Swiss, because a student at Wittenberg from 1524 to 1526, Erhard Hegenwald, reported in a letter to Grebel early in 1525 that he had inquired whether Luther would answer Grebel's letter. According to this student, Luther had replied that since he did not know how or what to answer Grebel, he had not intended to respond. Luther did, however, through Hegenwald, convey greetings to the Swiss Brethren, expressing the hope that the Swiss would not think that he was "ill-disposed" toward them, although he disliked some of their ideas. Luther no doubt referred to the Swiss's views on baptism and the Lord's Supper (Bender, *Conrad Grebel* 119). Luther's answer indicates that he knew at least some of what the Swiss Anabaptists believed and practised.

It was not long, however, before the relations between Wittenberg and the Swiss Anabaptists became clouded. Grebel and Hegenwald continued to exchange letters on such subjects as the Holy Spirit, the call to preaching, the Lord's Supper, and infant baptism. Hegenwald admonished Grebel not to be radical on these issues, and began to see him as someone who agreed with Karlstadt and others who denied the real presence in the Last Supper. He also announced that at the time Luther was writing a pamphlet on his understanding of the Last Supper, which would destroy all the arguments of the "enthusiasts."

In March 1525 Luther reported to Georg Spalatin about some fanatics who had come from the Low Countries, maintaining that the Holy Spirit was nothing but humans' natural reason and intellect. From this it is clear that these individuals were not Anabaptists but philosophical rationalists, and that Luther does not connect them with Anabaptism or with Karlstadt, showing that Luther was obviously on guard against any sign of the "spirit of Allstedt," meaning persons like Thomas Müntzer.

Toward the end of 1527 Luther characterized the Anabaptists as follows: "The new sect of Anabaptists is making astonishing progress. They are people who conduct themselves with very great outward propriety, and go through fire and water without flinching in support of their doctrines" (Coutts 114). For Luther, the good and pious life and steadfastness of the Anabaptists was a trick of the devil to lead sincere Christian souls astray. It is not known whether Luther's description of the life of the Anabaptists came from his personal knowledge of these people, or from what he had learned about them from other sources. From his letter to the two pastors, it seems reasonable to assume that around 1528 Luther had very little first-hand knowledge about the evangelical Anabaptists in general or the Swiss Brethren in particular.

When the Swiss reformers and the Swiss Brethren joined Karlstadt in his attack upon the real presence in the Eucharist, Luther released a treatise in 1527 entitled, *That the Words "This is my Body, etc." Still Stand. Against the Enthusiasts* (Werke 4, 335–480; LW 37, 3–150). In this carefully argued thesis Luther laments the fact that the various sects that oppose him claim to base their teachings on the Word of God. As far as Luther is concerned, they are all united in persecuting Christ. All his writings, he states, are of no avail against the fanatics; they despise him and do not even bother to refute his arguments from Scriptures. Their great success in winning adherents, he states, stems from the devil blinding the eyes of those who refuse to accept the plain truth. In writing against them, he is not trying to convert them from their errors, which is impossible, Luther adds, but he wishes to enlighten weak Christians and save them from perdition, and to demonstrate to all that he has nothing in common with these enthusiasts who deny that Christ's presence is real in the Last Supper.

Believing firmly that their doctrines are from the devil, Luther cannot help but condemn them. As soon as one looks with disapproval upon these radicals, Luther mocks, they feel persecuted and heap upon themselves all the crowns of glory. It is they who began the struggle with him, and then they accuse him of not keeping the peace. After all, who can keep the peace when such vital issues as the real presence are at stake? Luther does not believe that the enthusiasts are wilfully evil, but as far as he is concerned, they are blinded to such an extent that they cannot see that the devil is working in them. He feels sorry for them, for he knows that there are truly talented men among them. In conclusion, Luther warns all cities that harbour such fanatics to be on guard against them, for while these people may mean well, they have no control over the spirit that works within them. Müntzer may be dead, Luther states, but his spirit is not yet quenched.

As late as 1528, three years after the Peasants' War, Luther still believed that the only weapon against the Anabaptists should be the Word of God. These people should not be burned or murdered; they should be allowed to believe whatever they wished (WA 26, 145–6). Thus, while Luther was convinced that the

Anabaptists had been influenced by Karlstadt and Müntzer, he was well aware of the fact that many of them rejected war and violence and were more concerned about spreading their gospel than with effecting social change by force. He believed, however, that the peaceful intentions of the Anabaptists could not be trusted, for false teachings could lead easily to civil disobedience and strife.

◇◇◇◇◇◇◇◇◇◇◇

Peaceful and Revolutionary Radicalism

Was Luther correct in believing that there was a direct connection between most Anabaptists and such radical reformers as Karlstadt and Müntzer? There has been a tendency among some Mennonite writers to disown all radicals of the sixteenth century who failed to conform to the ideals and practices of the Swiss Brethren and of most Mennonites today. Some among these historians and theologians have been quite apologetic in discussing such "marginal" figures of Anabaptism as Hans Hut, Ludwig Hätzer, and even Hans Denck. The possible connection between Müntzer and the Swiss Anabaptists has been of some embarrassment in Mennonite historiography (Bender, "Die Zwickauer Propheten" 262ff.). While there is little or no substantial historical basis to Luther's assertion that the Zwickau prophets were the originators of the Anabaptist movement, it is equally wrong o disclaim any influence of the revolutionary radicals on the evangelical Anabaptists. It should be remembered that the entire radical movement at the time was seen as revolutionary. Both the quietistic and the more extreme groups were often desperate in their defensiveness as an outlawed movement, hence they were feared and seen as radicals.

Even the Swiss Brethren were not wholly free from excesses and extreme tendencies. For example, George Blaurock (1491–1529), one of the first and acclaimed leaders of the early Swiss Anabaptists, on January 29, 1525, attempted to usurp the pulpit from a Zwinglian pastor near Zurich. His first attempt failed, but on October 8 in another church Blaurock was more successful. He entered the pulpit while the pastor was absent, told the congregation that *he* had been sent by God to preach to them that day, not their pastor, and then delivered his sermon. Such radical behaviour in early 1525 was one of the contributing factors leading to the expulsion of the Anabaptists from Zurich and the arrest of Blaurock, Felix Manz, and some baptized farmers (Blanke, "Zollikon" 249–51; Zuck 211–26).

There were also some direct connections between the Swiss Brethren and the Wittenberg radicals. When Karlstadt was forced to leave Saxony and other territories in which Luther's influence was dominant, he went to Basel and Zurich where he met the Swiss reformers and the Grebel group. His writings on the Mass were well known among the Swiss Anabaptists and his views on the Last Supper agreed with theirs. Also, in an attempt to please the Grebel group, Karlstadt wrote a tract against infant baptism (Barge II, 205). But the influence of Karlstadt in Zurich was also felt in a more concrete way. In 1523, Ludwig Hätzer (1500–1529) published in that city a tract against the use of images in churches. This in part initiated the iconoclastic campaign in Zurich led by Zwingli. The tract, as Charles Garside has shown, depended wholly on the arguments of Karlstadt's pamphlet against images, published a year earlier in Wittenberg (Garside 20–36). It is also known that Karlstadt's influence on Zwingli's view about the Lord's Supper was more substantial than has been commonly assumed (Hillerbrand, "Andreas Bodenstein" 393). Thus the Swiss Brethren were indebted to Zwingli and Karlstadt for their understanding of the Last Supper. Moreover, Conrad Grebel was attracted to Karlstadt because this Wittenberg radical had accomplished in Luther's city what he and his group had attempted to do in Zurich (Bender, *Conrad Grebel* 109–10). Also, some of Karlsradt's writings against Luther were taken to Basel where, according to Gordon Rupp, they were "printed with the aid of the future Anabaptist leader, Felix Manz" (Rupp, "Andrew Karlstadt" 321).

MÜNTZER AND THE SWISS BRETHREN

⟪ **Did Thomas Müntzer** have any substantial influence on the Anabaptists in Switzerland, as some opponents of Anabaptism have claimed? The statement of Heinrich Bullinger (1504–1575), successor to Zwingli, that the Swiss Anabaptists made *personal* contact with Müntzer is highly suspect; it is falsification or gross error at best. Certainly Zwingli, to whose advantage it would have been to discredit Grebel and his group by connecting them with Müntzer, does not speak of any personal connection or association (Bender, *Conrad Grebel* 110–16).

It cannot be denied, however, that the Swiss Brethren were eager to establish some personal contact with Müntzer after they had read some of his theological writings on faith and baptism, as the following story demonstrates.

On September 5, 1524, Conrad Grebel, in the name of the Swiss Brethren in Zurich, wrote a most interesting letter to Müntzer, who at the time was the minister of Allstedt (Williams and Mergal 73–85). Although Grebel's letter did not reach Müntzer, the fact that it was written at all has considerably embarrassed those Mennonite historians who have wished to disassociate the Swiss Brethren from this revolutionary. Opponents of Anabaptism, on the other hand, have pointed to significant passages in the Grebel letter that seem to confirm their assumption that all radical and Anabaptist groups were influenced not only by the Wittenberg radicals and the Zwickau prophets, but also by Thomas Müntzer. What does the Grebel letter tell us about the Swiss connection to Müntzer?

In his biography of Conrad Grebel, Harold S. Bender has shown that there is no substantial evidence to suggest that Grebel and his group ever met Müntzer in person. In interpreting Grebel's letter to Müntzer, however, Bender becomes somewhat emphatic in his attempt to show that this letter "is sufficient to decide once and for all" that even Müntzer's literary influence on the origin of the Swiss Brethren was non-existent. Bender states further: "Those who insist on the close relationship between Grebel and Müntzer point to a few *isolated* [my emphasis] expressions in the letter, in which Grebel praises Müntzer as a 'true and faithful herald of the Gospel,' and as 'his faithful and dear fellow brother in Christ'" (Bender, *Conrad Grebel* 116–17).

Elsewhere in the biography Bender writes: "The epistle [Grebel's letter to Müntzer] has a peculiar double character. On the one hand it pays homage to Müntzer 'together with Carolostadio' [Karlstadt] as 'the purest heralds and preachers of the purest, divine Word.' On the other hand – and this is its primary purpose [which is questionable] – it constitutes a *strong criticism* [my emphasis] of Müntzer. In fact the whole epistle, except for the short introduction and the similarly short conclusion, is cast in the form of an admonition and instruction to Müntzer" (172). Summarizing the relationship between the Swiss Brethren and Müntzer, Bender concludes: "The best understanding of the relationship to Müntzer would be somewhat as follows: When the persecuted Brethren in Zurich who had been cast off by their 'unfaithful shepherds' [Zwingli et al.], looked out of the darkness of their circumstances into the World and saw there other men such as Carlstadt and Müntzer, who had also been cast off by their leader Luther and had yet not lost heart, they likewise took new courage and hastened without much consideration or careful examination to make friends with them. Their reaction to their discovery of these men was primarily an emotional (not theological) reaction [which is questionable], and one that is easily understood psychologically in the light of their situation at that time" (117).

In a close examination of Grebel's letter to Müntzer the following questions should be kept in mind: Does the letter in fact prove that Thomas Müntzer's writings had no influence on the origins of Swiss Anabaptism? Was the letter really "in essence a criticism of Münzer's position"? Are Grebel's praises of Müntzer only a few "isolated expressions in the letter"? And if Grebel's response to Müntzer was "primarily an emotional reaction," why then should the letter be full of theological considerations, comments, and interpretations of certain biblical passages? Some analytical comments on some issues in Grebel's letter may indicate that the Swiss Brethren wished to convey more to Müntzer than mere instruction and criticism, as Bender argues.

Grebel addresses Müntzer as follows: "To the sincere and true proclaimer of the Gospel, Thomas Müntzer at Allstedt in the Harz, our true and beloved brother with us in Christ" (Williams and Mergal 73). Having thus established the spiritual kinship between the Grebel group and Müntzer, the author proceeds to state the purpose of writing to him: First, Grebel desires to establish contact with the minister in Allstedt, requesting him "like a brother" to communicate with the Swiss Brethren in writing. Second, Grebel states that Christ, who is the master of all true believers, "has moved us and compelled us to make friendship and brotherhood" with Müntzer. Third, he wishes to bring certain points to Müntzer's attention. Fourth, Müntzer's writings of "two tracts on fictitious faith" have prompted the Brethren to write him. With reference to the "false forbearance" of the reformers, including Luther, the Grebel group was happy to learn that in Müntzer they had found someone who "was of the same Christian mind with us and dared to show the evangelical preachers their lack."

Grebel then expresses some criticism of Müntzer's practices, but in general the Grebel group agrees with him on major theological issues. Grebel, for example, does not like Müntzer's German version of the Mass and the use of hymns in the worship service. Since the apostles did not command singing,

Grebel states, Christians today ought not to do so either. Then he gives detailed instructions about how the Last Supper is to be understood and administered: not in priestly garments, nor by a minister but by a lay brother; not in "temples" [churches] but in houses; only worthy members are to participate; and ordinary bread is to be used. "The bread is nothing but bread. In faith, it is the body of Christ and the incorporation with Christ and the Brethren ... for the Supper is an expression of fellowship, not a Mass and sacrament." Looking up to Müntzer as his spiritual superior, Grebel adds somewhat apologetically: "Let this suffice, since thou are much better instructed about the Lord's Supper, and we only state things as we understand them. If we are not in the right, teach us better" (76–7).

Commenting on Müntzer and Karlstadt's opposition to the Wittenberg reformers, Grebel has nothing but praise for the two radicals: "Thou and Carlstadt are esteemed by us the purest proclaimers and preachers of the purest Word of God." Müntzer's devotional pamphlets have strengthened the Swiss Brethren and have instructed them beyond all measure, "us who are poor in spirit." Grebel continues: "And so we are in harmony on all points, except that we have learned with sorrow that thou has set up tablets, for which we find no text or example in the New Testament" (79). The reference to singing and stone tablets, containing the Ten Commandments, which Müntzer had apparently set up in his congregation, shows the importance the Swiss Brethren attached to the literal, non-symbolic reading of the Bible, hence their criticism of Müntzer's practice in this regard.

Of significance are Grebel's references to Müntzer's views on war and violence, issues certainly of great interest and importance to the peaceful Anabaptists. But strangely enough, this matter does not take up nearly as much space in the letter as the points concerning Müntzer's brave opposition to the evangelical preachers and the biblical teaching on baptism. According to Grebel, the gospel and believers are not to be protected by force of arms; the followers of Christ are like sheep among wolves, hence they must suffer persecution; also, with the New Testament, violence and killing have ceased among Christians. In a postscript to the letter Grebel states that he has heard that Müntzer has preached against the princes, "that they are to be attacked with the fist." This, it seems, is a reference to Müntzer's *Princes Sermon*. If the report is true, Grebel admonishes Müntzer to cease from such notions, especially if he should fall into the hands of his enemies, both Luther and Duke George of Saxony. In everything else about Müntzer, Grebel writes, he "pleases us better than anyone in the German and other countries."

In conclusion, Grebel rails against Luther who has made of the Bible, in Müntzer's mocking words, "Bible, Bubel, Babel," and urges Müntzer to defend himself with the Word of God "against the idolatrous caution of Luther." "May God give grace to thee and us," Grebel writes, for "our shepherds [Zwingli et al.], also are so wrath and furious against us, rail at us as knaves from the pulpit in public, and call us *Satanas in angelos lucis conversos* [Satans changed into angels of light]. We too shall in time see persecution come upon us through them." Grebel and his group sign the letter: "Thy brethren, and seven new young Müntzers against Luther" (85).

◇◇◇◇◇◇◇◇◇◇◇

Grebel's Letter to Müntzer

Although the letter written by the Swiss Brethren did not reach Müntzer, the fact that it was written and the nature of its content call for some comments. It might be stated that in certain important points Grebel and Müntzer were theologically far apart. On the question of a Christian's position on physical force and war, Grebel and Müntzer were diametrically opposed to each other. The realization that their beloved brother in Christ might in effect have advocated the killing of the godless filled the Grebel group with some misgivings about their spiritual superior, hoping, however, that these reports might only be rumours. In reading the passages that address the question of the sword, one gets the feeling that the possibility of Müntzer's militaristic position is treated as a hypothetical problem. In the postscript to the letter Grebel mentions that a "brother" has written about Müntzer's sermon against the princes, but then adds a question, "Is it true? If thou are willing to defend war, the tablets, singing, or other things ... then I admonish thee by the common salvation of us all that thou will cease therefrom" (83–4). The question of war is thus treated as a strictly theological or biblical issue alongside such subjects as persecution and suffering, the use of tablets and singing in the church, the Lord's Supper, and baptism. In fact, the matter of baptism, for example, on which Müntzer had written and which pleased the Grebel group so much, takes up much more space in the letter than the Swiss's concern that Müntzer might have unsound opinions about Christians and war. Then, after a lengthy explanation of what the Swiss believe about adult baptism, Grebel encourages Müntzer and Karlstadt to write more forcefully against infant baptism, calling it that "senseless, blasphemous form" of baptism that Luther and other "scholars" advocate.

It would seem, then, that the Grebel letter to Müntzer was generally an attempt to make contact with a man who, like the Swiss Brethren, had the courage to oppose those leading reformers who, according to the radicals' thinking, did not go far enough with their reforms. Grebel's criticism of Müntzer does not seem to be the primary object of the letter, as Bender would have us believe. The letter, in fact, expresses a feeling of oneness, fellowship, and solidarity with Müntzer in their labour, struggle, and potential suffering in the face of overwhelming odds. The Swiss Brethren reach out in an attempt to grasp the hand, as it were, of a resolute leader and, hopefully, conqueror in his struggle, believing that in unity there is strength and, they hoped, eventual victory. This expression of solidarity with Müntzer is reflected clearly in Grebel's words: "Regard us as thy brethren and take this letter as an expression of great joy and hope toward you through God, and admonish, comfort, and strengthen us as thou are well able. Pray to God the Lord for us that He may come to the aid of our faith, since we desire to believe. And if God will grant us also to pray, we too will pray for thee … that we all may walk according to our calling and estate" (Bender, *Conrad Grebel* 286).

As Bender rightly points out, the Swiss Brethren knew Müntzer only from his writings, and only those prior to the Peasants' War in 1525. It is thus likely that had the Swiss group known Müntzer's revolutionary agenda fully, or had they believed the reports about him, their letter would have taken on a different tone, or else it would have been left unwritten. But here we are conjecturing. If, on the other hand, the Grebel group thought that the reports about Müntzer's revolutionary views might be true, it comes as a surprise that the peace-loving Swiss Brethren still sought the fellowship of the preacher of Allstedt. No matter how one interprets the possible motives for writing the letter, this document will continue to haunt all those who wish to obliterate all evidence that might point in the direction of some influential connections and relationships between the Swiss Brethren and an important leader in the Peasants' War.

We have seen that even after the Peasants' War and Müntzer's leadership in it, many commoners, including some evangelical Anabaptists, continued to sympathize with Thomas Müntzer and mourned his death. For many, Müntzer had become the mouthpiece, however radical in its expression, of all those social and religious elements in sixteenth-century society that yearned for spiritual liberty and political and economic justice. It is thus most remarkable that evangelical Anabaptism was so restrained in the face of oppression and persecution. As Lowell Zuck puts it: "A remarkable aspect of early Anabaptism is thus not so much its occasional violence, as its frequent exhibition of sobriety and good sense amidst emotional upheaval and martyrdom" (Zuck 225).

To Baptize Babies or Adults

The most distinguishing mark of the evangelical Anabaptists was their rejection of infant baptism and their practice of adult baptism, or, as they preferred to call it, believers' baptism. With this they not only challenged the prevailing practice of baptizing infants, but also the belief in baptismal regeneration (the view that in the act of baptism the individual is saved or regenerated) held by Catholics and Lutherans alike. The Anabaptists claimed that infant baptism was an invention of the popes, but this is questionable. The belief in the remission of sins in connection with the baptismal act can be traced as far back as the early church. Several fathers of the early church, including Ignatius of Antioch, Justin Martyr, Tertullian, Cyprian, and St. Augustine believed in baptismal regeneration (Newman, *History* 3–5). Infant baptism seems to have been the rule from the fourth century on. That the practice was in use before this date, however, is evident from the writings of Tertullian (AD 197). Since Tertullian did not seem to believe in post-baptismal forgiveness of sins, he condemned pedobaptism, asking for a delay in baptism until adolescence or until after marriage (Be Vier, "Modes" 232–4).

In the fourth century several groups arose that attacked the sacraments, including baptism. The Donatist heretics believed that the validity of baptism depended on the moral character of the person baptizing, hence they rebaptized all those who joined them. St. Augustine called on the civil authorities for help against the Donatists when his efforts to secure unity in the church failed. The Paulicians and Jovinians rejected both infant baptism and baptismal regeneration. For them baptism was to follow conscious faith in the redemptive work of Christ and was believed to be an outward sign of the inner transformation of the believer. The Jovinians, who also denied the virginity of Mary, were condemned as heretics by Jerome, St. Augustine, Ambrose, and by a Roman synod in AD 390.

In the twelfth century Peter de Bruys of France and Henry of Lausanne, a Cluniac monk, followed in the footsteps of the fourth-century heretics. Referring to the activities of these two men, Peter the Venerable (1092–1156) lamented that wherever their influence held sway, people were re-baptized, churches were profaned, altars were overthrown, and monks were compelled by force to marry. Arnold of Brescia (ca. 1100–1155), student and defender of Peter Abelard (1079–1142), led a similar radical movement in northern Italy, and he also rejected the baptism of infants. By 1184 the Arnoldists had to some extent united with the Waldensians, who were not too clear about baptism. Some among the Waldensians re-baptized adults, but others simply laid hands on them instead of baptizing those who joined them, and still others practised infant baptism. Similarly, the Bohemian Brethren, who arose shortly after the Hussite wars (1419–34), practised both infant and adult baptism.

This historical sketch shows that opposition to infant baptism did not originate with the Anabaptists and that opposition to re-baptism was nothing new. As will be shown in another chapter, the old Justinian laws of the sixth century against re-baptizers, demanding capital punishment, were revived in the sixteenth century and enforced with the utmost severity against the Anabaptists.

The Anabaptists believed that their views on baptism were in harmony with Scripture. For their belief they were willing to suffer persecution, exile, and martyrdom. Menno Simons, the leader of the Dutch Anabaptists, wrote: "We are driven only by a God-fearing faith which we have in the Word of God to baptize and to be baptized, and by nothing else" (Simons 236). In his booklet *Christian Baptism* (1539), Menno elaborates on three reasons for baptizing adults and not infants: Christ commanded that faith should precede baptism; the apostles taught believers or adult baptism; and the apostles practised adult baptism only (Simons 229–87).

In his letter to Müntzer in 1524, Conrad Grebel gives us a clear picture of what the Swiss Brethren believed about baptism. Before a person is baptized, Grebel writes, he or she must have faith in the redeeming work of Christ, who forgives the repentant sinner. Water baptism is only a sign or symbol of what has taken place in the heart. "The water does not confirm or increase faith, as the scholars of Wittenberg say, and does not give very great comfort nor is it the final refuge on the death bed." The Grebel group rejected baptismal regeneration because it dishonours faith and Christ's suffering. As far as un-baptized children are concerned, they will be saved without conscious faith simply on the merit of Christ's death for them. The Anabaptists condemned infant baptism as "senseless," "blasphemous," and "contrary to all Scriptures" (Williams and Mergal 80–2).

Luther on Baptism

Luther did not quarrel much with the Catholic doctrine on baptism. He did not, however, believe, as the Catholics did, that after an individual had fallen into sin, the effects of baptism were erased and the sinner had to perform certain penitential works to come back to grace. Baptism, according to Luther, remains forever valid, for it is God's work and not man's. But as far as the individual's faith is concerned, Luther emphasized time and again that baptism without faith did not save the individual. In a sermon in 1522 he went so far as to say that baptism was "no more than an external sign to remind us of the divine promise." Baptism without faith is useless, according to Luther, comparing it to a letter to which seals are attached but in which nothing is written. Therefore, a person who has the sacramental sign but not faith has the seals only. In 1523 Luther wrote: "Baptism certainly does not justify without faith, but faith does not justify without baptism; therefore no part of justification may be ascribed to baptism." Moreover, since baptism signifies the drowning of the old human being, Luther wrote in 1519, children should really be immersed in water. This is demanded, according to Luther, by the significance of baptism, for baptism signifies that the old man and the sinful birth of flesh and blood are to be wholly drowned by the grace of God (WA 2, 727). While baptism, according to Luther's early views on the subject, does not automatically bring about a person's salvation, it signifies the washing away of sins and it demands that a life of sanctification and faith must follow to validate one's baptism. Luther valued baptism so highly because he derived from it the principle of the priesthood of all believers. Baptism, according to Luther, makes all believers equal before God, thus minimizing the sacerdotal function of the clergy (Dieckhoff 87–90).

Luther modified his early views on baptism when the Anabaptists appeared and began to diminish the two sacraments, the Eucharist and baptism. Luther, as has been shown, reduced the Catholic seven sacraments to two, namely baptism and the Lord's Supper. The "sacramentarians" (those who denied the sacraments) also attacked Luther's concept of the Eucharist, regarding it as a mere memorial service, and the Anabaptists demoted the sacrament of baptism to only a sign or symbol of what took place in a believer's conversion to God. Luther began to realize and emphasize that if the sacramentarians, including the Anabaptists, succeeded in doing away with the sacramental nature of the two remaining sacraments, there would be nothing concrete or objective left to which his and other believers' faith could cling.

This fear of Luther's is also the reason why he held on so firmly to the external, concrete Word of God in opposition to Müntzer, Schwenckfeld, and other radicals who stressed the spiritual, the inner Word. In baptism Luther began to see more and more a means of *receiving* the grace of God. This was best illustrated in the baptism of infants, who are completely passive in this act of God. Little children cannot boast of having done anything to acquire God's gracious forgiveness; they simply receive freely what God has offered.

The most concise and the best-known statement of Luther on baptism is what is in his *Small Catechism* of 1529 (Werke 3, 75–120). On the question, "What does baptism give or profit?" the *Catechism* answers that baptism "works forgiveness of sins, delivers from death and the devil, and provides eternal redemption to all who believe this, as the words and promises of God declare." It is not the water that produces these effects, the *Catechism* continues, but the Word of God that is in and with the water, and faith that trusts the Word of God. Without the Word of God the water is just water and not a baptism. But with God's Word it is a baptism, a water of life and a cleansing of regeneration in the Holy Spirit. Baptism signifies that by repentance the old person in us should be drowned and die with all sins and evil lusts, and that a new person should come forth and arise to live before God in righteousness and purity (Strohl 153–5).

Here Luther clearly defines what constitutes a sacrament. A sacrament must have two aspects to it, a material or physical aspect (water, bread, wine), and the Word of God spoken by Christ attached to it ("This do" and "This is"). Also, after his encounter with the Anabaptists, Luther maintained that there is no automatic salvation attached to a sacrament, but that faith and the Christian walk of a baptized believer ensured that the individual profited spiritually from the sacrament. In addition, as Dillenberger puts it, "The sacrament of baptism implies incorporation into the Christian community, the dying unto self and the new life in Christ" (Dillenberger xxxii).

At the question of two Catholic clerics from southern Germany in 1528 as to what should be done with the Anabaptists who infested their region, Luther found occasion to elaborate on the subject of baptism. In his open letter *Concerning Rebaptism*, Luther accuses the Anabaptists of killing the souls of Christians by denying the sacramental value of baptism; even the papists, according to Luther, are better in this, for they at least leave Christ to the people (WA 26, 148–9). To baptize upon an individual's confession of faith, as the Anabaptists preach and practise, is ridiculous, for how can one be certain that the person being baptized believes or does not believe? Such a baptism is actually a "baptism of adventure," according to Luther. One should not baptize on faith or on the profession of faith but on the sure foundation of the Word of God. Luther believes that since infant baptism had been practised ever since the beginning of Christianity, it should not be changed; he is certain that God would not have left Christians in the dark for so long about such an important matter.

Furthermore, how can the Anabaptists say that children cannot have faith when there is no scriptural basis for such an assertion? Does not the Bible speak of young children praising God their Father, and did not John the Baptist leap in his mother's womb as a result of faith (Luke 1:41)? After all, is it not possible for Christ to implant saving faith in the hearts of infants? Infant baptism, in fact, is most beautiful, Luther continues, for little children are not required to exert any kind of effort or do any kind of work; they are completely free, sure, and blessed alone through the glory of their baptism.

Luther compares infant baptism to circumcision in the Old Testament. Just as children under the old law were received into the covenant of God through circumcision, so are the children of the new dispensation received into the covenant of Christ through baptism. Since Christ commanded the disciples to go to all the nations to preach to them and to baptize them, he no doubt included children as well. Moreover, just as faith remains with an adult in his or her unconscious condition, such as sleep, for example, in the same manner faith can begin in infants even though they are unaware of it.

Also, the objections of the Anabaptists that many priests did not believe in Christ's saving grace while administering baptism, Luther refutes by stating that the validity of the sacraments does not depend on the moral character of the person administering them. It is the Word of God that is most important, not the human instruments through which the blessings flow. Judging from their gross errors, Luther concludes, in his *Concerning Rebaptism*, it is evident that the Anabaptists are blasphemers of God and messengers from the devil. The arguments of the Anabaptists about adult baptism do not convince him, for they have no sound basis for what they believe and practise. All they can do is hurl blasphemous names and expressions at those who believe in infant baptism, calling such baptism a "dog's bath," "a hand full of water," and other such names. And the devil knows that when the mad mobs hear blasphemies they will believe more readily than when sound arguments are presented.

The Anabaptists did not find Luther's arguments for the retention of infant baptism all that convincing either (Simons 126ff.). Is it absolutely certain, they asked, that infants were baptized in apostolic times? The statement in Acts that whole households were baptized does not prove that little children were included. Moreover, is it true that God would not allow gross errors to be perpetuated through the centuries? The errors of the medieval church did not mean that the church was dead; there were great men and women of God who, in spite of the general spiritual darkness at the time, still continued to live by the Spirit of God. God honoured the faith of these exceptional Christians even though they were ignorant about the true baptism. Then came the Reformation, the Anabaptists argued, in which attempts were made to bring back the church to its biblical foundations, including the correct practice of the sacraments. The Anabaptists were in no doubt that adult or believers' baptism, in which faith precedes baptism, was the biblically correct rite.

Luther's argument from the Old Testament practice of circumcising all male children in support of infant baptism seemed far-fetched to the Anabaptists as well. And Luther's insistence that Anabaptists could not be certain that the people they baptized had faith, negated the biblical order of first believing and then baptizing and not the other way around. Luther's attempt to prove that John the Baptist in the womb of his mother "leaped" because he had faith seemed insincere to them, or humorous at best. Menno Simons, in his *Foundation of Christian Doctrine* (1539), expressed surprise at Luther's talk about a "dormant faith" in infants of which the Bible had nothing to say: "If Luther writes this as his sincere opinion, then he proves that he has written in vain a great deal concerning faith and its power. But if he writes this to please men, may God have mercy on him" (Simons 126).

Although Luther pursued his later arguments on the subject along the lines outlined in his *Concerning Rebaptism* (1528), there were other points that he emphasized as time went on. In his *Small Cathechism* (1529), the reformer stated that it is not the water that saves the individual, but the Word of God that is attached to the sacrament, and the person's faith that accepts the Word. In 1530 he wrote that if adults only should be baptized, most people would live like pagans until the time of their death before asking for baptism. Throughout their life they would thus fail to come to hear the Word of God, for non-Christians are indifferent to spiritual things. For Luther, St. Augustine is a good example of this. The church father was not baptized until he was thirty years old, falling into the grave heresy of the Manichaeans and other sins as a result (EA 23, 163–5).

When the Anabaptists continued to deny the sacramental nature of baptism, Luther, in 1535, argued the contrary, stating that baptism had all three signs of a sacrament. It has the external element (water); it has the Word of God attached to the element; and, most important, it is backed by the command of Christ to baptize all people (EA 19, 108–13). Since this is so, neither our faith nor our unbelief affects the sacrament of baptism in any way. If the baptismal candidate believes, that is fine for him or her, but if the candidate does not have faith and refuses to believe after baptism, he or she will have received the life-giving sacrament for their own damnation.

In a letter of December 17, 1534, Luther asked Prince Joachim of Anhalt to stand as sponsor on his daughter's baptism in order to help "the poor little heathen out of her sinful state by nature into the most blessed new birth" (WA, Br. 129). This reference, with statements in the *Small Catechism*, indicates that Luther definitely believed in baptismal regeneration, but he never pressed the point, stating time and again that a living faith is the best evidence of a regenerate life.

In Luther's struggle with the Anabaptists' position on baptism, two considerations need emphasis. First, Luther's quarrel with the Anabaptists was not primarily over the issue of infant versus adult baptism. We have seen that at first the reformer had doubts about infant baptism, and only later, when the Anabaptists made an issue over "believers" baptism, did Luther begin to defend infant baptism. As we have seen from his treatise of 1528, *Concerning Rebaptism*, he had not studied the Anabaptists' position too well. Indeed, he may not have deemed the issue all that important, hence his at times weak arguments in favour of infant baptism.

Second, in Luther's arguments against the errors in the Anabaptists' thinking, the sacramental nature of baptism was more important than the question of infant versus adult baptism. While still an Augustinian monk, Luther wrestled for certainty, for assurance of salvation. Eventually he found this certainty in the promises of written Scriptures and in the sacraments that gave him something concrete to hold on to. In all his subsequent doubts and spiritual struggles he came back to these external means of grace, claiming divine pardon and assurance of salvation. The Zwickau prophets and Thomas Müntzer had devalued the external Word, emphasizing the inner Word; the sacramentarians had demoted the Eucharist to a mere memorial of Christ's death; and now the Anabaptists also considered baptism a mere sign of what happens spiritually in the life of believers. For Luther all this was a devilish conspiracy to rob Christians of the certainty of their salvation and to destroy the work of the Reformation.

Is the Church Free or Tied to the State?

Adult or believers' baptism was important to the Anabaptists, but there was more to it than mere rejection of infant baptism because they did not find it in the Bible. Their concept of a free church was tied to adult baptism. From reading the New Testament, the Anabaptists had come to the conclusion that the church must be composed of voluntary believers, men and women who freely chose to become followers of Christ and in so doing give their primary allegiance to God and his kingdom. Practically, this meant that while Anabaptists lived in society and took on their responsibilities as subjects of the state, they rejected all attempts on the part of the state to interfere in their Christian life and in the life of the church. In a word, church and state were to be separated, a principle that some believe began with the Anabaptists and which in time became a principle in modern democratic society. Infant baptism, Anabaptists believed, was against the idea of a free church because *all* baptized subjects belonged both to the church and to the state in which they resided.

In his defence of the thirteenth thesis against Dr. Eck in 1519, Luther asserted that the church, the *Una Sancta*, is the communion of all saints; those who truly believe belong to the church of Christ (WA 2, 190). In 1520 he wrote that Christ is the head of the church and only true believers are members of the church. Although all things, including evil people, are subject to God, "Christ cannot be the head of an evil community," that is, Christ is the head of a holy community only (WA 6, 301–2). In his "Lectures on Romans," Luther had spoken of a church as a persecuted small remnant. Between 1522 and 1527 Luther even attempted to establish a church composed of serious Christians who not only professed the gospel but actually lived it. He thought at first of entering the names of God-fearing people into a special book, thus separating them from the nominal Christians. He then proposed to be the minister of such a saintly group, while someone else would serve the larger body of professing believers. In the end, however, Luther concluded that he would not have a sufficient number of such dedicated people to realize his ideal (Bender, "Anabaptist Vision" 76–7). We do not know whether the princes would have tolerated such a small church within the larger church and the state. At any rate, such a church would have resembled medieval Christian conventicles, something that both Catholics and Protestants would not perhaps have accepted.

The ideal of a separate church, however, remained with Luther throughout his life. As late as 1538 he declared in a sermon that church and state must remain separated from each other if the true gospel and the true faith are to be preserved, for the nature of the Kingdom of God is very different from that of temporal kingdoms committed to princes and lords (WA 46, 734). But to carry out this principle in practice, Luther, of course, would have had to renounce all assistance from the secular princes, however well meaning their motives, and to rely on the power of the gospel only in his reform activity. However, to assure the course and success of his reform work, particularly after the Peasants' War, Luther accepted the assistance of his princely followers.

The idea of an alliance between church and state was of course not new. Ever since Constantine the Great (ca. 274–337), church and state had worked closely together off and on; the *Eigenkirchentum* (proprietary or private church system), against which the church reformers of the eleventh century had fought, was a clear case of the church's subjection to the state; and the Renaissance humanists' conception of a Christian state (including Erasmus) seemed to sanction the idea of the government's involvement in church affairs.

Luther, however, was never quite at ease about the surrender of the evangelical church to the state. To explain his awkward position somehow, he began to call the evangelical princes "emergency bishops" who were expected to assist in the work of the Reformation, not because they were princes but because they were also members of the Christian church, with special powers and authority. But Luther thought that as soon as the circumstances were more settled these princes would step back from their involvement in church affairs and leave the spiritual government to the clergy (Dieckhoff 182–3). This situation led Luther to speak of an "invisible church" which manifested itself in the preaching of the pure gospel and in the right administration of the sacraments and not necessarily in the faith and redemptive life of a Christian community. His early ideals about a church composed of only believers had thus given way to very real and practical considerations.

In contrast to Luther's "invisible church" and his increasing cooperation with secular governmenmts, the Anabaptists sought to follow the reformer's earlier ideal, of separating church and state, to its logical conclusion. Seeking to establish a concrete, visible, and, as far as possible, pure church composed of voluntary believers, they believed they needed to follow the New Testament example. According to the Anabaptists and other radicals, Constantine the Great had brought about the "fall" of the apostolic church by uniting it with the state. Their attempt to establish a church separate from the state was to follow the ideal of the primitive church (cf. Leithart).

The signs of a truly restored church, according to Anabaptist sources, are the following: a community of voluntary believers who become members by repentance, faith, and adult baptism; a pure theology or biblical doctrine; a scriptural administration of the sacramental signs (often called *ordinances* of baptism and the Lord's Supper); true discipleship, known as *Nachfolge*, or to follow Jesus in life; willingness to suffer persecution and if necessary dying for their faith; "brotherly love" for each other, which sometimes expresses itself in sharing material things in communal living; and withdrawal from the state and the "world" (Simons 739–42). Most of the evangelical or peaceful Anabaptists also included non-resistance or pacifism (non-violence, including refusal to go to war) as a mark of a true church. But some leaders, like Balthasar Hubmaier, also believed in just wars (usually defensive wars) and participation in combat on the side of a *just* government. For a short time, the Wadshut community in southern Germany, with Hubmaier as its leader, was such an Anabaptist state.

The Anabaptists' withdrawal from the world and the state drew upon them the suspicion of the magisterial reformers and magistrates, who accused them of conspiring against the secular powers. The Peasants' War, the fact that most of the later Anabaptists belonged to the lower strata of society, and the Anabaptist kingdom in Münster – all this seemed to give reason to believe that at heart every Anabaptist was a potential rebel. However, the evangelical Anabaptists were in principle and generally in practice submissive to the governments, basing their obedience to the state upon the teaching of the New Testament. They believed, like Luther, that God had instituted secular governments in order to preserve law and order, and that all true Christians are indebted as children of God and for love's sake to give to secular powers all obedience and submission. As one Anabaptist treatise put it: "All outward matters, even life and body, are subject to the outward powers, only the true faith in Christ may not be compelled or conquered" (Hillerbrand, "An Early Anabaptist" 31). When the Swiss Brethren were accused of disturbing the peace, Grebel and his group denied the charge categorically. And from Grebel's letter to Müntzer it is well known, as we have seen, how the Swiss Anabaptists felt about violence and war.

A document written in 1529 by one Clemens Adler gives some reasons why most Anabaptists did not take up arms against others: "For the love of Christ they [Christians] love their enemies, do good to them and pray for them, as Christ teaches them, and thus hearken to the voice of their shepherd. Even if the world rise up against them, yet they rage and storm against none; and if the world lifts up its sword against them, yet they take no sword against it nor against anyone, for they have made their swords into plow shares and their spears into pruning hooks" (Geiser, "Ancient Anabaptist Witness" 67). Anabaptist writers loved to quote biblical references to support their beliefs. But Luther was not convinced about the Anabaptists' profession of peacefulness and non-resistance or their refusal to carry lethal weapons even for self-defence. Luther is reported in his *Table Talks* as saying: "The Anabaptists are desperate and wicked fellows. They do not carry weapons and they boast of their great patience" (EA 62, 191). Luther, like many others, simply did not believe or trust them.

Having surrendered some of his earlier ideals to practical necessity, particularly in the realm of church–state relations, Luther began to view with contempt the Anabaptists' attempt to establish a free and pure church. "Where they want to go," Luther said of Anabaptist church discipline, "I am not disposed to follow. God save me from a church in which are none but the holy" (Coutts 184). In a sermon on the wheat and the weeds from Matt. 13:24–30 Luther compared the Anabaptists to the Cathari and Donatist heretics of old who had also tried to establish pure churches. This, according to Luther's interpretation of the parable, was quite impossible. The saints from Adam on have always had wicked people within their ranks; even Christ had tolerated Judas among the twelve disciples (SLA 12, 1234–7).

Luther's changed position on church and state matters and his belief that it was impossible to establish a pure church is understandable. But his attitude toward the Anabaptists in this regard is regrettable. The least the reformer could have done was to maintain a discreet silence; he need not have mocked the Anabaptists when they sincerely tried to put into practice what he himself had preached and tried to do earlier in his career. But given the social and political reality, Luther's personality and his combative nature, and the Anabaptists' desperate attempt to implement their understanding of the gospel in the turbulent times of the sixteenth century, perhaps peace between the two sides was too much to expect.

DOCTRINE OR ETHICS?

⟪ **The Anabaptists believed** that Luther's emphasis on justification by faith alone frequently led to loose morals among Lutherans. The evangelical Anabaptists certainly agreed with the reformer that men and women were saved and justified by the grace of God, but they rejected his idea of an enslaved will and maintained that a justified person ought to bring forth good works to give evidence of their justification and salvation. This gave Luther occasion to brand the Anabaptist as Romanists, but it was difficult for him to deny that there was often a marked difference between the Anabaptists' ethical life and that of his followers.

Luther, however, was not indifferent to the practical and ethical life of his followers. As early as 1521 he wrote to the Wittenbergers that it was necessary to live according to one's faith, not only to talk about it (EA 39, 136). From time to time he stressed that teaching the right doctrines would be of little use if godly life did not follow. In a sermon of September 14, 1538, Luther declared that Christ did not come so that men and women might remain in their sins and damnation; people will not be saved if they do not stop sinning. To be sure, sins are forgiven, but one must stop being a miser, an adulterer, or a fornicator (WA 47, 110). In 1546, shortly before his death, Luther declared emphatically that it is impossible to reach heaven without having seriously striven for sanctification here on earth (EA 16, 255–6). Luther was against "good works" only in so far as they tended to minimize the grace of God in the human experience of salvation.

Luther believed that the Catholic Church had neglected to teach salvation by grace alone and instead had emphasized "good works." In 1520 he wrote Pope Leo X that he had no dispute with anyone about morals, just about the word of truth, namely correct doctrine. In 1521 he wrote about his Catholic opponents: Whether they are good or bad does not concern him. But he will attack their poisonous and lying teaching, which contradicts God's Word (WA 7, 278–9). In 1524 he wrote to certain princes that he would have had little to do with the papists had they taught aright; their wicked life did not matter much to him (EA 53, 265). Luther believed that if justification by faith were emphasized a sanctified life would follow, for a justified person was sanctified by Christ and empowered to live a holy life. Luther knew of course that even after a person's justification the believer remained a sinner. But according to the reformer, a believer's sinfulness was not held against him or her whose sins were forgiven and who consequently now lived in a state of grace. Luther believed that his doctrine is pure because it is a gift of God. But in his followers' lives there is still punishable sinfulness. However, this sinfulness is forgiven and not held against the believer, but *remissio peccatorum* (remission of sin) is placed over it, and the sin is thus wiped out (WA 33, 371).

But Luther's teaching about justification without works undeniably resulted in confusion about the Christian life. Luther's advice in a letter to Melanchthon, "Be a sinner and sin boldly, but believe and rejoice in Christ even more boldly," was no doubt difficult for his followers to understand, even more so for his opponents. Or, "No sin will separate us from the Lamb, even though we commit fornication and murder a thousand times a day," no doubt shocked some of them. According to Strohl, "Extravagant statements like this one did not help clarify Luther's views to his opponents. He sounded like no friend to piety and moral probity" (Strohl 157).

It is well known that Luther's followers often denied with their lives what the reformer believed and taught, and there is little doubt that Luther's strong and constant emphasis on the principle of justification by faith alone often contributed to the lack of ethics among Lutherans. For example, some Bohemian Brethren expressed interest in the Reformation, but they found fault with the discipline and the moral life among Lutherans. When they complained to Luther about this, the reformer was annoyed at their plain speaking but promised to do something about the moral laxity among his followers. In 1524 Staupitz wrote to Luther, pleading with him not to disregard the moral aspect of Christianity: "I see that countless persons abuse the gospel for the freedom of the flesh." The poet Hans Sachs, a strong supporter of Luther, addressed the Lutherans in 1524 as follows: "There is much cry and little wool about you. If you have no use for brotherly love, you are no disciple of Christ. If you were really evangelical as you profess to be, you would lead a godly life like the Apostles" (Coutts 244).

Catholics and Anabaptists "faulted Luther's doctrines for failing to create a lively sense of piety in congregations that heard Luther and others preach year after year" (Marius 475). But among Luther's supporters and colleagues there was also disappointment about the lack of ethics among Lutherans. Melanchthon wrote in 1525 that the "common people adhere to Luther only because they think that no further religious duty will be laid upon them" (Horsch, *Mennonites* 28). In 1530, Luther blamed his "lazy and indifferent" ministers for the people's utter disregard of the sacraments. The longer the ministers preach the gospel, the deeper the people plunge into greed, pride and luxury (EA 23, 166–7). The bigamy of Philip of Hess and Luther and Melanchthon's embarrassing involvement in the case (EA 55, 258–264) are well known and need not be recounted here. In some instances even ministers were permitted to divorce and remarry with the reformer's consent. For example, a Lutheran pastor, Michael Kramar, lived in a bigamous relationship and married several times because, as he admitted, he was unable to be without women (Plummer 99–115). The Lutheran principle of justification by faith was often ignored, even abused, by those who were unable or had no desire to live by the demands of Christian ethics. Long after Luther, the justification by faith principle was often seen as the reason for Lutherans' loose living. An evangelical divine wrote in 1871: "Justification by faith is made to cover, in advance, all sins, even the future ones.... Hence we see not seldom the justified and the old man side by side, and the old man is not a bit changed" (P. Schaff, 667).

Luther knew that the moral life of some of his followers left much to be desired, and he did not find it difficult to acknowledge the well-meant criticism of his colleagues and friends. But when the Anabaptists attacked not only the life of Lutherans but also the doctrine of justification by faith, which they believed underlay this moral laxity, Luther defended his position, and in so doing went at times to extremes. Menno Simons' criticism of Luther's doctrine of justification and Lutherans' disregard of Christian living is typical of many Anabaptists' criticism: "For with the same doctrine [meaning justification by faith alone] they have led the reckless and innocent people, great and small, city dweller and cottager alike, into such a fruitless, unregenerate life, and have given them such a free rein, that one would scarcely find such an ungodly and abominable life among Turks and Tartars as among these people" (Simons 333). Alfred Coutts, interpreting the Anabaptists' opposition to the magisterial reformers' teaching, writes: "Just as Luther had traced all the moral chaos of his time to the errors of Rome, so the spiritual reformers found the explanation of the moral and spiritual degeneration of the Reformation age in the doctrinal errors of the Reformed Church" (Coutts 81).

But for Luther the criticism of the Anabaptists was a sure sign of their lack of the Holy Spirit, for the Spirit only condemns false doctrines and is patient with those who are "weak in the faith." In a sermon in 1533 Luther warned his listeners against the apparent godly life of the Anabaptists. The Anabaptists are like wolves in sheep's clothing. They do not curse, they despise the outward necessities of life, they pray and read the Word of God, are patient in suffering, and not vengeful against their enemies. All this is good and worthy of emulation. But one must be on guard against thinking that their outward piety is proof that their doctrines are correct. Luther lists what he considers to be their errors: They rely on their good works; they make God a liar by negating their first baptism and by baptizing again; they teach that in the Holy Communion there is nothing but bread and wine; they destroy the concept of marriage by insisting that the believing partner separate himself from the unbelieving spouse; they teach that it is sinful to own property; they despise governments as non-Christian institutions. In summary: they turn the three divine orders upside down and destroy them: the church, the state, and the household (SLA 13a, 799).

The piety of the sixteenth-century Anabaptists is reflected in many documents. Philip of Hesse, in whose realm many Anabaptists lived, wrote to his sister, the Duchess Elizabeth of Saxony: "I found more goodness in those so-called 'Enthusiasts' than in those who are Lutherans" (Coutts 256). Erasmus wrote to the Archbishop of Toulouse in 1529: "The Anabaptists are to be commended above all others for the innocence of their lives." And again: "This sect so hated ... preach repentance; they summon all men to amendment of life; they follow the examples of the Apostles" (Smithson, *The Anabaptists* 118). Franz Agricola, a Roman Catholic theologian, wrote in his *Against the Terrible Errors of the Anabaptists* in 1582: "As concerns their outward public life, they are irreproachable. No lying, deception, swearing, strife, harsh language, no intemperate eating and drinking, no outward personal display is found or is discernible among them, but only humility, patience, uprightness, meekness, honesty, temperance, and straight-forwardness in such measure that one would suppose that they have the holy Spirit of God" (117–8).

CONCLUSION

It bears repeating that Luther was not indifferent to the question of ethics among his followers. He had preached and written about the necessity of "good works" in the life of those who claimed to have experienced the grace of God, and he even became angry at times when his congregants did not heed his and other ministers' preaching. "What shall I do with you people of Wittenberg!" he thundered in a sermon on November 8, 1528. "I shall not preach to you the kingdom of Christ, because you don't take it up. You are thieves, robbers, merciless. To you I must preach the law.... Know this, you Wittenbergers, you are altogether empty of good works.... You ungrateful beasts are not worthy of this treasure of the gospel" (Marius 475). Sometimes Luther did go on strike and refused to mount the pulpit, "much to the consternation of his friends and his prince, who doubtless cherished Luther's continual preaching on obedience" (476).

In the light of this it is sad that Luther failed to appreciate the sincere attempts of the Anabaptists to put into practice what he himself had preached. And Luther had to agree that in the realm of discipleship the Anabaptists often put the Lutherans to shame. To believe, however, that Luther deliberately misrepresented the motives of the Anabaptists in an attempt to either justify the often all too loose living of his followers, or to warn people against what he considered their errors, is to misunderstand the reformer and the real issues involved. Just as Luther, in his break with Rome, was not primarily concerned with the alleged lack of ethics among Roman Catholics, so he was not overly impressed with the pious living of the Anabaptists. He certainly believed that doctrine led to conduct; but he also knew that right conduct was not necessarily a sign of right doctrine. Thus, when he examined the beliefs of the Anabaptists and found that they contradicted *his* understanding of Scriptures on the most vital points in *his* theology, he did not doubt for a moment that the devil was using the piety of the Anabaptists to lead sincere souls away from the gospel.

The Anabaptists' emphasis on discipline and good works detracted, as far as Luther was concerned, from the cardinal doctrine of the New Testament: justification through God's grace alone. Luther feared that as soon as the human element received priority in a Christian's life – and in Anabaptism he believed that it did – it would lead to human pride and to minimizing God's work in the life of individuals. That Luther's emphasis on *sola fide* often contributed to a disregard of ethical discipline and good morals among Lutherans, and that his belief in the enslaved will through sin was sometimes used as a pretext for carnal living, cannot be denied. Luther castigated this carnality among his followers. But on the issue of doctrine and works Luther remained clear and consistent to the end. Humans are saved and sustained by the grace of God; good works ought to be the evidence of God's grace in the lives of believers and expressions of gratitude for what God has done in Christ.

Ironically, the Anabaptists believed similarly, but they emphasized the necessity for Christians to live righteously, giving evidence to Christ's work of salvation in their lives. This difference in emphasis often blurred the issue of dogma versus practical living. Had both sides been more patient with each other, they could and should have been able to see that Lutheran and Anabaptist positions were not mutually exclusive. But this was surely too much to expect in a time when religion not only ran deeply in societies' veins, but that religious people would rather fight and even die for what they deeply believed than tolerate a group that believed otherwise.

"I Told You So"
Luther and the Anabaptist Kingdom in Münster

"I TOLD YOU SO!"

hen a group of **fanatical Anabaptists** erected their kingdom in Münster, Westphalia (1534–35), Luther's response was "I told you so." He regarded the developments in Münster as the logical outcome of what most Anabaptists believed and practised. Linking the Münsterites with Karlstadt and Müntzer, his attitude toward all Anabaptists continued to harden. He regarded the revolutionary activities of the Münsterites as God's punishment for the sins of Germany and the devil's attempt to destroy the Reformation. The Münster episode is important to our study in that it contributed to Luther's final assessment of the entire radical and Anabaptist movement. Up to 1534 Luther still seemed to differentiate between revolutionary radicals and the more peaceful Anabaptists. After Münster he, like other magisterial reformers, increasingly lumped all Anabaptists together and began to advise more severe measures against them. This final assessment of the Anabaptist movement persisted in historiography until the mid-nineteenth century when the Catholic historian C.A. Cornelius (1810–1903)

disentangled the historical threads and showed that the Münster episode was not at all characteristic of all Anabaptists. His *Geschichte des Münsterischen Aufruhrs* (1855) and other works on the Reformation influenced subsequent historians to write more objectively about the Anabaptist movement (ME 3, 780–2).

It is the purpose of this chapter to briefly sketch the story of the Anabaptist kingdom in Münster, comment on Luther's attitude toward the Münster events, and to consider any possible connections between the fanatics of Münster and the evangelical Anabaptists, including the followers of Menno Simons.

KINGDOM OF MÜNSTER BEGINS

⁜ **The Anabaptist movement** in the city of Münster, Westphalia, in northwestern Germany, stood in closest relation to the unrest of the time in general and the revolutionary tendencies within the city in particular. With a population of about 15,000 Münster was a major city with Bishop Franz von Waldeck (1491–1553) the civil ruler of the territory. Since the city enjoyed a large measure of self-government, radical changes were possible at almost any time. As early as 1525, during the time of the Peasants' War, the populace of Münster began to demand improvements in economic, social, and religious conditions. The formidable influence of the many guilds of craftsmen and merchants especially "created vital conditions for the rise of the Reformation and Anabaptist movements" (Haude 10). No important measures could be passed without the consent of the powerful guilds. It was the guilds or the unions with the support of the city mob that later gained control over the council and the bishop.

One of the priests of the city, Bernhard (Bernt) Rothmann (ca. 1495–1535) began in 1530 to advocate anti-Catholic reforms. He had been educated with the Brothers of the Common Life at Deventer, where he had also become acquainted with the New Testament. In 1531 he visited Wittenberg, and from there he went to Strasbourg where he was the guest of some Zwinglian reformers. Upon his return to Münster Rothmann began to preach with great success, so that the St. Maurice Church became too small to hold audiences and a pulpit had to be set up outside the church. The council gave Rothmann strict orders to preach inside the church only, but the enthusiastic preacher disregarded the council's ruling.

When the bishop outlawed Rothmann on January 7, 1532, the preacher asserted his Catholic orthodoxy. A few weeks later, however, he published a confession in which he defended Lutheran doctrines and advocated the establishment of a new state church along Lutheran lines. A cloth merchant and prominent member of the city council, Bernhard (Bernt) Knipperdolling (ca. 1490–1536) and a mob supported Rothmann in his defiance of the council and the bishop. On February 14, 1533, all the churches of the city, with the exception of the cathedral, were in the possession of the Lutheran radicals.

Before the close of the year a split occurred in the ranks of Rothmann's followers. The preachers began to favour Zwinglian and Anabaptist views on the Last Supper, whereas others continued to uphold the Lutheran version. Luther in a letter to the Council of Münster warned against tolerating Zwinglian and similar heresies, but it was no longer in the power of the magistrates to silence Rothmann. Through the influence of one Heinrich Roll, who had come to Münster from nearby Wassenberg, a "Melchiorite" centre, Rothmann's faction began in 1533 to advocate some Anabaptist views. The so-called Melchiorites were followers of Melchior Hoffman (ca. 1495–1544?), a former associate of Luther in Wittenberg. Hoffman was known for his apocalyptic visions and views on the speedy return of Christ. He became quite active in northern Germany and in the Rhine regions, preaching and baptizing with great success. However, he never advocated the use of violence, and later, while in prison in Strasbourg, he warned against the spirit of the Münsterites and counselled moderation.

Back in Münster, Rothmann's followers early in 1534 introduced some Anabaptist views and practices. Infant baptism was rejected and many adults were baptized. Within a brief period approximately 1,400 people submitted to baptism. According to C.A. Cornelius, the newly baptized renounced worldliness, practised community of goods, led good moral lives, and lived simply and piously (Wiswedel III 202). However, the principle of non-resistance was absent; there was infighting and struggle for control among the various factions. Opposition to the old order increased, the council and the bishop were defied, and like the Wittenbergers before them, the laity insisted on their right to participate in church reform. With the assistance of the ever-increasing number of persecuted refugees flocking to Münster from many parts of the empire, the radicals were in complete control of the city by the end of February 1534.

THE PROPHETS ARRIVE

⟪ Jan Matthys from Haarlem in the Netherlands had kept an eye for some time on the affairs in Münster. Similar to Thomas Müntzer, Matthys claimed to be divinely inspired by God and to receive revelations. After the example of Christ he sent twelve apostles into the world, ordering them to baptize and to preach that no Christian blood should be shed any longer, for the Kingdom of God was at hand. Early in January 1534, Bartholomaus Boekebinder and Willem de Kuiper, two of Matthys's messengers, arrived in Münster. On their way from Amsterdam to Münster they preached about the worthy example of the faithful in Münster who had taken matters into their own hands. In their preaching they encouraged their listeners to look forward to the great day of salvation and peace on earth when none would be persecuted for their faith and practising adult baptism.

Rothmann was greatly encouraged and strengthened by the arrival of these messengers of Matthys. On January 13 another of Matthys's apostles, Jan van Leyden (ca. 1509–1536), a young tailor and homespun comedian, came to Münster, and in February the chief prophet, Jan Matthys, himself appeared. At the time, the council was still feebly urging moderation and tolerance toward those who disagreed with the proposed changes. In February, at the regular election of the council, Bernt Knipperdolling was elected one of the two burgomasters, or mayors, of the city. Fearing that things would become worse, many Catholics and Lutherans left the city.

The time had come for Jan Matthys to disclose his plans for the defeat of the remaining unbelievers in the city, including killing them. Burgomaster Knipperdolling warned him that such rash measures would prove fatal for the new movement. Matthys was finally persuaded to lengthen the days of grace to the beginning of March, giving the "godless" an opportunity to leave the city. Many fled and others received baptism, not from conviction but as a matter of expediency. By March 1534 it was believed that the city was free of all opposing elements and church and state were united, with Matthys at the head. To assert his authority the prophet killed a man who dared to oppose him and called him a deceiver and lier.

JAN VAN LEYDEN AND POLYGAMY

❨❨ **While the Münsterites** were establishing their kingdom within the city, Bishop Waldeck led the siege outside the city walls. But Matthys, claiming to have received a vision from God to move against the enemy forces, led a small band of warriors against the besiegers. Needless to say, he was killed in the attack. Jan van Leyden was now the desired leader of the city. The city council was abolished and twelve men were ordained to become "the elders of the twelve tribes of Israel." The city was now turned into a well-organized military camp, with Jan van Leyden looking after the details of military operation. The new Kingdom of Zion proved its strength when in May the besiegers made an attempt to take the city by storm. The attack failed and some 100 of the bishop's forces were killed, while the Münsterites lost about 50.

Militarily strengthened in his position, the youthful prophet introduced polygamy. One reason for the innovation was that there were more than three times the number of women in the city than men. Jan van Leyden married Divara, Matthys's beautiful widow, although he was married at the time. He was soon the husband of seventeen wives. The introduction of polygamy was looked upon with horror and disgust by the better elements in the city, but the prophet argued from the practices in the Old Testament that plurality of wives was biblical, and he threatened to punish those who opposed him in the matter. Rothmann, who practised polygamy on a slightly more moderate scale than Jan van Leyden, also defended the practice on the grounds of the Old Testament. Jan van Leyden would not tolerate any opposition to his rule, but in July about two hundred men seized him, Rothmann, and Knipperdolling and demanded that polygamy be abolished. Jan's opponents were overpowered and the prophets were set free, after which a terrible bloodbath followed.

Once again in complete control and after another successful strike against the enemies outside the city, Jan van Leyden proclaimed early in September 1534 that he was to become the new King David of Zion. He surrounded himself with an imposing court, converted priestly garments into regal robes, erected a throne in the marketplace, and made his favourite wife Divara his queen. People sank to their knees wherever the king appeared. His authority was complete and unopposed except for the rebellion of one of his wives, Elisabeth Wandscherer, who tried to escape. She was apprehended, the king dragged her to the marketplace in full view of the Münsterites and accused her of falsehood and insubordination. The king then decapitated her with his sword and trampled her body with his feet (*Die Wiedertäufer* 232–3).

Toward the end of 1534 fate turned increasingly against the Münsterites. The bishop and his allies fortified their position and disease and famine caused untold hardships within the city. Jan van Leyden promised salvation and victory from above, and amused the hungry people with dances, music, and theatrical performances, but it was all to no avail in the long run. In the spring of 1535 old men, women, and children began to leave the city for the enemy camp where many of them were executed, while a few others were pardoned after they recanted their errors. On the night of June 25, some insider betrayed the city, a gate was secretly opened, and the combined forces of Bishop Franz von Waldeck, the City of Cologne, and Prince Philip of Hesse overpowered the surprised Anabaptists. Most of the male defenders, perhaps 1,000, were slaughtered and Jan van Leyden, Knipperdolling, and Bernhard Krechting were imprisoned.

In January 1536 the three men were severely tortured before they were executed. Only Jan van Leyden, apparently, accepted the offer of a bishop's priest to stay with him through the night before his execution. According to some reports, the priest found Jan much changed. "He greatly regretted his godlessness, his murders, his looting, his lack of discipline, and his shameful deeds. He admitted that he deserved the bitterest possible death ten times over and he renounced all his errors" (Arthur 176). After their execution, the bodies of the three men were placed in three separate iron cages and hung on St. Lambert's Church, where they still hang (without the bodies of course) presumably as a memorial of this tragic event nearly five centuries ago.

LUTHER AND THE MÜNSTERITES

⁅ **At first Luther was not too concerned** about the rising unrest in Münster. Rothmann's reform efforts, his views on church and government, and the declining influence of Catholicism in Münster must have given the reformer some satisfaction (Tillmanns 280). However, when Rothmann inclined to the Anabaptist view of the Last Supper, Luther became uneasy about the developments in Münster. In December 1532 he wrote a letter to the council of Münster, in which he warned against the Zwinglian and Anabaptist teaching about Holy Communion (WA Br. 6, 401–3). Referring to Rothmann he wrote that God had given the city some fine preachers, however they needed to be warned against false teachings, for the devil can lead good, pious, and scholarly preachers astray. Warning the Münsterites, Luther referred to radicals such as Müntzer, Ludwig Hätzer, and Hubmaier, who had been punished by God for their erroneous views on the Last Supper, and that the same might happen to them. He also mentioned others who had left the true faith, by becoming Zwinglians, Anabaptists, and rebels against the government. Luther's warning seemed to fall on deaf ears. The news from Münster continued to be most discouraging, with the Münsterites denouncing both the pope and Luther as "twin prophets of wickedness." Luther concluded his instruction that "Münster was reaping the whirlwind of all the storms which the older fanatics had unleashed" (Tillmanns 280). The reformer's personal letter to Rothmann at the end of the year 1532, in which he pleaded with the preacher to be moderate and to guard his congregation against the influence of the sacramentarians, was to no avail.

Luther wrote two prefaces against the Anabaptists in Münster, one to Urbanus Rhegius's *Confutation of the Münster Confession* (EA 63, 332–6), and the other to *News from Münster* (WA 38, 347–50). In the first preface Luther refers to the charges of the Anabaptists that he, Luther, is a false prophet, worse than the pope, and to the charge of the papists that he is the cause of the existing sects and rebels. The devils, Luther points out, were also angels at one time, yet God cannot be held responsible for their eventual apostasy. It should be noted that all heretics came out of the church of Christ and not from paganism. To a certain extent, Luther thus acknowledges his responsibility for the rise of the dissident groups, while at the same time insisting that he and the radicals are basically strangers to each other.

In his preface to *News from Münster,* Luther both censors and ridicules the Anabaptists' folly. The devil that tries to set up a kingdom in Münster, Luther mocks, must be very inexperienced, an ABC devil, who has not yet learned how to be successful. To succeed the devil should have put on a pious front, proclaimed days of prayer and fasting, taken no money from the people, eaten no meat, regarded all women as poisonous, shunned worldly amusements, and repudiated all use of force and violence. But to act as the devil does in Münster will deceive no one; the intent and the excesses of the evil one are too obvious. Luther's comment on how the Anabaptists should be combated is significant. He feels that the best way to fight the devil is with the sword of the spirit, for the devil is a spirit and is thus not impressed by a display of physical force. The bishops and princes, however, instead of preaching the Word of God and winning the hearts of people, strangle and kill the bodies of their opponents and leave the souls to the devil. Luther's apparent changed position from 1525, when he urged the princes to kill the rebellious peasants, seems surprising.

To conclude his preface to *News from Münster*, Luther attacks the doctrinal errors of the Münsterites, not so much their evil deeds. First, he holds it against them that they deny the human nature of Christ, believing that Mary was simply the channel through which the divine Christ came into the world. (It was Melchior Hoffman who had widely disseminated this view of Christ's incarnation throughout northern Germany and in the Rhine regions, influencing even Menno Simons that Jesus at his birth had retained his "heavenly flesh.") Luther points out that the Bible is clear on this issue, stating that Mary was "pregnant" and that Christ was "born," thus clearly implying that Christ was fully human and the Son of God at the same time. Second, they condemn the sacrament of infant baptism, making of it a human and pagan institution. It is strange, Luther concludes, that the same people who despise all that is human at the same time enjoy the gold of the godless, as the Anabaptists do in Münster. Third, they hold perverted views about marriage and polygamy. If the marriage of the "godless" is prostitution, as the Münsterites believe, it surely follows that the Münster Anabaptists are all illegitimate children. Fourth, their "kingdom" is so obviously rebellious that there is no further need to speak of it. Luther believes that Münster is God's way of chastising Germany for the purpose of needful repentance; but God is gracious and will not allow the devil to destroy the land.

The Münster debacle confirmed the suspicion that Luther had had all along about the whole Anabaptist movement. It proved to him beyond all doubt that every heretic and fanatic was also a rebel in disguise. They first sow lies, he argued, and later seal these lies with civil disobedience and murder. Münster also confirmed his belief that every Anabaptist, no matter how pious, is a concealed devil. The revolt of the Anabaptists in Münster had opened the eyes of the governments, and after that no one would trust even those radicals who claimed to be innocent and peaceful.

Many of Luther's sermons and writings after 1535 were filled with references to the Anabaptists' attempt to establish a kingdom on earth. In a 1539 sermon on Matthew 24 Luther brushed aside the dream of such people as Müntzer and the Anabaptists that Christ would set up an earthly kingdom in which the saints would reign. And what caused these Anabaptists to believe such notions? Luther asks. His answer is that it is the fact that the ungodly appear to be so fortunate in the world, possessing kingdoms, power, and wisdom, whereas Christians are of no account compared to them. So the Anabaptists believed that the ungodly must be destroyed so that the pious may live in peace (WA 47, 561–2).

WAS LUTHER CORRECT?

❊ **Luther's assessment of the Münsterites** was generally correct, but it did not apply to the peaceful Anabaptists who, after their emergence in 1525, were spreading within the empire. Ironically, these more peaceful radicals believed what Luther believed, namely that the Christian life was filled with persecution and martyrdom and that a follower of Christ was called upon to suffer patiently rather than take up arms against their oppressors. But past radicalism, the peasants' rebellions, and now Münster blinded Luther's eyes so that he saw nothing but evil in *all* Anabaptists. For Luther, unfortunately, the case of Anabaptism was closed; the Anabaptists had been tried and found wanting.

There can be no reasonable justification for what happened in Münster, but it is possible to understand the excesses in the Westphalian capital. As a result of severe persecution, apocalyptic expectations had become very strong among many Anabaptists. Most of them considered themselves to be at a crucial point in history, believing that God had assembled his people "for the decisive attack, but Satan too, arms with all his forces for the great conflict. All the forces of the *Civitas Diaboli* are let loose now upon the *Civitas Dei:* the old dragon and the great beast, the Anti-Christ, and the false prophets" (Stauffer 197). These eschatological visions and speculations were much stronger among the Dutch Anabaptists than among the Swiss. Many of the radicals, however, looked upon the end more in spiritual terms, expecting a heavenly kingdom established by Christ, not an earthly kingdom with an earthly king (Isaak). But a strong minority, influenced by the economic, social, and political conditions of the time, thought of and hoped for an earthly kingdom established by Christ with the help of his followers.

Luther himself believed that he was living at the end of the age. In 1520 he identified the pope with the Antichrist who, according to Scripture, was to appear in the last days (WA Br. 2, 167). In view of the dark prospect of his cause Luther wrote in 1521 that he was living in perilous times, worthy of the last days of which the prophet Daniel spoke (WA 7, 774). In 1522 Luther wrote that the Lord was beginning to destroy the Antichrist with the spirit of his mouth, and that Christians were waiting for the return of Christ, when the Antichrist would finally be defeated (WA 8, 554). Luther expected the Lord to return soon and encouraged all Christians to pray that God would soon utterly destroy the Antichrist and his sinful ways (WA 8, 185). In 1532 he expressed the opinion that the last day would come before the close of that year. In 1534 he expected to see certain signs that would precede the coming of Christ. For a time Luther even felt that the Turks, who threatened the eastern part of the empire, should not be resisted, for God would use them to usher in the end of the world.

The Anabaptists, then, were not the only ones in the sixteenth century whose apocalyptic expectations were ever real. Luther's views about the end times, however, seemed to correspond more closely with those of the New Testament writers who also believed that Christ's second coming was imminent; the revolutionary Anabaptists, on the other hand, believed that God had chosen them to usher in the Kingdom of God. This, according to Luther, is where they deviated from the biblical teaching on the subject.

About polygamy, it must be noted that not only the Münsterites but also some magisterial reformers held unorthodox views. Luther, as we have seen, agreed hesitantly to the bigamy of Philip of Hesse and Michael Kramer, justifying his position on the basis of the Old Testament. Moreover, in 1531 Luther advised Catherine of Aragon, the queen of Henry VIII of England, not to consent to the proposed divorce, suggesting rather that Henry VIII take another wife, after the example of the Old Testament patriarchs. Similarly, Melanchthon believed that holding more wives than one was not necessarily against the divine law (Horsch, "The Rise and Fall" 138–9). Some of the radical reformers, other than the Münster Anabaptists, were also charged with sexual immorality, the learned Anabaptist Ludwig Hätzer being one of them, and it is difficult to clear him of these charges altogether (Goeters 147–8).

ANABAPTISM AND MÜNSTERISM

⟪ **In spite of the evidence to the contrary** there are still those who follow the traditional line of thinking that there was little difference in the beliefs and practices of the various Anabaptist groups. Ronald A. Knox, for example, wrote some time ago that there is a contradiction between the Anabaptist doctrine of non-resistance and their blood-drenched history. He wrote that they preach non-resistance since they regard the state as part of the kingdom of darkness with which they have nothing to do. But when it comes to fighting the ungodly under "perfect" rulers or generals such as Müntzer or Jan van Leyden, they become as aggressive as others (Knox 132).

Comments such as these certainly cannot apply to the beliefs and practices of the peaceful Anabaptists. Writers such as Knox and others ignored all historical differentiation between the teachings and practices of the evangelical Anabaptists and the revolutionary trends in other groups. It is often overlooked that Münster was not the inevitable and final development of Anabaptism. Münsterism was largely an excrescence, an abnormal outgrowth of the Anabaptist movement brought about by the confluence of certain social and religious factors and the appearance of certain elements that were entirely foreign to the principles and ethics of such evangelical groups as the Swiss Brethren and most Dutch Anabaptists.

What were these unfortunate elements and how can they be accounted for? The violent suppression of the Peasants' Revolt had not destroyed the seeds of discontent among the common people; the lower classes remained as dissatisfied as ever, and governments even expected further uprisings after 1525. Münster was one such uprising, not necessarily only of peasants but of townspeople as well. While the religious element played an important role in the Münster episode, the socio-economic factors were an important aspect of what happened in the Westphalian capital (Zschäbitz 53–4). Luther himself referred to the greed and political ambitions of the Münsterites (WA 38, 347–50). In addition, it is significant that the Kingdom of Münster was preceded by a steadily mounting persecution of the Anabaptists in the Low Countries and to some extent in other parts of Germany. Also, when there were no longer able leaders such as Denck, Hut, Grebel, and Hubmaier, the Anabaptists were left without effective leadership. The result was that the more radical side was sidetracked in some instances from its New Testament ideals and then followed by more immature lay leadership. Moreover, the rapid expansion of Anabaptism sometimes introduced elements into the movement that had not become truly saturated with the essence of what these people stood for. Having quickly organized a congregation in one place, often under cover of darkness, the Anabaptist travelling evangelists left by early morning for another area, often leaving the immature but eager group of converts to inexperienced leaders. Hans Hut (ca. 1490–1527), for example, the Anabaptist apostle in Upper Austria, was very effective in spreading the Anabaptist gospel in the ranks of artisans, often baptizing those whom he convinced immediately after his sermon and then sending them out as evangelists to other areas (ME II, 847). The episode in Münster was not characteristic of the entire Anabaptist movement but the result of the ambitions of a few fanatical leaders. Münster was an isolated example of the worst aspect of radical Anabaptism; it was a caricature of the movement.

The above considerations are borne out when comparing the beliefs and practices of the Anabaptists and Münsterites. The Münster fanatics *forced* baptism on the people of the city; the Anabaptists, on the other hand, baptized only those who showed evidence of repentance and faith and wished to join Anabaptism voluntarily. The Münsterites believed in a state church with a king who combined the function of both church and government; the Anabaptists advocated a free and separate church and generally refused to serve in governmental offices altogether. The Anabaptist principle of liberty of conscience was foreign to the fanatics of Münster who they advocated the use of force and war against their enemies, which the evangelical Anabaptists repudiated. The Münsterites practised and defended plurality of wives; the Anabaptists sought to adhere to the conventions and laws regarding marriage, excluding those from their fellowship who offended along ethical lines.

There were other significant differences between the Münsterites and the Anabaptists. Whereas the Münsterites exalted the Old Testament above the New Testament, the Anabaptists were known for their adherence to the New Testament, particularly the principles of the Sermon on the Mount (Matt. 5–7). In his pamphlet *The Restitution*, it is significant that Rothmann ignored the Swiss Brethren altogether, but he pointed out that whereas it was Luther who had begun the restitution or restoration of true Christianity, it was "through our brother, John of Leyden [that] the truth has been gloriously established" (Horsch, "Rise and Fall" 134). The Anabaptists in turn disavowed the Münsterites, pointing out that there was no spiritual bond between them. Some Hutterian Brethren, for example, called both Luther and the Münster fanatics and false prophets. But the most outspoken opponent of Münsterism was Menno Simons (1496–1561) of Friesland in the Netherlands after whom the Mennonites are named.

MENNO SIMONS AND MÜNSTER

❰❰ **Ordained to the priesthood** when he was about twenty-eight years old, Menno had his first severe doubts about the Catholic faith in connection with the celebration of the Eucharist. At first he tried to dismiss the question of how the bread and wine could turn into the actual body and blood of Christ as a temptation of the devil. He began to study the New Testament with the Catholic doctrine of transubstantiation in mind and came to the conclusion that on the question of the Lord's Supper he had been following the "teachings of men." It was Luther who had taught Menno that "man-made laws do not bring about eternal death." In fact, Luther's influence on Menno Simons in his early years as a priest was profound. He read several works of the German reformer, possibly one of them being *On the Freedom of a Christian*, although Menno does not mention any specific titles. Menno adapted what he read in Luther to the various issues he dealt with, and while being grateful to Luther's insights and teachings, Menno criticized the "learned theologian" wherever he thought he was in error, and then followed an independent course (Simons 669, 692, 780).

Menno Simons accepted Luther's principle of justification by faith alone, but believed that Lutherans were so one-sided in their teaching of this doctrine that they neglected to stress the importance of Christian ethics. Ironically, on the question of baptism, Menno learned from Luther to doubt the validity of infant baptism. In his earlier references to baptism, Luther had stressed the necessity of faith, and in his later works he had contended that even children were capable of having faith. Comparing Luther's teaching on baptism with that of the New Testament and the Anabaptists led Menno to reject infant baptism and to embrace believers' baptism. In addition, the suffering and persecution of Anabaptists at the hands of both Catholics and Protestants made a lasting impression on him. In 1536, after the debacle of Münster, he decided to join the despised persecuted group in the Netherlands, becoming their teacher and leader. After 1535, when the authorities intensified their persecution of the Anabaptists, Menno Simons felt "called," as he puts it, to defend and support them. He purged the minds of many Anabaptists of the "apocalyptic fancies taught by many of their leaders ... inculcated the old ideas of non-resistance, of the evils of state control over the church, of the need of personal conversion, and of adult baptism as its sign and seal" (Lindsay 496). It is perhaps only partly true to say, as Tillmann does: "The disaster of the Heavenly Kingdom led Menno to his ... great doctrine: His teaching of non-resistance" (Tillmanns 281). The fact is that as a follower of the pacifist Melchior Hofmann Menno must have believed in non-resistance *before* Münster, but the events in Münster confirmed him in the view that violence is not the way of Christ.

Both at the height and in the aftermath of the Münster fanaticism Menno Simons became the champion of peaceful Anabaptism. Opposed to what Münsterism stood for, Menno particularly attacked the teachings, pretensions, and practices of Jan van Leyden. In a 1535 pamphlet entitled *The Blasphemy of John of Leyden* (Simons 33–50), Menno sought to invalidate the prophet's claim that he was the new King David. In the the tract's introduction, Menno states that necessity compels him to write against the Münsterites "because we cannot tolerate the shameful deceit and blasphemy against God that a man be placed in Christ's stead." Christ is the king of all; no man can usurp the divine throne. "Greater antichrist there cannot arise than he who poses as the David of promise." On the question of physical force, Menno states that if Christ fights his enemies with the sword of his mouth, "how can we, then, oppose our enemies with any other sword." Christ had no desire to be defended with Peter's sword. According to Scriptures, Christ will not destroy his enemies before the time of his coming, but Jan van Leyden proposes to destroy the enemies here and now. Warning his fellow Anabaptists, Menno concludes: "Let every one of you guard against all strange doctrine of sword and resistance and other like things which is nothing short of a fair flower under which lies hidden an evil serpent which has shot his venom into many. Let everyone beware" (Simons 34–9).

In many of his writings Menno tried his utmost to make the authorities aware of the differences between true Anabaptism and Münsterism. Writing in 1539 in his *Christian Baptism*, Menno states: "Therefore I say, if you find in me or in my teachings which is the Word of God, or among those who are taught by me or my colleagues any thievery, murder, perjury, sedition, rebellion, or any other criminal act, as were and are found among the corrupt sects – then punish all of us" (Simons 284).

The tragedy of Münster, however, stigmatized all Anabaptists as rebels and criminals and Menno's pleas for clemency for his co-religionists were not heeded. Many Anabaptists were executed after Münster. According to some estimates, in the sixteenth century about 4,000 Ananaptists were burned, drowned, or executed in some other way (Schnyder 116). According to some other estimates, however, in the ten years following the disaster in Münster, no fewer than 30,000 Anabaptists were executed in Holland and Friesland alone, although this number is now considered an exaggeration. In other areas such as Moravia and Hesse where Anabaptists had been generally tolerated before 1535, after the defeat of the Münsterites they were exiled and persecuted without necessarily being killed. Menno Simons himself became a fugitive, finally fleeing the territory of Charles V and finding refuge in Holstein under the protection of Count Bartholomew of Ahlfeld. There he was left free to preach, publish his works, and counsel both his own followers, who regarded him as their patriarch, and Lutheran believers (Tillmanns 232).

Some rulers differentiated between the violent Münsterites and the peaceful Anabaptists. In a mandate of 1544, Anna of Oldenburg, the regent of East Friesland, called the followers of Menno Simons "Mennists" instead of "Anabaptists" and protected them from persecution. Mennonites have gone by that name ever since. The Swiss and South German Anabaptists also adopted the name because it was associated with a faith and a way of life that was the opposite of what the revolutionary Anabaptists stood for.

Perhaps one should not be too critical of Luther, who saw the connections between revolutionary radicalism, doctrinal error, and the excesses at Münster but failed to appreciate the sincerity of the many peaceful groups. Given the circumstances and considering Luther's position of leadership within the Reformation, one can understand the reformer's attitude toward Münster and Anabaptism generally. However, his judgment of Anabaptism on the basis of a violent group of fanatics is lamentable. The great mass of Anabaptists were moderates; they consistently acknowledged civil governments as being from God, and paid their respect, obedience, and taxes to them; they merely wished to be left alone to practise their faith, including non-violence.

Ironically, most Anabaptists, not only the Münsterites, were charged with rebellion and bloodshed by those who did not believe in the principle of nonviolence themselves. Neither the Zwinglians and Lutherans nor other magisterial reformers shrank from using violence when it came to supporting, advancing, and defending their own causes. The Anabaptists were not blind to such inconsistencies. Menno Simons wrote: "Why do they indiscreetly accuse us of uproar while we are wholly innocent and clear of all uproar and they never pay attention to their own destructive, bloody murdering uproar. Again what bloody uproars the Lutherans have for some years made to introduce and establish their doctrine, I will leave to them to reflect upon. Nevertheless we, although innocent, must be accounted the tumultuous heretics and they the God-fearing, pious, peaceable Christians" (Horsch 68).

It is also ironic that in other matters the Münsterites and Lutherans had more in common than the Anabaptists and the Münster fanatics. For example, in matters of ethics the evangelical Anabaptists placed the Sermon on the Mount above the Old Testament; the Lutherans and the Münsterites regarded both the Old and the New Testament as equally authoritative in the area of ethics. In fact, in some important beliefs and practices, such as relations between church and state and sanctioning capital punishment for heretics, both Lutherans and Münsterites appealed to the Old Testament. Some went so far as to state that the Münster radicals were more imbibed with Lutheran ideas than with Anabaptism (Littell, *Free Church* 27). Thus, to lay the offences of the Münsterites to the charge of the Anabaptists on the grounds that both practised adult baptism, is, as Menno Simons pointed out, "as unreasonable as to accuse the Lutherans of the crimes of which some of the popes became guilty, on the ground that both were pedobaptists" (Horsch, *Mennonites*, 226).

Much Ado about Spirit and Matter
Luther and the Spiritualists

INNER AND OUTER WORD

The mysticism of the Zwickau prophets had been so pronounced and Thomas Müntzer's use of Scriptures so different from Luther's, that the reformer had little difficulty in detecting in these "enthusiasts," as he continued to call them, the work of evil spirits. According to Luther, these radicals clearly violated the will of God as expressed in the *written* Word. But when sane, educated, and sophisticated persons, who appeared to be sincere in their attempt to follow Scriptures, stressed the *inner* Word or the *inner* light as being more important than the written Word of God, Luther was compelled to re-examine his own position on this issue.

We have seen that for Luther the principle of *sola scriptura* was of great importance. On the basis of this principle he opposed medieval theology, the decisions of councils, the Catholic interpretation of Scripture, the position of the papacy, and the decrees of the emperor. He was bound in his conscience not to act contrary to God's Word. Some believe, however, that for Luther the Word of God and the Bible were not quite identical and that he began to stress the importance of the written Word only when he encountered spiritualists who de-emphasized it. It is known, however, that the young Luther inclined heavily toward mysticism, particularly admiring the *Theologia Deutsch* (1500), which he edited several times and recommended to all Christians. Luther called the book "a spiritual and noble booklet, which shows what the old and the new human being is, what Adam's and what God's child is, and how Adam ought to die and Christ rise in us." Volker Leppin observes that in Luther "mystic and Pauline theology merged, similar to St. Augustine's" experience of the Christian life (Leppin, LH 59).

Coutts finds Luther's leanings to the mystical side of the Christian life striking, "when it is remembered that in the *Theologia Germanica* there is no mention made of the supreme authority of the Scriptures, nor of justification by faith alone – foundation principles of the Reformation. Salvation is attained by the loss of self in the Divine" (Coutts 102). Coutts further observes: "For Luther himself, there was a twofold witness of the Holy Spirit for the authority of Scripture – the witness of the written Word itself, and the witness of the believing mind. But it is evident that he put the witness of the believing mind first, for everywhere the inspiration of Scripture was tested by the place it gave to justification by Faith, which was really the testimony of his own religious experience. The real authority Luther set up, though he did not clearly see it, was not the Scripture but his inward experience of Justification by Faith, which he found in Scripture, and to which Scripture gave witness. Where he did not find that doctrine, he found neither inspiration nor authority" (103–4).

There are references, particularly in Luther's earlier works, which seem to lend substance to the view that the reformer was subjective in his reading and interpretation of Scripture. In Luther's *Exposition of the Magnificat* in 1521 the reformer states that no one can understand God or his Word unless one has received such insight directly, without mediation (*ohne Mittel*), from the Holy Spirit, and no one can receive it from the Holy Spirit without experiencing, proving, and feeling it (Werke 6, 170).

There are, however, those who insist that to charge Luther with subjectivism is to misunderstand the reformer's view of Scripture. The fact that Luther opposed those radicals who stressed the inner Word above the written Scripture underlines the difference that existed between Luther's conception of the Word of God and that of such spiritualists as Hans Denck and Caspar von

Schwenckfeld (Siirala 122, 126–8). It is thus necessary to first sketch the views of some important spiritualists of the divine Word and then show Luther's position and his reason for opposing them.

HANS DENCK

⟪ **Among the more prominent men** who strongly advocated the inner Word in Luther's time, were Hans Denck, Sebastian Franck, and the Silesian nobleman Caspar von Schwenckfeld. The most attractive of the three was no doubt Hans Denck (ca. 1495–1527), rector of St. Sebald's School in Nürnberg. A Renaissance humanist and scholar, Denck had been greatly influenced by the medieval mystics, Luther, and Thomas Müntzer, among others. According to Coutts, Denck made the acquaintance of Müntzer at Nürnberg, although Walter Fellmann doubts that Denck ever made personal contact with Müntzer (Fellmann II, 10). Having become disillusioned with what he considered the unregenerate life of Lutherans in Nürnberg, Denck was increasingly drawn to Anabaptism, which seemed to him to stress Christian discipleship with great success. His individualism and mysticism, however, and his emphasis on the inner Word set him apart from the mainstream Anabaptists whose approach to faith and conduct, according to him, was too biblicistic and legalistic.

In contrast to Müntzer, Denck abstained from all recourse to violence; no one practised the principle of non-resistance as well as he. His life and writings spoke of God's love; he wrote reluctantly in answer to his enemies; and he confessed that he loved even those who persecuted him. "Persecution has severed me from a few men," he wrote, "but my heart has not been severed from them" (108). Not even Menno Simons, the leader of the Dutch Anabaptists, took his peace principle as far as this; Menno's writings against Catholics, Lutherans, and those Anabaptists with whom he did not agree theologically often betray an impatience, intolerance, and severity which ill become one who believed in love and peace (Simons 332–43).

In the autumn of 1523 the Council of Nürnberg had decided in favour of the Lutheran reformation, with the minister Andreas Osiander (1498–1552) becoming the spokesman of the new Lutheran movement. Toward the end of 1524, when some so-called "godless artists" in Albrecht Dürer's (1471–1528) circle were denounced, Denck was also mentioned in connection with heretical views. In January 1525 Denck had to submit a confession to the city council, which proved to be less than satisfactory to the Lutherans. As a result, he was banished from Nürnberg and forbidden "for ever" to return within ten miles of the city on pain of death.

Denck's *Confession to the Council of Nürnberg* (1525) leaves no doubt as to what the author believed about the inner Word and external things, including the Bible and the sacraments. As he writes, he "feels" that he is a sinful man, but he also "feels" that there is something within him that opposes his sinful nature and inclinations. There is something in him that compels him to believe Scripture; this is Christ within him, whom Scripture witnesses. Scripture is a lamp unto our feet, he states, but since it is written with human hands, it cannot remove the darkness completely. Only Christ in the heart of the believer can remove all darkness. Scripture can only be understood and interpreted through the Spirit of God in the heart. (This is similar to what Luther had written in his *Magnificat*.) Outward baptism, Denck states, cannot remove the sin of humans, and an inner baptism is necessary, for it is written that whoever believes and is baptized shall be saved. The external eating and drinking of the sacramental bread and wine may strengthen the outer person, according to Denck, but the *spiritual* eating of Christ gives strength to the soul. In fact, the partaking of the invisible cup and the love of God "deify the individual and humanize God" in the individual (Fellmann II, 20–6).

In a booklet called *Whether God Is the Cause of Evil* (1526) (Williams and Mergal 88–111), Denck gives more details on what he means by the inner and outer Word. The Kingdom of God, according to Denck, is within believers and whoever searches for it outside of the human heart will never find it, for apart from God no one can either seek or find God, and the person who seeks God already has him. But it is not enough that God lives in humans; humans must also be in God, that is, they must partake of the life of God. It is an illusion to believe that God is within if one does not honour him; it is of no avail to call oneself God's child if one does not believe like a child of God. Denck thus stresses, contrary to Luther, free will in a person's salvation. The individual hears the voice of God within *and* from the pages of Scripture, and then decides whether he or she will accept or reject God's salvation. But the truth in the heart is above Scripture, for Scripture testifies about the truth. "Therefore, whoever deems the testimony of greater importance than the truth itself, reverses the order, which is an abomination in the eyes of God." The light of God shines in all people; the Word of God is in all of God's creatures. Humans have no excuse if they do not see the light or don't hear God's Word; they have the ability to attune themselves, if they will, to his inner light and inner Word. The only evidence that one is obedient to the inner Word is the doing of God's will. Denck ends his booklet with the thought "The Word of God is with you before you seek. God gives before you ask, and he opens before you knock."

Denck's idea of the inner Word is most clearly expressed in his *Widerruf* (1527), a tract incorrectly translated as *Recantation*, a work in which he summarizes his theology (Fellmann II, 104–10). Denck holds the Holy Scripture above all human treasure, but not as highly as the Word of God, which is living, powerful, and eternal. The Bible is letter and not spirit; while it is useful to read the Bible, salvation is not tied to it. The outward Word cannot improve a wicked heart; but a pious heart, that is, a heart in which there is a "genuine spark of God's enthusiasm" (*götlichs eifers*), is improved through all things. While it is useful to preach and to read the Bible, an individual can be saved without preaching and Scripture. Ceremonies are of no use. Such things as outward baptism and the breaking of bread in communion are superstitions if one believes that they can lead to God. Infant baptism is merely a man-made practice. Christians are free to practise it if they wish, but baptism in itself is of no importance, for it is the life of a Christian that matters most of all.

Salvation, then, for Denck is wholly an inward process, initiated by God through the divine Word, the Christ within, whom we know outwardly as the historical Jesus and inwardly as the revealer of light, love, and faith. "But however audible the inner Word may be; however vivid the illumination; however drawing the love, there is never compulsion, the soul itself must hear and see and feel; must say *yes* to the appeal of Love, and must co-operate by a continuous adjustment of the personal will to the will of God and 'learn to behave as a child of God'" (Jones 27).

Rufus Jones concludes his study of Hans Denck as follows: "In an epoch in which the doctrine was new and revolutionary, he succeeded in presenting the principle of the Inward Word as the basis of religion without giving any encouragement to libertinism or moral laxity, for he found the way of freedom to be a life of growing likeness to Christ, he held the fulfilling of the law to be possible only for those who accept the burdens and sacrifices of love, and he insisted that the privileges of blessedness belong only to those who *behaved like sons*" (30). One might add, however, that Denck's mysticism was held in balance by his insistence that the Christian life must express itself in practical living. Like Luther before him, Denck was able to combine within himself perfect freedom in Christ and the discipline and subjection to the Christ who had redeemed him.

LUTHER ON HANS DENCK

⁜ **Denck's differentiation** between the inner and outer Word of God was at least in some measure, however small, in line with Luther's approach to the subject. But for Luther the spiritualist's view of Scripture, the inner light, and the sacraments was filled with dangerous heresies. In January 1525, Denck and the "godless artists," the brothers Sebald and Barthel Beheim and G. Pentz, were expelled from Nürnberg. On February 4 Luther wrote to J. Briessmann in Nürnberg that Satan had carried things so far in Nürnberg that some persons were denying that Christ is anything or that the Word of God is anything or that the Eucharist is anything or that the magistrates are anything, but that only God is something (WA Br. 3, 433). For Luther it was the spirit of Müntzer and Karlstadt that made its influence in Nürnberg felt. On the same day he wrote to Lazarus Spengler (1479–1534), a prominent supporter of the Reformation and the one who must have sent Luther the information about the city council's proceedings against Denck and the artists. In this letter Luther expresses joy and sorrow at the news from Nürnberg. He is happy to hear that Christ is able to protect his own from the wolves in Nürnberg, and he is sad to learn that the devil's messengers had succeeded in creating doubt about some articles of faith. It is good, however, Luther adds, to expose and then correct these things. In answering the question as to how the heretics should be dealt with, Luther feels that they should not be treated as blasphemers, which would mean the death sentence, but as Turks or misled Christians. However, if they should refuse to obey and to acknowledge the temporal powers, which would expose them as rebels and murderers, the authorities should not hesitate to proceed against them (432–3).

One could argue that Luther perhaps knew little about Denck and other spiritualists in Nürnberg, and that his judgment about them was based on hearsay only and thus unfair. From the two letters it is evident, however, that Luther was fairly well informed about the spiritualists in Nürnberg and that he understood their theological positions well. When Luther referred to the spirit of Müntzer and Karlstadt, he was not entirely wrong about what Hans Denck and other spiritualists believed. While Denck rejected Thomas Müntzer's program for establishing God's kingdom on earth, he was certainly influenced by the revolutionist's mysticism and view of the inner Word. And as far as Karlstadt was concerned, Denck was in agreement with the Wittenberg radical on the theology of the Lord's Supper, a point of utmost importance to Luther.

In addition, when Luther wrote that in Nürnberg some deny that Christ is anything and that the Word of God is anything, he was quite serious and troubled about it. Denck's differentiation between the historical Jesus and the inner Christ was no doubt confusing even to Luther and could be interpreted to mean that the inward Christ was of greater importance than the historical Jesus who, after all, had historically lived and died on the cross for the redemption of humankind. Similarly, Denck's stress on the inner Word in a sense diminished for Luther the importance of Scripture, which, according to the spiritualists, merely gives witness to the voice of God.

The spiritualists' individualism and stress on freedom must have seemed to Luther an attempt to put humans and their experience in the centre, thus denying any legitimate human authority over them. It may well be, as Rufus Jones points out, that in Denck's case the principle of the inner Word did not encourage libertinism or moral laxity, and that his freedom was the freedom of a follower of Christ. But Luther was not as optimistic about human nature as Denck seemed to be. With the social unrest and Peasants' War in 1525, Luther saw how individualism and freedom were abused on all sides by elements that were not governed by the ideals of Christian humanism or Christ's Sermon on the Mount, as Denck was.

CASPAR VON SCHWENCKFELD

❧ **Another spiritualist** who collided more directly with Luther was Caspar von Schwenckfeld (1489–1561), a Silesian nobleman from the duchy of Liegnitz. After studying in Cologne, Frankfurt on the Oder, and probably at the University of Erfurt, Schwenckfeld lived the life of a courtier, intending to make his success in a secular career. However, Luther's struggle against the Roman Church and his proclamation of justification by faith alone changed Schwenckfeld's life and he decided to become a follower of Luther and an active reformer in Silesia. As late as 1543, long after Schwenckfeld had been rebuffed by Luther, the nobleman admired the reformer and acknowledged his deep debt to him: "I owe to you in God and the truth all honour, love and goodwill, because from the first I have reaped much fruit from your service, and I have not ceased to pray for you according to my poor powers" (CS 1, 44–5).

Though influenced by Luther's reformation writings, Schwenckfeld blazed his own theological trail, attempting to maintain a middle course between Catholicism and Lutheranism. There were, however, several things in Luther and Lutheranism upon which he looked with dismay. He came to believe that Luther's emphasis on justification by faith alone was one-sided and led to a lax ethical life among Luther's followers. When Schwenckfeld spoke to Luther about this in 1525, the reformer agreed that something had to be done about this laxity among his people, but added: "Yes, dear Caspar, true Christians are not as yet all too common. I would like to see two together. I do not know of one" (CS 2, 281). This no doubt sarcastic comment may not have sat too well with the nobleman. Also, Luther's intolerant attitude toward those who dissented from him grieved Schwenckfeld to no end. He believed that it should be possible for Christians to resolve differences among themselves or at least to be tolerant toward co-religionists who held different views.

The most serious stumbling block for Schwenckfeld was Luther's rigid interpretation of Christ's words of institution in Holy Communion. His first nagging doubts about Christ's "real presence" came when he considered the part that Judas played in the first communion service. If the Eucharistic elements were in any way identifiable with the body and blood of Christ, the Silesian reasoned, then Judas must have actually eaten Christ, a thought that was repugnant to him (CS 2, 129–30). Eventually Schwenckfeld came to the view that the believers eat Christ spiritually and thus receive eternal life from such spiritual eating. John 6 in particular led him to the following conclusion: "He that eats my flesh and drinks my blood has eternal life; hence Judas could not have partaken of the real Christ because that would have conferred eternal life upon him, since the body and blood are never destitute of divine power but are spirit and life; the Word is an eternal Word of Christ" (CS 2, 130). The Lord's Supper, then, is a spiritual eating of the Lord, and only true believers can partake of the spiritual food. The outward celebration of the Lord's Supper is, according to this view, a mere memorial act, and the bread and wine remain mere physical emblems, *reminding* the communicant of the historic and redemptive facts of Christ's suffering and death.

Schwenckfeld had discussed his interpretation of the Eucharist with others in Silesia, including Valentine Crautwald (1465–1545), a humanist and biblical scholar and at the time the lector and canon at the cathedral at Liegnitz. Crautwald at first objected to Schwenckfeld's spiritual view of Christ's words of institution on the grounds that Scripture was plain on this issue and that this new approach would only confuse people. But after an extensive study, prayer, and "a vision from God," Crautwald was converted to Schwenckfeld's view "that from the necessity and nature of faith the communion in the Supper was spiritual and that the sacramental elements must not be confused with the actual body and blood of Christ" (131).

While the primary occasion for the disagreement between Schwenckfeld and Luther was their different views concerning the Last Supper, the basic issue dividing the two men was their different conception of matter and spirit. Schwenckfeld interpreted Scripture, the sacraments, the Christian life, and life itself spiritually. For him the spiritual was vastly superior to the material, an emphasis Luther could not accept. For Luther God was the creator of both spiritual and material things, and God used material to convey spiritual benefits to humankind. The *written letter* of Scripture conveyed to Luther the good news of salvation to the world. In the sacrament of baptism the Word of God was joined to the element of water for the spiritual benefit of the baptized; and in eating the bread and drinking the wine in the Last Supper, the believer partakes of the actual Christ. Luther and the spiritualists clashed over these different views of reality.

After working out his interpretation of the Lord's Supper, in the summer of 1525 Schwenckfeld sent Luther twelve questions or propositions for an examination and possible acceptance (129–40). They included, among others, the following points: The body of Christ is a spiritual food; only spiritual people are capable of appropriating such spiritual nourishment, and only faith is equal to an act of spiritual eating. Christ is the eternal life, "and he distributes through his flesh and blood nothing else than he himself is, viz., eternal life. On this account our Christian faith expresses on this wise, that life results from eating him, and he who eats must live for his sake." Since Christ is the heavenly light and the eternal truth, no unbeliever or carnal Christian can have a part of him. Christ dwells only in transformed hearts; he does not abide in any kind of earthly creature. Hence it follows, according to the Silesian, that unregenerate "persons can receive in the Supper only the bread of the Lord; but the bread which the Lord himself is and which he himself gives and distributes, they cannot taste" (133–8).

For some unknown reason Luther did not immediately respond to Schwenckfeld's twelve propositions. Hence the nobleman decided to visit Luther in person, arriving in Wittenberg on November 30, 1525. Selina Schultz writes in her biography of Schwenckfeld: "It required no small degree of courage and initiative to undertake to approach Luther at this juncture, particularly since he had ignored Schwenckfeld's letters and arguments" (Schultz 73). This may be so, but it should be remembered that from the time the twelve points were sent to Wittenberg and Schwenckfeld's arrival there, only four months had elapsed. Luther was preoccupied with the Peasants' revolts, the radicals in Wittenberg, his marriage, and his work on a reply to Erasmus on the freedom of the will, so it is not unreasonable to assume that the busy reformer had not had much time to study the propositions, let alone answer them. When Schwenckfeld reminded Luther of what he had written, Luther, according to the nobleman's diary of December 1–4, 1525, interrupted Schwenckfeld with two words: "Yes, Zwingli!" This seems to suggest that Luther was at least aware of Schwenckfeld's view on the Last Supper, namely that it was similar to that of the Swiss reformer, which Luther rejected.

Schwenckfeld's apprehension about meeting Luther in person must have been dispelled as soon as Luther and the Wittenbergers met the Silesian reformer. Luther was courteous, patient, and sympathetic toward his visitor's convictions. If the two men were unable to come to an agreement, the reason was not obstinacy on either side. The two men could not work out their differences because they proceeded from different premises, approaching reality from two different points of view, as their encounter shows.

MUCH ADO ABOUT SPIRIT AND MATTER

⟪ **Caspar Schwenckfeld conferred** with Luther and Johannes Bugenhagen (1485–1558), a Lutheran theologian and minister in Wittenberg, between December 1 and 4, 1525. When Schwenckfeld asked Luther for a time to see him, the reformer was most obliging: "Dear Caspar," he said, "I will be glad to confer with you, come tomorrow, as early as you wish, six, seven, or eight o'clock. Nothing shall hinder me. We will then give consideration to the matter [of the Lord's Supper]" (Schultz 75).

The next morning at the meeting Luther came directly to the point and asked the nobleman: "Tell me one thing, do you have a different ground [for interpreting the Last Supper] than Carlstadt and Zwingli?" Answering Luther in the affirmative, Schwenckfeld then began to argue that Christ's words cannot be understood in the literal sense but must be interpreted to mean his *spiritual* flesh and blood. Luther then picked up the Greek New Testament and pointed out the words about the cup and insisted that the meaning was quite clear. His guest opposed him, asserting that Christ could not have meant the cup or drink in the sacrament, but the blood shed for humankind on the cross, although he admitted that he was not well versed in the languages. Knowing that there could be no agreement, Luther did not wish to argue any further and said: "Dear Caspar, I will take all the material in care and send for the preacher [Bugenhagen]. We will study the problem together today, after which I will speak further with you." Schwenckfeld then left, appealing to Luther to give the matter more serious thought. But Schwenckfeld remained quite firm in his position. "By the grace of Christ," he wrote, "we were quite fully persuaded in our own minds and wished the same for him [Luther]" (36–8).

Since Luther wanted to discuss the matter with Bugenhagen, the Silesian went to see the Lutheran preacher himself. After some discussion with Schwenckfeld, Bugenhagen was summoned to Luther to confer with him about the matter. Luther then requested that Schwenckfeld send him the story of how Crautwald had received a revelation of the spiritual interpretation of the Last Supper. Schwenckfeld attached a note to the story which read in part: "Dear Doctor, I beg that you will carefully study this letter, and if anything is not clear kindly put it in writing.... It is my trust in God, that what he has begun he will also complete to his glory and to our betterment. The overthrow of the papal power is impossible as long as this article of the flesh and blood ... remains.... God grant you his divine grace to complete what has been begun, for which many devout brethren pray. God be with you" (78). The outcome of Bugenhagen's conference with Luther was discouraging to all. Bugenhagen reported to the nobleman: "You on your part claim a revelation. Others claim the same, and each party has a particular conclusion. There is no harmony. But the Spirit of the Lord is not a spirit of dissention. We also do not know otherwise than that we have the truth. Even if you have a good cause, you arouse suspicion since your views differ so widely" (79).

Luther's reply to Schwenckfeld, as reported by Schwenckfeld himself, shows consideration, openness, tolerance, and sympathy. Luther states that he had examined the matter, but could not give him an answer at this time until he had conferred with Melanchthon, who was away. Luther said that in less significant matters, such as the intercession of saints, he also yielded to Karlstadt, but in the matter at hand he needs to be convinced with good rational arguments. When the Silesian speaks of revelations, Luther does not want to be against God, but how can one be sure that it is God? Luther asks the nobleman to further think on the matter, as he too will pray that God might show him the full truth. God had promised him, Luther, not to let him err. "He will not forsake me in this matter and if it be His will thus to understand it, I hope He will grant it to me also. But that I should express myself [at this time] to favor you, is not fitting. For this is a matter of faith. I must first of all have and feel it in my conscience. Nevertheless, I will not condemn your opinion, although I cannot accept it, for proof is insufficient. The matter needs further study. If God grant, I will gladly agree with you.... Your opinion is plausible, it is very good, if it can be proved sufficiently, but you must see to that.... I must be convinced, particularly in such important articles, that it is to be thus understood and not otherwise" (92–3).

The lengthy quotation from Schwenckfeld gives rise to some comments. Luther's tolerance toward the Silesian nobleman's views must come as a surprise to those who see Luther as generally unyielding in matters of his theology in general and in important articles of faith in particular. This document, written by a man who disagreed with Luther profoundly on one of the most important issues of the Reformation, portrays the reformer as one who, while not accepting his opponent's point of view, nevertheless respects both the individual and his interpretation. Is it possible that Luther detected in Schwenckfeld an uncertainty about his interpretation of Christ's words of institution, hence wished to give him time to change his view in favour of his? Luther may also have thought that the Silesian reformer might in time become a promoter of the Lutheran reformation in Silesia.

There is no reason to doubt the accuracy of Schwenckfeld's account of what occurred between himself and Luther. Originally written in the form of a dialogue, the story was preserved and transmitted many years later, in 1540, when the break between the two reformers had become final and the Silesian had been condemned and despised in violent language by Luther and his followers (CS 14, 1030; WA Tr. 5, 300–1). The story of the encounter between the two men is, according to the editors of Schwenckfeld's writings, "charmingly told; it breathes with marked living qualities. It presents the great persons involved with a striking discrimination and with self-revelation of their dispositions and manners. Among the interlocutors one finds sweetness of temper, sometimes with a bit of dictatorial ruffling, but kindliness of expression, as well as conscientious earnestness" (CS 2, 238).

To understand Luther's eventual impatience with Schwenckfeld it is necessary to look at the nobleman's concept of reality, including ethics, faith, Scripture, the church, and his view of the sacraments. Like Denck, Schwenckfeld believed that "there is an inner and outer Word, gospel, preacher, ears, and hearing, corresponding to the inner and outer man." The true, eternal Word of God is spirit and life; it is none other than Christ. "The transitory, external letter is 'word of God' only in a derived sense, whether written in Scripture, spoken in the sermon, or portrayed in symbol, picture, and sign.... [The] inner Word is not conveyed by means of the outer and can brook no mixture with the external" (Maier 26; CS 2, 40–1). The influence of St. Augustine and Tauler is in evidence here. The inner Word, Christ, is shown by Schwenckfeld in his various functions. The Word gives new life to the inner person; the Word is food, nourishing the reborn soul; the Word washes away the sins of the old Adam; the Word is spirit, not letter; life, not death; light, not darkness. The elements in the sacraments (bread, wine, water, the letter of the Bible) are thus outward symbols of the inner Word and life. The Bible, to be sure, was inspired by God and is thus normative for Christian faith and conduct, but Schwenckfeld always emphasized the *demonstrative* function of Scripture.

Schwenckfeld's uncertainty about the correct understanding of the Last Supper culminated in 1526 in his, by now famous, *Stillstand* (standing still), a suspension of the celebration of Holy Communion until the Lord would reveal "a right understanding and true practice of it according to his will." This *Stillstand* was proposed in a public letter of April 1526, written jointly by Schwenckfeld, Valentine Krautwald, and other Liegnitz pastors (CS 1, 325–33). But the suspension did not ease the tension between the rival groups and so the nobleman continued to write on this issue for the next four years. The Duke of Liegnitz, who had supported Schwenckfeld from the beginning of the nobleman's ministry, came under increasing political pressure to draw closer toward the Wittenberg position. However, it was difficult to have a counsellor of so high a profile opposing a Lutheran position. Thus, in 1529, to save his duke any further embarrassment, Schwenckfeld voluntarily left his homeland of Silesia and moved to Strasbourg, a city known for its greater religious tolerance.

LUTHER AND THE WORD OF GOD

⁋ **Some critics of the reformer** believe that Luther's conception of the Word of God underwent considerable change, from a spiritual, almost mystical, view of the Bible to a greater emphasis on the written Word of God (Coutts 101–4). According to this view, Luther at first stressed the inner Word in accordance with his subjective experience of salvation, and interpreted Scripture according to God's voice within his heart. The written Word was thus subservient to the inner Word, that is, to a subjective, highly individualistic, interpretation of the Bible. Roman Catholics have frequently stressed Luther's subjective approach to Scriptures. But when Luther, according to this view, encountered the radicals who, like him, interpreted the Bible according to their own subjective experience, in opposition to the reformer, Luther saw the danger of such subjectivism and thus began to stress the *written* Word.

It is no doubt possible to see in Luther changes in emphases in his interpretation of the Bible. There are statements in his early writings that stress his subjective experience, identifying it with the Word of God in his heart. In fact, for Luther the Word of God and individual faith could not be separated; faith was the Word of God in the human heart (WA 18, 626). But are changes and different interpretations subjectivism, mysticism, or even spiritualism? Luther always taught that the Bible must be read according to its "plain sense," be it literal, allegorical, or symbolical, according to what the text demands. To understand Scriptures correctly, according to Luther, the reader must be enlightened and guided by the Holy Spirit and see the Word of God as law and gospel, and understand that Scripture points from the Old Testament to Christ the redeemer of humankind (LH 362–71).

In his exposition of the *Magnificat* (Luke 1:46–55) in 1521 (Werke 6, 161–248), Luther stated that it is only the Holy Spirit that can properly interpret the Word of God and inscribe it in the human heart. No one can correctly understand God or his Word unless one has received such understanding directly from the Holy Spirit. But no one can receive it from the Holy Spirit "without experiencing, proving and feeling it." In such experience the Holy Spirit instructs one as in his own school, outside of which nothing is learned but empty words. Luther, to be sure, stresses the individual experience of Mary, but this experience is tied to God, his Word, and the Spirit who is the mediator between the individual and God. This being so, we must, according to Luther, approach the study of God's Word with due modesty and without preconceived notions of our own. In his exposition of Jeremiah 23:5–8 in 1526 Luther warns against heretics who bend Scripture according to their own notions. Instead, we should hear the Word of God with fear and study it with humility; we should not pounce upon it with our own ideas of what is right or wrong. It would be better to fall into sin than into self-conceit, so dangerous and damaging is it to read one's own notions into the Word. The Word of God insists that it be honoured and observed.

In an exposition of John 6:63 in 1531 Luther stated that the Word of God and the Holy Spirit are always in agreement. If someone claims to be inspired by the Spirit but is opposed to what Scriptures teach, that is from the devil. The Holy Spirit always comes through Scriptures in an orderly fashion. We must test all human notions against Holy Scriptures. No matter how interesting an interpretation appears to be, if it is not grounded in and commanded in the Bible, it means nothing. All subjectivism is thus excluded. In his open letter to the two pastors about Anabaptism in 1528, Luther stated that even our faith is not more important than God's Word, for faith comes from hearing the Word of God. Faith may waver and change, but the Word remains forever.

In 1533 Luther stated that only the Word of God made him sure that he was right. Without the Word one must fall into despair, for one lacks divine assurance for what one is called upon to do and is borne onward only by the egotism of one's heart. In a sermon of 1528 Luther spoke of the manner in which God reveals himself. According to the "enthusiasts," the "internal" Word comes before the "external" Word, but God, according to Luther, does not reveal himself in the heart except through the external Word. This is why the external Word must be the beginning and end of our consideration and enlightenment. Otherwise human notions replace what God has spoken.

As Alfred Beutel observes, "For Luther there are only two answers to the question of the Word of God: No or yes, unbelief or faith" (LH 371). In the believer God's Word affects not only faith and salvation, but also opens the door to eternal life in the end. For the unbeliever, however, the Word of God is also damnation, for "it closes the door of heaven and denies him" eternal life.

SCHWENCKFELD AND THE WORD OF GOD

⁌ **In opposition to Luther,** Schwenckfeld believed that "the inner word of the spirit must be differentiated from the external word spoken by the preacher; that the living Word of God is not the Scriptures, but Christ; that the Scriptures must be interpreted spiritually; that external ceremonies, services and ministers are of value, but must be distinguished from the power and service of Christ, the living Word" (Schultz 330). Schultz points out this difference between Luther and Schwenckfeld as follows: "Luther not only called the literal, external, printed word the Gospel, but also emphatically stated that the preached word from the pulpit was the genuine, inspired Gospel. Schwenckfeld maintained that the preached word about the Gospel was no more the true Gospel than the preached word about Christ was the genuine Christ. He denied that Luther's preached gospel, accepted through faith, had any saving power, and that ministerial services are indispensable in the fostering of faith and the Holy Spirit."

Schultz's comment is valid as long as one keeps in mind that for Luther the Holy Spirit uses the written Word and the proclaimed gospel to touch the hearts of the hearers or readers and thus brings them to a saving knowledge of Christ. For Schwenckfeld and other spiritualists, preaching and the reading of the written Word were merely *useful* functions, but not essential for salvation, which depended on the *inner* Word and the spiritual Christ in the hearts of believers.

Schwenckfeld's opposition to physical things and externals went so far that he not only spiritualized the sacraments and Scriptures, but also aroused suspicion about his view of the nature of Christ. He stressed the oneness of Christ to the extent that he believed Christ's human nature was divine, entirely different from sinful carnality. Luther charged him and other spiritualists with the heresy of Eutychianism. This heresy went back to Eutyches of Constantinople (ca. 380–456) who believed that in Christ his human nature was overcome by his divine nature, thus essentially making Christ all divine. Schwenckfeld denied that he believed in Eutychianism, answering Luther's charge in his *Answer to Luther's Malediction* that he had been badly misunderstood.

Schwenckfeld writes: "I recognize nothing of creation or creatureliness in Christ but rather a new divine birth and natural Sonship (*kindschafft*) of God. Wherefore I cannot consider the Man Christ with his body and blood to be a creation or a creature. Rather, I believe and confess with Scripture that he is wholly God's only-begotten Son and that Christ, the Son of God, his Heavenly Father, the whole person indivisibly (*unzertailig*) God and Man, was born in time of the virgin Mary; also that he suffered and died for us opon the cross in personal unity and wholeness, and as such rose again and ascended into heaven, that he sits at the right hand of God and rules also in his human nature wholly with God his father in divine glory, unity and essence" (Williams and Mergal, 180–1). Sinful humans then derive their nature from Adam; the spiritual man in Christ derives his divine nature from Christ, the new Adam who was without sin.

Believing himself in essential agreement with Luther's view on the nature of Christ, in 1543 Schwenckfeld sent Luther some of his pamphlets on the doctrine of Christ and a letter in the hope that a friendly understanding between the two men could be brought about. Luther's answer in a letter of December 6, 1543, was most disheartening for the Silesian reformer. The letter was not even addressed to Schwenckfeld personally but to Hermann Riegel, the messenger who had delivered the spiritualist's material to Luther (WA Tr. 5, 300–1). Luther accuses Schwenckfeld of preaching and teaching when no one had called or sent him. According to Schwenckfeld, however, as early as 1522 Luther had approved of the nobleman's ministry in Silesia. "I am glad to hear," Luther had written, "that you have become a preacher. May you continue in God's name, and may He grant you His grace and blessing" (Schultz 15). Similarly, Bugenhagen had written to the nobleman: "It is well that you are preaching, insofar as you seek the honor of God; and I consider that your calling is good."

In his 1543 letter Luther becomes downright abusive: "And the mad fool, possessed of the devil, does not understand anything; does not know what he is babbling. But if he will not cease, so let him leave me unmolested with his booklets which the devil excretes and spews out of him" (Williams and Mergal 163). Luther concludes his short letter by pronouncing a final curse on the spiritualist: "The Lord punish Satan in you, and your spirit which has called you, and your course which you are following." Even Luther's wife Katie found Luther's letter too coarse, but Luther replied that the fanatics teach him to be coarse and that the devil does not deserve a better answer (WA Tr. 5, 300).

Schwenckfeld replied to Luther's abusive letter with his *An Answer to Luther's Malediction* in which he attempts to clear himself of the charges against him, particularly on his views about the Lord's Supper and the humanity of Christ (Williams and Mergal 163–81). The nobleman advances no new arguments in favour of his position; he simply reiterates that the divine mysteries, including the sacraments, the nature of Christ, and Scripture must be viewed and experienced spiritually, not materially or physically. Both the language of the pamphlet as well as Schwenckfeld's attitude toward Luther speak well for the nobleman, expressing sadness and sorrow for his opponent, whom he had come to love and admire. To the very end Schwenckfeld held fast to his Lutheran–Augustinian–Pauline convictions and in the basic Protestant principle of justification by faith (Williams, *Radical Reformation* 203).

In 1529 Schwenckfeld went to Strasbourg, hoping that the theologians there would accept his theology "and be won over also to his theory of an external and an internal baptism which he and Crautwald had worked out" (383). He was treated there well by the reformers, including Wolfgang Capito (1478–1541), in whose house he stayed for a while, attended the preaching of Matthew Zell (1477–1548), and assisted in the services at the cathedral. When the Swiss reformers, including Zwingli and Oecolampadius, travelled to Marburg in 1529 for the Eucharistic colloquy, they stopped off at Strasbourg, where they heard Schwenckfeld's views on the sacraments. At the colloquy, the case Luther contra Schwenckfeld would have been thoroughly discussed. On their return from Marburg, having heard from Luther what he thought about the Silesian nobleman, most of the Swiss and Strasbourg reformers became quite cool toward Schwenckfeld, no doubt "in the interest of Protestant summit harmony" (384).

In her biography of Schwenckfeld, Selina Schultz assesses the role of the Silesian reformer among other reformation figures, most notably Luther. The lengthy quotation from her is significant: "In the Reformation century, Schwenckfeld was without doubt the pre-eminent exponent of the spirit, and the greatest champion of religious liberty. His contemporaries, like Pharisees, could not and would not understand him. They were engrossed in building great churches of external things through preaching, baptism, and the Sacraments, saying: Lo! here is Christ. Lo! there. Schwenckfeld answered: Believe it not, for the kingdom of God is within you; Christ is the Word of God; external ceremonies, sacraments, services, ministers, and preaching, although of great value to the carnal man, have no divine or saving power, and must therefore be distinguished from the power and service of Christ, the living Word. The preachers of his time were almost unanimously of the opinion that by this doctrine he was destroying their prestige. This was the cause of their relentless bitterness toward him to the end of his life" (Schultz 334–5).

CONCLUDING COMMENTS

❅ **Selina Schultz** is correct in her summary of Schwenckfeld's beliefs, sincerity, and ministry. He was definitely the "pre-eminent exponent of the spirit," and his exemplary life as a Christian believer was exceptional in an age of social, political, and religious turmoil. One might consider it most tragic that he and Luther failed in the end to accept each other as colleagues in the work of reform. But Selina Schultz is mistaken in stating that the preachers, meaning the Lutheran and Reformed theologians, opposed the spiritualists because their doctrine "was destroying their prestige."

As we have seen, Luther at first welcomed the reformation in Silesia in general and Schwenckfeld's work in particular. Schwenckfeld encouraged Luther theologically to look deeper into the relationship between the inner and the outer Word. Also, Luther had no reason to fear Schwenckfeld as a social or revolutionary activist. By 1525 Luther was well established as the foremost reformer in Germany and beyond, so that he need not have feared that someone else might destroy his "prestige." In the end Luther opposed the Silesian reformer because of his unacceptable theology.

Luther understood the spiritualists well. He knew that the difference between their theology and his was not merely a difference of some minor doctrinal points. Both sides appealed to Scriptures for what they believed, but in their basic orientation they stood far apart. It is too simple to suggest that Luther was merely concerned about building churches by preaching the external Word. He, too, emphasized time and again that the Kingdom of God is in the hearts of men and women, that the sacraments must be appropriated in faith and experienced in the heart. Luther also believed that only the Holy Spirit must open the Scriptures to individuals, thus bringing them to repentance, faith, and holy living. But he also realized that the emphasis of the spiritualists on the inner Word and spirit would destroy the concept of the New Testament church, that is, a local congregation of believers where the Word of God is preached and the sacraments are rightfully administered.

Luther believed that once the "real presence" of Christ in the sacrament was denied and the written Word undermined, there was nothing objective left for the believer to cling to, and everything depended on subjective experiences. "What a precious and noble thing it is," he stated in 1533, "to have the Word of God on our side! For such a person can be safe and happy, however much he may be tried." Acording to Luther, God has always worked with material and physical things. Whenever he wanted to do something with us, he did it through the Word and physical matters (WA 27, 60). To minimize external means through which God has chosen to work, and to rely instead on the inner Word, subjective experiences, and revelations, was, for Luther, to put man and not God in the centre. This is why Luther even hesitated, perhaps mistakenly, to stress holiness, sanctification, perfection, and divinity in human beings, for he saw that it was so easy to boast of human works and achievements and thus minimize one's complete dependence on the grace of God. These were some of the real and fundamental issues that separated Luther and Schwenckfeld.

Three in One or One in Three?
Luther Opposes the Rationalists

THE SPIRITS LUTHER HAD CALLED UP

In a poem, "The Sorcerer's Apprentice" (*Der Zauberlehrling*), by the German poet Goethe (1749–1832), the young apprentice of magic has learned from his master the magic words to make the broom haul water for a bath. But when the broom has filled the bathtub, the young man has forgotten the correct formula to stop the broom's work. The water soon overflows and floods the whole house. When the master at last appears, the apprentice cries out in despair: "Master, I'm in trouble! The ghosts I called up, I now can't get rid of" [*Herr, die Not ist gross! / Die ich rief, die Geister, / Werd' ich nun nicht los.*] (Goethe's Werke 1, 279; cf. Brendler 282–3).

Similarly, Luther never knew that when he enunciated the principles of his reformation such as the priesthood of all believers, *sola fide* and *sola scriptura*, in the early stages of his career, and gave each believer the right to interpret Scriptures, that many of his followers would interpret the Bible differently from and often in opposition to him. Throughout his career Luther struggled with the many spirits he had called up, namely papists, enthusiasts, fanatics, peasants, radicals, humanists, revolutionaries, baptists, spiritualists, rationalists, antinomians, and others. Unfortunately for Luther, there was no sorcerer with a magic wand or formula to come to his help to stop the work of these spirits!

The Antinomians

Antinomianism was a term coined by Luther from the Greek, *anti* (against) and *nomos* (law), meaning to be against the law. During the Reformation the term was specifically applied to the view that under the gospel dispensation of grace, the Old Testament moral law was no longer necessary for New Testament believers because faith alone is necessary for salvation. But this was not Luther's view. As Markus Wriedt puts it, "By law Luther understands all statements of Scripture that uncover the sin of humans and accuse them. In contrast, the gospel includes all statements that promise comfort, redemption, and the grace of God" (Wriedt 106). The antinomians pushed Luther's doctrine of justification by faith alone to what they thought was its logical conclusion, asserting that since good works are not necessary for salvation, so do evil works neither hinder nor work against it. According to them, Christians were necessarily good, justified, and sanctified by their very vocation and profession as being in Christ. They were incapable of losing their justification, spiritual holiness, and final salvation by any violation of the law of God. The antinomians thus preached freedom from any of God's laws, emphasized the gospel over the Old Testament, and rejected any moral coercion or discipline as part of the Christian life. In fact, they appealed to Luther who, according to them, was the one who had freed them from all legalism in the first place.

Luther encountered a certain kind of antinomianism as early as 1525 when one Eloy Pruystinck (d. 1544) of Antwerp, a slate roofer by trade, came in the middle of March of that year to Wittenberg to see what the reformer would make of his antinomian views, in fact, hoping that he would get Luther's endorsement for his doctrine (WA 18, 244). A disputation took place in Luther's house between the Lutherans and Eloy, with the result that the heretic's views were exposed for what they were. In a letter of April 1525 Luther wrote to his followers in Antwerp, warning them against the dangerous heresies of the *poltergeists* (ghosts of disturbance) and the "new prophets" at Antwerp. He writes that he has heard about how their country is agitated by spirits who are full of errors. They devote themselves to resisting and opposing the progress of the Christian truth. Among them has come a demon that wants to make them fall into darkness and divert them from the true gospel (541–50).

George Williams summarizes Luther's letter about what the Loists (as Eloy and his followers were called) believed: "According to Luther, the Loists held (1) that every human being has the Holy Spirit, (2) that the Holy Spirit is none other than the person's own reason and understanding, (3) that everyone believes, (4) that this belief is to wish for one's neighbor what one wishes for oneself, (5) that there is no hell or condemnation except for the flesh, (6) that all souls will enjoy eternal life, (7) that sin is not committed so long as one does not so intend, and (8) that whoever has not the Holy Spirit (likewise) has no sin, for such a person has no reason" (Williams, *Radical Reformation* 536). Luther, according to Williams, is confident that Eloy is a restless and deceiving spirit, full of bravado and insolence; he first affirms something and then immediately denies it. It is difficult to pin him down to a reasonable answer as to what he actually believes. But it seems certain that Eloy and his followers were dualists who separated the physical and spiritual natures, claiming that the one had little or no influence on the other. The final goal of the Loists was to vanish into the divine being.

Luther's letter to the Antwerp group found a practical response. On his return to Antwerp Eloy and nine of his followers (two of them were women) were examined by the Inquisition in February 1526. All recanted their heresy publicly, but Eloy continued to circulate libertine works for several more years. In 1544 Eloy was condemned and burned alive, and in 1545 three leading Loists were executed, bringing the sect to an end in the Low Countries, although some Loists fled to England. George Williams believes that the execution of the last Loists in Antwerp may have contributed to Calvin's decision in 1545 to write a major treatise in French against all the libertines, *Conte la secte phantastique et furieuse des Libertines qui se nomment Spirituels,* published in Geneva (904ff.).

Johannes Agricola

The leader of the antinomian party in Luther's camp was Johannes Agricola (1499–1566), a former student of Luther and later teacher in Eisleben. In the autumn of 1536 Luther approached Agricola about a possible position as university professor at Wittenberg. Obviously feeling highly honoured, Agricola left Eisleben immediately with his wife and nine children, was received in Luther's house, and that year substituted for Luther both at the university and in the pulpit. Before long, in March and June 1537, the preacher offended orthodox people by using a "new vocabulary" in his sermons and particularly by stating that the preaching of the law should be banned from the churches (WA 50, 461). In a July 1535 sermon, Luther preached against "our antinomians" without mentioning Agricola's name, stating that some people conclude from Romans 2:4 that repentance comes from preaching the gospel and not from the law, and that first of all the grace of God should be preached and only later should people hear about the wrath of God. Agricola published a number of theses in which he advocated the abolition of the Old Testament law. According to Agricola and his followers, the gospel was to be preached in all its "sweetness," without any reference to the Decalogue or the Ten Commandments, and sinners should be counselled and admonished only in private and not criticized from the pulpits.

Between 1538 and 1540 Luther held five disputations against the antinomians without again mentioning the names of his adversaries, but he was at times disappointed and angry when Agricola did not even appear at the sessions. In the disputation of September 13, 1538, Luther admitted that in his earlier years he had emphasized the gospel of Christ because at that time Christians were generally weak and in need of comfort and assurance, whereas now they needed the strong hand of the law. It was thus a matter of emphasis for him, not a basic belief that the law was superfluous for Christians. The abolition of the Ten Commandments from all preaching, Luther stated, would discredit the gospel, ruin all governments and church life, do away with all repentance and salvation, and result in Müntzerism and complete anarchy (EA 61, 28–36). Even Christians need to observe the law; although they are made holy through grace, they nevertheless live in a sinful body. And because of this remaining sin, they must be admonished, rebuked, and sometimes terrified by the law of God. Luther advised the magistrates to take action against the antinomians, accused Agricola of hypocrisy and of destroying all moral discipline and order, and finally demanded that his opponent revoke his heretical views (WA 50, 465).

Several attempts at reconciliation were made between Luther and Agricola. In December 1538 Agricola again asked to be reconciled with Luther, no doubt motivated in part by fear that the elector might cut off his stipend. To make certain there would be no misunderstanding about the sincerity of his apology, Agricola even asked Luther to prepare the text of his recantation, which he would then be happy to sign. Luther then wrote the treatise *Against the Antinomians* (1539) in the form of a letter to a friend in Eisleben, one of Agricolas' fiercest opponents. To Agricola's dismay, Luther included a few humiliating sentences: "He [Agricola] declared himself willing to do this [to recant]; but since he feared that he could not compose a statement that would command sufficient respect, he urged me to do it. He also said that I should do it as I saw fit and he would be entirely satisfied" (LW 47, 108).

Against the Antinomians

Luther's *Against the Antinomians* (LW 47, 107–14) is addressed to the reformer's "good friend in Christ," Dr. Caspar Güttel (1471–1542), preacher at Eisleben. It is not just a personal letter to Güttel, Luther advises his friend, but is "especially to those who are unable to read.... I have no other way of opposing the devil," Luther adds. "In various writings he constantly presents a false picture of me and my views." No wonder Agricola was hurt by Luther's tract and felt betrayed by the reformer.

Luther laments the fact that his opponents appeal to his writings in support of their heretical views, thus making him, in effect, their patron. He finds it ironic and surprising to hear that he had allegedly abolished the Ten Commandments when throughout his life he taught the law, preached on the necessity of it, included it in his *Catechism*, and repeated it daily like a child. He did of course teach that sinners should be brought to repentance through sermons and contemplating Christ's suffering, but this must be done to show the wrath of God against sin which had necessitated the death of Christ. How else can one know sin without the law? And how can one learn of Christ and grace without the law? The law must be preached so that our conscience is terrified and thus driven to the grace of God.

Luther further laments what his adversaries are doing with his writings; when he sees this he comes close to the despair of Job. At times he had wished he had not written anything. In his struggles he has come to the conclusion that the devil is lord of this world. From the very beginning of the Christian church the devil sought to extinguish the Word of God. He, Luther, alone, not to mention the many men of God before him, has had to endure more than twenty storms from the devil. First there were his difficulties with the papacy; as soon as he was no longer afraid of the pope, the devil broke into his house with Müntzer and the rebels, which nearly extinguished the light; then came the struggles with Karlstadt; after that came the Anabaptists, breaking in the door and the windows in the hope of destroying the gospel; now it is the antinomians through whom the devil seeks to extinguish the candle of the gospel. Luther, however, is confident that the church will stand forever, for Christ, and not a human leader, is the lord of the church. The tragic end to which Müntzer and the Anabaptists of Münster came, Luther states, should be a warning to all that the devil is at work, and a reminder that human works come to no good.

Even after Agricola had retracted his heresy, the controversy was far from over. It was not just Agricola who felt that he was badly treated by Luther. In fact, his academic colleagues sympathized with him as well. They even proposed that Agricola become the dean of the faculty of arts at the university. Luther, however, blocked the project, upon which Agricola first appealed to the rector of the university and on March 31, 1540, he asked the elector for an impartial investigation of the matter. Luther was angry and wrote *Against the Eislebener*, meaning Agricola (WA 51, 429ff.), in which he portrayed Agricola as dangerous to the ethical order of society and that antinomianism was not to be tolerated. The elector at last initiated an inquiry and ordered that Agricola not leave Wittenberg until the dispute was settled. But in August 1540, weary of the controversy, Agricola fled to Berlin, where he became the court preacher of Elector Joachim II of Brandenburg.

Eventually, Agricola withdrew his complaint against Luther, submitted a theological retraction that Melanchthon helped him to draft, "and was reinstated – at least formally – in the good graces of both the political and theological authorities of Electoral Saxony" (106). But the breach between the two men was never repaired. Several years later Agricola sought another reconciliation with the reformer, but Luther refused to receive him. With tears in her eyes Agricola's wife pleaded with Luther to give in somewhat, and the Elector of Brandenburg also spoke for Agricola, but the rift between the two men had become too wide for healing (EA 61, 123-4). A gifted teacher, preacher, theologian, and administrator, Agricola's character was marred, as Luther observed, by vanity, contentiousness, and moral weakness (WA 50, 474).

LAW AND GOSPEL

⟪ **Throughout his long ministry,** Luther never failed to differentiate between the function of the law on the one hand and the gospel on the other, and stressed the necessity of teaching both. According to Luther, Christian maturity is required to distinguish correctly between the law and the gospel. By "law" the reformer understood the Word of God and the commandments that demand the obedience and service of men and women. The "gospel," on the other hand, is the Word of God, which does not demand human works but simply bids men and women to receive the offered grace of forgiveness and eternal salvation as a gift (WA 36, 30–1).

The gospel, according to Luther, is the message about the incarnate Son of God. It is the word of salvation, grace, joy, and peace, whereas the law is the word of perdition, wrath, sadness, pain, unrest, and malediction. The law is the ministry of wrath; the gospel is the ministry of grace. The law is the letter; the gospel is the spirit. The preaching of the law is not only necessary; it is the first thing a sinner must hear. Once sinners have been convicted of their sinfulness by the law, they must hear the gospel in order to find pardon for their sins (WA 22, 188). A penitent sinner should no longer be terrified with the law, but hear the gracious words of the gospel. Moreover, when the subject of preaching is righteousness, life in Christ, and eternal salvation, the law must be put out of sight as if it had never existed (WA 4, 1, 490). And yet, while the law and the gospel are far apart, they are nonetheless most intimately joined together in the heart. Nothing is linked more closely together than fear and confidence, sin and grace, law and gospel (WA 40, 1, 527). In his exposition of Galatians in 1531

Luther stated that it is difficult to keep the law and the gospel together and at the same time apart: "Oh, for the man who can distinguish well here and does not look for law in the gospel but keeps the two as far apart as heaven is distant from the earth! This difference is easy, certain, and plain by itself; but for us it is difficult, in fact, almost incomprehensible" (WA 40, 1, 141).

From the above it is easy to see how and why antinomians like Agricola preferred to emphasize the gospel instead of the law. Luther did emphasize the gospel, the love of God, and justification by faith more than the necessity of performing good works and the law of God. But at no time did Luther question the validity of the law and the necessity of good works as evidence of a redeemed life. As early as 1519, in his exposition of the first twenty-two Psalms, he insisted that as human beings we must not tamper with the law of God, but keep it *God's* law, pure and unadulterated (WA 5, 32). His *Small Catechism* (1529) examines the Ten Commandments and their importance in the life of Christians, urging that they be committed to memory. In a sermon of 1537 on Matthew 22, at the beginning of the antinomian controversy, Luther taught that in Christ there is freedom from sin and the demands of the Old Testament law, but this does not mean that a Christian is free to sin or disobey the law. It is God's will that the Ten Commandments be kept, and Christ enables Christians to keep the law of God. The freedom in Christ is not license, Luther states: We, too, who are now made holy through grace, nevertheless live in a sinful body. And because of this remaining sin, we must permit ourselves to be rebuked, terrified, slain, and sanctified by the law until we are lowered into the grave (WA 51, 440). Human nature, according to Luther, is always the same. The church of the Old Testament needed the law, and the church of the New Testament must likewise keep it. The antinomians, who hold that the teaching of the law is to be thrown out of the churches, are not to be tolerated, for they advocate license and thus pervert the liberty in Christ (WA 39, 1 356).

Agricola's antinomian teaching and writings have not had an appreciable effect on the general understanding of the relationship between law and the gospel, especially his attempt to banish the law from the salvation process. Luther's sharp criticism of Agricola, calling him a Satan, and grouping him with Müntzer, Karlstadt, and the Münsterites, contributed to his loss of reputatation after his initial rise as a follower of the reformer and a popular teacher and theologian (Peters, LH 133).

CONCERNING THE TRINITY

One would think that the Christian theological article on the Trinity, the view that the Godhead consists of one God but in three persons (God, Son, and Holy Spirit), would be the one article of faith that Luther never doubted. But Earl M. Wilbur states that even the conservative leaders of the Reformation inquired into the scriptural basis of this traditional doctrine. Luther, according to Wilbur, "disliked the term *homoousios* [same substance or same essence] as being a human invention, not found in Scripture, and he preferred to say 'oneness.' Trinity, he said, has a cold sound, and it would be far better to say God than Trinity. He therefore omitted these terms from his Catechism, and the invocation of the Trinity from his Litany. Hence Catholic writers did not hesitate to call him an Arian" (Wilbur I, 15).

Wilbur goes on to assert that Melanchthon, Calvin, and other leaders of the Reformation at first doubted the scripturalness of the doctrine, but since the Protestant cause depended "upon the sympathy and support of the German Protestant Princes as against the Catholic Emperor, it could not afford to do anything to alienate the former, nor to furnish the latter with gratuitous grounds of attack" (17). Thus Luther, according to Wilbur, was at first less than orthodox about this doctrine, but dared not deviate from the Nicene and Athanasian Creeds on this point for fear of alienating the conservative populace and doing damage to his cause.

Without overstating the point, it is fair to say that few theologians of the Reformation era have stressed the doctrine of the Trinity more strongly and consistently than Luther. True, in many statements on the subject he referred to the problem of adequate expression. He was not quite satisfied with the designation "persons" in the Trinity, but concluded that there was no better term to express the thought that there were indeed three distinct persons but only one God or a single Godhead (WA 46, 550). About human terms used to designate the Trinity, he wrote in 1537 that it is not very good German and does not sound well to designate God by the word *Dreifaltigkeit* (threefoldness). Even the Latin *Trinitas*, according to Luther, does not sound right. But since there is no better word, we must speak as best we can (WA 21, 508).

In a sermon of 1538 on Luke 9:19–36, Luther stated: "We should stay with the true, ancient belief that there are three distinct Persons – Father, Son, and

Holy Ghost – in the eternal Godhead. This is the most sublime and the first article of the Christian faith.... But to say that God is threefold is very poor language, for in the Godhead the highest Oneness exists.... Augustine, too, complains that he has no fitting word for the mystery.... To be sure, a threeness does exist in the Godhead, but this threeness exists in the Persons of the one Godhead.... I cannot give this Being a fitting name" (Plass III, 138).

If Wilbur refers to passages like these, he may indeed find Luther's dissatisfaction with terms describing the divine mystery, but these references do not in any way cast doubt on the reformer's orthodoxy about the Trinity. Not only did Luther see the Trinity revealed in the New Testament, he also saw it dimly discerned in Old Testament times and believed by the prophets (WA 4, 443; WA 50, 278). In fact, Scripture, according to Luther, opens with the revelation of the triune God, namely, the Father who creates the universe through his Word the Son, and the Holy Spirit who broods over all things (WA 42, 8). In the New Testament, John 1:1–3, which speaks of the Word that was in the beginning with God, was for Luther the triune God who created the universe in the first chapter in Genesis.

In 1523 and 1526 Luther wrote about the German Mass and the order of the "Gottesdienst" (divine church service) as it was practised in Wittenberg (Werke 7, 151–202). He was especially concerned that young people and simple men and women ("die Einfältigen") be encouraged to come to the divine services not only to hear the Word of God but also to learn the articles of faith. Music and singing, according to Luther, were important enticements for people to come to church. Among the articles of faith to be learned through hymns was the doctrine of the Trinity. One of the hymns that taught belief in the Trinity was Luther's "The German Confession of Faith," which may have been the first hymn Luther also wrote the music for (Werke 8, 57). This hymn speaks of God the creator in the first stanza, of Jesus Christ his Son in the second, and of the Holy Spirit, who is with God the Father and the Son, in the third (57–8). In another hymn, "God the Father be with us" (58–9), which Luther took from the Catholic Church and changed to a German and evangelical text, the three persons in the Godhead are asked to remain with us (*wohn uns bei*). There is thus no doubt that Luther accepted the belief in the triune God unreservedly.

ANTI-TRINITARIANS

❧ **It is not known** when Luther first came in touch with anti-Trinitarians. Wilbur states that this heresy appeared in Protestant circles in Nürnberg as early as 1524, suggesting that Hans Denck may have been one of the anti-Trinitarians. However, in Denck's writings there is no evidence that he denied the Trinity, although he may have associated with some anti-Trinitarians in the city. When asked by the city council of Nürnberg as to what to do with those who deny the doctrine, Luther, according to Wilbur, ascribed this heresy to the influence of Karlstadt and Müntzer and advised regarding the persons involved as Turks and apostates (Wilbur 23–9). The first Protestant to express anti-Trinitarian views may have been Martin Cellarius (1492–1564). He was attracted to the reformers in Wittenberg and was influenced by the Zwickau prophets, but left in 1525 for East Prussia where he defended Anabaptism and was subsequently imprisoned for his radical views.

Luther's direct encounter with anti-Trinitarians came in the person of Johannes Campanus (1500–1575) who came from the Lower Rhine area of the duchy of Jülich, leaning toward a spiritualistic interpretation of Christian beliefs. According to Karl Rembert, "Campanus impressed upon the entire movement in Jülich the stamp of his spirit. He was the driving force and spiritual leader until displaced by Menno Simons and his followers who turned the movement into a different direction" (ME I, 499). He was not an Anabaptist, but some of his ideas were similar to some Anabaptists' beliefs. According to Robert Friedman, "Campanus belonged to the group of humanistically trained theologians ... who between 1520 and 1535 shifted so much in their position from Catholicism to Lutheranism, then into the direction of Anabaptism ... and finally to a free and near gnostic Christianity."

In 1528 Campanus enrolled as a student in Wittenberg and was a staunch follower of Luther. However, in 1529 he antagonized both Luther and Melanchthon when he pushed himself into the Marburg Colloquy where the Swiss and Lutheran theologians discussed the nature of the Last Supper (Williams, *Spiritual* 147). Campanus soon drifted into unorthodox thinking, questioned the Trinity, denied the personality of the Holy Spirit, attacked Luther's doctrine of justification by faith and his understanding of the sacraments, and believed he had rediscovered the truth that had been lost since the time of the apostles. In

1532 he wrote a book entitled *Against the Whole World since the Apostles*, which was followed by an abridged version under the title *Restitution*. The booklet covers Campanus's system of theology and is distinctly anti-Lutheran. Excluding the Holy Spirit as a person from the Godhead, Campanus postulates an eternal binity of persons, God the Father and Christ the Son in one essence and nature, just as husband and wife are two persons but one flesh. According to Campanus, the passage of Genesis 1:26–7 explains the mystery of the relationship between God and Christ well. The words, "Let us make man in out image, after our likeness ... male and female he created them" point out the two persons in the Godhead and the relationship between the two. Just as Eve was subject to Adam, so Christ is subject to his Father. The Holy Spirit is not a person but the common bond between Father and Son. Campanus believed that when the church lost this biblical view of God and humans, it fell and is thus now in need of restitution (Williams, *Radical Reformation* 404–5).

Neither Luther nor Melanchthon was impressed with Campanus's ideas. Melanchthon, for one, suggested that Campanus should be hanged on the highest tree, but Luther advised paying no attention to this blasphemer lest he become puffed up over his own importance. As Luther put it, Campanus, this damned piece of dirt [*Unflath*] and scoundrel [*Bube*] one should only despise and not write against, for when one writes against him he becomes more bold and daring (EA 61, 5). In his tract *Against the Antinomians*, Luther mentions Campanus together with anti-Trinitarian Michael Servetus as persons who stormed against the old teachers, the pope, and Luther (WA 50, 475). Luther thus considered anti-Trinitarianism as a dangerous storm that threatened to extinguish the light of the gospel.

Michael Servetus

Michael Servetus (1511–1553), perhaps the most famous anti-Trinitarian during the Reformation, came from Villanueve in Spain. He was well acquainted with the large settlements of Jews and Moors (Moslems) in Spain whom the Catholic Inquisition sought to covert to Christianity. To become Christian, these monotheistic groups, whose belief in only one God went back for centuries, had to not only receive baptism but also accept the Christian belief in a triune God, which for them meant worshipping three deities. Over the years the church had shed much blood in trying to convert them. Already as a young man Servetus had been appalled at the violence and cruelty Jews and Muslims had to endure because of their ancient beliefs and their refusal to convert to Christianity. When Servetus studied the Bible with these questions in mind, he discovered that, as far as he was concerned, neither the Old Testament nor the New Testament taught the doctrine of the Trinity.

Not only did Servetus doubt and ultimately reject this Christian belief, but he also came to realize that the church and the state had become so intertwined as to have lost all meaningful distinctions between the spiritual and secular aspects of life. This insight came to Servetus in 1530 when he watched the coronation of Charles V by the Roman pope. Charles kissing the hand of the pope symbolized the unity of the spiritual and temporal realms, which Servetus found not only shameful but also blasphemous. Christ had been a humble servant of people on earth, but the pope has himself carried by others. "He does not touch the ground with his feet, lest his holiness be polluted – to be carried on the shoulders of men and thus to make himself to be adored on earth as God," Servetus wrote. At this Servetus cries out in a language that would certainly not endear him with the Catholic Church: "O vilest of all beasts, most brazen of harlots!" (Williams, *Radical Reformation* 55–6). But many radicals at the time, including the various groups of Anabaptists, held similar views about the Church of Rome. And for Luther the pope was the veritable Antichrist as well.

In 1531 Servetus published in Strasbourg his *On the Errors of the Trinity*, a work consisting of seven volumes. In the first book Servetus propounds his conception of Christ as the natural Son of God, begotten, not eternally, but in a mysterious way through the operation of the Holy Spirit. The Holy Spirit is here thought of as the seed of God through which Mary conceived, not as a distinct person of the Trinity. Christ, in Servetus's view, remains the great saviour of the world to whom God gave all power in heaven and on earth, and can thus legitimately be called divine, but he is not, as Catholics and Protestants believed, a person in the Godhead equal to God the Father.

The remaining six books develop the anti-Trinitarian theme, and attack Luther's doctrine of justification by faith in strong and disrespectful language, stating that the reformer's emphasis on faith only and his disregarding of good works, weakened the importance of sanctification in believers. Moreover, Servetus believed in baptismal regeneration of adults, rejected infant baptism as not being biblical, and believed that adults should not be baptized until age thirty like Jesus. The Eucharist was for Servetus food that comes from eating the celestial body of Christ. According to Williams, it was for this God, who was visible in the person of the historic Jesus and experienced in the breaking of the Eucharistic body, that Servetus was prepared to live and die as a martyr.

Having escaped from prison, where he was briefly held by the Catholic Inquisition, in 1553 Servetus foolishly passed through Geneva, hoping to communicate with Calvin some theological matters close to his heart, especially anti-Trinitarianism. Perhaps he even hoped that Calvin might be swayed to accept his interpretation of Scriptures on the Trinity. But in this hope Servetus was woefully mistaken. When he arrived he was at once apprehended and imprisoned, and charged by Calvin with Anabaptism, anti-Trinitarianism, pantheism, and psychopannychism (the belief that the soul sleeps in death). In addition he was charged with other "crimes," but the court found him guilty of only two heresies, namely Anabaptism and anti-Trinitarianism, both of which, according to the sixth century Justinian Code, were considered crimes deserving death. Seeing his life at an end, Servetus asked to be executed by the sword, for he was afraid that protracted agony might make him recant his beliefs. Even Calvin agreed that he could be executed swiftly, but the city council insisted that he be burned alive and die a slow death. He was then tied to a stake, fairly green wood was placed around him, and because the wood burned slowly, Servetus suffered for two hours before he died. In his agony he prayed, "O Jesus, Son of the eternal God, have pity on me." He thus remained true to his anti-Trinitarian faith to the end.

Michael Servetus did not occupy a prominent place in Luther's life and thinking. His *Table Talks* deal at length with Karlstadt, Müntzer, the Anabaptists, the sacramentarians, Zwingli, Agricola, Erasmus, and Campanus, but Servetus is not mentioned by name. It is not known whether Luther had read Servetus' *On the Errors of the Trinity* (1531), but he knew of him and his anti-Trinitarianism. In his *Against the Antinomians,* Luther referred to Servetus as one who had attacked both him and the pope, and in a disputation of 1544, which dealt primarily with the Trinity, the reformer again referred to Campanus and Servetus. In his *Against the Antinomians* Luther emphasized again that human reason is inadequate to deal with the mystery of the Trinity. It is dangerous to reason about it and we must avoid assuming any distinction between the three persons because each person is the very God and God in his entirety (WA 39, 2, 253). For Luther this article of faith was a matter of either believing it or of being lost (WA 50, 278). As early as 1529 he had explained: "We could never attain to a knowledge of the Father's favour and grace except through the Lord Christ, who is a mirror of His Father's heart. Outside Christ we see in God nothing but a wrathful and terrible Judge. But about Christ we could know nothing if the Holy Spirit had not revealed it to us" (Plass III, 1389).

There was little religious tolerance in the Reformation century. All groups believed in tolerance when it came to their own beliefs, but denied it to others when they were in power. When Luther broke away from Roman Catholicism he claimed, on the basis of Scriptures, that he needed to oppose the church on many issues, but when other individuals and groups opposed him, he was less willing to grant them toleration. Some historians, including Harold S. Bender, claim that the Anabaptists were the first true advocates of religious liberty. They certainly would not kill anyone for their beliefs. But were they tolerant to the extent of accepting other believers whose theology differed from theirs as their brothers and sisters? The issue of tolerance and religious liberty, particularly in Luther and his opponents, needs to be more fully investigated, which the following chapter seeks to do.

{xii}

To Believe What You Like?
Luther and His Opponents on Tolerance and Religious Liberty

LUTHER'S EARLY VIEWS ON TOLERANCE

Critics of Luther are almost unanimous in stating that the reformer was tolerant toward religious dissenters when he himself was in danger of persecution or death, but that he changed to being intolerant when his own cause was in danger and certainly when Lutheran Protestantism became the established religion of the realm (Kühn 72–139; Holl 288–380; Bainton, *Hunted Heretic* and *Travail of Religious Liberty*). The argument runs as follows: In his early works Luther advocated religious liberty, that is, patience and fairness toward groups whose religious opinions and practices differed from the accepted dogma of the church. However, his early language on behalf of religious liberty was dictated by his constant fear of persecution, assassination, poisoning, or murder. Only later, when he had passed from the status of a fugitive to that of a builder of a church, did he express his true views on the question of personal beliefs and coercion. At the beginning of his reformation work, when Luther pleaded for clemency toward heretics, it must be accepted that he spoke and wrote primarily in his own behalf and that of his cause. There is no doubt that Luther changed his views toward persecution and heretics. His later statements on the subject are as much an embarrassment to his followers as his harsh writings against the peasants in 1525 and his other opponents, particularly the Jews, toward the end of his life.

In the *Ninety-Five Theses* (1517) Luther stated that the burning of heretics is contrary to the will of the Holy Spirit. A little later he went so far as to state that there has never been a heresy that has not expressed some truth. In 1520 he wrote in his *To the Christian Nobility* that one should overcome heretics with the Word of God and not with fire. If it were scholarly to conquer heretics with fire, he wrote, then the executioners would be the most learned doctors on earth (WA 6, 455). In the same year he wrote in his *The Babylonian Captivity of the Church:* "I say, then, neither pope nor bishop, nor any man whatever has the right of making one syllable binding on a Christian man, unless it be done with his consent. Whatever is done otherwise is done in the spirit of tyranny.... I cry aloud on behalf of liberty of conscience, and I proclaim with confidence that no kind of law can with any justice be imposed on Christians, whether by men or by angels, except so far as they themselves will; for we are free from all" (Wace and Buchheim 196).

In a Pentecost sermon in 1522, Luther taught that the sword has no power over the hearts of human beings and that heresy cannot be fought with carnal weapons. Secular rulers ought not to meddle in purely spiritual things; the ministers of the Word of God must capture the love and delight of the human heart and thus win men and women for the truth. Princes and bishops are foolish when they use force in an effort to press and compel people to believe (WA 10, 3, 156). Faith is personal and free; all outward compulsion in matters of faith must be excluded. As he wrote in his treatise on *Secular Authority* (1523), in matters of faith we are dealing with free actions toward which no person can be forced. Faith is a divine action of the Spirit of God, and it is therefore out of the question for an external power to obtain it by force. One neither can nor should compel anyone to believe (WA 10, 264). Similarly, heresy is something spiritual and not physical. One cannot strike it with iron, burn it with fire, or drown it in water. Only the Word of God can overcome it (WA 11, 268).

As late as 1525, during the height of Luther's struggle with the radicals, he was still against the use of force in religious matters. Interpreting the parable of the weeds and the wheat (Matt. 13:24–30) in a homily, Luther stated: "As to heretics and false doctors, we must not pluck them out or destroy them. Christ tells us plainly to allow them to grow. The Word of God is our only recourse, for in this field whoever is bad today may become good tomorrow. [Even a heretic may eventually be touched by the Word of God and be saved.] But if a heretic is burnt or eliminated, his conversion has been made impossible. He is cut off from God's Word and he who otherwise might have been saved is of necessity lost. That is why the Lord said that the good grain might be uprooted with the tares. This is abominable in the eyes of God and absolutely indefensible" (Lecler I, 152).

Even Karlstadt and Müntzer, wrote Luther in 1524 to the princes of Saxony, should be allowed to preach as much as they wish; the Word of God must go to battle; let the spirits battle with one another; some will no doubt be led astray, for that is what happens in the real course of war; when there is strife and battle, there some must fall (WA 15, 218–19). When in 1525 some Anabaptists in Switzerland were drowned in mockery of adult baptism, Luther did not approve of such cruelty (Bainton, *Travail* 61). Writing in 1528 to two pastors about the Anabaptists, Luther expressed unease about putting these people to death. Let every one believe what they like, for if they are wrong they will have punishment enough in hell. *Unless there is sedition and outright rebellion* (my emphasis) one should oppose them with God's Word only (WA 26, 145–7). Further, in a letter to Wenceslaus Link, a friend of his in Nürnberg, Luther wrote in July 1528: "You ask whether the magistrates may kill false prophets. I am slow in a judgment of blood even when it is deserved. In this matter I am terrified by the example of the papists and the Jews before Christ, for when there was a statute for the killing of false prophets and heretics, in time it came about that only the most saintly and innocent were killed.... I cannot admit that false teachers are to be put to death. It is enough to banish" (Oyer 107).

By 1528 a new element had entered Luther's thinking about capital punishment, namely that while rebels against the governments should be put to death, heretics should only be exiled or banished. Is there some inconsistency between what Luther believed and practised earlier and later? Both Müntzer and Karlstadt, for example, became fugitives during the unrest among the peasants, and in 1525 Luther advocated the death penalty for the rebellious peasants. But in 1528 he still believed that heretics should be allowed to believe what they wished, provided they did not undermine the legitimate secular authorities. As to the question of banishing dissenters from the official religious belief, it seems clear that at no time had Luther advocated freedom of public or open worship. Dissenting individuals and groups could believe what they wished, but they were not allowed to express or practise their beliefs, especially if that religious practice was considered detrimental or dangerous to what was commonly believed to be the true faith. But, it might be asked, is there really freedom of conscience if one cannot express that freedom openly and in public worship?

ECCLESIASTICAL VISITATIONS

⦅ **Someome historians have ponted out** that Luther's "ecclesiastical visitations" (Lutheran ministers visiting their parishes), initiated in 1527, registered the reformer's increasing impatience with religious dissent (Lecler I, 158–60). There are, to be sure, many statements in this connection that could be interpreted as expressions of Luther's changed views on freedom of conscience. In 1529 he wrote to Joseph Lewin Metzsch, who took part in visiting the parishes, that even if people are not Christians, they should be compelled to come to hear sermons in order to learn at least some practice in attending church services (WA, Br. 6, 136–7). And writing to Thomas Lösscher, a parish priest of Milau, Luther insisted that people should go to hear sermons, so that they may learn political obedience and social duties, whether they believe in the gospel or not (137).

In 1533, Luther described in a letter to a parish priest in Zwickau how the visitations were conducted in Wittenberg: "By the authority and in the name of the Most Serene Prince we usually frighten and threaten with punishment and exile those who are negligent in religion and do not come to the sermons. This is the first step. If they do not improve, we instruct the priests in charge to set them a time limit, one month or more, that they may listen to reason. After that, if they remain obstinate, they are excluded from the community and all contact with them ceases, as if they were pagans" (Lecler I, 159–60). The letter is remarkable, as Joseph Lecler comments, in that it foreshadows the principle of *cujus regio, ejus religio* ("whose region, his religion") of the Peace of Augsburg (1555).

In a lengthy exposition of Psalm 82 in 1530, Luther explains his position in more detail (LW 13, 42–72). He first makes it clear that no person should be forced to believe this or that; an individual's belief or unbelief is their private matter. However, when it comes to teaching falsehoods or to blaspheming, the secular authorities should step in. A blasphemer should go to where there are unbelievers and not be allowed to disturb the peace in Christian territories or lands. To preserve the peace, each region should have but one religion. The papists and the Lutherans should not be allowed to carry on their religious activities in the same region. If the Lutherans are not wanted in a certain location, they should leave voluntarily, for God's Word should not be forced upon people. If, on the other hand, both the Catholics and Lutherans insist that they will carry on their activities in a certain region, the magistrates should arrange a hearing between the two, listen to the views of both sides, and then decide between the one or the other on the basis of which side has the better scriptural arguments. It is not advisable to tolerate two types of preaching, as this causes confusion, hatred, and the formation of sects. The "corner preachers," as Luther calls the Anabaptists, spiritualists, and radicals who conducted their activities in secret, should not be allowed to preach and teach. They should in fact be reported to the parish minister or priest, for tolerance toward them could lead to disturbances of the peace. Had Müntzer and Karlstadt been restrained in time, Luther continues, the misfortunes that resulted from their activities would not have happened. Only the duly elected and ordained ministers should be allowed to preach. He, Luther, would gladly discontinue his own ministry, but since he is a doctor of theology and God's minister, he must preach and teach, however difficult it might be at times. Luther concludes the first major point of his exposition by stating that he is in no way strengthening the hands of the magistrates against the believers in spiritual matters. According to him, Christian magistrates will not punish anyone except those who disturb the peace *and* blaspheme God.

The exposition of Psalm 82 is significant as a document clarifying Luther's distinction between liberty of conscience and liberty of worship. On the question of personal beliefs, he had not changed from his formerly held position. An individual was free to believe or to disbelieve. However, when it came to proclaiming or advocating a certain creed or to expressing certain beliefs publicly, the outward consequences had to be taken into account. In an age of religious fanaticism, different religious opinions often led to public disorder and social disturbances. The breaking of images here and there was only one example of such religious zeal. Add to this the political and social implications of certain ideologies and emphases in preaching and religious instruction, as exemplified in the later Münster fanatics, and it is not difficult to understand the reformer's apprehension about what he believed were anti-Christian preachers and notions.

WHAT TO DO WITH HERETICS

❦ **In 1531 the theologians at Wittenberg,** headed by Melanchthon, prepared a document on the question of whether Anabaptists and other dissident groups should be punished by the sword, and sent it to Johann Frederick, Elector of Saxony. Melanchthon definitely demanded capital punishment for heretics, including Anabaptists, especially those who were found guilty of blasphemy and sedition. The Wittenberg reformers defined *blasphemy* to mean the teaching of certain doctrines that were contrary to Scripture, rejection of an article in the Apostolic Creed, rejection of infant baptism, and the denial of hereditary sin. For all practical purposes this meant that people who did not believe or practise the accepted creed were liable to prosecution by the authorities. *Sedition* was defined as refusal to participate in war or to serve in the magistracy, the belief in community of goods, and any act that undermined or threatened legitimate governments (WA 50, 10–13; Schraepler 24–9).

Blasphemy and sedition were to be dealt with by the secular state, while the church was to deal with purely theological matters according to Christ's directives in Matthew 18:16ff. Applying the Justinian Code to sixteenth-century heretics, the 1531 document read, in part: "We may therefore conclude that my gracious Lord is entitled to apply to them [the heretics and rebels] in good conscience the penalties laid down by the Code, law II (L. I, tit. 5)" (Lecler I, 162). Luther signed his name to the document, but added the following significant note: "Although it is cruel to admit that they be punished by the sword, it is more cruel still on their part that they wish to condemn preaching, propagate dangerous doctrines, suppress orthodox teaching and seek the overthrow of the kingdoms of this world." It is not known whether Luther was fully convinced that the document he signed was directed only against religious fanatics, who were religiously and politically dangerous people. The note he added seems to indicate that he had his doubts about the justice of inflicting the death penalty on those whose religious views and actions differed from the official version of faith. It is to his credit that he remained sensitive toward those who did not fit in with the established order.

SEDITION AND BLASPHEMY

❡ **The erection of the Anabaptist kingdom in Münster** confirmed Luther in his thinking about the danger of tolerating the teaching of heretical views and beliefs. He seems to have fully concurred with the action of the Catholics and Lutherans against the Anabaptists following their defeat in Westphalia. But not all secular princes were certain that all Anabaptists deserved death. The Landgrave Philip of Hesse, for one, asked the Wittenberg theologians what he should do with some Anabaptists who had just been arrested in his domain. In answer to this question, the Wittenberg theologians released in 1536 a document that bore the title: *That Christian Princes Must Repress the Anabaptists by Corporal Punishment: Some Considerations at Wittenberg* (WA 50, 6–15). This document is a clear statement of what the reformers at Wittenberg understood by sedition and blasphemy, and the reason for their severity against the Anabaptists.

The document first makes it clear that only the temporal authorities are responsible for the social and political well-being of their subjects. But when subjects meddle in worldly affairs, as Müntzer and the Münsterites had done, they become guilty of rebellion. It is the duty of governments to punish those who seek the destruction of worldly states. The document goes on to differentiate between sedition among the Anabaptists and blasphemy. The following beliefs and practices among the Anabaptists were considered seditious: Christians should not serve in government; Christians should not even swear (which was seen as disloyalty toward governments); Christians should not own property; Christians may leave their wives if they do not wish to become Anabaptists. These articles were considered seditious because they undermine the social and political structure and thus lead to chaos, as happened in Münster. Governments thus do not punish these people for what they privately believe, but for what their beliefs lead to.

Then there are doctrinal articles advocated by the Anabaptists that are blatant blasphemy: the rejection of infant baptism; the denial of original sin;

illumination of the Holy Spirit outside of God's Word, and other heretical views. These beliefs and practices are both blasphemous and dangerous, for they are contrary to the clear teaching of Scriptures and they destroy, as sedition does, not only the social structures but also the church. Some may object that the civil authorities should not meddle in spiritual matters, which is true; but it is also true that both church and state must work together to the glory of God. As the document puts it: "Princes must not only protect the goods and material existence of their subjects, but their most essential function is to promote the honour of God and to repress blasphemy and idolatry. That is why in the Old Testament the kings, and not only the Jewish kings, but also kings converted from paganism, had the false prophets together with the idolaters put to death. Such examples apply to the function of princes, as St. Paul also teaches: 'The law is good, for the chastisement of the blasphemers'" (Lecler I, 163).

The parable about the weeds and the wheat, which had earlier been an argument in favour of toleration, is now interpreted to mean the opposite: The word that both the weeds and the good grain should grow together does not apply to the temporal authorities, but to the ministers of God only who should not exert any physical compulsion. In conclusion, the document points out confidently: "From all this it is clear that the secular authority is bound to repress blasphemy, false doctrine and heresy, and to inflict corporal punishment on those that support such things." The document ends by stating that the heretics should be banished or put to death, but only after all attempts at converting these erring people have failed. It also warns that those who hold erroneous views concerning governments may indeed be "pregnant with the Münster spirit."

The 1536 document, demanding severe measures against Anabaptists, was signed by the Wittenberg theologians, including Luther, Bugenhagen, Caspar Creutzinger, and Melanchthon. However, before Luther signed, he again added a postscript, perhaps indicative of his unease about agreeing to killing Anabaptists: "This is the general rule of how to deal with the Anabaptists, but may our gracious lord at all times let mercy exist besides punishment, according to circumstances and cases" (WA 50, 15).

LUTHER'S CHANGED VIEW

❰❰ **It is a sad fact** that Luther's earlier pronouncements in favour of religious liberty had later given way to supporting the suppression of beliefs and practices which, according to him, undermined the religious, social, political, and economic institutions of the time. According to Lecler, from the point of religious freedom, Luther's Reformation did not show appreciable progress. "There was liberty of conscience in the evangelical States, if you like, but freedom of worship did not exist. But can one really speak of freedom of conscience if one is not allowed to give expression to one's belief or to show it in outward acts of worship?" (Lecler I, 164). No doubt Luther knew that he had changed his earlier views on tolerance to those of sanctioning persecution, but throughout he remained most uneasy about it, and in his later life he came back to his earlier statements, namely, that banishment and imprisonment were sufficient penalties for heretics (Bainton, *Travail* 64). Various circumstances and his encounter with Karlstadt, Müntzer, the peasants in 1525, and the Münsterites, left Luther "in a state of distraught nerves," as Bainton puts it, hence his belief that all Anabaptists were enemies of the Reformation he led (63).

Not all Anabaptists, as we have seen, were revolutionaries intent on overthrowing the constituted governments, certainly not the peaceful Anabaptists, but many of them insisted on the separation of church and state, thus in effect advocating the principle of a holy community separated from the world, including the secularized state. But Luther viewed such separation with grave misgivings. According to him it was not only impossible to reach perfection on earth by thus separating from the world, but such separation was also undesirable because it led to human pride on the one hand, and to a withdrawal of the Christian influence on the other. For Luther, as well as for other magisterial reformers, both the church and the state existed under God, and Christian magistrates were not only responsible for the maintenance of law and order, as Christians they also shared the spiritual concerns and obligations of the church.

The Anabaptists' separation of church and state, on the other hand; their rejection of infant baptism, which in Luther's view, withdrew the grace of God from a large section of society; their refusal to participate actively in matters of state; their rather unorthodox views and practices with regard to private property – all this made Luther fearful about what the consequences of tolerating the Anabaptists might be. After the Münster uprising Luther might have seen the difference between those revolutionaries and most of the peaceful Anabaptists who took the Christian life as seriously as he did. However, in an age of strong religious convictions, theological differences, and political and social turmoil, little room was left for objectivity, forbearance, and Christian love and understanding. When it is remembered that humanists such as Zwingli and Melanchthon were most severe in their condemnation of the Anabaptists, Luther's relative moderation in the treatment of heretics (as expressed in his reluctance to agree with the death penalty against them) is remarkable.

The anti-Anabaptist writings of the Wittenberg theologians had their dreadful effect not only in electoral Saxony, the centre of the Lutheran Reformation, but also in other areas of the empire. To justify the execution of Anabaptists and other sectarians, the rulers often appealed to the teaching of the leading reformers on the subject. Philip of Hesse was one of the few princes who did not resort to harsh measures against the more peaceful groups. He did not see them as rebels and blasphemers, but only poor people who erred in their faith. As late as 1545 Philip was unable to persuade himself to inflict the death penalty on the heretics, since, as he put it, "over night a man may be instructed and turn from his error. If we should condemn such a one so summarily to death we fear greatly that we should not be innocent of his blood" (Bainton, "The Parable" 87). In his last will, this prince distinguished between the peaceful and the rebellious Anabaptists – something the magisterial reformers seldom did – and advised the educated to win the dissenters back to the true doctrine, for to "kill anybody because he's of false belief, this we have never done and wish also to warn our sons against it" (Littell, *Anabaptist View* 33). Philip's tolerant measures paid off well. In his territory many Anabaptists were won back to the Lutheran fold, and many more contributed to the economy of the land through good farming and other occupations (Littell, *Origins* 35–6).

Although Philip of Hesse cannot be hailed as a champion of religious liberty, among Lutherans he was one of the few who at least questioned the wisdom and justice of persecuting those of other religious persuasions. He was also an example of a temporal ruler who was one of the first to see the practical benefits of dealing justly with religious dissenters. Sadly, as far as Luther was concerned, he not only betrayed his earlier tolerance, but with other magisterial reformers he left a legacy of Anabaptist persecutions and the loss through exile of some of the best people and communities. It now remains to be seen whether the dissidents and opponents of the magisterial reformers were true champions of religious liberty, as some have claimed.

ANABAPTISTS ON TOLERANCE

❊ **Most Protestant and Catholic theologians and historians** do not believe that there were any religious groups in the sixteenth century that were genuinely tolerant toward creeds other than their own. Some go as far as to state that it was not until two hundred years later that a German poet and critic, Gotthold Ephraim Lessing (1729–1781), fought for complete tolerance toward non-Christian and other confessions of faith. His drama *Nathan the Wise* (1779) is a fervent plea for religious tolerance. Still others see the institution of freedom and religious liberty coinciding with the inauguration of the American constitution in the eighteenth century (Pfeffer ix).

There are, however, writers who see the birth of religious liberty in some of the radical reformers. Smithson feels that "an unprejudiced examination of the work and teaching of the Anabaptists reveals them as outstanding pioneers in the struggle for religious liberty" (17). Harbison states that it was the Anabaptists who first caught the vision of religious freedom (65). Mennonite historian Henry Smith makes Anabaptism "the essence of individualism," for these radical reformers believed that "the greatest degree of liberty must be granted the individual conscience in spiritual matters" (21). Franklin Littell looks upon the Anabaptists as people who consistently championed religious liberty in the modern sense (*Anabaptist View* 66). And Harold S. Bender goes so far as to say: "There can be no question but that the great principles of freedom of conscience, separation of church and state, and voluntarism in religion, so basic to American Protestantism, and so essential to democracy, ultimately are derived from the Anabaptists of the Reformation period, who for the first time clearly enunciated them, and challenged the Christian world to follow them in practice" (Bender, "Anabaptist Vision" 68). Bender's claim that the Anabaptists were the forerunners of American Protestantism is no doubt an enthusiastic statement, but perhaps it can be said that the early Anabaptists *contributed* to the modern principles stated in the quotation.

In considering tolerance and religious liberty among the radicals, it should be stated at the outset that certain individuals and groups knew nothing of tolerance. The Anabaptists of Münster, for example, used lethal force and taught that the "godless" must be killed to make room for their followers. It was these revolutionaries who made the entire Anabaptist movement suspect in the eyes of the leading reformers and of society. But how about some of the peaceful Anabaptists and certain spiritualists? Were they truly tolerant toward persons and groups who did not share their beliefs? Tolerance here does not mean indifference or neutrality in religious matters, but a willingness to let others believe and practise their creeds as they see fit, and not to interfere with those beliefs by any force whatsoever. Whether *respect* for those beliefs must be part of tolerance is another matter and is perhaps too much to ask of religious groups during the Reformation century.

The evangelical or peaceful Anabaptists were against any form of physical compulsion in religious matters in principle. We have seen from the letter of Conrad Grebel to Müntzer (1524) that the Swiss Brethren repudiated all forms of physical violence. The Anabaptist and the Mennonite congregations, however, practised excommunication, their only weapon against spiritual offenders in the church. During the period that Balthasar Hubmaier was persecuted as an evangelical preacher, he wrote a pamphlet entitled *Concerning Heretics and those who Burn Them* (1524). The tract is one of the earliest pleas for complete toleration of all dissenters. Menno Simons also wrote against the persecution of heretics; he even went so far as to challenge the moral basis of capital punishment, as Bender argued ("Anabaptists and Religious Liberty" 94). And one Hans Mueller of Medikon stated before the Zurich authorities: "Do not lay a burden on my conscience, for faith is a free gift given freely by God and is not common property. The mystery of God lies hidden, like the treasure in the field, which no one can find but he to whom the spirit shows it. So I beg you, ye servants of God, let my faith stand free" (Lindsay II, 441–2).

According to Heinrich Bullinger (1504–1575), a Swiss reformer and an avowed enemy of the Anabaptists, the Swiss Brethren taught that one cannot and should not use force to compel anyone to accept religious faith; that it is wrong to put anyone to death for the sake of their erring faith; that the temporal kingdom should be separated from the church; that no temporal ruler should exercise any authority in the church; that God has commanded simply to preach the gospel, not to compel anyone by force to accept it; that the true church of Christ has the characteristics that it suffers and endures persecution, but does not inflict persecution on others (Bender, "Anabaptist Vision" 68–9). Pilgram Marpeck (ca. 1495–1556), an Anabaptist leader in south Germany, when accused of refusing to recognize other religious groups as scriptural, defended himself as follows: "It is not true that we refuse to count as Christians those who disagree with our baptism and reckon them as misguided spirits and deniers of Christ. It is not ours either to judge or condemn him who is not baptized according to the command of Christ" (Smithson 127).

While testimonies such as these appear to be genuine pleas for religious liberty, one cannot help but suspect that they are the isolated expressions of some men under duress and not characteristic of the entire evangelical Anabaptist movement. According to many other documents, Anabaptist tolerance did not extend to those who remained true to the state churches, whether Catholic or Protestant. An anonymous Anabaptist writer, for example, in a tract entitled *Christian Baptism*, condemns the churchmen of his day, regarding them as instruments of the devil because they uphold an unscriptural state church (Wenger, "Three Swiss" 282–4). Another anonymous pamphlet, *Concerning Evil Overseers*, warns its readers against ministers such as the humanist Hans Denck, who regard infant baptism as an insignificant point, not worth causing strife on account of it (280–1). In yet another tract, *The Hearing of False Prophets or Antichrist*, the writer warns against listening to Luther and other state church ministers, for it is like drinking poison and true Christians must guard against it (276–8).

Even Menno Simons (1496–1561), well known for his theology of non-violence and peace in northwestern Europe, and who gave Mennonites their denominational name, found it difficult to tolerate certain individuals and groups within the Anabaptist movement, and his criticism of the state churches was at times most severe. In reviewing the doctrines of the Catholics, Lutherans, and Zwinglians, Menno comes to the conclusion that these three groups might rightly be considered as "sects," for their teachings and lives are contrary to God's Word (Simons 332–55). Pleading for tolerance on behalf of his persecuted followers, Menno tells the magisterial churchmen that their "office and service are not of God and His Word but issue from the bottomless pit" (207). This seems similar to the language Luther used in describing his enemies. As the Russian-Mennonite historian

Peter M. Friesen wrote in 1911: "On the whole, Menno's polemical writings do not belong to those that one reads with spiritual pleasure, indeed one cannot read them without a painful feeling of spiritual uneasiness. He was no less intolerant than Luther, Calvin and their followers" (P.M. Friesen 18). The difference between the peaceful Anabaptists and the magisterial reformers was that the Anabaptists did not sanction killing anyone for their wrong faith or unbelief, whereas Luther, Zwingly, and Calvin did.

TOLERANCE PROBLEMATICAL DURING THE REFORMATION

☾ **The Anabaptists and later Mennonites** did not understand liberty of conscience to mean a general tolerance of all creeds, but took "liberty of conscience to mean and to imply the separation of church and state and the rejection of all persecution" (Horsch, *Mennonites* 323). It must be remembered, however, that while the Anabaptists taught that Christians should not take part in government affairs, the point was only a theoretical issue because in those days no Anabaptist could have become a magistrate even if they had wanted to. Heretics were automatically excluded from all governmental offices and privileges; they were not even considered full citizens but only subjects of the state. However, when, much later, religious liberty was granted in Holland, Switzerland, and Prussia, some Mennonites in Europe began to participate fairly freely in state affairs, in some cases even serving in the military.

As for the use of force in matters of faith among the Anabaptists, the sixteenth century provides some telling examples. Hans Hut (ca. 1490–1527), for example, an overly zealous Anabaptist, was for a time imprisoned by a fellow Anabaptist, Leonhard von Liechtenstein (1482–1534), the Lord of Nikolsburg in Moravia (Smith 41). Balthasar Hubmaier, who had earlier written in favour of religious toleration, approved of Hut's imprisonment, setting forth his views in a pamphlet entitled *On the Sword*. Hubmaier even argued in support of the actions of the Christian magistrates in matters of religion, including the use of force and going to war in self-defence. Some among the Anabaptists did not agree with Hubmaier, which then resulted in the formation of two groups among them: the *staebler*, the staff-bearers (those who carried only a staff for protection) and the sword bearers, *schwertler*, those who carried a sword for protection. Stayer's *Anabaptists and the Sword* (1972, 1976) deals with this issue, demonstrating that Anabaptism was not a homogeneous movement, but consisted of diverse groups with multiple beliefs and practices. Peter M. Friesen speaks of Menno Simon's "painful" observation of Anabaptists' proclivity to quarrel and divide because they could not tolerate differences even among themselves. Friesen calls this the "Anabaptist illness" (31, 108).

TOLERANCE AMONG SOME SPIRITUALISTS

Among the spiritualists in the sixteenth century there seem to have been at least a few individuals who advocated and practised what amounted to genuine tolerance. Hans Denck of Nürnberg, for example, believed in extreme non-resistance and the separation of church and state, yet this did not prevent him from cooperating and having fellowship with Balthasar Hubmaier, who did not share his views about the sword and the separation of church and state. Denck testified that he could not associate with godless people and pronounced heretics, but admitted that he might be in error about some article of faith and that other believers who did not share his views could be right in certain points. The humility and tolerance of this Christian humanist were exceptional in an age of bigotry and fanaticism. His patient love included not only his friends but also his persecutors, against whom he did not vituperate, as Menno Simons and some other Anabaptists did; he stated that nothing could separate him from people who were not of his mind. Denck believed that Christians should not quarrel over such rites as baptism and the Lord's Supper, but practise Christian love toward each other and all human beings. Before he died, still a young man in his early thirties, he went so far as to express regret for having caused strife and divisions by his zeal for what he had believed to be theologically true. After all, Denck stated, his adversaries worship the same God and honour the same redeemer in Christ. Denck's expression of tolerance no doubt rings true (Fellmann 108).

Sebastian Franck (1499–1542), another spiritualist, came from Donauwörth in Bavaria. He first followed Luther's teaching, but soon turned against Lutheranism and all other organized religious groups. The following factors seem to have contributed to his decision to follow an independent course. In Luther's dispute with Erasmus on free will, for example, Franck sided with the humanist; the horrors of the Peasants' War and Luther's siding with the princes and his later persecution of the Anabaptists affected Franck deeply; the many divisions provoked by the Reformation, with each group claiming to possess the absolute truth, made him cautious about religious claims and protestations; and the weakness of the Reformation on an ethical level caused Franck to question the scripturalness of Luther's *sola fide* principle (Lecler I, 166–7).

In 1531 Franck published his *Chronica* or *Bible of History* in which the author seeks to prove that throughout the ages many devout men and women had been persecuted as heretics. According to the *Chronica*, persecution is an unmistakable sign of heresy. Both Protestants and Catholics saw themselves implicated by this work, and as a result Franck himself was forced to flee for his life. Rejecting all outward authority, Franck championed the complete freedom of a believer. According to him, God wants human beings to be free to such an extent that they do nothing from compulsion. Whatever is done under pressure of any kind is not from faith. Franck praised God for giving him love and understanding for all human beings and religious groups, even those who did not agree with him on certain theological issues. "I reject no heretic," he wrote in his *Chronica*, "at the risk of throwing out the grain with the rest, that is, the truth with the falsehood, but I do separate the gold from the mud. For there is hardly a pagan, a philosopher or a heretic who did not have a glimpse of something good" (175).

In 1539 Franck wrote: "To me, anyone who wishes my good and can bear with me by his side, is a good brother, whether Papist, Lutheran, Zwinglian, Anabaptist, or even Turk, even though we do not feel the same way, until God gathers us in his own school and unites us in the same faith.... Let no one try to be master of my faith and to force me to follow his belief.... I reject no one who does not reject me.... I do not stand apart from any sect, knowing full well that God's community cannot be pointed out like a sect of which it can be said that it is here or there, but I believe in a holy Christian Church, a communion of saints; I love and consider as my brother and neighbor every man, especially those who, among all sects, beliefs and peoples, belong to Christ."

Joseph Lecler observes: "In the history of the freedom of conscience, Sebastian Franck occupies a radical position. It is surprising that such a definite religious individualism could develop already in the beginning of the sixteenth century" (176). It is all the more remarkable when it is considered that Franck's individualism was not that of a pure humanist, skeptic, or rationalist, but that of a deeply spiritual Christian. Franck's tolerance was the result of mystic spirituality and a sense of realism, as paradoxical as that may seem. All human beings were dear to him in so far as they lived sincerely for God. He did not ask anyone what they believed, but how they lived. He stated: "I am so accustomed to errors and mistakes in all men that, because of these, I do not hate anyone on earth, but I deplore, admit and see in them my own misery and condition" (175). There seems to be no doubt about the sincerity of Franck's tolerance.

Like Sebastian Franck, Caspar Schwenckfeld insisted, as we have seen in his clash with Luther, on the invisible character of religion. According to him, God's Word was completely free and not attached to such visible things as the sacraments and an outward ministry. As a result, in matters of faith there was to be complete freedom. While Schwenckfeld did establish small groups for prayer, instruction, and the practice of charity, he maintained, contrary to Luther, that the church was invisible. He refused to become a leader of any specific group, and he was opposed to those who, like the Lutherans and Anabaptists, organized into structured congregations. He frequently wrote against the civil authorities' practice of interfering in religious matters. In a letter of 1533, he argued that if the Christian religion was to consist of outward worship, justice, and prescriptions, the civil authorities have the power to command and punish, even with weapons, in religious things. Since, however, Christianity is based on inward justice, faith, devotion, and freedom of conscience, the state has no power to order or prohibit in such matters (CS 4, 752–3).

Both Schwenckfeld and Luther made use of the expression "freedom of conscience," but understood the concept differently. Luther believed that while the Christian conscience was set free from all human regulations, especially those of "papism," it was the more strongly bound to the Word of God (WA Br 4, 28). And a conscience bound to God's Word would submit to scriptural teaching on matters of church and state, including obedience to temporal powers. Schwenckfeld, on the other hand, did not have the same respect for the "letter" of the Bible. For him religious freedom was primarily concerned with the use of outward things. Since faith is a highly individual matter, the outward expression of faith must be left up to the individual. No outward force may therefore interfere in the practice of one's religion (CS 3, 140–469).

Although Schwenckfeld had some strong theological convictions, in his writings and personal conduct he adhered to his principle of religious liberty. He did not want to found a religious denomination because he believed in the freedom of the spirit and individual faith. He was criticized, attacked, and sometimes persecuted, but he never resorted to revenge or violence. He was sad to see Lutherans and other magisterial reformers persecuting heretics, including the Anabaptists. He wished to be tolerant of other creeds as long as he could practise his own faith freely. In 1534 he wrote to Philip of Hesse: "I only ask to be a brother and a friend to anyone who has the zeal of God, loves Christ with all his heart, clings to the truth and is devoted to piety" (Lecler I, 184). The Anabaptists, according to Schwenckfeld, were not to be persecuted but persuaded by gentleness, to which Philip of Hesse agreed (CS 3, 79). Because of his tolerance and leniency toward others, Schwenckfeld frequently had to clear himself of the charge of being an Anabaptist. Nevertheless, he visited Anabaptists in prison, and to the end insisted that the magistrates had no right to interfere in spiritual affairs. According to Franklin H. Littell, it was Schwenckfeld's teaching on, and example of, tolerance that was not only exemplary in the sixteenth century, but also had a profound influence on later generations.

A NOTE ON PERSECUTION

⁅ **The persecution of heretics** was nothing new in the sixteenth century. Men and women of heterodox beliefs and practices had been persecuted by both church and state ever since the fourth century, when Emperor Constantine legalized Christianity and promoted it as the religion of the Roman state. The Roman Church now had to decide whether it could tolerate persons who deviated from the Christian faith. Church fathers of the second, third, and early fourth centuries, such as Irenaeus, Tertullian, and Eusebeus of Caesarea sought to refute heresies by writing treatises against them. In 325 Constantine convened the Council of Nicaea to settle the main doctrines of the church and then issued an edict banning heretics. From banning heretics to killing them was but a short step. In 385 Priscillian (ca. 340–ca. 385), a saintly Spanish bishop, became the first person to be executed for heresy.

St. Augustine, the church father Luther most admired and revered, was the first influential theorist of persecution. In his youth he belonged to the Manichaean heresy, a heresy that went back to Mani of Baghdad (ca. 216–ca. 276), who taught a dualistic view of good and evil and that God was not necessarily omnipotent, but would conquer the devil and the forces of darkness only at the end of time. When Augustine joined the Catholic Church in 387 and then became a bishop, he at first advocated peaceful methods in fighting Manichaean, Pelagian, and Donatist heresies. By about 400 Augustine began endorsing more drastic measures, calling for the persecution of heretics. He interpreted the parable of the wheat and the weeds (Matt. 13:24–30) to justify using force to keep the church doctrinally pure, but without success. Throughout medieval times the church continued to grapple with heresy. Christians even went to war with the support of popes to keep the church pure, one of the bloodiest examples being the Albigensian Crusade in France (1209–29). Pope Gregory IX assigned the examination and interrogation of heretics to the Dominican order in 1233, thereby establishing the dreaded Inquisition. It was the church that first examined the heretic. If found guilty he or she was handed over to the "secular arm" to be dealt with appropriately, which often resulted in torture and death. This method of dealing with heretics was continued in the sixteenth century among both Catholics and Protestants, although with some notable differences between the two churches.

As we have seen, in the end, after some hesitation, Luther agreed to sign the Wittenberg theologians' document demanding the death penalty for unrepentant Anabaptists. Claus-Peter Clasen (*Anabaptism* 358–422) has investigated the persecution of Anabaptists at great length, including when and where Anabaptists were most numerous, number of persons executed, and differences in persecution between Catholics and Protestants. Some of Clasen's findings have been challenged, as for example his assertion that "The Anabaptists had no discernible impact on the political, economic, or social institutions of their age," or his argument that on the basis of their low numbers the Anabaptist movement "cannot be called more than a minor episode in the history of sixteenth-century German society" (Clasen 428). The fact that both Catholic and Protestant churches and states took the Anabaptist threat to their religious, economic, and political institutions very seriously, no doubt shows that these "sects," as Clasen repeatedly calls them, were a movement to be reckoned with (Haude 150). It is also worth considering that the Free Church movement, including the Baptists and many other evangelical churches in modern times, had its roots in the radical reformers of the sixteenth century.

For the number of Anabaptists executed between 1525 and 1618 in Switzerland, south and central Germany, Austria, Bohemia, and Moravia we are indebted to Clasen's careful research. His number of Anabaptist martyrs in these regions and time frame is 845, with 488 known and "probable" executions occurring between 1527 and 1530. Clasen admits, "It is possible that the records of the executions of about 200 to 300 Anabaptists have been lost," which would bring the number to well over 1,000.

To these numbers must of course be added the Anabaptists and Mennonites who died in the Netherlands and northern Germany after the 1530s, as Brad S. Gregory has shown (Gregory 197–249). According to Jonathan Sailing, between 2,000 and 2,500 Anabaptists were executed in the sixteenth century, with about half of them in the Netherlands and the other half in the southern regions of central Europe. This number of Anabaptist martyrs comprises about 50 percent of all religious martyrs in this period of European history. Of interest is that 30 percent of Anabaptist martyrs were women, a much higher rate than women martyrs of Protestant and Catholic persuasion.

There was a considerable difference between Anabaptist persecutions in Catholic and Protestant territories. The executions of Anabaptists in Catholic south-central Europe between 1527 and 1533, especially in Tirol, Austria, and Bavaria, account for 80 percent of all Anabaptist executions. Only in Catholic territories were Anabaptists burned at the stake, while women were generally drowned; but sometimes women were buried alive. Generally the majority of executions took place with the sword. According to Clasen, 68 percent were burned at the stake, and of those who were beheaded with the sword 12 percent were women (Clasen, *Anabaptism* 370–1). According to Brad Gregory, although the apprehended Anabaptists did not *seek* martyrdom, many of them went to their death willingly and often joyfully, believing that their martyrdom was a sign of God's approval of their faith and life (Gregory 223–4).

Some Protestant writers did not agree that willingness to suffer or constancy in death for one's religious convictions was a sign of God's favour. Luther, for example, "stated that even if individuals were to die for the doctrine that good works contribute to salvation, and for human righteousness and free will, 'they would not be God's martyrs, but rather their own and the devil's, just like pagans who died for the sake of temporal rights, possessions, and honor'" (323–4). The Protestant divines, therefore, sought to persuade the Anabaptists to leave their errors and return to the true faith. In most Protestant territories, especially in Hesse, where many Anabaptists had fled to avoid capture, "gentle" means, such as instruction, were at first used to bring the erring back to the Lutheran fold. Such instructions were very time-consuming, but this method of dealing with Anabaptists was preferred to harsher means, such as those in Catholic territories (Clasen, *Anabaptism* 365). Only if instruction and attempts at pesuasion failed were the heretics either expelled from the territory or sometimes jailed. Some Anabaptists recanted under pressure. In Protestant Zurich the death penalty was applied to the Swiss Brethren, with Felix Mantz being one of the first Anabaptist martyrs (1527), and in Calvin's Geneva Michael Servetus was executed for denying the Trinity and for Anabaptism.

CONCLUSION

⟨⟨ Although Luther had advocated religious liberty in his earlier writings, he modified his views on tolerance when he realized that allowing views contrary to his own would threaten not only his work of reform but also the social and political order of the time. Luther the heretic had become a persecutor himself. Luther was no exception in this and he was not the first. There had been advocates of tolerance and liberty of conscience since the beginning of Christianity. For example, as we have seen, such church fathers as Tertullian and St. Augustine had spoken in favour of religious toleration when the Christian church was in the minority and oppressed; but when the church was later accepted in society, these very same men counselled coercion and even physical punishment, for, according to them, allowing heretics freedom would jeopardize the salvation of Christian souls.

The Anabaptists, who remained a minority group in the sixteenth century, cannot be considered genuine champions of religious toleration because for most of them their sectarianism was often too exclusive and sometimes even fanatical. This is certainly how Schwenckfeld felt about them (Littell, "Schwenckfeld" 383). Nevertheless, it can be said that the Anabaptists and spiritualists laid the *foundation* of religious liberty by insisting that church and state must be separate, that only believers were to be baptized, that Christians must reject all violence, and that the individual is primarily responsible to God and not to any human authority. Through suffering persecution, Anabaptists and spiritualists eventually contributed to the realization among persecutors that most coercion in matters of mind and spirit is useless as a method for achieving desired objectives. For example, as Bainton points out, it was believed that persecution would bring about the salvation of the heretic's soul, vindicate the honour of God, as Calvin taught, and bring about orthodoxy and unity within the church. As time went on, however, persecution proved ineffective in achieving these desired ends. And the later Enlightenment undermined some of the principles underlying the theory of persecution (Bainton, *Travail* 17ff.).

Some of the spiritualists were perhaps the only true advocates of liberty of conscience, for they conceded freedom of belief and practice to all those who dissented from the status quo. They not only wrote against all coercion in religious matters, but also admitted that others who differed from them might be able to shed as much, if not more, light on certain theological issues as they. Such humility and understanding may well be the touchstones of sincerity. Our modern concept of religious liberty owes much to the spiritualists of the sixteenth century.

Ironically, Luther contributed perhaps *indirectly* to at least the *necessity* of religious tolerance. When Luther experienced the grace of God and was justified by God without human good works or any human or churchly intermediary, resulting in his principles of *sola fide* and *sola scriptura*, he became the model for other individuals to experience God and salvation. The result was a multitude of Protestant individuals and groups, all of them claiming not only to have experienced the grace of God directly, but also that the truth that they derived from the Word of God was absolutely true. Luther advised his followers to read the Bible. The reader enlightened by the Holy Spirit would then know God's will for his or her life. Luther believed that readers of Scriptures would understand God's Word as he understood it, for the biblical text, according to him, was clear. But in time Luther found that other individuals understood Scriptures differently from him, which resulted in the formation of different groups that not only opposed Catholicism and Lutheranism, but also other groups within the Reformation movement. The clash between Catholicism and Protestantism and between other groups led to dissension and wars after the Reformation for decades and centuries to come.

To preserve the peace, the states and the church had to devise a way for their citizens and subjects to live together. As Robert Glenn Howart has argued in a recent article (Howard 91–108), recognizing and accepting different religions in regions and states became necessary. Thus, today, while holding to the truth of their own interpretation of the Bible, the various churches and religious groups must tolerate each other, for not to do so would mean continued persecution, religious wars, and general chaos. And this "peace" between religions is maintained by the secular state, which Luther, who believed in the different roles of the state and church, would perhaps approve of.

{xiii}

"Drive Them Out of the Land!"
Luther on the Jews

About Luther's book *On the Jews and their Lies*, which appeared in 1543, just three years before the reformer died, the esteemed Reformation scholar Roland H. Bainton wrote more than half a century ago: "One could wish that Luther had died before ever this tract was written" (Bainton, *Here I Stand* 297). The Evangelical Lutheran Church in America, indeed Lutherans throughout the world, are not only embarrassed about Luther's anti-Judaism, but also unreservedly condemn the reformer's attitude and his later writings against the Jews. Especially after the Holocaust nothing could be said or done to excuse or mitigate the reformer's hateful writings against the Jews. All that Christians in general and Lutherans in particular can do now is to acknowledge Luther's obvious evil with regard to the Jewish people and in humility and contrition seek to explain how this could have happened.

A chapter on Luther and the Jews is obviously difficult to write, especially for anyone who is generally sympathetic toward Luther's work as a reformer. However, all decent human beings, be they Lutherans, Catholics, Mennonites, Christians of all stripes, or non-Christians, must deplore the reformer's unchristian thoughts and writings against a group of people who did not share his religious faith. At the same time, in a book about Luther and his opponents, one cannot sweep under the proverbial carpet what is both negative and painful. In what follows, an attempt is made to briefly report on and interpret Luther's anti-Judaic writings as objectively as possible, although there are some who believe that after what happened to the Jews during the Second World War it is impossible to be objective on the subject.

A PERSONAL EXPERIENCE

❰ **In April 1997,** I had the privilege of visiting the centre of the Lutheran reformation for the first time. Entering with anticipation "Luther's church," the *Stadtkirche* or city church of Lutherstadt-Wittenberg, I stopped first to view the history-laden sanctuary, contemplating on how Luther would have seen the audience that had come to hear their pastor expound the Word of God and the great themes of the Reformation. On this occasion the church was empty and just dimly lit, only a man in working clothes moving between the pews, dusting them and sweeping the floor. Seeing the raised pulpit to the right, I felt a desire to step behind the historic pulpit for just a moment, but a chair had been placed at the foot of the steps, obviously to indicate that access to the pulpit was not allowed. I approached the janitor, told him that I had published on Luther, and that I would love to see the auditorium from where Luther had preached. To my pleasant surprise, the kind gentleman allowed me to ascend the pulpit, from where I could imagine the sixteenth-century audiences to whom Luther preached on many occasions.

Outside again, I walked around the church, touching the ancient walls to make physical contact with nearly 500 years of Protestant history. As I looked up to the high roof, I discovered on the southeast corner a sandstone relief I had not known about. About eight meters above ground level, just below the roofline, there appeared a badly weathered sculpture known as the *Judensau* (Jewish sow) with several Jews vulgarly represented beneath and behind the animal. Just above the relief I read in carved Hebrew words, *Rabini Schem Hamphoras* (the Rabbi's expounded name of God), a name derived from the *Kabbalah*, an old Jewish body of mystical writings (Shachar 30). As I knew that pigs were considered unclean to Jews, I was not only shocked to see this hideous relief on Luther's church, but also wondered why Luther had not removed it during his tenure as pastor there.

As a counterpoint to the *Judensau* on the church and in memory of the terrible events of the Holocaust, the city of Wittenberg had placed in 1988 a memorial on the ground just below the sculpture. The memorial consists of a large metal square of four plates in the form of a cross. Along the joints of the plates there is a representation of blood oozing out, and on the margins of the memorial a German text reads: "God's true name / the reviled Schem-Hamphoras / which Jews before the time of Christianity / held inexpressibly holy / perished in six million Jews / under the sign of the cross" (Lindberg 369).

When I visited Lutherstadt-Wittenberg in October 2011 again, I did not find the *Judensau* or the commemorative plaque where I had seen them before. As the exterior of the church building was being renovated, I thought perhaps workers had removed these objects – and perhaps for good! But when I enquired at the city later, asking what had happened to the relief, I was informed that once the renovations were completed, the scupture and the metal plaque below would be replaced. The city no doubt felt that however ugly, shameful, and painful the objects were, they needed to be preserved for their historical value and as a reminder of what had happened to millions of Jews during the Holocaust.

THE JUDENSAU OF WITTENBERG

❰❰ **Luther, who often preached in this church** and knew the sandstone relief on the church well, described it in a 1543 treatise against the Jews as follows: "Here at Wittenberg on our parish church is a sow carved in stone, and lying under her are young piglets and Jews who suckle there. Behind the sow stands a rabbi, who lifts up the sow's right leg and with his left hand pulls the sow's rump toward him, bends down, and with great interest looks at the Talmud under the sow's rump, as if to read and learn something difficult and special" (Brecht 3, 346–7).

Luther scholar Martin Brecht is correct in stressing that Luther's writings about the Jews must not be taken out of context. Like other Protestant Reformation scholars, he also believes that Luther's attitude toward the Jews did not change from the time he wrote his positive tract *That Jesus Christ Was Born a Jew* (1523) and his later anti-Jewish writings. His unfortunate writings about the Jews in his later years, including his shocking comments on the sandstone relief, were no doubt the culmination of his anger against the Jews and disappointment about their unwillingness to accept his Christian message. Some students of Luther have also argued that the reformer's old age and ill health would have contributed to the tone and content of his later writings, including those he wrote against the Jews.

The exact date as to when the *Judensau* relief was placed on the Wittenberg church is not known, but some scholars have determined that it was placed there early in the fourteenth century, perhaps 1305. We know that the choir of the church was completed around 1300 and that the Jews were expelled from Wittenberg in 1304. It is possible that the sculpture was placed there to celebrate or commemorate the expulsion of the Jews from that city (Shachar 30–1). Wittenberg was not the only city that displayed the ugly symbol. The representation of Jews sucking, or sometimes riding, a sow occurs frequently in German sculpture and painting from the thirteenth to the sixteenth century. The vulgar caricature in its various forms was found mostly in German-speaking territories and cities, including Cologne, Erfurt, Basel, Regensburg, Wittenberg, Salzburg, Vienna, and others. Most of the representations were placed in or on church buildings and cathedrals, but some were also seen on bridges and public and private houses, intended to keep Jews from entering Christian places of worship and residences.

Jews in Luther's Time

The cultural–social reasons for Christians' hatred and caricature of Jews are complex. Throughout medieval times the Jews were seen as the people who had killed Christ and who continued to reject the Christian faith (Dietrich 15–59). According to many Christians at the time, including Luther, Jews blasphemed Christ and the Virgin Mary by calling Jesus the son of a whore. Rich Jews were also feared and hated as religious competitors as well as business people who made great profits from usury (excessive taking of interest or profiteering). Many rulers, however, benefited financially from the presence of Jews in their territories; they borrowed money from them and exacted high protection taxes from them. During plagues, like the Black Death in the fourteenth century, Jews were often accused of contaminating wells and placing curses on Christian communities. Jews were often charged with killing Christian children and mixing their blood with the Passover meal. In his anti-Jewish writings Luther repeated such accusations and malicious gossip (Hsia 131–5).

In many European countries Jews were expelled and tortured, and their religious books, synagogues, and houses destroyed (Johnson 233–48). Jews were expelled from England in 1215 and 1290, from France in 1315 and 1348, from Spain in 1492, and from most German free imperial cities and states between 1480 and 1500 (*Oxford Encyclopedia* 1, 54). In the sixteenth century Jews were again expelled from some German cities, including Magdeburg and Regensburg. One of the largest expulsions took place in 1519 in Regensburg at the instigation of the cathedral pastor there, Balthasar Hubmaier (1485–1528), who later converted to Anabaptism and became an influential leader among the Anabaptists. Jews had to leave the city within four days, their synagogue was razed to the ground, and in place of its rubble a "Chapel of the Blessed Mary" was erected (Oberman *Roots* 7, 75–8). In his book *On the Jews and Their Lies*, Luther referred to many of these expulsions with evident approval (LW 47, 266, 272).

The Reformation did not change society's views and feelings toward the Jews much, although the breakup of the Roman Church's monopoly in matters of Christian faith seemed to a certain extent to favour religious dissidents and outsiders. Also, renewed interest in Hebrew studies among reformers and humanists contributed some sympathy toward educated Jews and Hebrew scholars like Johannes Reuchlin (1455–1522), whom Erasmus, Luther, Melanchthon, and others respected greatly. Luther and fellow reformers were sometimes accused by their Catholic opponents of working under the influence of "Judaizers" toward the destruction of the Roman Church (*Oxford Encyclopedia* 2, 339–45). There were Jews who hoped that through Luther's criticism of Rome the Reformation might trigger a conversion of Christians to Judaism. There may have been some grounds for such hope. Luther's writing *Against the Sabbatarians* was about Christians who accepted the Sabbath as part of their faith and is a clear indication that the reformer and other Christians felt religiously threatened by Jewish efforts to make converts among them.

Luther was known for writing harshly against those he opposed and considered his or the Reformations' enemies, including the pope, the radicals, the peasants, the Anabaptists, humanists like Erasmus, and the Turks. Thus Luther's anti-Jewish writings did not seem to overly shock many of his contemporaries. Among Luther's close followers only Justus Jonas, Andreas Osiander, and to a certain extent Luther's right-hand man Philipp Melanchthon, showed sympathy for the Jews and mildly criticized the reformer for his harshness against them. Other fellow reformers agreed with Luther's attitude toward the Jews. Martin Bucer (1491–1551) of Strasbourg, for example, advised Philip of Hesse that if the Jews in his realm continued to reject the Christian faith, they should be forced to perform the most menial and difficult work. Even the Christian humanist Erasmus was not altogether free of anti-Judaism; he expressed the hope that some day Christian Europe might be free of Jews. Hatred of Jews and Judaism was widespread in both Catholic and Protestant society in sixteenth-century Europe.

Luther's Writings Against the Jews

There are those who believe that Luther's views about the Jews changed between 1523, when the reformer wrote his sympathetic tract *That Jesus Christ Was Born a Jew* and some twenty years later in 1543 when he wrote his hard-hitting book *On the Jews and Their Lies*. However, most Luther scholars argue, correctly I think, that the reformer's attitude toward the Jews remained fairly constant. As early as his lectures on the Psalms in 1513–15, Luther asserted that the Jews continued to suffer the wrath of God because they rejected Christ, and that efforts to convert them would be in vain. The Jews, according to these lectures, were blasphemers of Christ and their interpretations of Scripture were lies and must not be tolerated. Luther expressed similar sentiments in 1515–16 in his *Lectures on Romans* (LW 47, 126–7). Martin Bertram observes, "the evidence indicates that the Luther of these earlier years shared to the full in the medieval prejudices against the Jew" (LW 47, 127). This prejudice continued and increased as the reformer became older and more impatient and irritable.

In his 1523 tract *That Jesus Christ Was Born a Jew* it becomes clear that Luther had a missionary motive in writing the piece. He states that if one deals kindly with the Jews "and instructs them carefully from Holy Scripture, many of them will become genuine Christians." The Jews, Luther states, will not believe the Roman Church, but they may well consider the new-found faith of the reformers positively. "Our fools, the popes, bishops, sophists, and monks – the crude asses' heads," he writes, "have hitherto so treated the Jews that anyone who wished to be a good Christian would almost have had to become a Jew. If I had been a Jew and had seen such dolts and blockheads govern and teach the Christian faith, I would sooner become a hog than a Christian" (LW 45, 200). At this time Luther still believed that the Jews were capable of accepting the grace of God, and would turn to him and become Christians.

To teach them in the way of salvation, Luther proceeds to "instruct" the Jews in Old Testament passages that according to his interpretation definitely refer to the coming of the Messiah. For example, the "seed of the woman" in Genesis 3 and Abraham's "seed" in Genesis 22 refer, Luther states, to Christ and to the spiritual Israel, the church, respectively. Luther argues at length that the "young woman who is with child" in Isaiah 7 is a prophecy about the Virgin Mary who will give birth to the man-God Jesus, the Messiah. According to the "seventy weeks" in Daniel 9, Luther writes, the Messiah has actually appeared, after which Jerusalem and its temple were destroyed. After the destruction of Jerusalem by the Romans in AD 70, Jewish life as it had existed until then came to an end. After the destruction of their holy places, according to Luther, the Jews have been without prophets for fifteen hundred years, a sure sign that there is no other Messiah to wait for (228).

To Luther's disappointment and chagrin, however, Jews did not take kindly to the reformer's Christological interpretation of their Scriptures, and there were not many Jews who left Judaism in favour of Christianity. In fact, there is some evidence to suggest that some Jews continued to proselytize among Christians (LW 47, 59–62). Some radical reformers like Oswald Glait and Andreas Fischer, for example, emphasized the importance of the Ten Commandments and included Old Testament practices, such as keeping the Sabbath, in their Christian worship services. These "Sabbatarians," as they were called, were of great concern to both Catholics and Protestants. As Luther wrote in 1535: "In our time there arose in Moravia a foolish kind of people, the Sabbatarians, who maintain that the Sabbath must be observed after the fashion of the Jews." He adds sarcastically, "Perhaps they will insist on circumcision too" (60). In his treatise *Against the Sabbatarians,* published as an open letter in 1538, Luther attacks both the Jews and the Christian Sabbatarians (57–98). Because they have rejected Christ, the Jews, according to Luther, have been abandoned by God: "[It] is evident that [God] has forsaken them, that they can no longer be God's people" (97). According to Luther, "the Jews and their apes, the Sabbatarians," are wrong in their attempts to observe the ceremonial laws of Moses, for with the destruction of Jerusalem and the Jewish exile after that, these laws have come to an end (60).

A new note has come into Luther's thinking: he is apparently becoming convinced that the Jews have been forsaken by God and are no longer God's people. The chill that had come over Luther's attitude toward the Jews in the late 1530s finds crass expression in the reformer's relationship with a well-known and prominent Jewish leader in Strasbourg, Rabbi Josel of Rosheim (ca. 1478–1554). According to Luther's *Table Talks*, Rabbi Josel had written Luther a letter requesting that the Elector of Saxony grant him and other Jews safe entrance and passage through the elector's territory. Luther's response was most unkind and negative: "Why," Luther snapped angrily, "should these rascals, who injure people in body and property and who withdraw many Christians to their superstitions, be given permission? In Moravia they have circumcised many Christians and call them by the new name of Sabbatarians" (61). To Rabbi Josel Luther wrote that in the past he had tried to intercede on behalf of the Jews, but in return the Jews have shamefully misused his kind and friendly services, have not turned to Christ, and do things that Christians simply cannot tolerate (62).

In 1543, just three years before he died, Luther published three treatises concerning the Jews in rapid succession: *On the Jews and Their Lies, On Shem Hamphoras* ("On the Ineffable Name"), and *The Last Words of David.* His writings about the Jews prior to 1543 were largely theological, the writings of a theologian, a Christian pastor, and Bible expositor who not only opposed the Jews' understanding of their Bible, but who also sought to convince them of the rightness of Christianity. Historians like Oberman and Brecht, who argue that Luther's anti-Judaism had little or nothing to do with racism nor with modern anti-Semitism may be right when Luther's earlier writings are taken into account and when his 1543 anti-Jewish pieces are given the most generous reading possible. His anti-Jewish writings of 1543, however, appear, on the surface at least, full of hate and venom, written with a red-hot pen, as it were, by a reformation leader who no longer wished to convert the Jews to the Christian faith, but who demanded that they be expelled from German territory, even killed if necessary (Rose 4–8).

To make its contempt for the Jews most visual, the title page of *On the Jews and Their Lies* had an illustration by the Lutheran artist Lucas Cranach depicting a horned, full-bearded Moses in a fool's dress playing a keyboard instrument. While such pamphlet and cartoon illustrations were commonly used by both Catholic and Protestant contestants to make fun of their enemies and opponents, negative depictions of Jews were designed to hurt an entire people who had suffered throughout the Middle Ages (Shachar 43). Luther, however, was convinced that in writing against the Jews and depicting them as evil people who were ruinous to Germany, he served both his German people and God. He knew that he was severe in his writing against them, but he saw it as a "sharp mercy," a "mercy" that pronounces harsh judgment upon them.

In the first part of *On the Jews and Their Lies* Luther exposes what he considers Jewish lies and boasts about their special status as God's people. They claim to have descended from Abraham, their covenant with God is symbolized in circumcision, they boast of having received the Law of Moses, and that God has given them the land of Canaan, Jerusalem, and the temple. However, the Jews, according to Luther, have lost all this because of their sins and their rejection of Christ. "So it became apparent," Luther states, "that they were a defiled bride, yes, an incorrigible whore and an evil slut with whom God ever had to wrangle, scuffle, and fight" (LW 47, 166).

In the second and third parts of this book Luther speaks of the Jews' blasphemies against Jesus, Mary, and God himself. According to Luther, the Jews do not even believe God who speaks from their own Scriptures. Not only do the Jews blaspheme the Holy Trinity in their homes and synagogues, but they also wish and pray that God might kill their enemies, the gentile Christians. Moreover, the Jews are lying about how they are being treated in the countries where they came to live, accusing Christians of holding them captive and persecuting them. "If you cannot tolerate a person in a country or home," Luther asks, "does that constitute holding him in captivity? In fact they [the Jews] hold us Christians captive in our own country. They let us work in the sweat of our brow to earn money and property while they sit behind the stove, idle away their time, fart, and roast pears [expression for laziness]. They stuff themselves, guzzle, and live in luxury and ease from our hard-earned goods. With their accursed usury they hold us and our property captive" (266).

In the last part of the book Luther asks, "What shall we Christians do with this rejected and condemned people, the Jews?" (268ff.). He makes several recommendations about what is to be done: The Jewish synagogues and schools should be burned and whatever will not burn should be covered with dirt, "so that no man will ever see a stone or cinder of them." Their houses shall be razed to the ground or destroyed. Their prayer books and Talmudic writings, in which such idolatry, lies, cursing, and blasphemy are taught, shall be taken away from them. Their rabbis must be forbidden to teach on pain of loss of limb and life. Luther further advises that Jews be denied safe conduct on the highways, that usury should be prohibited to them, and that all cash, silver, and gold should be taken from them. Luther recommends that young Jews, both male and female, be put to work so that they "earn their bread in the sweat of their brow" and not with usury. When all else fails, as a "final solution" the Jews should be expelled from the country (135).

Luther concludes his hateful book by saying, "If I had power over the Jews, as our princes and cities have, I would deal severely with their lying mouth" (289). "I wish and ask that our rulers who have Jewish subjects exercise a *sharp mercy* [my emphasis] toward these wretched people" (292). As for the ordinary Christian, Luther expresses the hope that his book will provide "enough material not only to defend himself against the blind, venomous Jews, but also to become the foe of the Jews' malice, lying, and cursing, and to understand not only that their belief is false but that they are surely possessed by all devils" (305–6).

After reading *On the Jews and Their Lies*, Rabbi Josel of Rosheim wrote: "Never before has a scholar advocated such tyrannical and outrageous treatment of our people" (135). The rabbi petitioned the magistrates of Strasbourg to prohibit the circulation of the book in that city, a petition that was granted. Although the book did not have large sales, many of Luther's recommendations about what was to be done were carried out by some German rulers. In some territories, including electoral Saxony, the right of safe conduct for Jews was withdrawn, and Elector John Frederick revoked certain concessions he had made to the Jews in 1539; he cited Luther's book as having alerted him to the Jews' wicked designs. Even Philip of Hesse, one of the most tolerant of Lutheran princes, introduced new measures prohibiting Jews from engaging in money-lending and requiring them to attend Christian sermons (135). Fortunately, most authorities were not willing to act upon Luther's recommendations, not because they were more tolerant toward the Jews and felt compassion for them, but because the Jews played an important role in their economy.

Luther reached the depth of vulgarity and obscenity in a tract entitled *On Shem Hamphoras and the Generation of Christ*, written a few months after the publication of *On the Jews and Their Lies*. This tract was intended to refute a medieval Jewish chronicle, *The Book of the Life of Jesus* (in Hebrew, *Sefer Toledot Yeshu*), written in Hebrew and translated into Latin. This chronicle portrays Jesus most negatively, namely, that he was born illegitimate, that he was a heretic, and that he died a disgraceful death. During medieval times and into the Renaissance, this "history" of Jesus became the object of a most acrimonious controversy among Jews, Christians, and atheists. Thus Luther was not the first to use this chronicle as a counterattack against the Jews. Luther's *On Shem Hamphoras* includes translated passages from *Toledot Yeshu* and many references to the *Judensau* motif of Wittenberg which he describes in great detail and mocks the Jews and judaizing Christians in gutter language, as, for eaxample, the following: "Now where are they, the immoral Christians who have or who want to become Jews? Hither! To the kiss! ... the Devil has ... emptied his belly once more. This is a proper sacred relic [that] the Jews, and whoever wants to be Jew, should kiss, gobble up and drink and adore. And in turn, the Devil may gobble up and drink that which his disciples spew out, above and below" (Shachar 43, 86).

Luther then, in the form of questions and answers, explains with biting sarcasm and crude humour the "real" origin and meaning of the Wittenberg *Judensau*. The Jewish rabbis, according to Luther, get their cabbalistic insights about the holy name of God and their interpretation of their holy books, the Talmud, from the sow's behind. "From this, certainly, they got their *Sham hamephorash*." Commenting on the expulsion of Jews from the Wittenberg area some two hundred years earlier, Luther writes: "[I]n the past there have been very many Jews in these lands, as is indicated by the names of hamlets and villages, also of burghers and peasants, which are Hebrew to this day." And with regard to the origin of the *Judensau* relief, Luther states: "[S]ome learned and esteemed man, who was an enemy of the dirty lies of the Jews, had such sculpture made. For the same is said ... among the Germans of one who shows off wisdom without justification: Where has he read this? (To be rude) in the sow's behind." "Explaining" the meaning of *Shem Hamphoras* (the ineffable name), Luther uses a witty word play based on the two words: "This is how the Devil makes fun of the Jews his prisoners, he lets them say *Shem hameforash,* believe in it and hope for great things. But *he* [the devil] means 'Sham haperesh,' meaning [in Hebrew]: 'here is dirt'; not the kind that lies in the streets, but that which comes out of the belly" (Shachar 43–4, 86–7).

Some of Luther's friends and colleagues were embarrassed, shocked, and most critical of the reformer's stooping so low in using such language and imagery to demean the Jews. Melanchthon shook his head in disbelief and exclaimed: "Look at what he is doing now" (Brandler 368). The churches of Zurich prepared a public document, stating that had the treatise been composed "by a swineherd, rather than by a celebrated shepherd of souls, it might have some – but very little – justification" (LW 47, 123).

With regard to Luther's bizarre "interpretation" of the *Judensau*, Isaiah Shachar is no doubt correct when he writes: "There is no need for us to take the interpretation more seriously than its author meant it and turn his joke into a valid explanation of a scene carved more than two centuries earlier." However, it is a sad fact that Luther's writing about the Wittenberg relief, together with his other anti-Jewish writings, were not only taken seriously by many of his followers and some influential Catholic writers, but also used as weapons against the Jews. "Luther's reference to the sow as the Talmud in which the Jews, deceived by the Devil, find their great mysteries, was regarded as profound and authoritative, and learned elaborations soon followed" (Shachar 45). According to Shachar, beginning with one Fabricius, a professor of Hebrew at the University of Wittenberg in the late sixteenth century, many interpeters of the *Judensau* followed Luther's "interpretation" of the relief. Stories, poems, and dramas were written about the *Judensau,* and the motif appeared in books, on broadsheets, and even playing cards. By the eighteenth century, however, representations of this motif declined as an abusive image; it was no longer in good taste. It is interesting to note, however, that even when political and racial anti-Semitism emerged in Germany in the 1860s and 1870s, the obscene caricature was no longer used for propaganda purposes, although abusive and hate-filled labels like "Saujud!" (Jewish pig) persisted until well into the Nazi period (64).

The Jews continued to occupy Luther's thinking and writing to the end of his life. In his tract *Last Words of David,* Luther calls the Jews "children of the devil, who have perverted everything" (LW 15, 344). In 1546, three days before he died, Luther added an "Admonition against the Jews" to the last sermon he preached in Eisleben. In it he stated again that the Jews are open enemies of Christians; that they continue to blaspheme Christ; that they call Mary a whore and Jesus a bastard. And "if they could kill us all," Luther adds, "they would gladly do so. And they often do." Luther concludes, "We want to practice Christian love toward them and pray that they convert." But those who refuse to convert "we should neither tolerate nor suffer among us" (Brecht 3, 350). Luther had only two alternatives for the Jews: they either submit to baptism or else be driven out of the land (Kirn 223).

While Luther's basic views about the Jews remained constant during his lifetime, in the early 1540s his interpretation of Paul's passages in Romans 9–11 about the Jews seemed to change. Eric Gritsch states that, "Luther succumbed to the evil of anti-Semitism through a theological failure of nerve" (McNutt 43). Luther had always taught that God is sovereign in all things, including in the act of salvation, and that human beings do not know whom God foresees, elects, and redeems. But when it came to the Jews, Luther seemed to know that they were not only hardened by God but also rejected by God, which surely went against his earlier theology, hence Gritsch's calling it a "failure of nerve."

Thomas Kaufmann agrees, but goes a step further by showing that with his harsh writings Luther wished to make a personal confession and to "relieve his conscience" about what he had written earlier in favour of the Jews, and which had resulted in their favourable treatmet when the general populace continued to be hostile toward them. As McNutt writes, "Put simply, Luther believed he had been too lenient earlier with such a stubborn people, and his conscience could not bear a passive approach to those who defamed Christ" (McNutt 45).

Martin Brecht refers to the revision of the Luther Bible in 1541 in which the reformer, referring to Romans 11, expressed a more promising view of the Jews. According to Brecht, the Jews are not denied life and the door of grace is not closed to them. According to Paul, the Jews are not to be abandoned entirely and God's mercy remains open to his people. Christians must thus go and preach and baptize both Jews and gentiles, for they do not know what God will do: "Let God alone, we cannot fathom his decree" (Brecht 3, 340). But in Luther's 1543 writings against the Jews the reformer did not seem to "let God be God" but decided that the Jews had been definitively abandoned by God.

As is evident from his writings, Luther carried on his attack against the Jews on two levels, the economic-political level and the moral-religious level. On the economic-political level, he accused the Jews of extorting money from the already severely exploited German people, a financial burden that commoners, especially, had to bear. Luther's accusation endeared him not only to the peasants and craftsmen but also to his Protestant rulers. According to Paul Rose, Luther and his followers knew that Jewish money was enabling Emperor Charles V to proceed against those German princes who had embraced the evangelical faith. While the emperor and the Catholic princes were also concerned about preserving their old faith, the economic and political questions were no doubt of greater importance to them. In fact, it was the political rulers, including the Elector of Saxony, who encouraged Luther to stress the economic factor in his later writings (Edwards, "Luther's Last Battles" 135).

On the moral-religious or theological level, Luther saw the Jews as the worldly agents of the devil, the deadly enemies of the gospel that he and his fellow reformers proclaimed. Being a theologian and religious reformer, the theological concern with the Jews was uppermost in Luther's mind. It is significant that in his writings against the Jews he also included the Christian Sabbatarians who, though not Jews, embraced aspects of the Jewish faith. This seems to agree with Oberman, Brecht, and other defenders of the reformer, that the nature of Luther's writings against the Jews, while harsh and anti-Christian, was more theological than racial. As Martin Brecht writes: "In advising the use of force [Luther] advocated means that were incompatible with his faith in Christ.... Luther, however, was not involved with later racial anti-Semitism. There is a world of difference between his belief in salvation and a racial ideology. Nevertheless, his misguided agitation had the evil result that Luther fatefully became one of the 'church fathers' of anti-Semitism and thus provided material for the modern hatred of Jews, cloaking it with the authority of the Reformer" (Brecht 3, 351).

Luther and the Holocaust

As noted earlier, there are those who think that after the Holocaust it is almost impossible to comment objectively on Luther's writings about the Jews, especially those who believe that Luther's concerns and writings were of religious and theological and had little to do with economic and social issues, and certainly not with racial anti-Semitism. According to this view, Luther contended for the Christian faith, opposing the Jews because of their unwillingness to accept the Christian religion and for posing a threat to the church and his Christological view of the Bible. While Luther's language against the Jews may have been unworthy of a Christian pastor and theologian, the reformer, unfortunately, often expressed himself harshly, violently, and vulgarly against his opponents.

However, Luther's writings about the Jews had a *Wirkungsgeschichte,* a historical legacy, that continued until well into the first half of the twentieth century when the *Shoah,* the Holocaust, happened. Luther's anti-Jewish writings were used for anti-Jewish ideological and political purposes. In 1570, for example, a Lutheran pastor, G. Nigrinus, used his tract *Der Judenfeind* to promote anti-Jewish politics. In 1577, Nikolaus Selnecker, promoter of a strict Lutheranism, published a new edition of Luther's anti-Jewish writings to warn Christians against the enemies of the endtimes, Jews, Calvinists, and "enthusiasts." And in 1613 and 1617, when the Jews were driven out of Frankfurt on the Main and Worms, Luther's late anti-Jewish writings were again republished (Kirn 223). In the age of Enlightenment, Jews enjoyed more freedom and respect, although it was still hoped that Jews would convert to Chistianity. After the 1870s, however, during the emergence of racial anti-Semitism, Jews again became targets of violent anti-Jewish propaganda, which reached its height under National Socialism (Nazism) in the 1930s (224).

While Luther's anti-Judaic writings cannot be seen as a direct cause of the Holocaust, they were nevertheless used by anti-Semites in their propaganda against German Jews and as a justification for their destruction. In a sermon of 1539, Luther was already using ominous words that could later be used to justify killing Jews: "I cannot convert the Jews. Our Lord Jesus Christ did not succeed in doing so; but I can close their mouths so that there will be nothing for them to do but lie upon the ground" (Rose, 351). These ambiguous terms, while no doubt metaphorical, are open to a physical interpretation. For later anti-Semites and the Nazi criminals such terms were only too gladly used in quoting the German reformer as being in favour of eliminating the Jewish people in territories under German control. Luther's anti-Jewish writings were certainly intended by him to lead to the death of Judaism as a religious faith; but in the 1930s these writings lent support to Germany's genocidal policy, resulting in the destruction of Jews simply because they were Jews. It is of significance to note, that when synagogues were destroyed and Jews were harassed and killed during *Reichskristallnacht* (the night of broken glass) of November 9–10, 1938, considered the prelude to the Holocaust, a leading Protestant churchman, Bishop Martin Sasse, approved of the Nazis' action and wrote: "On November 10, 1938, on Luther's birthday, the synagogues are burning in Germany." The German people, he urged, ought to heed the writings "of the greatest antisemite of his time, the warner of his people against the Jews" (Goldhagen 111).

Paul Rose writes, "as the first great national prophet of Germany and the forger of the German language itself, Luther ... shaped the overwhelming pejorative, indeed demonic, significance of the word *Jude* [Jew]. Through the influence of Luther's language and tracts, a hysterical and demonizing mentality entered the mainstream of German thought and discourse" (Rose 7–8). This may be an exaggeration, but there is no doubt that in Hitler's Germany a demonizing mentality developed that made "the final solution" possible. Whether there would have been a Holocaust without Luther's anti-Jewish writings cannot be known, but that Luther's writings contributed to and justified violent anti-Semitism among Hitler's henchmen cannot be denied. Considering that anti-Judaism and anti-Semitism were prevalent throughout Europe and that Jews were both ridiculed and hated in many other countries, it is irresponsible to focus on Germany alone and on Luther in particular. To be sure, there was anti-Semitism in Germany as well as elsewhere in Europe prior to the 1930s, but it was Hitler and his cohorts who through their ideology and propaganda were able to mobilize this evil and use it for the destruction of the Jews.

At this point it might be useful to ask how much the German people knew about Luther's anti-Judaic writings before Hitler's coming to power in 1933. It appears that in the 1930s there were many churchgoing Lutherans who did not know about Luther's writings against the Jews, including some prominent clergymen and theologians. According to a recent biography of Dietrich Bonhoeffer, for example, both Bonhoeffer and his friend Eberhard Bethke, both committed Lutherans and opponents of the Nazi regime, "were unaware of the anti-Semitic ravings of Luther." Biographer Eric Metaxas writes, "It was only when the arch-anti-Semite propagandist Julius Streicher (1885–1946) [publisher of the Nazi newpaper *Der Stürmer*] began to publish and publicize them that they became generally known. It must have been shocking and confusing for devout Lutherans like Bonhoeffer to learn of these writings. But because he was so intimately familiar with everything else Luther had written, Bonhoeffer most likely dismissed the anti-Semitic writings as ravings of a madman, unmoored from his own past beliefs" (Metaxas 94).

Certainly, the average Lutheran Church member did not know much, if anything, about Luther's writings about the Jews. Some of Luther's works, including the ten-volume edition of *Luthers Werke* (1905), did not include any of Luther's anti-Jewish writings. Did the editors feel that these writings portrayed the reformer in too negative a light or that they would not edify faithful church members? (cf. Werke 4, 119). Be that as it may, for the Jewish people who suffered as Jews during the Holocaust it did not matter whether Luther's writings against them were "theological" or "proto anti-Semitic" in nature, or whether many or few people in Germany even knew of them. The fact is, they were used by the Nazis to justify their crimes against them – and they remain to this day a shameful blot on Luther's reputation as a Christian reformer.

It might be added that it was not only the "German Christians" who supported the National Socialist policies and shared their anti-Semitism. The modern descendants of the radical reformers, who in the sixteenth century were condemned and persecuted by both Catholics and Protestants, also became guilty of collaboration in the "final solution." Historians have shown that some Mennonites in Germany and Russia both sympathized with the Nazis' actions against the Jews and took part in their elimination. Barbara Beuys expresses sadness that even the followers of the peaceful Menno Simons, the Mennonites in Germany, not only welcomed and were jubilant about the rise of Hitler, but also officially expressed their support, including to go to war and die for the Führer (Beuys 528–9). Gerhard Rempel, in a recent research paper, has shown that some Mennonites in Germany and Ukraine were not only sympathetic to Hitler and his regime, but also collaborated with the Nazis in eliminating Jews during the Second World War (Rempel; see also Foth). Tragically, the devil of anti-Judaism and anti-Semitism that assaulted Martin Luther also affected many of his Christian followers through the centuries.

The Cross and the Crescent
Luther Opposes the Turks and Islam

THE TURKISH THREAT

During the time of the Reformation, the Ottoman Turks continued their advance through southeastern Europe, causing western Christendom much fear and anxiety. Under their leader Süleyman I, the Magnificent, the longest reigning sultan of the Ottoman Empire (1520 to his death in 1566), the Turks occupied Luther's mind throughought his career as a reformer. In his *Table Talks* Luther frequently spoke about the Turkish threat as one of the signs of the apocalyptic end he anticipated soon. In 1529 Vienna was besieged by the Ottoman Turks, their farthest advance into southeastern Europe. In 1532 Luther followed the news of the Turkish advances in Hungary. When the Catholic King Ferdinand of Austria suffered losses of territories, and then in 1537 an ignominious defeat at the hands of the Turks, Luther was certain that God was punishing him for opposing the Protestant Reformation. Luther advised his elector to contribute military assistance to fight the Turks, but he did not think that King Ferdinand deserved much help because he was incompetent and incapable of defeating the enemy. Instead, Luther advised that people pray, as Martin Brecht observes, "that God's punishment would be limited and not lead to a breakdown of the political order or to a religious war in Germany, as the pope wanted. In these circumstances God alone could help, and only the evangelicals [Protestants] were able to pray to him in hopes that he would hear them" (Brecht 3, 352).

Both the pope and Emperor Charles V were naturally expected to wage war against the Turks, but other prominent individuals at the time disagreed for various reasons. For some critics such combined action and cooperation between the church and the empire was reminiscent of the bloody and unholy crusades of past centuries. Ulrich von Hutten (1488–1523), scholar, poet, reformer, and outspoken critic of the Roman Church, for example, was against the pope participating in a war against the Turks. He believed that the politics of the popes in the past had prevented the German emperors from achieving notable successes in the crusades, eventually resulting in the loss of the Holy Land. Erasmus, in his *On War Against the Turks* (1530), made suggestions similar to Luther's, that before rushing into war against the Turks, whom he called "half-Christian" barbarians, Christians should fight the "Turks" within their own ranks and see the Turks as God's anger and punishment for their many sins which called for repentance (Rummel 315–33).

The Anabaptists were, in principle, against Christians participating in any war. The position of some of their leaders on the Turks is both interesting and significant in that it contrasts and agrees in part with Luther's view of church and state. When Michael Sattler (1490–1527), a prominent leader of the Swiss and South German Anabaptists, was tried for heresy by the Roman Catholic authorities in 1527, he was accused, among other things, of speaking against going to war against the Turks. In his defence Sattler stated: "For it is written: Thou shalt not kill. We must not defend ourselves against the Turks and others of our persecutors, but are to beseech God with earnest prayer to repell and resist them." Sattler then added boldly: "But that I said that, if warring *were* right, I would rather take the field against so-called Christians who persecute, capture, and kill pious Christians than against the Turks was for the following reasons. The Turk is a true Turk, knows nothing of the Christian faith, and is a Turk after the flesh. But you who would be Christians and make your boast of Christ persecute the pious witnesses of Christ and are Turks after the spirit!"

(Williams and Mergal 141). That sealed Sattler's fate as a heretic and he was condemned to die at the stake, which was carried out in 1527.

Luther was not a pacifist, but he was cautious in his pronouncements about fighting the Turks. In 1517 he opposed the papal indulgences and criticized the raising of crusade taxes because they extracted money from Germany, not for fighting the Turks but simply to fill the coffers of the papacy. Moreover, he spoke of the popes who dream of warring against the Turks but at the same time were not willing to deal with their own sins, or see the Turkish threat as a punishment from God. In his 1520 bull *Exsurge Domine*, Leo X, according to Luther, deliberately falsified the reformer's meaning about the Turks, namely that to fight them was against God who is punishing the church through them (Raeder 226). Luther was not against fighting the Turks, but against *ecclesiastical* leadership in the war, as happened during the crusades for centuries when the popes actually led in the wars against the "infidels" (Jensen 234).

In 1523 Luther wrote his treatise *Temporal Authority: To What Extent It Should Be Obeyed* (Werke 7, 223ff.) in which he speaks of the two realms or kingdoms, the spiritual and the temporal. Christians who are part of the spiritual kingdom must live and act according to the gospel and Christian love, but as members of a secular society Christians, according to Romans 13, must obey their governments, who at times must use the sword to protect their subjects against aggressors and to punish the wicked. In his 1526 tract *Whether Soldiers, Too, Can be Saved* (Werke 7, 383ff.), Luther justifies Christians going to war against aggressors. In doing so, a Christian fulfills Christ's commandment of love for one's neighbour in that he fights and possibly dies for his neighbour. About going to war against the Turks, Luther notes at the end of this tract that the time has not yet come for him to write against the Turks. After the Battle of Mohacs in 1526, the Turks had withdrawn and the immediate threat to Christendom had eased somewhat. But Luther leaves no doubt that the time will come for him to address the Turkish threat and that he will urge Christians to go to war against the Ottoman empire.

In addition to his frequent references to the Turks in his *Table Talks* and letters to individuals, Luther wrote three tracts about the Turks: *War Against the Turks* (1529), *War Sermon Against the Turks* (1529), and an *Appeal for Prayer Against the Turks* (1541). Generally, Luther was opposed to waging wars against the Turks. Like other thinkers at the time, he knew that in the past Christians had organized crusades against Islam under the banners of both the church and the states, a situation that not only expressed the corruption and wordliness of the papal church, but also brought about the slaughter of many Muslims' lives, which was contrary to the gospel, especially Jesus's Sermon on the Mount (Werke 7, 435). However, while Luther was against religious and holy crusades, he nevertheless believed and taught that all Christians should support their rulers, even going to war for them against their enemies –*not as Christians in a holy war*, but as subjects of their secular princes who were responsible for maintaining law and order and for protecting their subjects and lands.

In all his writings about the Turks, Luther saw the Turks as agents of God's punishment of sinful and wordly Christianity and as "black devils" who, together with the papal Antichrist, signalled the end of the age. Luther never expressed any hope that the Christian West would ever win the war against the Turks. All Christians could do is to pray for the Turkish people, possibly testify to them about Christ, fight against them alongside other Christians for their princes and the emperor when called upon to do so – but they should never think that they are fighting in a religious war. This kind of separation of church and state in matters of war seems new in the sixteenth century, coming close to what the Anabaptists believed and practised, except that Anabaptists like Michael Sattler rejected participation in *any* war altogether.

WARS AGAINST THE TURKS

❡ **In a letter of October 9, 1528,** Luther dedicated and sent his tract against the Turks to the Landgrave Philip of Hesse, but the printing of the treatise was delayed and not published until March 1529. In the dedicatory letter, Luther mentions the reasons for writing against the Turks at this time. "About five years before," he writes, "some had asked me to write against the Turks and to urge our people to fight them. And now that the Turks are coming closer, my friends too are urging me to write, especially since there are clumsy [*ungeschickte*] preachers among our Germans, as I unfortunately hear, who make the rabble believe that one should not fight against the Turks; there are even some so mad [*toll*] as to teach that it is inappropriate for Christians to wield the temporal sword" (Werke 7, 438). In addition, Luther observes, there are people who actually believe that to live under Turkish rule would be preferable, and that he, Luther, is blamed for such a misconception. People thus look for an occasion to blaspheme the Holy Spirit and the known truth, for which they deserve to go to hell and not to receive forgiveness for their sins. Luther concludes the letter by stating that he dedicates the treatise to his "famous and powerful prince," the Landgrave Philip of Hesse, so that the booklet may find a wide readership and prepare people if it should come to a campaign against the Turks.

The treatise appeared at the end of April 1529, and less than half a year later, in September, Vienna was besieged by the Ottoman Turks. Luther knew that the situation for Christian Europe looked grim. To add to his pessimism about the political and military situation, there were the quarrels and disunity among European rulers and the developing alliance between Francis I of France and Süleyman the Magnificent. Luther's treatise thus appeared at a time when both the evangelicals and the Protestant rulers needed advice from the reformer as to how to think and what to do about the serious threat from the non-Christian East.

Luther begins his booklet *On War Against the Turks* (Werke 7, 433–91) with a reference to Pope Leo X, who condemned him in 1517 for saying that fighting the Turks is the same as resisting God, who punishes us for our sins. Luther admits that at the time he had written about not fighting the Turks, but the accusations of the papists were made out of context and without any reference to what he, Luther, actually believed about their spiritual and temporal powers and their obligations in society. In the meantime, Luther states, he had written on temporal authority (1523) and what the obligations of secular princes were. In fact, Luther prides himself that no one since the time of the apostles, except perhaps St. Augustine, had written so clearly as he about the duties and privileges of the temporal powers. Even his late prince, Frederick the Wise, Luther adds, had valued the booklet so highly that he had made a copy of it for himself (Werke 7, 440–1).

Luther had dealt clearly with how a Christian was to live in the two kingdoms. Among other things, as Christians they are not to resist evil, and they are to endure all things, give away all property, and not take revenge or retaliate when personally injured. However, the duty of temporal governments is to protect their subjects and lands, with force if necessary, something that Christians *as* Christians cannot do. They would rather suffer than go to war and shed Turkish blood. The popes and the cardinals, according to Luther, had never seriously intended to fight the Turks; they used the Turkish danger to rob Germany of money by selling indulgences. Had they been serious about the Turkish threat, they could have gone to war themselves and used their own means and resources (442). What concerned Luther most was that a "Christian army" was urged to go to war against the Turks, which was against the teaching of Christ. For popes and bishops to preach war against the Turks puts Christ to great shame and dishonour, for the church is called upon to fight the devil only with God's Word and prayer. The church is forbidden, Luther writes, to fight with the sword against flesh and blood. Like Christ, who rejected an earthly crown, Christians are not to kill in war but to preach and care for souls. The two callings or offices, the spiritual and the temporal, Luther stresses, need to be kept strictly separate (444–5).

Luther then asks how well Christians have actually succeeded in their past wars against the Turks. In fact, Luther states, they have now lost almost all of Hungary and much of the German territories besides. If Christians will not learn from Scriptures about how to live and act, they will need to learn from the "Turks' scabbard" until they learn to their own hurt that Christians are not to make war or resist evil. Fools must be taught with clubs! Luther has heard from soldiers that when they went to war in the name of the church and its bishops, they were thoroughly beaten by their enemy. If he were a soldier and saw a priest fighting beside him, Luther states, he would run as though the devil were chasing him. Even a wicked pope like Pope Julius II (1503–1513) did not succeed militarily and had to call on Emperor Maximilian to take charge of the war, despite the fact that Julius had more money, arms, and people then the emperor. And Pope Clement, whom people considered a god of war, in the end lost Rome and all his wealth on May 6, 1527. Luther's conclusion is that Christ teaches Christians not to make war. Instead, Christians become hardened and unrepentant until they are defeated and destroyed – to which Luther says a hearty "Amen, Amen!" (448).

HOW TO WAGE WAR AGAINST THE TURKS

❦ **As the foregoing has made clear,** Luther was not a pacifist nor was he in principle against going to war against enemies, but he wanted to make it perfectly clear that the church and Christians have no business waging war or shedding blood per se. The church's function is to use its resources to relieve the plight of the poor and needy, to preach the gospel, and to care for the souls of its members. So if the church, the pope, or the bishops ask Christians to go to war under their *Christian banner*, then, Luther quips, they should run away and say, "I do not know this coin." But if, on the other hand, the banner is that of the Emperor Charles V or of a prince to whom subjects have sworn their obligatory allegiance, the Christian subjects must obey and go to war under the command of their *temporal* rulers (Werke 7, 448).

But before Luther exhorts Christians to go to war against the Turks, he will teach them how to fight with a good conscience. In the first place, he states, it is certain that the Turks do not have the right to attack lands that do not belong to them. Such aggression is nothing but an outrage and robbery with which God is punishing the world. The Turks do not fight from necessity or to protect their own land, but like pirates, robbers, and highwaymen. Second, whoever goes to war against the Turks must be sure that God is calling him and that he truly lives as a Christian. He must not enlist for the sake of personal revenge or for some other reason, so that, win or lose, "he may be found in a state of grace" (449).

There are two supreme commanders in this war against the Turks, Luther explains: one commander's name is "Christianus" (Christian), and the other is called "Emperor Carolus" (Charles V). In a curiously realistic twist of logic, Luther argues that since the Turks are God's punishment of Christians, and that the Turks' lord is the devil, it is only Christianus, "that is, the pious, holy, dear body of Christians," who is armed to defeat the devil. The devil cannot be beaten with armour, guns, horses, or men. Only God, through the Christians, who have repented for their sins to avert God's punishment, can beat the devil and ultimately perhaps the Turks as well. Luther fears that if the devil, who is the Turks' god, is not beaten first, the Turks will not easily be defeated (450).

This war then must begin with repentance and reformed lives among Christians, Luther continues, or else they will fight in vain. The reformer then cites many examples from the Old Testament where God's people repented, cried to God for help against their enemies, and then God often heard them and helped. Since the war against the Turks is also a spiritual battle, prayer, Christian living, and witnessing about Christ are necessary. Luther gives examples of how Christians living under Islam or in Turkish captivity are deprived of their freedom to worship or witness to their Christian faith, all the more reason to consider the war against the Turks as a spiritual struggle, because the Turks' religion is a spiritual matter as well (454).

MOHAMMEDAN BELIEFS

⟪ **First,** Luther speaks about the faith of the originator of Islam, Mohammed (570–632), who wrote the Mohammedans' Bible, the Koran, calling it a foul and shameful book. However, in time Luther intends to translate the Koran into German. Mohammed, according to Luther, praises Jesus and his mother Mary as biblical figures on the one hand, but on the other he considers Jesus as just another prophet, like Jeremiah or Jonah, and denies that he is the Son of God, nor does he believe that Christ is the world's saviour. Christ's work ended with his death, according to the Koran, and now it is the prophet Mohammed whose task it is to carry his faith to the rest of the world. If, however, people reject the Mohammedan faith they become the enemies of Islam and will be destroyed. Anyone can see, Luther states, that Mohammed is a destroyer of Christ and his kingdom. Islam's faith is a patchwork of three religions, according to Luther: Judaism, Christianity, and paganism. From Christianity Mohammed gets the story of Jesus, the apostles, and the saints; from Judaism he gets their dietary laws about not drinking wine, and fasting on certain days. The largest part of Islam's religion comes from paganism. Luther expresses surprise that some people believe and accept such a blasphemous religious faith (Werke 7, 458).

Second, the Koran teaches that not only the Christian faith is to be destroyed, but also the temporal governments, and that occupying Christian lands and killing Christians is considered a noble work. The Turkish faith has not made its progress by preaching and working miracles, as in the Christian gospels, but by the sword and killing, and its success has been due to the wrath of God against sinful Christians (460). The fanatics of old and in more recent times, Luther states, were also driven by the "spirit of lies and murder" and influenced Christians to do evil. Luther refers to the Arians and Donatists in St. Augustine's time, and to Thomas Müntzer, who sought to "become a new Turkish emperor" in more recent times. Even the popes and archbishops of the church, according to Luther, became worldly lords and practised killing and murder by setting kings and princes against each other. Why? Luther's answer: "Because the spirit of lies never acts in any other way" (461).

Third, the Koran thinks nothing of marriage, but permits men to take many wives. In Turkey women are held immeasurably cheap and are despised, even bought and sold like cattle. Not all Turks make use of this polygamous marriage practice, Luther admits, but anyone can do it if he wishes. Such a law of marriage is not true marriage because there is no intention of staying together for always, as Genesis 2:24 commands: "The man shall cleave to his wife and the two are one flesh." Luther mocks the Turks by saying that their men like the "chaste life" of soldiers who live with their harlots; for Turks are soldiers and they must live like soldiers: "Mars and Venus, the poets say, want to be together" (463).

Luther says that he has learned these three points about Islam's faith and practices from the Koran; he will not report on what else he has heard about the Turks from other sources, for he is not sure whether they are true. But he has also heard that some Muslims are faithful, friendly, and honest people. No doubt they also have other virtues, for no person is so bad that there is not some good in them. But then the devil can hide in a cloak and appear as an angel of light, thus easily deceiving good people into believing that even Turks live virtuous lives; and in many instances the Turks are better people than Christians. They do not keep and worship images, for example, and they even go to war with the battle cry "Allah! Allah!" which in essence means that they do all things in the name of God. Yet while they call upon God to help them in their battle against Christians, they destroy Christ and all of God's words and works (465).

Luther concludes that he wanted to say all this to the First Commander named "Christianus," namely the community of Christians. Christians must know how much need there is for prayer. They must also first destroy the Turks' Allah, that is the devil, thus destroying his might and divinity. Christians do not fight the Turks with just carnal weapons, as the pope and his people do and teach. Christians recognize the Turks as God's rod and wrath and must then fight them spiritually with tears, repentance, and prayer (466).

THE EMPEROR MUST LEAD THE WAR

⁋ **In a war against the Turks,** it is the Second Commander, Emperor Charles V, who must lead his troops under his banner and in his name only. To obey the emperor is to obey God. Whoever dies under his banner dies in a good and spiritual state, for the emperor and the princes are there to protect their subjects, not to fight the Turks just because they are not Christians. The emperor's sword has nothing to do with faith, but only with temporal things and statecraft. People must remember the great suffering that Christians in the past have caused by crusading against Islam (Werke 7, 469).

Luther laments the fact that kings and princes do not seem to take the Turkish threat all that seriously. They must remember that these enemies are powerful and that no one is able to resist them, unless God works a miracle. But God will not help with a miracle unless Christians seriously change their ways and honour God's Word. Moreover, in going to war, the emperor and princes must not seek their own gain, but must humbly pray to God that he might help them. And when they succeed they must give God the credit and honour. But Luther is not all that confident that the emperor and princes, to say nothing of the common soldiers, will mend their sinful ways, seek God in prayer, humble themselves, and give God alone the honour and glory in their undertaking. What is more, Luther knows that there are German people who welcome the coming of the Turks because they think that their life under them would be better than under the emperor or under their own princes. To confront the Turks with such traitors in the Christian ranks would be nothing short of disastrous. Pastors and preachers need to exhort and instruct their people about the great danger in which they find themselves and the wrong they are doing, including the great sin of disobeying their divinely instituted governments. Anyone who willingly turns away from his overlord and takes the side of the Turks can never do so with a good conscience (475–6). Even worse, such people then make themselves partakers of all the abominations and wickedness of the Turks and become blasphemers of Christ and his gospel. It is far better to die in obedience to one's emperor or overlord than to become a willing subject of the Turks. Such traitors, Luther warns, will not fare well among the Turks, but will become their slaves.

Interestingly, Luther compares the popes to the Turks. Both are evil and godless, but the popes at least have no weapons to attack their enemies with, and must rely on the emperor and princes to do their dirty work for them, as it were. No doubt thinking of his own war against the papacy, Luther says that "Sir Christian," that is, the Christian people, has been aroused against the popes because of their errors and wickedness and therefore now attacks them boldly with prayer and God's Word. The papacy, according to Luther, has now been wounded and the axe is laid to the papal tree. The tree must now be uprooted before it bears bad fruit (483).

Luther expresses pessimism about defeating the Ottoman Turks because of the disunity and divisions that exist within the Christian ranks. But his pessimism turns to hope, for the Turkish threat heralds a new day, namely the apocalypse, and Christ will at last establish his own kingdom. The Turk is in fact the "Empire's token of farewell," a parting gift to the Roman Empire (484). But this does not leave the emperor off the hook yet, for he must still do all he can to protect his subjects by fighting and checking the Turkish advances and holding them off as long as possible (485). Luther is clearly on the emperor's side and is angry with the kings and princes who are unwilling to fight in the emperor's ranks, instead seeking their own gain. According to Luther, they deserve the same punishment that the peasants received in 1525 when they rebelled against their feudal overlords.

Luther concludes his treatise by trying to impress his readers with how powerful the Turks are and that they need to be taken seriously. The Turks, according to Luther, have among their people many friends and more land and resources than all the Christian states put together. If the Christian kings and princes were to agree among themselves, unite, form a sizable force, and call upon God for help, the emperor would be equal to the Turkish forces, all of which would give Luther much hope (489). But Luther is certain that "the Turk is at our throat," whether he will come this year or later, he will surely come. Yet at the Diet of Speyer (1529), Luther laments, the princes, instead of dealing with the pressing issue of the Turkish threat, were discussing religious matters and about how they could "harrass Luther and the gospel," which is none of their business. But for his part, Luther, by writing this booklet against the Turks, has cleared his conscience and told his Germans the truth and what to do. It may well be, Luther concludes, that this will be the end and usher in the Last Judgment, and Christ will "smite both the Turks and the pope, together with the tyrants and all the godless, and deliver us from all sins and all evil! Amen" (490-1).

SÜLEYMAN THE MAGNIFICENT

❦ **There is an interesting story** about what the sultan thought of Luther and his writings against the Ottoman Turks. At the end of his treatise Luther had a comment to the effect that if his book were to come before the sultan, he, Luther, would certainly not find a "gracious lord" in him (491). In a footnote to this comment, there is a story first told by Luther scholar Julius Köstlin, according to which a certain person by the name of Schmalz, who had been to Turkey with a western delegation, had said in 1532 that the sultan had asked about Luther's person and age. When told that Luther was forty-eight years old, the sultan had apparently replied: "I wish he were still younger, for he would find in me a gracious lord." When Luther was informed about what the sultan had said, he made a cross, no doubt expressing horror, and exclaimed, "May God deliver me from this gracious lord."

The last Luther heard about the negotiations between the Christian West and the Turkish East was that the emperor in October 1545 had ceded Hungary to the Turks and then concluded an armistice with the sultan. Luther was disappointed and angry, especially when he heard about the various negotiations that had preceded the armistice. He wrote to some friends in July 1545: "Just listen to this, if you still don't know it: the pope, the emperor, the French and [King] Ferdinand sent a glorious delegation with expensive gifts to the peace negotiations with the Turks!" Luther then continues, no doubt sarcastically: "And what is most beautiful, honourable, and worthy of an eternal memory is this: they [the western delegates] took off their own clothes, and after Turkish custom put on and decorated themselves with long gowns. These are those [people] who till now decried the Turks as enemies of the Christian name, extorted money [from Christians] to fight them, and excited the world against the Turks.... O you Christians, no, more than that, you hellish and devil's images! Don't you see that the empire's destruction and the day of our salvation is approaching? Let us be happy and rejoice! The end of the world has come. God be praised from everlasting to everlasting! Amen." Grisar calls the story a "fable" (Grisar 495). Perhaps it is, but it certainly rings true!

WAR SERMON AGAINST THE TURKS

❴ **As with almost everything else in Luther's life and work,** his thinking on the Turkish problem was theological in nature. While Luther's writings about the Turks had an effect on the politics of his day, the reformer was not a politician nor did he lay any claim to political expertise in statecraft. He saw the Turks and their threat to Christendom as a Christian and as a student of the Bible. But he interpreted the Bible in the light of his understanding of the religious and political situations of his time. And for him the religious and political situations related to what he considered were the greatest threats to Christianity and the gospel, namely Roman Catholicism and Islam, which for him were the visible signs of the endtime.

Soon after the siege of Vienna in 1529, Luther published a tract entitled *War Sermon Against the Turks* (1529). What in the *War Against the Turks* were some occasional and general comments become in this tract a main theme, namely that the Turks and the Roman Church are the two anti-Christian forces of the endtime (Raeder 229–30). In line with the medieval interpretation of the Prophet Daniel, Luther saw the four beasts in Daniel 7 as four successive empires: the Babylonian, the Medo-Persian, the Macedonian of Alexander the Great and his successors, and the Roman (WA 30, 2). The ten horns of the fourth beast embody the ten kingdoms of the Roman Empire. The small horn that appears among the ten horns and subdues three horns represents, according to Luther, Mohammed's reign, which now included Egypt, Greece, and Asia. The ten eyes of the small horn, Luther explains, represent the Koran, in which there is no divine eye but only human reason. The horn, according to Daniel, will change the times and the law, which for Luther means changing the gospel and Christian teaching. The mouth of this horn speaks words against the Most High, which Luther sees as the terrible blasphemies of Mohammed, who sets himself up above Christ. Like the horn in Daniel that persecutes the saints, so the Turks persecute Christians. However, after many victories, the Turks will not be able to conquer the Roman Empire before the Day of Judgment arrives (Raeder 229).

For Luther it is important that in fighting the Turks Christians need to enter the war with a truly Christian attitude. With such a godly attitude, Luther assures Christian soldiers, whoever kills a Turk can be certain that he has killed an enemy and blasphemer of God. For Luther this is not a return to the ideology of crusading. As we have seen, he rejects war against the Turks in the name of Christianity. However, whoever dies in such a war now, dies as a martyr in obedience to God's commandment. Even little children who are cruelly killed by the Turks become saints. Luther then turns to the Christians who are or might become prisoners of the Turks. To prepare for possible imprisonments among the Turks, Christians should memorize the Ten Commandments, the Lord's Prayer, and the Confession of Faith so as to be able to withstand the teachings of Islam and remain faithful to Christ.

Luther then speaks of the fascination that some Christians have for Muslims. The spiritual leaders of the Turks lead such commendable lives, that the lifestyle of some Christian priests and monks seems like a joke in comparison. The prayer sessions of the Turks, for example, are disciplined, quiet, and beautiful. But then it is better, according to Luther, to have less order in Christian worship than more beautiful gestures without faith; it is certainly better to have less prayer in faith than many prayers without faith. The Turkish lifestyle, Luther states, is marked by integrity and honesty: "They don't drink wine, don't booze and gobble [*saufen und fressen*] as we do, don't dress so frivolously ... don't build [their houses] so lavishly ... don't curse so much ... and keep their outward life in order the way we in Germany would like to have it" (230). Luther also finds words of praise for the Turks' family life and sobriety, but then adds that it is better to be in Christ and drink wine moderately and be happy, than to live soberly without Christ.

When Sultan Süleyman occupied the larger part of Hungary in 1541, Germany feared another attack would follow. Luther now wrote another piece on the Turks, *An Appeal for Prayer Against the Turks* (1541). Historian Mark U. Edwards may be right in stating that in all his writings against the Turks the reformer's primary target was not the Turks but the popes (CCL 202). Indeed, for Luther the Turks and the papacy were the enemies of Christ in two incarnations, as it were. As he wrote, "If we fall under the Turk, we go to the Devil;

if we remain under the pope, we go to hell" (Brady 362). Nevertheless, Luther is also concerned about Christians who find themselves prisoners in Turkish lands and thus seeks to comfort them. He writes that in the willing services of Christians among the Turks, he sees a wordless form of witness for Christ. However, at no time ought Christians agree to render the Turks military assistance in their war against the West. The Catholic critics, on the other hand, faulted Luther and the Lutherans for not doing enough to assist in the defence against the Turks.

CONCLUDING OBSERVATIONS

Perhaps because Luther saw the Turks as God's punishment of wicked Christendom and a clear sign of the coming Last Judgment, he did not believe that the West could prevail against their might. What is ironic, perhaps even contradictory, is that he nevertheless urged that the emperor and the princes prepare for and wage war against the Turks. When the western allies failed to fight the Turks and eventually negotiated what Luther believed to be an inglorious peace treaty, he was disappointed and angry. For Luther this reflected not only on the miserable weakness and disunity among the western allies, but also on his belief in a great and majestic God. No wonder Luther was both depressed toward the end of his life and believed that the end of the age was at hand. Nevertheless, as we have seen, Luther was also happy to see that the Day of the Lord and of salvation was at hand.

Though not a politician, Luther was a realist and deeply immersed in the political issues of the day. Both the spiritual and the earthly aspects of life were for him part of God's overall plan and design. However, his working so hard at trying to convince the western allies of the need to stem the tide of the Turkish advance seems inconsistent with Luther's view of God's hidden will and foreknowledge, according to which all things are predestined and cannot be changed by humans. But then Luther might of course reply that since humans do not know God's *hidden* will they must do all they can to do what is right and pray that they might obey God's *revealed* will in Scripture. And the revealed will in Scripture is known or should be known to the church, namely that Christians must resist evil and godlessness.

The booklets on the Turks are not only Luther's encouragement for Christians to fight the Turks and to comfort those who found themselves in Turkish captivity, but also an instructive summary of what he believed were the responsibilities of the two sides in the spiritual and temporal kingdoms. In the past, the church and the empire united in the crusades to fight the Turks. Luther believed that Christians had no business going to war and shedding blood *as* Christians. It was the temporal powers' duty to protect their territitories and subjects from aggression, or rebellion, fight in just wars, and lead their subjects under the imperial banner. Luther had not changed this view throughout his career. Luther even justified his harsh tract on killing the rebellious peasants on the basis of his view of the two distinct kingdoms. The Anabaptists and other radicals, who also believed in the two kingdoms, separated the functions of church and state more consistently than Luther. While obeying their temporal governments according to Romans 13, as Luther did, they would not go to war because for them Christ had forbidden all killing. They preferred to die rather than inflict suffering or death on others.

Luther's view of the two kingdoms was also consistent with his opposition to crusading against Islam, condemning the popes for preaching against the Turks and promising martyrdom status for Christians who were killed in the crusades against Muslims. In this Luther was well ahead of his time, for even today the West's wars in the Middle East are, for many, fought like the past crusades, only today they are fought to defend or promote "western values and democracy." Muslims today see these wars as Christians crusading against them, reminiscent of what Christians did to them in the past. In an interesting note, Luther, like Erasmus, advocated that the West not only pray for the Turks, but also send Christian witnesses to them. But Luther differed from Erasmus in that he did not hold out much hope that Muslims would convert to Christianity.

The commendable things Luther had to say about the Muslim way of life might suggest how today western and eastern societies could approach each other to bridge the cultural and religious divides between them. It may be that the religious differences, so important in the sixteenth century, may not be all that significant today in western democratic societies, but the cultural differences are still there and need to be made harmless as the West and the East seek to live and function together. Many Muslims take their religious faith seriously and will not tolerate insults to their religion. When the Prophet Mohammed or the Koran are mocked and caricatured, as happens in western countries time and again, in the name of "free speech," some Muslim faithful will express their anger and even kill in retaliation. Luther taught that while Christians reject the Mohammedan faith, they must respect some of Muslims' values and even see some good in them.

With Muslim immigrants seeking to live in western countries, it is democratic governments' responsibility, not the churches and the mosques, to see to it that religious and cultural differences are accepted and legally tolerated. The principle of pluralism of Christian religions, or the absence of any religion, which has become acceptable in the West since the Enlightenment, must also apply to eastern religions like Islam, to keep the peace. Here again Luther would agree that the state must see to it that there is peace in the land. However, sadly, Luther's general leniency toward and limited respect for Islam did not extend to the papacy, which he fought throughout his life as a reformer, at no time more ferociously than in the last few years of his life. The next chapter deals with this sad story.

{xv}

"An Institution of the Devil"
Luther's Last Battle Against the Papacy

As Luther entered the 1540s he was more than ever convinced that he was engaged in the climactic battle between the church of Christ and the 'synagogue of Satan.' Everywhere he read signs of the approaching End Time. Before his death he felt that he must make his final testament against the enemies of God" (Edwards CCL, 202). Among the enemies Luther saw were the papacy, the Jews, the Turks, and those who dissented from him in his own camp. His worst enemy, however, was no doubt the papacy. Luther battled the Roman Catholic Church with his pen throughout his career as a reformer, beginning in 1517 when he posted his Ninety-Five Theses to the door of the Castle Church in Wittenberg and ending with his last writings, Against Hanswurst (1541) and Against the Roman Papacy, an Institution of the Devil (1545). In all his writings against the Roman Church Luther is not only severely critical of its doctrines, institutions, and deeds, he also condemns the papacy as non-Christian and evil. In fact, for Luther, the papacy was the Antichrist of the endtime.

The language Luther uses against the papacy has shocked not only Catholics but also Luther's evangelical contemporaries. His coarse and vulgar writings against the papacy and his other enemies toward the end of his life have been attributed to the reformer's old age and ill health. There seems little doubt that Luther's physical and mental condition was in part responsible for his increasing impatience, irritation, anger, and even vulgarity. However, while Luther's abusive language cannot be excused, his theology, knowledge of history, and his ability to write clearly and forcefully to the very end were apparently not affected by his physical and mental condition and are nothing short of amazing (Edwards, CCL 204–5).

AGAINST HANSWURST

⁅ **Toward the end of Luther's life** the German states were beginning to split into two camps, with the Catholics and Protestants confronting each other not only religiously but also politically. Ever since the Diet of Worms (1521) and the Diet of Speier (1529) it had become evident that the Protestants and Catholics would not unite but go their separate ways. There were signs that there would eventually be war between them. The Diet of Augsburg (1530) was called by Emperor Charles V to discuss religious differences between the Catholics and Protestants and to deal with the threat of the Ottoman Turks in the East, for which united action was necessary. This diet was significant for the Lutheran cause: it resulted in the Augsburg Confession of Lutheran dogma, and it saw the establishment of the military Schmalkaldic League, consisting of Protestant princes and territories for protection against the Catholic and imperial forces of the emperor. The war of pamphlets continued unabated, with each side ridiculing, mocking, and insulting the other side. It was only a matter of time before the paper war would turn to bloodshed and armies invade opposing territories.

Henry the Younger (1489–1568), Duke of Brunswick-Wolfenbüttel, was a supporter of the emperor and of the Catholic cause and one of the most aggressive dukes, intent on ridiculing, slandering, and fighting the Protestants whenever he could. He was well known for his unscrupulous behaviour toward neighbouring territories and in his private life. It was said that he had set fire to the holdings of his enemies, in which hundreds of people died, and that he lived a sexually dissolute life, including having concubines and fathering children outside his marriage. The occasion for Luther's writing against Henry of Brunswick, whom he disrespectfully and mockingly calls "Heinz" (a boor or rustic) throughout his work, was Duke Henry's slanderous writings against the Landgrave Philip of Hesse and the Elector of Saxony, John Frederick, both evangelical rulers and strong supporters of the Reformation. He accused the landgrave of heresy, of being an enemy of Catholicism, and of bigamy. The latter was sadly true, and, what was worse, the Wittenberg theologians were not only embarrassed about it, but also tried to keep it secret. Duke Henry also accused the Elector of Saxony of heresy for leaving the Catholic faith and of being a drunkard.

According to Duke Henry, Luther had at one time called his elector "Hans Worst" (Jack Sausage). This was an often-used designation in jest or humour for someone who acted like a clown or baffoon. But now Luther used the word "Hanswurst" as a title for his tract against the Catholic duke, not in jest but in dead seriousness, to show the duke up for what he was and what the reformer thought of him. More important, however, Luther uses the tract against Duke Henry to battle the Roman Catholic Church once again and to compare it to the true evangelical church of the reformer.

Luther's booklet is very coarse and severe in its criticism of both the duke and the Catholic Church. For Luther the duke is the embodiment of all evil and malice. Luther just wanted to write a "short and gentle booklet," as he put it, but it turned out otherwise. He wrote to Melanchthon: "I have re-read my book and wonder how it happened that I have been so moderate [*mässig*]. I ascribe it to my headache at the time, which hindered my spirit to be more frank and to hit much harder" (Werke 4, 254). (Here we may have some evidence that Luther's ill health in his old age may have been one reason for his vulgar language against his enemies.) The booklet is not only severe and harsh, but also filled with foul language, invective, name-calling, and verbal abuse. As we know, Luther was not alone in the sixteenth century in using such language to attack opponents and enemies, not only to ridicule but also to hurt and if possible to destroy them. The Reformation age, with its emotionally intense faith issues, accepted and welcomed such "direct speaking" in the name of "truth." In fact, unless speakers and writers were repetitive, loud, graphic, and shrill, they would often not be seen nor heard (254). But Luther was known for outdoing all other pamphleteers at the time and often going over the top.

While Luther ridicules, dispises, and demeans Duke Henry for what he is and does, he remains the theologian, concerned about the Reformation in general and the nature of the true church in particular. When Duke Henry accused the Elector of Saxony of heresy and of betraying the Catholic Church, Luther, in this tract, finds occasion to talk about the nature of the true church, and then concludes that it is not the Catholic Church that is the true church, but the evangelical church redeemed by the grace of God.

Luther begins his booklet *Against Hanswurst* (Werke 4, 248–334) by stating that his piece is in response to Duke Henry's "slanderous" pamphlet against his sovereign, the Elector of Saxony. Duke Henry, this "dirty fellow," is not worth being answered with a single word, but Luther will write his booklet so that his own, Luther's, people will have something to talk about. Luther is happy that his writings have angered his enemies to such an extent that these devils now rave and scream about what he has accomplished as a reformer. The writings of his enemies can be answered with but one little word: "Devil, you are a liar!" It was a lie that he, Luther, had called his elector a "Hanswurst," a word that is generally well known and used, but he had never applied the word to any person, neither friend nor foe, and least of all to his sovereign. But now he is using the "Hanswurst" name for the stupid and lying "asses and pigs" of the Duke of Brunswick's type (257–9).

The major first part of the booklet is Luther's analysis of the true and false church. To begin with, the true church is the one that endures much persecution, opposition, and lies hurled at it by the false church, as is evident in what "Hanswurst," the Duke of Brunswick-Wolfenbüttel, is doing. The true church is thus happy that it is maligned by the likes of Duke Henry, for such treatment is a certain sign that God is with it. Also, Duke Henry, who with his writing against the Elector of Saxony stabs himself in the heart, shows that with his lies and slander he belongs to the false church. Luther then asks how the true and false churches can be recognized. He refers to St. Augustine, who saw the two churches existing from the very beginning in the persons of Cain and Abel, the sons of Adam and Eve, with the true church coming from Abel and the false church from Cain, who murdered his brother.

Luther begins by pointing out that both Catholics and Lutherans came originally from the first and true church. Both churches practise the correct baptism and the true Eucharist; both believe in the keys Christ gave to Peter to bind and to loose from sins; both were given the Word of God to preach, and both have similar worship services where prayers are said, including the Lord's Prayer; both teach that the temporal governments were instituted by God and that subjects must obey them for their own good; both honour the institution of marriage; both are persecuted in the world because they are Christian; both teach that Christians should love their neighbour and not take revenge or kill others. "With this we have shown," Luther states, "that we [both Catholics and Protestants] are the true old church. One body and one church of the saints" (272–3).

Then Luther proceeds to show that the present Roman Church is *not the first* and certainly not the true church, but one that has left the first and true church. The Church of Rome has left the first and true baptism and has added other requirements for salvation, things like monasticism, pilgrimages to so-called holy places, and other additions; it has introduced indulgences and told the faithful that by paying money for them, their sins and those of their loved ones will be forgiven, which is a lie; it has introduced holy water (*Weihwasser*) and salts to wash away sins, established various fraternities (*Bruderschaften*) of lay people for financial and religious purposes, and for performing good works, as if Christ's work of salvation were not sufficient; it has given the sacrament to the laity in one kind only while the priest takes the bread and drinks the wine in communion, contrary to the commandment of Christ; it has introduced new and false teachings and has added good works, thus nullifying Christ's work of salvation; it has created a pope, making him head of the church when only Christ is to be its head; it commits idolatry by making many saints and worshipping them when only Christ is to be worshipped; it has condemned marriage by introducing celibacy for the priesthood; it has gone to war with the sword, something it has not learned from the apostles, who conquered the world with the Word of God only. Luther has the past crusades and the warring Renaissance popes in mind. He ends by saying that the true church will not teach lies and error as the present one does.

Luther then directly addresses Duke Henry's accusations against the Elector of Saxony and the Landgrave Philip of Hesse. Even a true and holy church is not without sin, Luther explains, but it must be certain that it is founded on the rock of Christ, not the rock of St. Peter, as Rome teaches (290–1). That his master, the Elector John Frederick, is a drunkard, as Duke Henry claims, is a blatant lie. True, this prince likes his drink, but that is nothing out of the ordinary among the princes of Germany. "All of Germany is plagued with addictions to drink" (316). He, Luther, and his ministers have often preached against the not-so-holy life of their princes and nobles, but, alas, often to no avail. Other than taking the occasional drink with his guests and friends, the elector's life is most exemplary. He leads, thank God, a disciplined life, he always speaks the truth, has an open hand to support churches, schools, and to help the poor, has a constant and true heart to honour God's Word, looks after law and order in his realm, and leads an examplary married life as pure as that of monks. In his household the Word of God is heard and read, and the prince and his family pray and praise God daily. "Do you hear, Devil Heinz, and Heinz Devil?" Luther shouts at Duke Henry. "Such Christian, princely and honest life you cannot call that of a drunkard, unless you do it with a tongue that disgraces and blasphemes both God and [the elector]" (314).

Compared to the elector's exemplary lifestyle, that of Duke Henry's life, as the whole world knows, is literally abominable, Luther writes. The duke treats his wife badly, commits adultery, and whores around with many other women. Such shameless behaviour he has learned from his equally wicked companion, the Archbishop Albrecht of Mainz, and together they commit shameless deeds.... And Duke Henry wants to lecture the upright and good Elector of Saxony about drinking wine with his friends? (315).

Luther then seeks to defend the Landgrave Philip of Hesse, the most powerful supporter and friend of Luther and of the Reformation. Duke Henry had accused him of serious moral failing, namely of bigamy, and of being an Anabaptist, a charge that put him in the camp of the Münsterites. Luther does not go much into defending the landgrave about his bigamy, an offence that had serious legal implications. But he speaks to the issue of Duke Philip's "heresy" and alleged Anabaptism. The landgrave is no heretic for leaving the false church and becoming a member of the Lutheran and true church. As for the charge of Anabaptism, nothing could be more ridiculous and blasphemous than such an allegation and lie; it shows how stupid a buffoon Duke Heinz really is. Luther actually praises the landgrave for his courageous involvement in the Peasants' War (1525) and his military action against the Münsterites (1535). The fact that Philip of Hesse did not deal as harshly with the rebellious Münster Anabaptists as the crueller Catholics did should not be held against him nor make him a suspected sympathizer of Anabaptism.

Luther ends his tract against "Hanswurst" by quoting Psalm 64, which is a prayer for deliverance from secret enemies, an indication no doubt that the reformer felt the darts of his Catholic enemies more and more as he got older. The Psalm ends with the promise that "God will shoot at [his enemies] with an arrow; suddenly they will be wounded.... The righteous man ... will take refuge in Him" (339ff.).

THE POLITICS OF HANSWURST

⁅ **In March 1541,** the booklet *Against Hanswurst* was ready for the printer, and early in April Melanchthon reported that it was being eagerly read by the public. In the first year after its publication it was reprinted three times, and the part about the true church was also translated into Latin (254). To the evangelicals, Luther's distinction between the true and the false churches was generally convincing. His biblically based arguments, backed by his graphic and peppery language and his condemnation of the papacy as a whore, especially left no doubt as to which side the evangelical readers wanted to be. However, the evangelical representatives at the Diet of Regensburg felt that Luther's involvement in politics detracted from his reputation as a serious theologian. Luther and his elector thought otherwise. After the death of Duke George of Saxony in 1539, Duke Henry's writings against John Frederick and the evangelicals revealed the duke as the most formidable foe of the Reformation. Luther thus felt that with his booklet against Duke Henry he had helped the evangelical cause and church (Brecht 3, 222).

In 1542, Duke Henry continued his attacks against the territories around him, confirming his long-time reputation as an arsonist and murderer. The Elector of Saxony and Philip of Hesse, with Luther's approval, decided to go to war against him and to conquer the duchy. The victory over Duke Henry's forces was surprisingly easy and the duke fled. Luther considered the victory an act of God and an answer to prayer. But he became quite angry when he heard of the allied soldiers' acts of pillage and other unchristian and disorderly behaviour. Plans were made by the evangelicals to introduce the Reformation to

Brunswick-Wolfenbüttel, with Luther being involved in appointing the superintendent in the duchy (321). But in 1545 the elector informed Luther that Duke Henry was preparing to reclaim his land and that there would be war again. "Never before did I sleep less over a war," Luther later admitted (322). Fortunately, it did not come to a major battle, for Duke Henry was captured by the forces of Philip of Hesse and imprisoned, a sign again for Luther of God's intervention.

In this volatile political and religious situation, the elector requested that Luther write something on the subject of Duke Henry's capture so it could be used against the enemies of the Reformation. Chancellor Brück was charged not only with seeing that the letter was prepared at once, but also that "nothing undesirable was contained in the politically relevant" piece (323). At the end of December 1545 Luther published an open letter, *To the Elector of Saxony and the Landgrave of Hesse on the Imprisoned Duke of Brunswick,* advising the princes not to release Duke Henry unless he changed his mind and repented of his sins. But Luther also admonished the evangelicals' side not to become arrogant, for God had not given them the victory because they were more pious than the papists. The evangelicals, however, at least had the Word of God on their side, whereas the papists had perverted God's Word.

Martin Brecht writes: "This letter is one of the few things Luther wrote that speaks directly to a political question. One can say that he thereby made theology a means of politics. The theological reasons for imprisoning Henry were consistent. There is no hint that he was improperly intoxicated with victory; on the contary, critical admonition of the victors is not missing." Brecht's comment is most charitable toward the reformer, but also debatable. Like most magisterial reformers, Luther used his theology not only in the service of the church but also to advance the political interests of the Reformation, often appealing to the temporal powers to help him in his cause and in turn being grateful when their support came. His two-kingdom theology clearly separated the functions of the two realms, but he believed that the temporal rulers, as Christians, were also responsible for advancing the cause of the gospel.

BACKGROUND FOR *AGAINST THE PAPACY*

❰❰ **The editors** of the ten-volume edition of Luther's works (Berlin 1905) seek to justify their inclusion of the reformer's polemical writings, whose language might offend modern readers' sensibilities, on the grounds that "No one should be able to say that we have presented just a made-up, a castrated Luther." They trust that the reasonable reader will take into account that in Luther's time the use of obscenity and swearing in speech and writing was common. Also, Luther's crude and hard-hitting language against his enemies speaks of the reformer's sincerity and zeal for the evangelical faith and his reformation (Werke 4, 117). This is partly true and portrays Luther's character correctly, but it is also true that there were many other writers at the time, including humanists like Erasmus, who were more circumspect in their writing. Luther's polemical writings are exceptionally crude compared to others at the time.

Like the booklet *Against Hanswurst*, Luther's *Against the Roman Papacy, an Institution of the Devil* (Werke 4, 117–248), was part of the reformer's final reckoning with the Catholic Church as an institution. The book is not against a specific pope as a person, but against the Roman Catholic institution, which Luther, in despair, abandoned as incapable of change, convinced that it was not the church of Christ but that of the devil. The Roman Church, with its false teaching and practices, could not be reformed, according to Luther, but in writing against it he wanted to inform his own followers, the evangelicals, who their real enemies were. Of the two enemies of the endtime, the Turks and the papacy, it was the papacy that was the greatest and more dangerous to Christ's church. In about 1542 Luther wrote "a children's hymn to be sung against the two archenemies of Christ and his holy church, the pope and the Turks": "Lord, keep us steadfast in thy Word / And curb the Turks' and papists' sword / Who Jesus Christ, thine only Son, / Fain would tumble from off thy throne" (Brecht 3, 357).

The occasion for writing *Against the Roman Papacy* was as follows: At the Diet of Speyer in June 1544 Emperor Charles V, seeking the support of the evangelical princes against the French, with whom he was on bad terms at the time, promised to recognize them as equal partners in discussions at a forthcoming general council. In August of that year, Pope Paul III wrote an angry letter to the emperor, demanding that he withdraw his promise to the evangelicals, for the Protestants were heretics who sought to destroy the church and thus divide the empire. The pope also demanded that the emperor not deal with matters of religion in any future council, as it is the pope's prerogative to deal with spiritual things. Moreover, it is the emperor's duty to punish heretics, support the pope in his effort to keep the unity of the church, even militarily, and certainly not favour those who seek to destroy it.

Granvelle, the chancellor of the emperor, sent the pope's letter to the Elector of Saxony, thus making Luther aware of the pope's objections and designs. An additional papal letter to the emperor, dealing with the pope's aversion to plans for a general council, became known to Luther as well, making it perfectly clear that Pope Paul III, like many popes in the past, would not submit to temporal rulers and councils calling for reform. The elector forwarded the pope's letter of August 24 to Luther, with the express order "to do something with it," which meant that Luther should respond to the letter in some form. Chancellor Brück and Luther discussed the main points the reformer would write about, and by the beginning of March 1545 the booklet was completed (Werke 4, 120).

It might be added that the next general council was not held in Germany but on Italian soil. This council is known as the Council of Trent (1545–63), which initiated the so-called Counter-Reformation. Catholic dogma, including the seven sacraments, was reaffirmed, measures were taken to reform the morals of the church, and an aggressive missionary outreach throughout the world was begun. The Council of Trent convened in December 1545, just a couple of months before Luther died in February 1546.

CONTENT OF *AGAINST THE PAPACY*

⁋ **Luther begins his booklet against the papacy,** not with the customary address of "to the most holy Father," but with the words to "the most hellish Father, S. Paulus Tertius [St. Paul III)], who pretends to be the bishop of the Roman church." Luther then refers to the two angry letters the pope had written to Emperor Charles V, showing how wicked and devilish the pope actually is. Luther accuses the pope of refusing to submit to a council for a most needful reformation of the church. But he is not surprised because the popes have always acted that way: they do not want the emperor or any council to dictate to them, for such interference from outside diminishes their power and would force them to change their wicked lives. Instead, the popes' claim of being the only legitimate head of the church is denied when a council is allowed to dictate to them (122–3).

For the popes, according to Luther, there are three unacceptable words with regard to councils: the words "free," "Christian," and "German." When council members are *free* to speak and they seek to implement *Christian* measures, and their place of meeting is in *Germany*, the popes fear for their power. At the Council of Constance (1414–18) on German soil, the popes saw what could happen when councillors are free to speak and call for reform in the church, and even tell the popes what is to be done. During the Council of Constance three popes ruled at the same time (the period of the so-called papal schism), thus causing division and strife in the church. These popes were forced by the council to abdicate so as to restore at least a semblance of unity and recognize just one pope. Though this council ended the papal schism, it also clipped the wings of papal power by ruling that a council is *above* the popes and not the popes above the council, a ruling that drove "terrible fear" (*scheußlich graut*) into the popes, according to Luther. Future popes intended to restore their power over the councils. Luther also mentions as an aside that at the Council of Constance Jan Hus, the Bohemian reformer, was condemned and executed (124–5). Luther's readers knew of course that the reformer had been compared by his enemies to Jan Hus and thus implied that the fate of Hus might await the heretic Luther as well.

Luther then shows, from the history of the church, that the pope was not the head of Christendom before the seventh century. While Catholics maintain that St. Peter was the first pope of Rome, Luther argues that the popes had their beginning during the time of the evil eastern Emperor Phocas (reign 602–10). Phocas had murdered his predecessor Maurice, his wife, and his sons and daughters, and in 607 conferred upon the bishop of Rome, Boniface III, the title "head of all churches" (138). This evil beginning in Rome continued under subsequent popes, as visitors to Rome testified when they returned home. According to Luther, those who return from Rome have a "papal conscience," that is, "an epicurian faith," meaning a pagan faith. When Luther himself had visited Rome years ago, we are told, he heard on the streets people freely talking about the wickedness of the popes, saying, "if there is a hell, then Rome stands on it, and after the devils there are no worse humans than the pope and his people" (140). It is thus no wonder that the popes are afraid of councils where delegates are free to speak. Becoming vulgar, Luther writes that the pope-ass "hellish father," "craps," "farts," and "shits" on the devil. "Fie," Luther exclaims in disgust, "how the pope-ass has crapped in his pants." And again, "You are a crude ass, you pope-ass, you remain an ass!" (142–3).

After his lengthy introduction (some thirty pages) of denouncing and demeaning the papacy as an institution, Luther at last answers three questions about the papacy: whether the pope is the head of the church; whether anyone can judge or depose the pope; and whether the pope has brought the Roman empire from Greece to Germany. The first question Luther answers at some length (some sixty-one pages), but the last two answers are much shorter (some thirty-five pages) as he does not feel all that well and thus may not have had the energy to complete them, another indication of his ill health toward the end of his life.

THREE QUESTIONS ABOUT THE PAPACY

⁅ **The first question** is whether it is true that the pope of Rome is, as he claims to be, the head of Christianity, councils, emperors, angels, and everything else. It is easy to prove, Luther begins, that the pope is not the head of Christendom, nor the lord of the emperors and councils. From history and from the writings of the church fathers, including St. Jerome, St. Augustine, and Cyprian, we know that before Boniface III the bishops of Rome were simply bishops. As Jerome said, all bishops are equal, for *all* are the inheritors of the seats of the holy apostles. When Pope Gregory the Great (590–604) was offered the title, he declined, saying that no one should be called the highest bishop over all the others. He was the last bishop of Rome, after whom there were no more bishops but only popes, all masked devils, as Luther puts it. In fact, in many of his writings Gregory condemned the papacy, although he is pictured wearing the papal tiara, which is a lie, for he never wanted to be called pope. In 607 Emperor Phocas made Boniface III pope, after whom all other popes followed. But subsequent popes feared that whatever an emperor grants can again be withdrawn by another emperor, so they decided that they should not receive the title of pope from any human being, be it an emperor or a council, but only from God. And so the popes claimed that the papacy was founded by Christ when he told Peter in Matthew 16 and John 21 that he was the rock upon which the church would be built and that he was to feed his sheep.

Since according to Catholic teaching the popes are founded on St. Peter, the popes now set up rules, laws, and regulations that church members had to obey and follow if they wanted to receive salvation and forgiveness of sins. In effect, all this is nothing but deception and lies, for according to the Word of God it is not works that save us but only faith in Jesus Christ. After the popes had subjected all bishops to their rules and service, they began to subject the worldly rulers to themselves as well, making them kiss their feet and demanding that they submit to their teaching or else be punished with a ban or an interdict. Here it becomes evident that the papacy is nothing but a human invention and an institution of the devil.

To prove that the papacy is not founded on Christ through St. Peter, Luther goes into detail interpreting the words of Christ to Peter and the other disciples in Matthew 16:13–19, the passage that Roman Catholics use in their claim that Peter was the first pope of Rome. According to the passage in Matthew, Jesus asks his disciples what the people say about who he is. When Peter answers, "You are the Christ, the Son of the living God," Jesus tells him, "I also say to you that you are Peter, and upon this rock I will build my church." According to Luther, what Christ says to Peter is spoken to all the disciples, not just to Peter, for Peter merely speaks for all the others. And the rock, an allusion to Peter's name (petra), is not Peter but Christ himself upon whom the church is built. This means that the church is not a human institution like the papacy, with its many rules, regulations, and works, but a divine institution based solely on faith.

Luther then interprets the keys in this passage which the papacy interprets as Christ having given Rome absolute power "to bind and to loose" all things on earth. Throughout the centuries this claim has given the papacy power over churches and temporal rulers. For Luther, however, the keys simply mean that the church that preaches human sinfulness and God's forgiveness can pronounce the forgiveness of God when a sinner repents, or pronounce damnation when a sinner refuses to repent (181, 196). Moreover, the keys are not given to Peter alone, but to all apostles and all future pastors anywhere in the world. In fact, there were many great Christian churches throughout the world, including

Jerusalem, Antioch, and Alexandria, yet the popes claim that Rome was chosen by God to become the centre of the Christian world. Also, there have been great Christians, church fathers, martyrs, teachers, and writers, all greater than what Rome could ever produce, yet none aspired to become popes.

Christ commanded Peter to feed his sheep (John 21:17), but the popes have fed the church anything but wholesome food. In this connection Luther goes into detail about the kind of food the popes have fed the church. Also, Christ makes it clear to Peter that before he can feed the sheep he must love Christ, but the popes neither love Christ nor do they love and feed the sheep, certainly not with nourishing food. Their sheep stall is foul and stinks. In fact, whatever comes from the Roman popes, their popish faith, works, and decrees, was "born from the devil's behind," hence nothing good has come from the papacy, just the destruction of Christian faith, lies, idolatry, blasphemy, murder, sorrow, and shameful immorality, which is most apparent in Rome to this day. In disgust, Luther exclaims in horror and most obscenely: "I was terrified when I heard a great thunder, it was a loud and dreadful fart the pope-ass let go; he must have pushed with great might to produce such thunder-fart. A wonder it did not tear his hole and belly!" (213).

Luther closes this part of his book with the words of 1 Peter 5, where Peter as a "fellow elder" admonishes fellow pastors to "shepherd the flock of God ... not as being lords over those entrusted to you, but being examples to the flock." Luther feels he has thus conclusively shown that St. Peter was not the first pope but a humble fellow elder with many other elders, seeking to feed the true flock of Christ, and that the Roman Church was founded by the devil.

Luther then answers the second question about whether it is true that no one can judge the pope because he claims to be above all others in the church and in the world. Because of his age and ill health Luther will answer this question briefly. Any baptized Christian, Luther argues, either themselves or through a sponsor, has promised in baptism to renounce the devil and his works. Now, since the pope's doings and works are of the devil, even a baptized child is above the pope and the devil and thus can and must judge, avoid, and flee from both. Further, the popes, being most ignorant, do not know anything about faith, the Word of God, or theology; they are stupid asses who certainly cannot pronounce true judgment, so how can they presume to judge in matters of faith and morals? Even a donkey that carries a sack of grain to the mill knows that it is a donkey and not a cow. "But the raging and desperate pope-asses at Rome do not know that they are asses.... In sum, they know nothing except how to found monasteries, gobble up the world's goods, rob and steal the kings' crowns, and do the devil's work and ways" (231–2).

The Lord is perfectly clear about what to do when someone sins, namely that the sinning brother needs to be admonished first, and if he will not repent and mend his ways, he is to be regarded as a pagan. The popes have obviously sinned gravely, and now ordinary Christians must judge them, not the other way around. In fact, the pope is not a Christian, and he wants to judge others? He is neither a bishop nor a Christian, but a pagan and a wild bear-wolf who tears to pieces and destroys all that is in his path. The jurists should urge their lords, kings, and princes to demand that the damned pope give back all that he has robbed from the very beginning of his rule. And if the pope will not restore what he has stolen, he should pay with his hide, the way foxes are treated when they steal. Luther says that his blood rages and he wishes to see the pope punished, but there is no punishment enough for the popes' crimes (237–9).

Luther now answers the third question: whether the pope has transferred the empire from the Greeks to the Germans. According to Luther, the popes' claim that they have created the Holy Roman Empire is a blatant lie, for the popes had nothing to take from Constantinople and nothing to give to the Germans. He then goes on to review the history to show that after Constantine the Great had moved his capital from Rome to Constantinople, Italy was overrun by the Goths, Lombards, and Vandals, and in 410 Alaric sacked and plundered Rome. This sorry state in Italy continued for centuries, until the popes appealed to the Franks to help them against the Lombards and other tribes. When Pope Leo III was in trouble with his enemies in Rome in 799, he appealed to Charles the Great (Charlemagne), king of the Franks, to come to his aid. On Christmas Day 800, while Charles was praying in the papal basilica, Pope Leo III placed a crown on his head, thus not only crowning Charles but, in effect, nullifying the legitimacy of Empress Irene's rule and laying the foundation for the Holy Roman Empire. From then on there were two Roman empires, the eastern empire with its capital in Constantinople and the western with its capital in Aachen, Germany. Each empire continued to lay claim to the other until in time both recognized the political reality for what it was. They then exchanged embassies and sought to live in peace side by side (243–7).

Luther is correct, in part, to argue that the popes have not transferred the Greek empire to the Germans, but that it is historical circumstances, as Luther has reviewed them that have brought about the Holy Roman Empire. At the same time it is true that the popes were involved in creating the Germanic empire by inviting the Frankish king to come to their assistance in Italy, in the end crowning Charles the Great as emperor. Luther, however, admits that it was a mistake by both Charlemagne and subsequent emperors to accept the popes' annointing (*schmiere*), thus accepting the popes' blessing and dependence on them. The emperors did not need this symbolic subservience to the pope, for they were elected by the German electors, not appointed by the popes (248).

At the end of the book Luther writes: "Here I must end: in another booklet I shall do better. But if I should in the meantime die, may God grant that another will write a thousand times worse [about the papacy]. For the devilish papacy is the last misfortune on earth.... God help us! Amen" (248). Luther did not write another piece against the papacy. He died the following year. But the Church of Rome, which Luther wished dead, did not die. Instead, with the Council of Trent's reform measures, it experienced a kind of new life. With the sacrificial work of the Society of Jesus (Jesuits) at home and abroad the church reclaimed much lost spiritual territory in Europe; it even expanded into foreign areas with its missionary outreach. More important, the seven sacraments, reaffirmed by Trent, proved to be resilient and continue to hold a central position among the Catholic faithful to this day. As a Luther biographer states, "the sacramental experience of Catholic worship maintains an impressive hold on its adherents. The sacraments have an existence independent of the pope and papal pronouncemets" (Marius 482). Even some Mennonites, including Reformation scholars, who have left their church for Roman Catholicism, testify to the continuing attraction of the Church of Rome (Martin 167–95).

A NOTE ON CATHOLIC WRITERS AGAINST LUTHER

⁋ **Hartmann Grisar,** in his biography *Martin Luther: His Life and Work* (1930), speaks of the discouragement of Catholic writers who were exposed "to the vulgar invectives to which Luther and his disciples resorted" (Grisar 453), and complained about the difficulties of having their writings in defence of the

Catholic faith published. Johannes Cochlaeus (1479–1552), an eloquent Catholic controversialist, wrote in 1540: "For twenty years there was nothing more disadvantageous for us Catholic authors, in contrast with the heretics, than the great unreliability of our publishers.... The publishers were almost all Lutherans, and we were able to obtain their services only at a great outlay of money" (457). Nevertheless, Catholic authors did respond to Luther's work and writings and managed to have their many pamphlets and books published. Cochlaeus, according to Grisar, deserves credit for his Latin *History of the Acts and Writings of Luther*, which appeared in 1549, three years after Luther's death.

There were several early Catholic opponents of Luther and his work. The Dominican Hieronymus Emser (1477–1527), secretary to Duke George of Saxony at Leipzig, a staunch defender of Catholicism, was one of Luther's early opponents. In fact, there was much bad blood between Emser and Luther, with the reformer calling Emser the "Leipzig goat" (Emser's crest was a goat's head) and an inferior writer and scholar. Emser had translated the New Testament into German, but had much relied on Luther's New Testament translation, which was no doubt superior to Emser's. Emser also called Luther names, one being "The "Wittenberg bull," and accused him of being a heretic in the tradition of Jan Hus, who in the end was burned at the stake. The Franciscan Thomas Murner (1475–1537) was another early opponent of Luther. He was a brilliant satirist who at first directed his satire at the corruption of his own church in the hope of contributing to its reform, but when he saw that Luther's work was tearing the church apart, he turned against Luther and satirized him in 1522 in a well-written work, *About the Great Lutheran Fool – and how Doctor Murner exorcised him*.

The popular opponent of Luther, Dr. Johann Eck (1486–1543) of the University of Ingolstadt, produced the *Manual Against the Lutherans* that went through fifty editions and was in general use up to 1600. Eck also argued that the beliefs of Luther and Jan Hus were similar. Another writer, Johann Faber (1478–1541), who became bishop of Vienna in 1530, was quite successful in preaching and writing against Luther and the Lutherans and in advising Catholic princes in matters of theology. Beginning in 1535, Faber wrote against the Lutherans, defending the Mass, the priesthood, Catholic faith, and good works.

Some of Luther's literary opponents were at first drawn to the reformers, especially to Luther and Erasmus, but after they came back to the Catholic faith, they not only wrote against Luther and other evangelicals, but also hoped to heal the break between the old church and the Protestants (458–60). Georg Witzel (1501–1573) of Mainz, for example, was influenced by Reformation ideas, including the writings of Erasmus, embraced Lutheranism, and married, but then, after learning more of the aims of Luther and seeing the moral decline that often followed Luther's teaching, returned to the old faith in 1533. He published treatises on good works, justification, and on the church. At the Council of Trent he was critical of the theologians who refused to consider his ideas about establishing peace between Catholics and Protestants (458–9).

Another Catholic writer, Friedrich Staphylus (1512–1564), had studied at first at Wittenberg as a Protestant and was greatly influenced by Luther's teaching. He married, but in 1552 he became a Catholic convert and then helped to restore Catholicism in Bavaria and Austria. In 1558 he wrote a caricature of Luther's theology, *Epitome of the Doctrine of Luther* (*Theologiae Martin Lutheri Trimembris Epitome*), in which he especially attacked the splintering nature of Protestantism, the people's veneration of Luther, and religious subjectivism, such as justification through faith only.

Both Franciscan and Dominican writers and orators were in a spiritual struggle to countenance Luther and the evangelicals and to keep Catholicism alive after the colossal breach caused by the Reformation. The Franciscan Johann Wild (1497–1554), for example, was a gentle and popular preacher at Mainz, writing effective commentaries and sermons in defence of the old faith. It was largely due to his preaching that Mainz remained Catholic. His preaching and saintly life impressed many, including the Lutheran Albert of Brandenburg, who in 1552 occupied Mainz. Many priests and other religious fled the city, but Father Wild remained. Prince Albert solicited the preacher to give up his religious habit. "For many years I have worn it," Wild said in imitation of the second-century martyr Polycarp of Smyrna, "it has never done me any harm, why should I now abandon it?" Struck by Father Wild's apostolic zeal, Albert granted the priest anything he wished. Wild asked that the Franciscan building in the city might be spared from desecration and destruction. His request was granted (CE vol. 15).

Writers such as these, among many others, contributed greatly to the restoration and reformation of the old faith, not only through their writings but also through their exemplary lives and faithfulness to their church.

{xvi}

Conclusion and Evaluation

RADICAL REFORMERS VINDICATED

The various groups of radical reformers, including the Anabaptists, were persecuted during the Reformation throughout Europe. Although more persons died at the hands of the Catholic states and churches, there were also many who had to endure the wrath of Martin Luther and other magisterial reformers throughout the sixteenth century and beyond. For almost four hundred years they had to bear ridicule, suspicion, discrimination, reproach, and sometimes persecution and death. Lutheran Protestantism especially, to which the radicals had appealed, has sinned against them most, for it failed to appreciate that they sincerely endeavoured to follow Luther's early Reformation principles to their logical conclusion and live in accordance with the precepts of the gospel as they sincerely understood them. As late as the nineteenth and twentieth centuries, the descendants of the radical reformers were compelled to leave their soil, country, home, and property, just to be able to live their lives according to the dictates of their conscience. The general attitude toward them, however, was bound to change in their favour. In 1905 the Baptist historian Henry Vedder wrote: "The time is rapidly approaching when the Anabaptists will be as abundantly honoured as in the past four centuries they have been unjustly condemned" (Vedder 21). Since that time the Anabaptists and their heirs, the Baptists, the Mennonites, and the so-called Free Church movement, have been at least partly vindicated.

The Catholic scholar C.A. Cornelius was one of the first, in the middle of the nineteenth century, to speak an effective word in mitigation of judgment upon the radicals, and declared that their real history was yet to be written. Others soon followed Cornelius to the Anabaptist sources – which had been largely neglected until then – and soon discovered what Sebastian Castelio (1515–1563), humanist scholar of Savoy, had already found in the sixteenth century. In a manuscript he addressed to Theodore Beza (1519–1605), a French Protestant theologian and heir of John Calvin in Geneva, Castelio wrote: "With regard to the Anabaptists I would like to know how you know that they condemn legitimate marriage and the magistracy and condone murders. Certainly it is not in their books and much less in their words. You have heard it from their enemies.... I do not believe what you say about the Anabaptists.... Neither should people be held responsible for a position which they have themselves repudiated, anymore than you, Beza, should be reproached for the amatory verses of your youth" (Hershberger 319).

All persons and groups against whom Luther spoke and wrote have been defended and in many instances rehabilitated or vindicated by historians and theologians. Hermann Barge, among others, has shown that the Wittenberg radicals, especially Karlstadt, were not merely misguided people whose sole ambition was to destroy what Luther had carefully built up, but sincere individuals who believed they were putting into practice what Luther had advocated and preached. Radical theologians like Thomas Müntzer have been shown not only to have complemented Luther in his reform efforts but also to be proposing new ways of applying the biblical message, not only to magistrates and princes but also to the common people. Müntzer, far from being a misguided and idealistic rebel, as he was misrepresented by Luther, stood up for the socially and politically oppressed peasants whose suffering he sought to alleviate in accordance with God's Word. "Luther and Müntzer no longer appear to be mutually exclusive. Müntzer must be understood as a corrective of Luther. For Müntzer stood for another and highly important aspect of Protestantism: he carried the Protestant protest into the social area" (Nigg 316). In recent decades Thomas Müntzer scholarship has experienced a veritable renaissance, with conferences and publications dealing with this seminal thinker and activist (Goertz, Stayer, et al.).

The spiritualists and mystical Anabaptists, notably Schwenckfeld and Denck, have also been vindicated in numerous works. As we have seen, they may have been the only individuals and groups during the Reformation period who were truly tolerant in the midst of religious and theological strife and bigotry. The anti-Trinitarians, or Unitarians, as they are known today, have also found their defenders among reputable scholars. Wilbur's *History of Unitarianism* and Bainton's *Hunted Heretic*, which tells the tragic story of Christian persecution, have left their mark in favour of these "stepchildren of the Reformation." And Mennonite historians and theologians have not failed to do their part in clearing the Anabaptists of the charges against them, portraying them as advocates of a biblical Christianity. Many journals, among them *The Mennonite Quarterly Review* (Goshen, Indiana), the *Mennonitische Geschichtsblätter* (Hamburg, Germany), the *Journal of Mennonite Studies* (Winnipeg, Manitoba), and the *Conrad Grebel Review* (Waterloo, Ontario), continue to publish the results of research into the life and faith of the radical reformers, including the Anabaptists and related groups. Today, the once estranged children of Luther and other magisterial reformers enjoy a greater reputation than ever before; both Roman Catholic and Protestant historians and theologians acknowledge their contribution to the church and western culture and society.

Only a few excerpts from their writings will be cited. The late E.A. Payne (1902–1980), General Secretary of the Baptist Union of Great Britain and Ireland, wrote about the Anabaptists: "The doctrine of the church as a fellowship of believers, free from the control of the state; [the] emphasis on the spirit of man as the candle of the Lord; the claim for toleration and freedom of conscience; the recognitions of the obligations resting on all Christians to charity, community and evangelism; these ideas, with varying degrees of emphasis, have become influential in all parts of the world" (Hershberger 315). A noted scholar and biographer of Luther, Roland H. Bainton (1894–1984), although stating that the radical reformers may have advocated tolerance because they were a persecuted lot, nevertheless observed correctly, perhaps with a touch of exaggerated good will: "The Anabaptists anticipated all other religious bodies in the proclamation and exemplification of three principles which are on the North American continent those truths which we hold to be self-evident: the voluntary church, the separation of church and state, and religious liberty" (317).

Of the sixteenth-century radicals in general, Philip Hughes, one of the world's leading Catholic historians, wrote about the Anabaptists: "They were the means of preserving what, in the nature of things, would seem to be the aim and the first justification of Luther, Calvin, and of all the other successful reformers who were their deadliest foes: the principle, that is to say, that men have the right to form their own religious groups, to join a group or not to join, to leave it when they choose; that these groups are equal in their rights and subject to no authority but that they themselves choose; that the groups are free to choose the way they shall worship; that every individual is free to choose what he shall believe. Whatever the theologians may need to say ... about the value of these principles they have had a great history ... nor is that history at an end" (Hughes 143).

Lutheran scholars have also come to see that the reformer's principle of justification by faith alone may have been one-sided, as the Anabaptists have claimed. Lutheran Hans Georg Fischer wrote: "Only too often have we reviled the alleged works-righteousness of the Anabaptists while we ourselves have been all too forgetful and negligent concerning the divine commandment of brotherly love. Over all the joy and satisfaction of justification by faith alone, we have forgotten the call for sanctification of our lives" (Fischer 38). Even the question of infant versus adult baptism did not die with the radicals of the sixteenth century. Reformed theologians such as Karl Barth and Emil Brunner have raised several questions about this subject, and what they have said has caused some anxious debate in various circles (Barth). And Dom Gregory Dix and Kenneth Kirk, both of the Anglican Church, "have come to feel that the rites of baptism and confirmation must be brought more closely together again" (Hershberger 315).

THE OTHER SIDE

There is, however, another side, as we have seen throughout our story. Seeking to correct the bad or incomplete image of peaceful Anabaptism, sympathetic historians of the movement have succeeded well in their task, but often at the expense of Luther's side of the story. In their treatment of the struggle between Luther and the radicals, the reformer sometimes does not come off well. He is either shown as a heartless enemy of all those who opposed him, or else his reasons for attacking them are oversimplified. A good example of such oversimplification of Luther's theology is the following: "In his haste to establish the doctrine of justification by faith rather than by works Luther downgraded good works; the only place he had left for good works was at the very end, as a sort of postscript or appendage, something that needed attention after salvation was an accomplished fact. We meet in Luther, to put it theologically, a very heavy emphasis on the forensic aspect of salvation [merely declared or imputed by God] and a correspondingly light emphasis on the moral aspect. Luther was primarily interested in pardon, rather than in renewal.... There is an imbalance in the theology between what God does *for man* and what He does *in man*" (Verduin 12).

The quotation, while generally correct as a one-paragraph summary of Luther's doctrine of justification, is misleading as it stands. Luther did not, as we have seen, establish his doctrine of justification by faith in haste, nor did he downgrade good works. His salvation, for which he struggled for many years, was for him a matter of life or death. In the end Luther realized that it is God who declares the sinner just, but before that it is the individual who struggles with self, sin, and even the devil, as Luther did. Good works, though not necessary for salvation, were important to Luther, but he believed that they would follow after God's grace and justification, a belief for which he had biblical support. When his followers failed to live up to the gospel, as Luther himself often admitted that they did, he advised his pastors to preach the necessity of ethics and moral precepts more often. Luther himself often castigated his parishioners for their lack of Christian ethics and even threatened to go on strike and not preach to them anymore (Marius 475).

However, what Luther saw among those who seemed to belittle the principle of justification through faith alone and emphasize the importance of good works, was a legitimate concern for the reformer. According to Luther, an emphasis on good works not only diminished God's sovereignty and glory but also led to legalism. As much as the Anabaptists and the Mennonites believed in salvation through God's grace, their insistence that good works must follow often led to legalism in individual members and their churches. Luther and other reformers saw the Anabaptist movement as a new monasticism because of their stress on the necessity of good works. In reading Menno Simons on discipline and the ban (excommunication), the tendency among early Anabaptists toward moralistic legalism becomes obvious, and some Mennonite churches suffered from such legalism through much of their history (Peters "The Ban").

Luther's struggle with the antinomians within his own camp is a clear indication that the reformer was not indifferent to the practice of good works. It will be remembered that in connection with those who dismissed the law and good works, Luther expressed his greatest agony, saying that it might have been better had he never written anything than to endure the onslaught of the devil in this respect. His earlier emphasis on Christian freedom from the law disappointed Luther because people continued to live sinfully. In 1529 he told his Wittenbergers, "I do not want to be the shepherd of such pigs." Despite endless admonitions and instruction, as Brecht writes, "the people could not be diverted from their godlessness and brought to repentance; instead, they sinned that much more, seemingly 'to spite' Luther." By 1530, Luther was so "exhausted by the godlessness of the Wittenbergers," that he announced he would not preach anymore, a promise he kept for several months (Brecht 2, 288).

Luther's clash with the various radicals did not spring from his capriciousness or jealousy, or because of a mere difference of opinion about the principle of justification, as some critics have alleged. As we have seen repeatedly, the heart of the problem was Luther's agonizing conversion experience and his understanding of the gospels, especially Paul's writings. Not to recognize this is to fail to understand fully the life and death struggle between Luther and his opponents (Zeeden 8–9). For Luther, the doctrine of justification was of such importance that not to accept it was to blaspheme God and to repudiate the Christian religion. In view of this, the radicals' emphasis on outward piety, the freedom and work of the spirit, the separation of church and state, and social reform was, in Luther's opinion, missing the very heart of the Christian faith (Troeltsch II, 756). He was mainly concerned with establishing a right relationship with God. But once a right relationship between the believer and God was established, good works would or at least *should* follow. Sadly for Luther, this did not always happen.

LUTHER'S TRAGEDY

☾ **As a result of his salvation experience and study of the Bible,** Luther at first loudly proclaimed the Reformation principles of *sola fide* and *sola scriptura* and advocated with conviction complete religious liberty of conscience. When he realized, however, that some of his earlier followers, co-workers, and colleagues understood and applied these principles differently from him, Luther felt that he had no choice but to oppose them. And when some of them, particularly Thomas Müntzer, became associated with the Peasants' War, Luther was certain that his attitude and actions against them were justified. But the issues were not quite as simple as that. At first Luther even sympathized with the lot and cause of the rebellious peasants. They believed that they were acting according to the reformer's principles of justice and freedom and that the time had come to have their difficult feudal existence alleviated. As a student of the Bible Luther should have realized that the gospel was clearly on the side of the "common man" and against the oppressors, and that it would have been in the interest of a truly genuine reformation to combine with the goals of a Thomas Müntzer. But Luther did not see it that way. Therein lay the tragedy.

What Luther considered spiritual values only was often applied by the peasants and many other radicals to material and social conditions. And when the peasants translated their grievances into concrete and even violent actions against their oppressors, in Luther's view the divinely instituted rulers, he was convinced that they had overstepped their bounds. Luther warned the rebels before he urged the princes to attack them, even pleading with them not to resort to violence and explaining what he had meant by freedom and justice in Christ. But it was too late and his pleas fell on deaf ears. According to Luther, the rebellious peasants abused the gospel by using it as a cover for their purely selfish, social, economic, and in some cases, political goals. He felt he had to separate himself from them and their cause lest the conflict undo the work of the Reformation.

It is at this point that the critics of Luther may be correct: the reformer allied himself with the princes because he saw the success of his work in jeopardy. Luther's violent and anti-Christian attitude and language against the peasants cannot be excused, however sympathetic one might feel toward the reformer and his cause. When one realizes, however, that Luther saw in the destructiveness of the rebels not only a threat to the Reformation but also a threat to all other institutions, it should at least be possible to understand the fury with which he moved against the rebels. Any doubts that Luther may have had about his harshness toward the revolutionary radicals and the peasants was definitely dispelled when the fanatical Anabaptists established their kingdom in Münster. Luther was thus confirmed in his thinking that all dissenting groups were not only "enthusiasts" and fanatics, but dangerous rebels against legally constituted governments. As far as he was concerned, unscriptural theological views on the faith mysteries such as the sacraments went hand in hand with religious and civil disobedience and rebellion.

Luther's attitude toward all the Anabaptists, including the peaceful groups, received its initial hue from his encounter with the Wittenberg radicals, including Karlstadt, the Zwickau prophets, Müntzer, and the rebellious commoners. Some have suggested that had the reformer first met such peaceful groups as the Swiss Brethren, whom he actually never really got to know well, he would perhaps have been more lenient and tolerant toward the whole "left wing" of the Reformation (Geiser 279–80). This may be debatable, but Payne observes correctly when he states that the revolt of the Münsterites was the "main cause of Anabaptism's passing under a cloud of obloquy and shame, thus preventing any honest facing of the basic issues raised by the Swiss Brethren and their more responsible followers" (Hershberger *Recovery* 307). It must also be remembered that in the sixteenth century the distinction between the various radical groups was not as clear to Luther and other magisterial reformers as to today's historians. As we have seen, there were several points of contact, even connections, between the various individuals and groups within the radical Reformation.

For Luther the views of the radicals on the sacraments, Scripture, church–state relations, and the place of law and grace in preaching the gospel were not mere opinions with little or no spiritual consequence, but weighty matters that concerned the salvation or damnation of the people who held them. When, for example, Luther insisted on the "real presence" in the Eucharist, he was in effect fighting to maintain the certainty of his own salvation; in the real body and blood of Christ in the Last Supper he experienced the real Redeemer. Similarly, in the baptismal water, Luther saw a tangible manisfestation of God's grace, which the infant experienced without any action on his or her part. The real Christ and the written Word were also the issues in his struggle with the spiritualists. For Luther to give in to the spiritualists was not only to fall prey to subjectivism, but also to elevate human reason and the mere opinions of humans above Scripture.

While Luther believed that the secular state had no business in purely religious matters, the radical reformers' kind of separation of church and state was for Luther both unscriptural and dangerous. In his cooperation with the princes, Luther was no doubt led by the reality of the circumstances in which he found himself. He believed, however, that the principle of the priesthood of believers also applied to the Christian magistrates who had a share in the building of the church in their realm. Moreover, the removal of the state from the church would, in Luther's view, bring about chaos and a complete secularization of many human institutions, a fear that later proved well founded. While the absence of the religious in many functions of the state and society is taken for granted today, during the Reformation secularization was just beginning to make inroads, which the magisterial reformers, including Luther, sought to prevent, ultimately with little success.

Luther's fear of and struggle against those groups, who at one time had appealed to him and his writings, can only be understood when it is considered that the dissidents were *radicals* in the true sense of the word, proposing to turn the long-established order and institutions upside down. And Luther, though a radical himself for his break from Rome, was religiously conservative at heart. Commenting on the persecution of the Anabaptists by the church and state, Philip Hughes states: "Let it once be believed in any society that a particular group is really threatening to overthrow the distribution of property, to introduce a new conception of right and wrong, to prohibit and to crush all ways of life but its own, and the society will react savagely" (Hughes 140). To this may be added that the radicals' idea of a free church and their opposition to official Christendom were so clearly against the still dominant medieval idea of a social order as expressed in the concept of the church and empire, that many at the time could see in the radical groups "nothing less than the destruction of the very basis of society itself" (Troeltsch II, 704).

According to some documents, there are some who believe that there was "a real possibility that Anabaptism, if unimpeded by the sword of the magistrate, might have become the prevailing form of the church in Germany" (Hershberger 321). This may be speculation or wishful thinking on the part of some Mennonite historians, but the fact is that Anabaptism in all its forms was feared by both church and state. To further speculate, had Anabaptism triumphed, it is difficult to say what would have happened to the state, the principles of nonresistance or pacifism, religious toleration and liberty, and the idea of a free church. The fact seems to be that persecution contributed in no small measure to what the radical reformers later became, and many of the positive traits we today find praiseworthy in the Anabaptist-Mennonite movement are the result of past hardships and hostilities toward them.

RIGHTS AND WRONGS

☾ **In the nineteenth century** the German poet Heinrich Heine (1797–1856) stated: "Luther was wrong and Müntzer right" (Nigg 315). In many ways Heine was right, and historians, especially those on the left, concur with this view. In the twentieth century the same view has been expressed about the other sixteenth-century radicals. Verduin states that in his book he has given the radicals of the Reformation a sympathetic treatment because "history has to a large extent demonstrated that they were in a large way right" (*The Reformers* 276). He then goes on to say that Protestantism has come to endorse the emphases for which the radicals pioneered: "The free Church, the Church by voluntary association, the missionary Church, and a host of other features for which the Stepchildren agonized, have become part and parcel of the Protestant vision – so much so that men are often surprised to learn that it was not always thus" (277).

While to a large extent history may have vindicated the many radical individuals and groups, it is not the purpose of this study to assign guilt to any of them or to absolve any from guilt, but to see the struggle between Luther and his opponents in its historical and theological contexts and to remind writers that in their zeal to correct the image of the radical reformers they sometimes become one-sided and less than charitable toward the magisterial reformers. If we wish to speak of right and wrong in connection with Luther and his opponents, it may be suggested that we have here a case of two rights and two wrongs. The radicals, including Karlstadt, Müntzer, the peasants, and the Münsterites, were, according to Luther, wrong in what he thought was their misapplication of the gospel to their religious, social, and political views and their perversion of the intentions of his writings; according to the radicals, Luther was wrong and certainly unchristian in moving with fury and violence against them. Some of the radical reformers, particularly the spiritualists and peaceful Anabaptists, thought they were right in believing that individuals should have the freedom to live their faith according to the dictates of their conscience; Luther believed he was right in insisting that the freedom of a Christian did not include the right to destroy social structures and political institutions. Moreover, while some theological differences between Luther and the dissidents were fundamental, other theological issues were often a matter of different emphases and different interpretaions. But whether they were core differences or mere differences in emphases, they were felt strongly by the two sides. In the heat of battle at the time, compromise, tolerance, and understanding were largely unknown or forgotten.

At a deeper level, the difference between Luther and most radical reformers was a difference in their views of God and human nature. Luther, generally pessimistic about human nature and medieval in many of his views, approached God as a helpless sinner in need of forgiveness and healing. He believed implicitly in the sacramental value of the Eucharist and baptism, experiencing in the sacraments tangible expressions of God's grace and love for the sinner. Most dissidents, on the other hand, were radical to the point of severing most connections with medieval Christianity. Their more rational explanations of the sacraments and such concepts as the Trinity and the incarnation of Christ and their stress on practical living rather then on dogma, seemed to reveal them as Christian humanists, although most of them would have repudiated the term. Paradoxically, however, Luther, generally pessimistic about human nature, considered all reality and life as given by God, and thus worthy of acceptance and enjoyment; many Anabaptists, on the other hand, turned away from the secular world and emphasized the inward reality of the spirit.

It is to be hoped that the religious fanaticism and intolerance of the Reformation period are things of the past. In an age of increasing religious indifference and skepticism it may indeed appear incredible that the struggle between Luther and the radical reformers was fought with such deadly seriousness on both sides. And yet, it may have been because of this profound seriousness that throughout history both the Lutheran and the radical tradition have continued to contribute significantly to the development and richness of Protestant religious thought.

OTHER OPPONENTS

Luther's struggle against the radical reformers was severe and long-standing. But there were also struggles with other foes, equally as intense, which had lasting results. As we have seen, Luther's bitter tangle with Erasmus about free will, his writings against the Ottoman Turks and the Jews, and his final literary blast against the papacy revealed the best and the worst in the character and work of the great reformer.

On Luther and Erasmus's debate concerning free will, the jury is still out about who had the better arguments. Luther claimed that his book *Bondage of the Will* was the best he had written, and he believed that he had defeated Erasmus the Renaissance humanist with better arguments. Luther's painful salvation experience, his reading of St. Augustine and St. Paul, and his belief that Erasmus did not fully understand God's Word, especially the theology of the cross, convinced the reformer that his view was the correct one. But other thinkers at the time and later were of a different opinion. Erasmus and the Roman Catholics held to a semi-Pelagian position, believing that both God and the human individual cooperate in salvation and the Christian life. Even in Luther's camp there were those who, like Melanchthon, were sympathetic toward the arguments of Erasmus. And most of the radicals, while accepting Luther's justification through God's grace, stressed free will because, according to them, it made ethics and following Jesus in practical living possible.

Luther's writings against the Jews remain a permament blot on Luther's character and work as a reformer. Like the legendary ink spot on the wall of the Wartburg Castle, retouched from time to time for tourists interested in Luther's struggle with the devil, the reformer's anti-Judaic writings stand as a lasting witness not only to Luther's but also to Christianity's evil actions against the Jews. Luther's writings against the Turks, on the other hand, are mild in comparison to his fulminations against the Jews. In fact, they are relevant today because they show a way for western society to learn from Muslims and from Islam to appreciate eastern values, thus benefiting economically and culturally from these new immigrants to the West. However, Luther's attitude toward and writings against the papacy come close to his animosity toward the Jews. While Luther considered Roman Catholicism as having had a Christian beginning as a church, he saw the entire papal system as totally corrupt, that is, "theologically, juridically, ecclesialistically, and politically" polluted, as Martin Brecht puts it. According to Brecht, "Although Luther did not consider using force against the pope – unlike against the Jews – among his last great battles the one against the pope was the fiercest, for the pope embodied for him the eschatological principle of the Antichrist" (Brecht 3, 367). Ironically, Luther saw the Turkish threat to Europe and the evil of the papacy as visible signs of the endtime – and he rejoiced in it, for it would be the glorious beginning of God's ultimate reign.

Today the West is again facing Muslims and Islam, in the form of their religion and way of life. Questions of tolerance and acceptance of alien ideas are perhaps as real today as they were in Reformation times. In the sixteenth century the Ottoman Turks were a threat to Christendom from *outside*; today many Muslims have come to live *within* the borders of western countries. The two communities generally coexist peacefully, but after 9/11 (September 11, 2001), when the twin towers in New York were destroyed by Muslim-inspired terrorists, western societies remain fearful and suspicious of what to expect next, especially when western bigots continue to provoke Islam's Prophet and its holy book. It is apparently difficult for religiously indifferent westerners to understand how seriously Muslims take their religious values and that they are prepared to kill and die for them. It will take time and sincere effort for westerners and Muslims to live together. Again it will be the responsiblility of governments to see to it that there is relative peace between the two communities.

Among Luther's opponents dealt with in this book, the question of who his greatest opponents were may not be all that clear, but as far as the reformer was concerned, all of them were dangerous enough to be seen as "devils" against whom he hurled the legendary inkwell all his life. Luther's pen and words were powerful und effective, but as we have seen, they often also boomeranged and hit him, causing him severe pain, so much so that he often despaired at having written anything at all. †

| Epilogue

Many in today's society not familiar with Reformation history might wonder what the religious fuss was all about. Most people in western societies are used to letting everyone believe (or disbelieve) about God, religious faith, or religious and cultural practices as they see fit. Among the major western religious denominations, such as Catholicism, Lutheranism, Reformed, and Anglicanism, and the free church groups such as the Baptists, Mennonites, Amish, Hutterites, Schwenckfeldians, Pentecostals, among others, there may still be polite discussion about theological differences, but there is little if any animosity toward each other. Even churchgoing people are generally often indifferent toward the beliefs of others, echoing the quip of the tolerant and religiously indifferent Prussian King Frederick II (1712–1786) that every one should be allowed to practise his faith "in his own fashion."

On the other hand, there are significant recent signs that the earlier tension, even hostility, between Luther, Catholics, and dissident groups is thankfully receding in favour of a better understanding and acceptance of each other, in the name of Christian ecumenicity and charity. In 2009, for example, in a meeting in Chicago, Catholic, Lutheran, and Methodist church leaders marked the tenth anniversary of an agreement on the doctrine of justification by faith, the doctrine over which the unity of the church was destroyed in Luther's time: "Together we confess: By grace alone, in faith in Christ's saving work and not because of any merit on our part, we are accepted by God and receive the Holy Spirit, who renews our hearts while equipping and calling us to good works" (United Methodist News Service). Neither Luther nor the sixteenth-century popes could have foreseen the possibility of such a statement of theological agreement.

There are also encouraging signs about Lutherans and Anabaptists coming together in acts of forgiveness and reconciliation. In May 1983, for example, Werner Lech, the bishop of Thuringia, expressed regret about what Luther did to the Anabaptists, stating: "Our thankfulness for the legacy of Martin Luther is linked with a plea for forgiveness from all against whom our fathers in the heat of the Reformation sinned." And, more significantly, in a reconciliation ceremony during the 11th Lutheran World Federation Assembly in Stuttgart, Germany, on July 22, 2010, some 480 Lutheran delegates from around the world acknowledged "the harm that our forebears in the sixteenth century committed to Anabaptists, for forgetting or ignoring this persecution in the intervening centuries, and for all inappropriate, misleading and hurtful portraits of Anabaptists and Mennonites made by Lutheran authors, in both popular and scholarly forms, to the present day."

Lutheran President Mark S. Hanson called on delegates to vote by standing or kneeling. The resolution passed unanimously with a number of delegates "dropping to their knees." Mennonite World Conference president Danisa Ndlovu of Zimbabwe, faltering with emotion, said that Mennonites too do not come with "heads held high; we also stand in need of God's grace." He continued, "We believe that today God has heard your confession and is granting your appeal for forgiveness. We joyfully and humbly join with God in giving forgiveness" (Rempel–Burkholder, 32).

The subject of Luther and the Jews has been an important issue in both academic and popular Luther studies, especially since the Second World War. But here, too, Lutherans in the twentieth century have acknowledged the sins of Luther against the Jewish people and have asked for forgiveness. The Church Council of the Evangelical Lutheran Church of America, on April 18, 1994, adopted the following document as a statement on Lutheran–Jewish relations, which reads in part: "In the long history of Christianity there exists no more tragic development than the treatment accorded the Jewish people on the part of Christian believers. Very few Christian communities of faith were able to escape the contagion of anti-Judaism and its modern successor, anti-Semitism.... [We] who bear [Luther's] name and heritage must with pain acknowledge also Luther's anti-Judaic diatribes and the violent recommendations of his later writings against the Jews.... [We] reject this violent invective, and yet more do we express our deep and abiding sorrow over its tragic effects on subsequent generations." The document suggests practical ways of carrying on mutually useful dialogue and cooperation with Jewish communities.

There are still severe critics of the Roman Catholic Church, which Luther and others sought to reform in "head and members." Long-time Catholic liberal theologian Hans Küng, for example, continues to press for more reforms in the Church of Rome, including, among other things, decentralization of the power of the papacy, the ordination of women to the priesthood, and permission for the clergy to marry. Thus, for Küng and other critics of the Catholic Church, the reformation that began some 500 years ago has not yet ended. In his recent book, *Ist die Kirche noch zu retten?* (Can the Church still be saved?), Küng argues that the Catholic Church can only be saved as a relevant institution if the pope and the curia are willing to reappropriate the spirit of Jesus and the apostles (Küng). With the election of Pope Francis in 2013, the papacy shows signs of becoming more open to dialogue not only with non-Catholic churches and communities, but also with Jews, Muslims, and even atheists. Such openness from a Catholic pope would have been unthinkable in the sixteenth century.

Finally, it might be asked whether Luther and Reformation issues are passé or whether they are still relevant after five centuries. There are writers today, including agnostics and the so-called "new atheists," who maintain that it is religious faith – any religious faith – that is causing strife and wars throughout the world, and that religious beliefs should be eliminated to allow a more tolerant society to emerge. Many of them also believe that in the face of suffering, the many wars that brought misery and death to millions of innocent people, and especially the evils of the Gulag and the Holocaust, no rational human being can still believe in the existence of a benevolent and omnipotent God.

It is significant that after the Second World War (1939–45), with its destruction and a bleak future, some thinkers turned to Martin Luther and other Reformation figures for possible answers to the question of God's love in a brutal world. For example, Jürgen Moltmann (b. 1926) served in the German military, was taken prisoner of war by the English, and in the United Kingdom came under the influence of Christian thinkers. Upon his return to his home in Hamburg he was confronted not only with the destruction of his city but also that of many other cities in Germany. In 1948–49 he enrolled at the University of Göttingen to study Luther and the Reformation. He wanted to find some answers to the many questions he had about the collapsed and suffering world around him, including such evils as the Holocaust. With many other postwar thinkers he asked himself whether God had been absent in all the suffering of the war years. In Luther he found at least some answers, and the result was his influential book *The Crucified God*, published in 1973. According to Moltmann, Luther speaks of a God hidden in suffering, "the apparent absence of God in the cross of Christ, yet his hidden presence in the suffering of Jesus, working through it the salvation of the world" (Tomlin 178). This view of God is the opposite of the triumphalist thinking about an all-mighty and all-loving God of former times. According to this view, God is not the traditionally omnipotent deity, but an apparently weak and suffering God, a God who understands and suffers with suffering humankind. Luther believed that only at the final end will all suffering and evil be overcome, and he yearned for that day of God's victory over evil and redemption (Oberman, *The Reformation* 68).

Similarly, in Japan, another country that was on the losing side during the Second World War, Christian thinkers have reflected on an apparently absent or hidden God in the face of destruction and human suffering. Some of them also found Luther's theology of comfort and help in understanding the postwar world. Kazoh Kitamori (1916–1998), a theologian, pastor, and university teacher, wrote an important book titled *Theology of the Pain of God* (1946) in which he developed, on the basis of Luther's thought, "the notion of a God who embraces and forgives sinful people, despite the pain that it causes him" (Tomlin 178). Both Moltmann and Kitamori learned that to understand the Christian God, they needed to begin "with the wounds of Christ," as Staupitz once told Luther when the reformer struggled to find a gracious God (178–9).

More recently, philosophers like the Marxist theorist Slavoj Žižek and the radical theologian Boris Gunjevic have reflected on Luther's attempt to understand the complexities of human existence and the role that God plays in it. In their book, *God in Pain: Inversions of Apocalypse* (2012), these thinkers speak of a suffering God, "not a triumphalist God who always wins in the end … but a God who – like the suffering Christ on the cross – is agonized, who assumes the burden of suffering, in solidarity with human misery" (Žižek 156). Quoting the German philosopher F.W.J. Schelling (1775–1834), Žižek states that "Without the concept of a humanly suffering God … all of history remains incomprehensible." According to Slavoj Žižek, "This is the philosophical background of Dietrich Bonhoeffer's deep insight that after the Shoah, 'only a suffering God can help us now'" (157). Thus Luther's theology of the cross reaches across the centuries and tries to make sense in a new way of the pain and often senselessness of modern human existence.

The ideas and beliefs of Luther's opponents did not die with them, but live on today in many forms. The free church movement that was born with the spiritualists and the Anabaptists of the sixteenth century continues today in the evangelical churches, especially in developing countries, where Christianity, unlike in the West, is far from retreating, , but is numerically and in importance on the increase. In the mid-sixties Harvard professor Harvey Cox was confident that religious faith was no longer relevant in the "secular city" and was on the way out (Cox, *The Secular*). But recently Cox has come to the opposite conclusion with his book *Fire from Heaven* in which he documents the phenomenal growth of the Pentecostal movement, which next to Catholicism is the largest Christian movement in the world today with over 500 million adherents (Cox, *Fire*).

Other Anabaptist contributions have come to fruition in the modern world. The separation of church and state and the democratic principles of free speech and belief, for which the Anabaptists contended, are taken for granted today in democratic societies. And not to forget the importance of the sixteenth-century "revolution of the common man" that left its lasting mark in the labour movements with their drive for justice, equality, and positive legislations throughout the western world.

Both Luther and his opponents derived their faith and views from the Christian tradition, with its theology rooted in the gospel, especially the theology of the cross, with its accompanying suffering, including that of God in Christ. The cross of Christ has no parallel in any other religion. The cross as the means of salvation was important to both Luther and his Christian opponents. This theology of divine and human suffering still has an appeal to many people throughout the world who are faced with suffering and the question of evil in the world. It is in this gospel that Christians still find a source of strength and purpose of living.

The world of the Reformation has changed dramatically after five centuries. Both Catholics and Protestants hold on to beliefs and principles of the Christian faith that may seem naïve and outdated to many. The shrill voices of the materialists, secularists, and atheists seek to drown out the voices of those who still believe that there is another reality, a spiritual reality that provides answers that the materialistic world cannot provide. Especially in times of crises, wars, suffering, and search for meaning, men and women still turn to the God of Luther, especially his Christian opponents, and find there what makes their life worth living. What is more, the descendants of the former opponents are beginning to extend their hands to each other in forgiveness, respect, tolerance, and love.

Selected Bibliography

PUBLISHED SOURCES

Corpus Schwenckfeldianorum. 19 vols. Published under the auspices of the Schwenckfelder Church, Pennsylvania. Leipzig and Pennsburg, PA, 1907–1961.

Dillenberger, John, ed. *Martin Luther: Selections from his Writings, edited and with an Introduction.* New York: Anchor 1961.

Enders, Ernst Ludwig, ed. *Dr. Martin Luthers Briefwechsel.* 10 Bände. Calw/Stuttgart, 1884–1903.

Fellmann, Walter, ed. *Hans Denck Schriften: Religiöse Schriften.* Band II. (Quellen und Forschungen zur Reformationsgeschichte, XXIV). Gütersloh, 1956.

Kidd, B.J., ed. *Documents Illustrative of the Continental Reformation.* Oxford: Oxford University Press, 1911.

Loserth, J., ed. *Quellen und Forschungen zur Geschichte der oberdeutschen Taufgesinnten im 16. Jahrhundert. Pilgram Marbecks Antwort auf Kaspar Schwenckfelds Beurteilung des Buches der Bundesbezeugung.* Wien, 1929.

Luther, Martin. *First Principles of the Reformation or the Ninety-five Theses and the Three Primary Works.* Translated and edited by Henry Wace and C.A. Buchheim. London: John Murray, 1883.

———. *The Letters.* Selected and translated by Margaret A. Currie. London: Macmillan, 1903.

———. *Reformation Writings.* Translated by Bertram Lee Woolf. 2 vols. London: Lutterworth Press, 1952.

———. *Sämmtliche Werke.* 65 vols. Erlangen and Frankfurt a.M: Heyder & Zimmer, 1826–1855.

———. *Werke. Kritische Gesammtausgabe.* Weimar: H. Böhlau, 1883–1948.

———. *Werke. Kritische Gesammtausgabe. Briefwechsel.* Weimar: H. Böhlau, 1930–1948.

———. *Werke. Kritische Gesammtausgabe. Die Deutsche Bibel.* Weimar: H. Böhlau, 1906–1961.

———. *Werke. Kritische Gesammtausgabe. Tischreden.* Weimar: H. Böhlau, 1912–1921.

———. *Luthers Werke.* 10 Bände. Berlin 1905. C.A. Schwetschke und Sohn. Auslieferung für Amerika: Wartburg Publishing House, Chicago.

———. *Luther's Works.* Concordia Publishing House and Fortress Press, 1956–.

Rummel, Erica, ed. *The Erasmus Reader.* Toronto: University of Toronto Press, 1990.

Schwenckfeld, Caspar. *Eight Writings on Christian Belief.* Edited by H.H. Drake Williams III. Kitchener, ON: Pandora Press, 2006.

Simons, Menno. *The Complete Writings.* Translated from the Dutch by Leonard Verduin. Edited by John Christian Wenger, with a biography by H.S. Bender. Scottdale, Pennsylvania, 1956.

Wenger, John C., trans. and ed. "Three Swiss Brethren Tracts." *MQR,* XXI. (Oct. 1947): 276–85.

Williams, G.H., and Angel M. Mergal, eds. *Spiritual and Anabaptist Writers.* Library of Christian Classics, Vol. XXV. Louisville, KY: Westminster John Knox Press, 1957.

Zieglschmid, A.J.F., ed. *Die älteste Chronik der Hutterischen Brüder. Ein Sprachdenkmal aus frühneuhochdeutscher Zeit.* Ithaca, NY: Cayuga Press, 1943.

SECONDARY LITERATURE

Acton, J.E.E. *Essays on Freedom and Power.* Selected and with an introduction by Gertrude Himmelfarb. Glencoe, Illinois, 1948.

Albornoz, Paul. *Luthers Haltung im Bauernkrieg.* Darmstadt, 1952.

Augustijn, Cornelis. *Erasmus: His Life, Works, and Influence.* Translated by J.C. Grayson. Toronto: University of Toronto Press, 1991.

Arnold, Gottfried. *Unparteiische Kirchen- und Ketzerhistorie vom Anfang des Neuen Testaments bis auf das Jahr Christi 1688.* 2 Bände. (Reprographischer Nachdruck der Ausgabe Frankfurt a.M. 1729). Hildesheim, 1967.

Arthur, Anthony. *The Tailor-King: The Rise and Fall of the Anabaptist Kingdom of Münster.* New York: St. Martin's Press, 1999.

Bainton, Roland H. *Christian Attitudes Toward War and Peace: A Historical Survey and Critical Re-evaluation.* Nashville: Abington Press, 1960.

———. "The Left Wing of the Reformation." *Journal of Religion,* XXI, April 1941.

———. *Here I Stand: A Life of Martin Luther.* New York: Mentor Books, 1950.

———. "The Parables of the Tares as the Proof Text for Religious Liberty to the End of the Sixteenth Century." *Church History*, I (June 1932), 67–87.

———. *The Travail of Religious Liberty: Nine Biographical Studies.* Philadelphia: Westminster Press, 1951.

———. *Hunted Heretic: The Life and Death of Michael Servetus 1511–1553.* Boston: Beacon Press, 1953.

———. *The Reformation of the Sixteenth Century.* Boston: Beacon Press, 1953.

———. *The Age of the Reformation.* An Anvil Original. Princeton, NJ: Van Nostrand Reinhold Company, 1956.

Barge, Hermann. *Andreas Bodenstein von Karlstadt.* 2 vols. Leipzig: Friedrich Brandstetter, 1905.

Barth, Karl. *The Teaching of the Church Regarding Baptism.* London: SCM Press, 1956.

Bax, E. Belford. *The Peasants' War in Germany 1525–1526.* London: Swan Sonnenschein, 1899.

———. *The Rise and Fall of the Anabaptists.* London: Swan Sonnenschein, 1903.

Bender, Harold S. "The Anabaptist Vision." *MQR*, XVIII, April 1944: 67–88.

———. *Conrad Grebel ca. 1498–1526: The Founder of the Swiss Brethren, Sometimes Called Anabaptists.* Scottdale, PA: Herald Press 1950.

———. "Church and State in Mennonite History." *MQR*, XIII (April 1939), 83–103.

———. "The Anabaptist Theology of Discipleship." *MQR*, XXIV (Jan. 1950): 25–32.

———. "The Anabaptists and Religious Liberty in the 16th Century." *MQR*, XXIX (1955): 83–100.

———. "Die Zwickauer Propheten, Thomas Müntzer, und die Taeufer." *Theologische Zeitschrift*, Heft 4 (1952), 262ff.

Bensing, Manfred. "Müntzer, Thomas." *Encyclopaedia Britannica* XII. 1980, 619–20.

———. *Thomas Müntzer und der Thüringer Aufstand 1525*, 3rd ed. Leipzig, 1983.

Bergmann, Werner. *Geschichte des Antisemitismus.* München: Verlag C.H. Beck, 2002.

Bergsten, Torsten. *Balthasar Hubmaier. Seine Stellung zur Reformation und Täufertum, 1521–1528.* Kassel: J.G. Oncken Verlag, 1961.

Beutel, Albrecht. "Wort Gottes." *Luther Handbuch.* 2010, 362–71.

Beuys, Barbara. *Und wenn die Welt voll Teufel wär: Luthers Glaube und seine Erben.* Rowohlt: Rowohlt Verlag, 1982.

Be Vier, William A. "Modes of Water Baptism in the Ancient Church." *Bibliotheca Sacra*, CXVI (July–Sept. 1959): 230–40; "Water Baptism in the Ancient Church." (April–June 1959): 136–44; "Summary and Conclusions Concerning Water Baptism in the Ancient Church." (Oct.–Dec. 1959): 317–21.

Blanke, Fritz. "Täuferforschung: Ort und Zeit der ersten Wiedertaufe." *Theologische Zeitschrift*, Heft 1, 1952: 74–6.

———. "Zollikon 1525. Die Entstehung der ältesten Täufergemeinde." *Theologische Zeitschrift*, Heft 4, 1952: 241ff.

Blickle, Peter. *The Revolution of 1525: The German Peasants' War from a New Perspective*. Translated by Thomas A. Brady and H.C. Erik Midelfort. Baltimore: Johns Hopkins University Press, 1981.

———. ed. *Der deutsche Bauernkrieg von 1525*. Darmstadt: Wissenschaftli- che Buchgesellschaft, 1985.

———. *Die Reformation im Reich*. 2. überarbeitete und erweiterte Auflage. Stuttgart, 1992.

Bloch, Ernst. *Thomas Müntzer als Theologe der Revolution*. Berlin: Aufbau Verlag, 1962.

Boehmer, Heinrich. *Martin Luther: Road to Reformation*. Translated from the German by J.W. Doberstein and T.G. Tappert. New York: Living Age Books, 1957.

Böhme, Helmut. "Albrecht Dürers Traumgesicht von 1525." In Gerhard Härle (hg.), *Grenzüberschreitungen, Friedenspädagogik, Geschlechter-Diskurs, Literatursprache-Didaktik*. Festschrift für Wolfgang Popp. Essen, 1995.

Bornkamm, Heinrich. *Luther and the Old Testament*. Translated by Eric W. and Ruth C. Gritsch. Edited by V.I. Gruhn. Philadelphia: Fortress Press, 1969.

———. *Luther's World of Thought*. Translated by M.H. Bertram. St. Louis, MO, 1958.

Brady, Thomas A. Jr. *German Histories in the Age of Reformations, 1400–1650*. Cambridge: Cambridge University Press, 2009.

Brecht, Martin. *Martin Luther*. 3 vols. Vol. 1: *His Road to Reformation 1483–1521*. Translated by James L. Schaaf. Minneapolis, MI: Fortress Press, 1993; Vol. 2: *Shaping and Defining the Reformation 1521–1532*. Fortress Press, 1990; Vol. 3: *The Preservation of the Church 1532–1546*. Fortress Press, 1993.

———. *Martin Luther*. "Luther und die Türken." In *Europa und die Türken in der Renaissance*, herausg. von Bodo Guthmüller und Wilhelm Kühlmann. Tübingen, 2000.

Brendler, Gerhard. *Martin Luther. Theology and Revolution*. Translated by Claude R. Foster, Jr. Oxford: Oxford University Press, 1991.

Brentano, Franz-Funk. *Luther*. Translated from the French by E.F. Buckley. London: Cape, 1936.

Bubenheimer, Ulrich. *Thomas Müntzer. Herkunft und Bildung*. Leiden: E.J. Brill, 1989.

Clasen, Claus-Peter. *Anabaptism: A Social History, 1525–1618*. Ithaca and London: Cornell University Press, 1972.

———. "Executions of Anabaptists, 1525–1618: A Research Report." *MQR*, XLVII (Apr. 1973): 115–52.

Cooper, J. C. "Some Radical Elements in Luther's Theology." *Lutheran Quarterly* (May 1968): 194–201.

Cooper, Terry D. *Paul Tillich and Psychology: Historic and Contemporary Explorations in Theology, Psychotherapy, and Ethics*. Macon, GA: Mercer University Press, 2006.

Cox, Harvey. *Fire from Heaven: The Rise of Pentecostal Spirituality and the Reshaping of Religion in the 21st Century*. Boston: Da Capo Press, 2001.

———. *The Secular City: Secularization and Urbanization in Theological Perspective*. New York: Macmillan, 1965.

Coutts, Alfred. *Hans Denck 1595–1527: Humanist and Heretic*. Edinburgh: Macniven & Wallace, 1927.

Crous, E., et al. *Gedenkschrift zum 400-jährigen Jubiläum der Mennoniten oder Taufgesinnten 1525–1925*. Ludwigshafen am Rhein, 1925.

Deschner, Karlheinz. *Abermals krähte der Hahn. Eine kritische Kirchengeschichte*. München: Goldmann Verlag, 1996.

Dieckhoff, A.W. *Luthers Lehre von der kirchlichen Gewalt historisch dargestellt*. Berlin: Verlag von Gustav Schlawitz, 1865.

Dietrich, Donald J. *God and Humanity in Auschwitz. Jewish–Christian Relations and Sanctioned Murder*. New Brunswick, NJ: Transaction Publishers, 1995.

Dix, Gregory. *The Shape of the Liturgy*. 2nd ed. Westminster: Dacre, 1945.

Durant, Will. *The Reformation: A History of European Civilization from Wycliffe to Calvin: 1300–1564* (The Story of Civilization, Part VI). New York: Simon & Schuster, 1957.

Edwards Jr., Mark U. *Luther's Last Battles: Politics and Polemics, 1531–46*. Ithaca, NY: Cornell University Press, 1983.

———. "Luther's Last Battles." *Concordia Theological Quarterly*, Vol. 48 (Apr.–July 1984): 125–40.

———. "Luther's Polemical Controversies." In *The Cambridge Companion to Martin Luther*. Edited by Donald K. McKim. Cambridge: Cambridge University Press, 2003.

———. *Printing, Propaganda, and Martin Luther*. Berkeley, Los Angeles, London: University of California Press, 1994.

Eisenstein, Elizabeth L. *The Printing Press as an Agent of Change: Communications and Cultural Transformation in Early-Modern Europe*. Vol. 1. Cambridge: Cambridge University Press, 1979.

Elliger, Walter. *Thomas Müntzer. Leben und Werk*. Göttingen: Vandenhoeck & Ruprecht, 1975.

Elton, G.R., ed. *The New Cambridge Modern History*. Vol. II. Cambridge: Cambridge University Press, 1958.

The Encyclopedia of Judaism. Editor-in-chief Geoffrey Wigoder. New York: Macmillan, 1989.

Erb, Peter C. *The Life and Thought of Kaspar Schwenckfeld von Ossig*. Pennsburg, PA, 1997.

———. ed. *Schwenckfeld and Early Schwenckfeldianism*. Papers Presented at the Colloquium on Schwenckfeld and the Schwenckfelders. Sept. 17–22, 1984. Pennsburg, PA, 1986.

Eriks, Garrett J. "Luther and Erasmus: The Controversy Concerning the Bondage of the Will." *Protestant Reformed Theological Journal*, 32, no. 2 (April 1999).

Estes, James M. *Peace, Order and the Glory of God: Secular Authority and the Church in the Thought of Luther and Melanchthon, 1518–1559*. Leiden: E.J. Brill NV, 2005.

Fast, Heinold. *Der Linke Flügel der Reformation. Glaubenszeugnisse der Täufer, Spiritualisten, Schwärmer und Antitrinitarier*. Bremen: C. Schünemann, 1962.

Fife, Robert Herndon. *The Revolt of Martin Luther*. New York: Columbia University Press, 1957.

Fischer, H.G. "Lutheranism and the Vindication of the Anabaptist Way." *MQR*, XXVIII (Oct. 1940): 195–213.

Foth, Helmut. "Juden, Täufer, Mennoniten. Ein Ueberblick über ihre 500 Jahre währende Beziehungsgeschichte." *Mennonitische Geschichtsblaetter*, 2013, 23–54.

Friedmannn, Robert. "Anabaptism and Protestantism." *MQR*, XXIV (Jan. 1950): 12–24.

———. "The Encounter of Anabaptists and Mennonites with Anti-Trinitarians." *MQR*, XXII (July 1948): 139–62.

———. "The Schleitheim Confession (1527) and Other Doctrinal Writings of the Swiss Brethren in a Hitherto Unknown Edition." *MQR*, XVI (April 1942): 82–98.

———. "Thomas Müntzer's Relation to Anabaptism." *MQR*, XXXI (Apr. 1957): 75–87.

Friesen, Abraham. *Erasmus, the Anabaptists, and the Great Commission*. Grand Rapids, MI: Eerdmans, 1998.

———. *Reformers, Radicals, Revolutionaries. Anabaptism in the Context of the Reformation Conflict*. Elkhart, IN: Institute of Mennonite Studies, 2012.

———. *Thomas Müntzer: A Destroyer of the Godless*. Los Angeles and Oxford: University of California Press, 1990.

———. "Thomas Müntzer and the Anabaptists," *JMS*, Vol. 4 (1986): 143–61.

Friesen, Peter M. *The Mennonite Brotherhood in Russia (1789–1910)*. Translated from the German. Fresno, CA: Board of Christian Literature, General Conference of Mennonite Brethren Churches, 1989.

Furcha, Edward J. *Schwenckfeld's Concept of the New Man: A Study in the Anthropology of Caspar Schwenckfeld as Set Forth in His Major Theological Writings*. Pennsburg, PA, 1970.

Gane, E.R. "Luther's View of Church and State." *Andrews University Seminary Studies* (July 1970): 120–43.

Garret, James Leo. "The Nature of the Church According to the Radical Continental Reformation." *MQR*, XXXIV (Apr. 1958): 111–27.

Garside, Charles. "Ludwig Haetzer's Pamphlet Against Images: A Critical Study." *MQR*, XXXIV (Jan. 1960): 20–38.

Gassmann, Günther. "Luther in the World-Wide Church Today." *The Cambridge Companion to Martin Luther.* Edited by Donald K. McKim. Cambridge: Cambridge University Press, 2003.

Gatiss, Lee. "The Manifesto of the Reformation. Luther vs. Erasmus on Free Will." Online at https://leegatiss.wordpress.com/2009/10/22/luther-vs- erasmus-on-free-will/.

Gazzaniga, Michael S. *Who's in Charge? Free Will and the Science of the Brain.* New York: Ecco, 2011.

Geiser, Samuel. "An Ancient Anabaptist Witness for Nonresistance." *MQR*, XXV (Jan. 1951): 66–9, 72.

Gerdes, Hayo. *Luthers Streit mit den Schwärmern um das rechte Verständnis des Gesetzes Mose.* Göttingen: Emanuel Hirsch, 1955.

Gibbon, Edward. *The Decline and Fall of the Roman Empire.* New York: Modern Library, 2003.

Goertz, Hans-Jürgen. *Das schwierige Erbe der Mennoniten: Aufsätze und Reden.* Leipzig: Evangelische Verlags-Anstalt, 2002.

———. *Der Mystiker mit dem Hammer. Die theologische Begründung der Revolution bei Thomas Müntzer.* 1974.

———. *Deutschland 1500–1648. Eine zertrennte Welt.* Schöningh UTB, 2004.

———. *Innere und äussere Ordnung in der Theologie Thomas Müntzers.* Leiden, 1967.

———. *Thomas Müntzer: Apocalyptic, Mystic and Revolutionary.* Translated by Jocelyn Jaquiery. Edited by Peter Matheson. Edinburgh: T. & T. Clark, 1993.

———. hrsg. *Umstrittenes Täufertum 1525–1975 Neue Forschungen.* Göttingen: Vandenhoeck & Ruprecht, 1975.

Goeters, Gerhard J.F. *Ludwig Haetzer (ca. 1500–1529) Spiritualist und Antitrinitariar. Eine Randfigur der frühen Täuferbewegung.* Quellen und Forschungen zur Reformationsgeschichte, XXV. Gütersloh, 1957.

Goethes Werke. "Hamburger Ausgabe." 14 Bände. München: Verlag C.H. Beck, 1974.

Goldhagen, Daniel Jonah. *Hitler's Willing Executioners: Ordinary Germans and the Holocaust.* New York: Alfred A. Knopf, 1997.

Gregory, Brad S. *Salvation at Stake: Christian Martyrdom in Early Modern Europe.* Cambridge, MA: Harvard University Press, 1999.

Grisar, Hartmann. *Martin Luther: His Life and Work.* Adapted from the 2nd German Edition. Westminster, MD: Newman Press, 1955.

Grislis, Egil. "Martin Luther and Menno Simons on Infant Baptism." *JMS*, Vol. 12 (1994): 7–25.

———. ed. *The Theology of Martin Luther: Five Contemporary Canadian Interpretations.* Winnipeg: Lutheran Council of Canada, 1985.

Gritsch, Eric W. "Luther and the Jews: Toward a Judgement of History." In *Stepping-Stones to Further Jewish–Lutheran Relations.* Edited by Harold H. Ditmanson. Minneapolis, MI: Augsburg, 1990: 104–19.

Gritsch, Eric W. *Reformer Without a Church: The Life and Thought of Thomas Müntzer 1488 [?]–1525.* Philadelphia: Fortress Press, 1967

———. "Luther and Schwenckfeld: Towards Reconciliation by Hindsight." In *Schwenckfeld and Early Schwenckfeldianism.* Edited by Peter C. Erb. Pennsburg, PA, 1986: 401–14.

———. *Martin Luther's Anti-Semitism: Against His Better Judgement.* Grand Rapids, MI: Eerdmans, 2012.

———. *Reformer Without a Church: The Life and Thought of Thomas Müntzer 1488[?]–1525.* Philadelphia: Fortress Press, 1967.

———. *Thomas Müntzer: A Tragedy of Errors.* Philadelphia, Fortress Press, 2006.

———. "Thomas Müntzer and the Origins of Protestant Spiritualism." *MQR,* XXXVII (1963): 172–94.

Gutteridge, Richard. *Open the Mouth for the Dumb!: The German Evangelical Church and the Jews 1879–1950.* Oxford: Oxford University Press, 1976.

Harbison, E. Harris. *The Age of Reformation.* Ithaca, NY: Cornell University Press, 1955.

Haude, Sigrun. *In the Shadow of "Savage Wolves": Anabaptist Münster and the German Reformation during the 1530s.* Boston: Humanities Press, 2000.

Heick, Otto W. *A History of Christian Thought.* 2 vols. Philadelphia: Fortress Press, 1965–66.

Hershberger, Guy F. ed. *The Recovery of the Anabaptist Vision.* Scottdale, PA: Mennonite Publishing House, 1957.

Hillerbrand, Hans J. "Andreas Bodenstein of Carlstadt. Prodical Reformer." *Church History,* XXXV (Dec. 1960): 404–23.

———. ed. "An Early Anabaptist Treatise on the Christian and the State." *MQR,* XXXII (Jan. 1958): 28–47.

———. "Luther's Deserting Disciples: An Anniversary Reflection on the Anabaptists of the 16th Century." *McCormick Quarterly* (Nov. 1967): 105–13.

———. "Thomas Müntzer's Last Tract Against Luther." *MQR,* XXXVIII (1964): 20–36.

Hinrichs, Carl. *Luther und Thomas Müntzer. Ihre Auseinandersetzung über Obrigkeit und Widerstandsrecht.* Berlin: W. De Gruyter, 1962.

Horsch, John. *Mennonites in Europe.* 2nd ed. Scottdale, PA: Mennonite Publishing House, 1950.

———. "The Rise and Fall of the Anabaptists in Münster." *MQR*, IX (April 1935), 92–103; (July 1935), 129–43.

———. "Menno Simons' Attitude toward the Anabaptists of Münster." *MQR*, X (January 1936), 55–72.

Howart, Robert Glen. "The Double Bind of the Protestant Reformation: The Birth of Fundamentalism and the Necessity of Pluralism." *Journal of Church and State*, 47, no. 1 (2005): 91–108.

Hsia, Po-Chia. *The Myth of Ritual Murder: Jews and Magic in Reformation Germany*. New Haven and London: Yale University Press, 1988.

Huch, Ricarda. *Das Zeitalter der Glaubensspaltungen*. Berlin/Zürich, 1937.

Hughes, Philip. *A Popular History of the Reformation*. New York: Image Books, 1960.

Huizinga, J. *Erasmus of Rotterdam*. With a selection from the letters of Erasmus. London: Phaidon Press, 1952.

Hyma, Albert. *The Brethren of the Common Life*. Grand Rapids, MI: Eerdmans, 1950.

Isaak, Helmut. *Menno Simons and the New Jerusalem*. Kitchener, ON: Pandora Press, 2006.

Iserloh, Erwin, et al. *Reformation, Katholische Reform und Gegenreform*. Freiburg/Basel/Wien, 1967.

Jensen, Janus M. *Denmark and the Crusades 1400–1650*. University of Southern Denmark, 2005.

Johnson, Paul. *A History of the Jews*. London: Weidenfeld & Nicolson, 1993.

Jones, Rufus M. *Spiritual Reformers in the 16th and 17th Centuries*. Boston: Beacon Press, 1959.

Jung, Martin H. *Die Reformation. Theologen, Politiker, Künstler*. Göttingen: Vandenhoeck & Ruprecht, 2008.

Jungmann, Joseph A. *The Mass of the Roman Rite: Its Origin and Development*. Translated by F.A. Brunner; revised by Charles K. Riepe. New York: Benziger Brothers, 1959.

Kamen, Henry. *The Rise of Toleration*. New York and Toronto: McGraw-Hill, 1967.

Katz, Steven T. *Historicism, the Holocaust, and Zionism: Critical Studies in Modern Jewish Thought and History*. New York/London: New York University Press, 1992.

Kaufmann, Thomas. "Luther und Erasmus." *Luther Handbuch*, 2010: 142–52.

———. "Luther and the Jews." In *Jews, Judaism, and the Reformation in Sixteenth-Century Germany*. Edited by Dean Phillip Bell and Stephen G. Burnett. Leiden: E.J. Brill, 2006: 69–104.

———. *Martin Luther*. München: Verlag C.H. Beck, 2006.

Keller, Ludwig. *Die Anfänge der Reformation und die Ketzerschulen*. Berlin: R. Gaertner (H. Heyfelder), 1897.

———. *Ein Apostel der Wiedertäufer*. Leipzig: S. Herzel, 1882.

———. *Die Reformation und die älteren Reformparteien.* Leipzig: S. Herzel, 1885.

Kirn, Hans-Martin. "Luther und die Juden." *Luther Handbuch* 2010: 217–24.

Kittelson, James M. "Luther and Modern Church History." *The Cambridge Companion to Martin Luther.* Edited by Donald K. McKim. Cambridge: Cambridge University Press, 2003: 259–71.

Kiwiet, Jan J. *Pilgram Marbeck. Ein Führer in der Täuferbewegung.* Kassel, 1957.

Klaassen, W. "Anabaptism and the Reformation." *Canadian Journal of Theology* (Jan. 1962): 34–42.

———. "Hans Hut and Thomas Müntzer." *Baptist Quarterly*, XIX (1962): 209–27.

———. *Michael Gaismair: Revolutionary and Reformer.* Leiden: E.J. Brill, 1978.

———, and William Klassen. *Marpeck. A Life of Dissent and Conformity.* Scottdale, PA: Herald Press, 2008.

Knox, R.A. *Enthusiasm: A Chapter in the History of Religion.* New York: Oxford University Press, 1950.

Kohnle, Armin. "Luther und die Bauern." *Luther Handbuch,* 2010: 134–9.

Krahn, Cornelius. *Menno Simons (1496–1561) Ein Beitrag zur Geschichte und Theologie der Taufgesinnten.* Karlsruhe, 1936.

Krajewski, Ekkehard. *Leben und Sterben des Züricher Taeuferführers Felix Manz.* Kassel, 1957.

Kramm, H.H. *The Theology of Martin Luther.* London: James Clarke, 1947.

Kreider, Robert. "Anabaptism and Humanism. An Inquiry into the Relationship of Humanism to the Evangelical Anabaptists." *MQR,* XXIV (Apr. 1952): 123–41.

Kroeker, Greta Grace. *Erasmus in the Footsteps of Paul: A Pauline Theologian.* Toronto: University of Toronto Press, 2011.

Küng, Hans. *Ist die Kirche noch zu retten?* München: Piper Verlag, 2011.

Langton, Edward. *History of the Moravian Church: The Story of the First International Church.* London: George Allen & Unwin, 1956.

Lau, Franz, ed. *Der Glaube der Reformatoren. Luther, Zwingli, Calvin.* Bremen, 2008.

Lecler, Joseph. *Toleration and the Reformation.* Translated by T.L. Westow. 2 vols. New York, 1960.

Leithart, Peter J. *Defending Constantine: The Twilight of an Empire and the Dawn of Christendom.* Downess Grove, IL: IVP Academic, 2010.

Leppin, Volker. *Das Zeitalter der Reformation. Eine Welt im Übergang.* Darmstadt: Theiss Verlag, 2009.

———. "Humanismus." *Luther Handbuch,* 2010: 67–70.

———. "Mystic." *Luther Handbuch,* 2010: 57–61.

Lexutt, Athina. *Die Reformation. Ein Ereignis macht Epoche.* Köln/Weimar/Wien: H. Böhlau, 2009.

———. *Luther.* Köln/Weimar/Wien: H. Böhlau, 2008.

Liechty, Daniel. *Andreas Fischer and the Sabbatarian Anabaptists: An Early Reformation Episode in East Central Europe.* Waterloo, ON: Herald Press, 1988.

Lindberg, Carter. *Beyond Charity: Reformation Initiatives for the Poor.* Kitchener, ON: Augsburg Fortress Publishers, 1993.

———. "Luther's Struggle with Social-Ethical Issues." *The Cambridge Companion to Martin Luther.* Edited by Donald K. McKim. Cambridge: Cambridge University Press, 2003: 165–78.

Lindsay, Thomas M. *A History of the Reformation.* 2 vols. Edinburgh: T. & T. Clark, 1907.

Littell, Franklin H. "The Anabaptist Doctrine of the Restitution of the True Church." *MQR*, XXIV (Jan. 1950): 33–52.

———. *The Theology of Anabaptism: An Interpretation.* Waterloo, ON: Herald Press, 1973.

———. *The Anabaptist View of the Church: A Study in the Origins of Sectarian Protestantism.* 2nd ed. Boston: Starr King Press, 1958.

———. *The Free Church.* Boston: Starr King Press, 1957.

Loewen, Harry. "The Divine Comedy of a Reformation Principle: Luther, the Anabaptists and Bonhoeffer on *sola fide*." *The Theology of Martin Luther: Five Contemporary Canadian Interpretations.* Edited by Egil Grislis. Lutheran Council in Canada, 1985.

———. "The 'Judensau' of Wittenberg: Martin Luther and Anti-Judaism." Unpublished paper presented at Okanagan University College. Kelowna, BC, 1998.

———. *Luther and the Radicals: Another Look at Some Aspects of the Struggle Between Luther and the Radical Reformers.* Waterloo: Wilfrid Laurier University Press, 1974.

Lohse, Bernhard. "Die Stellung der 'Schwärmer' und Täufer in der Reformationsgeschichte." *Archiv für Reformationsgeschichte.* Jahrgang 60, Heft 1 (1969), 5–26.

Lortz, Joseph. *Die Reformation in Deutschland.* 2 vols. 3rd ed. Freiburg: Herder & Co., 1940.

MacCulloch, Diarmaid. *Christianity: The First Three Thousand Years.* New York: Viking Penguin, 2010.

McGriffin A.C. *Martin Luther: The Man and His Work.* New York, 1914.

MacKensen, H. "Historical Interpretation and Luther's Role in the Peasants' Revolt." *Concordia Theological Monthly* (April 1964): 197–209.

McNutt, James E. "Luther and the Jews Revisited: Reflections on a Thought Let Slip." *Currents in Theology and Missions*, 38, no. 1 (Feb. 2011): 40–7.

Maier, Paul L. *Caspar Schwenckfeld on the Person and Work of Christ: A Study of Schwenckfeldian Theology at Its Core.* Assen, The Netherlands: Royal Van Gorcum, 1959.

Man, John. *The Gutenberg Revolution. The Story a Genius and an Invention That Changed the World.* London: Review/Headline Book Publishing, 2002.

Marius, Richard. *Martin Luther. The Christian Between God and Death.* Cambridge/London: Harvard University Press, 1999.

Martin, Dennis D. "Retrospect and Apologia." *MQR*, LXXVII (April 2003): 167–95.

Matheson, Peter. "Review Essay: Recent German Research on Thomas Müntzer." *MQR*, LXXXVI, 1 (2012): 97–109.

The Mennonite Encyclopedia. Edited by H.S. Bender et al. 5 vols. Scottdale, PA: Herald Press, 1957; 1990.

Meisner, Michael. *Martin Luther. Heiliger oder Rebell.* Lübeck, 1981.

Meusel, Alfred. *Thomas Müntzer und seine Zeit. Mit einer Auswahl der Dokumente des grossen deutschen Bauernkrieges.* Berlin, 1952.

Michelbach, Philip A. "Democracy as Vocation: Political Maturity in Luther and Hegel." *Journal of Democratic Theory*, 1, no. 4 (2011): 1–33.

Mittig, Hans-Ernst. *Dürers Bauernsäule: Ein Monument des Widerspruchs.* Frankfurt/Main: Fischer Taschenbuch Verlag, 1984.

Mueller, John Theodor. "A Survey of Luther's Theology." *Bibliotheca Sacra*, CXIII (Apr. 1956), 153–61; (July 1956), 227–38.

Nauert, Charles Garfield. *Humanism and the Culture of Renaissance Europe.* Cambridge: Cambridge University Press, 2006.

Neusner, Jacob, ed. *In the Aftermath of the Holocaust.* New York/London: Garland, 1993.

Newman, Albert Henry. *A History of Anti-Pedobaptism.* Philadelphia, 1897.

Nigg, Walter. *The Heretics.* Edited and translated by Richard and Clara Winston. New York: Alfred A. Knopf, 1962.

Nitsch, Thomas O. "Dr. Martin Luther's intrusion into the realm of political economy (Das Reich der politischen Oekonomie). *American Review of Political Economy*, 5, no. 2 (Dec. 2007): 31–8.

Oberman, H.A. *Man Between God and the Devil.* Translated by Eilee Walisser-Schwarzbart. New York: Doubleday, 1992.

———. *The Reformation: Roots and Ramifications.* Translated by Andrew Colin Gow. Grand Rapids, MI: Eerdmans, 1994.

———. *The Roots of Anti-Semitism in the Age of Renaissance and Reformation.* Translated by James I. Porter. Philadelphia: Fortress Press, 1984.

O'Rafferty, Nicholas. *Instructions on Christian Doctrines – The Sacraments*. New York: Bruce Publishing Company, 1939.

Oyer, John S. *Lutheran Reformers Against Anabaptists*. The Hague, 1964.

———. "The Writings of Luther Against the Anabaptists." *MQR*, XXVII (Apr. 1953): 100–10.

Peachey, Paul. *Die soziale Herkunft der Schweizer Täufer in der Reformationszeit*. Karlsruhe: H. Schneider, 1954.

Peters, Christian. "Luther und seine protestantischen Gegner." *Luther Handbuch*, 2010: 121–34.

———. "Luther und Müntzer." *Luther Handbuch*, 2010: 139–42.

Peters, Frank C. "The Ban in the Writings of Menno Simons." *MQR*, XXIX (Jan. 1955): 16–33.

Pelikan, Jaroslav. *Spirit versus Structure: Luther and the Institutions of the Church*. New York: Collins, 1968.

Pfeffer, Leo. *Church, State and Freedom*. Boston: Beacon Press, 1953.

Pietersen, Lloyd. *Reading the Bible after Christendom*. Harrisonburg, VA/Waterloo, ON: Herald Press, 2012.

Pinomaa, Lennard. "Die Heilung bei Luther." *Theologische Zeitschrift*, Heft 1 (Jan.–Feb. 1954): 30–50.

Plass, Ewald M. (ed.). *What Luther Says: An Anthology*. 3 vols. Saint Louis, MO: Concordia Publishing Company, 1959.

Plummer, Marjorie Elizabeth (ed. with Robin B. Barnes). *Ideas and Cultural Margins in Early Modern History*. Essays in Honor of H.C. Erik Midelfort. Surrey: Ashgate, 2009.

Price, David Hotchkiss. *Albrecht Dürer's Renaissance: Humanism, Reformation, and the Art of Faith*. Ann Arbor, MI: University of Michigan Press, 2003.

Probst, Christopher. "Martin Luther and the Jews: A Reappraisal." In *The Theologian: The Internet Journal for Integrated Theology*, 2005. http://www.theologian.org.uk/churchhistory/lutherandthejews.html.

Raeder, Siegfried. "Luther und die Türken." *Luther Handbuch*, 2010: 224–31.

Ranke, Leopold von. *Deutsche Geschichte im Zeitalter der Reformation*. Im Wien: Phaidon-Verlag. Ungekürzte Textausgabe (n.d.).

Rempel, Gerhard. "Mennonites and the Holocaust: From Collaboration to Perpetuation." *MQR*, LXXXIV (Oct. 2010): 507–49.

Rempel-Burkholder, Byron. "Lutherans and Anabaptists reconcile in service of repentance and forgiveness." *Canadian Mennonite*, 14, no. 16 (Aug. 23, 2010): 32.

Ritter, Gerhard. *Luther, Gestalt und Tat*. 6. Auflage. München, 1959.

Rose, Paul Lawrence. *Revolutionary Antisemitism in Germany from Kant to Wagner*. Princeton: Princeton University Press, 1990.

Roth, John D., and James M. Stayer, eds. *A Companion to Anabaptism and Spiritualism, 1521–1700*. Leiden: E.J. Brill, 2007.

Rupp, Gordon. "Andrew Karlstadt and Reformation Puritanism." *Journal of Theological Studies*. New Series, X (1959): 308–26.

———. *Patterns of Reformation*. London: Epworth Press, 1969.

Russell, Bertrand. *A History of Western Philosophy*. New York: Simon & Schuster, 1972.

Sachar, Abram Leon. *A History of the Jews*. New York: Alfred A. Knopf, 1964.

Schaber, Will, ed. *Weinberg der Freiheit. Der Kampf um ein demokratisches Deutschland von Thomas Müntzer bis Thomas Mann*. New York: Frederick Ungar Publishing Company, 1945.

Schaff, Harold H. "The Anabaptists, the Reformers, and the Civil Government." *Church History*, I (March 1932): 27–46.

Schaff, Philip. *History of the Christian Church*, Vol. VII. Reproduction of the 2nd ed., revised. Grand Rapids, MI: Eerdmans, 1953.

Schiff, Otto. "Thomas Müntzer und die Bauernbewegung am Oberrhein." *Historische Zeitschrift*. Band 110. München/Berlin, 1913.

Schilling, Heinz. *Martin Luther. Rebell in einer Zeit des Umbruchs. Eine Biografie*. München: Verlag C.H. Beck, 2012.

Schnyder, Caroline. *Reformation*. Stuttgart: Verlag Eugen Ulmer, 2008.

Schorlemmer, Friedrich. *Hier stehe ich. Martin Luther*. 2003.

———. *Selig sind die Verlierer. Friedrich Schorlemmer im Gespräch mit Meinhard Schmidt-Degenhardt*. Zürich: Pendo-Verlag, 1996.

Schraepler, Horst W. *Die rechtliche Behandlung der Täufer in der deutschen Schweiz, Südwestdeutschland und Hessen, 1525–1618*. Tübingen, 1957.

Schramm, Brook and Kirsi I. Stjerna, eds. *Martin Luther, the Bible, and the Jewish People: A Reader*. Philadelphia: Fortress Press, 2012.

Schultz, Selina G. *Caspar Schwenckfeld von Ossig (1498–1561): Sprirtual Interpreter of Christianity, Apostle of the Middle Way, Pioneer in Modern Religious Thought*. Norristown, PA, 1946.

Schwiebert, E.G. *Luther and His Times*. Saint Louis, MO: Concordia Publishing House, 1950.

Scott, Tom. *Thomas Müntzer: Theology and Revolution in the German Reformation*. New York: St. Martin's Press, 1989.

Seiling, Jonathan. "Verfolgung." Online in mennlexV.de.

Shachar, Isaiah. *The "Judensau": A Medieval Anti-Jewish Motif and Its History*. London, 1974.

Shirer, William L. *The Rise and Fall of the Third Reich: A History of Nazi Germany*. New York: Simon & Schuster, 1960.

Sider, Ronald J. "Karlstadt's Orlamünde Theology: A Theology of Regeneration." *MQR*, XLV (July 1971): 191–218.

Siirala, Aarne. *Gottes Gebot bei Martin Luther*. Helsinki: Savon Sanomain Kirjapaino Oy, 1956.

Smith, C. Henry. *The Story of the Mennonites*. 3rd ed., revised and enlarged. Newton, KS: Mennonite Publication Office, 1950.

Smith, Preserved. *The Life and Letters of Martin Luther*. Boston: Houghton Mifflin, 1914.

———. *Erasmus*. New York: Harper & Brothers, 1923.

Smithson, R.J. *The Anabaptists: Their Contribution to Our Protestant Heritage*. London: J. Clarke & Co., 1935.

Snyder, C. Arnold. *Anabaptist History and Theology: An Introduction*. Kitchener, ON: Pandora Press, 1995.

———. ed. *Commoners and Community: Essays in Honour of Werner O. Packull*. Kitchener, ON/ Scottdale, PA: Herald Press, 2002.

———. *The Life and Thought of Michael Sattler*. Scottdale, PA, 1984.

Stauffer, Ethelbert. "The Anabaptist Theology of Martyrdom." *MQR*, XIX (July 1945): 179–214.

Stayer, James M. *Anabaptists and the Sword*. Lawrence, KS: Coronado Press, 1972, 1976.

———. *The German Peasants' War and Anabaptist Community of Goods*. Montreal & Kingston: McGill-Queen's University Press, 1994.

———. "Terrorism, the Peasants' War and the 'Wiedertäufer.'" *Archiv für Reformationsgeschichte*, LVI (1965): 227–29.

Steinmetz, David C. *Luther in Context*. Grand Rapids, MI: Baker Books, 1995.

———. *Reformers in the Wings*. Philadelphia: Fortress Press, 1971.

———. "Scholasticism and Radical Reform." *MQR* (April 1971): 123–44.

Stockhausen, Alma von. *Der Geist im Widerspruch. Von Luther zu Hegel*. Weilheim-Bierbronnen: Gustav-Siewerth-Akademie, 1990.

Strohl, Jane. E. "Luther's Spiritual Journey." *Cambridge Companion to Martin Luther*. Edited by Donald K. McKim. Cambridge: Cambridge University Press, 2003.

Strübind, Andrea. *Eifriger als Zwingli: Die frühe Täuferbewegung in der Schweiz*. Berlin: Duncker & Humblot, 2003.

Stupperich, Robert. *Das Münsterische Täufertum. Ergebnisse und Probleme der neueren Forschung*. Münster: Aschendorff, 1958.

Thomson, Bard. *Humanists and Reformers: A History of the Renaissance and Reformation*. Grand Rapids, MI: Eerdmans, 1996.

Tillich, Paul. *The Shaking of the Foundations*. New York: Scribner's, 1948.

Tillmanns, Walter G. *The World and Men Around Luther*. Minneapolis: Augsburg, 1959.

Tomlin, Graham. *Luther and His World*. Lion Publishing, Oxford: Oxford University Press, 2002.

Torvent, Samuel. *Luther and the Hungry Poor: Gathered Fragments*. Philadelphia: Fortress Press, 2008.

Troeltsch, Ernst. *The Social Teaching of the Christian Churches*. Translated by Olive Wyon. 2 vols. London, 1931.

United Methodist News Service. http://www.umc.org/news-and-media/methodists-lutherans-catholics-mark-historic-agreements-anniversary.

Vedder, Henry C. *Balthasar Hübmaier the Leader of the Anabaptists*. New York: G.P. Putnam's Sons, 1905.

———. *The Reformation in Germany*. New York: Macmillan, 1914.

Verduin, Leonard. *The Reformers and Their Stepchildren*. Grand Rapids, MI: Eerdmans, 1964.

Vogler, Günther. "Thomas Müntzer und die Gesellschaft seiner Zeit." Mühlhausen: Thomas Müntzer Gesellschaft, Veröffentlichungen 4, 2003.

Wappler, Paul. *Die Täuferbewegung in Thüringen von 1526–1584*. Jena: Eugen Diederichs, 1913.

Watson, Philip S. *Let God Be God! An Interpretation of the Theology of Martin Luther*. Philadelphia: Muhlenberg Press, 1949.

Weber, Max. *The Protestant Ethic and the Spirit of Capitalism*. Published in 1905 in German; translated later.

Welsh, Frank. *The Battle for Christendom: The Council of Constance, the East–West Conflict, and the Dawn of Modern Europe*. Woodstock & New York: Overlook Press, 2008.

Westin, Gunnar. *The Free Church Through the Ages*. Translated from the Swedish by Virgil A. Olson. Nashville: Broadman Press, 1958.

Weydmann, L. *Luther, ein Charakter-und Spiegelbild für unsere Zeit*. Hamburg und Gotha: bei Friedrich und Andreas Perthes, 1850.

Whitford, David M. "Luther's Political Encounters." *The Cambridge Companion to Martin Luther*. Edited by Donald M. McKim. Cambridge: Cambridge University Press, 2003.

Die Wiedertäufer zu Münster Berichte, Aussagen und Aktenstücke von Augenzeugen und Zeitgenossen. Jena: Eugen Diederichs, 1923.

Wilbur, Earl Morse. *A History of Unitarianism. Socinianism and Its Antecedents*. 2 vols. Cambridge, MA: Harvard University Press, 1945.

Williams, G.H. "'Congregationalist' Luther and the Free Church." *Lutheran Quarterly* (Aug. 1967): 283–95.

———. *The Radical Reformation.* 3rd ed. Kirksville, MO: Sixteenth Century Publishers, 1992.

———, and Angel M. Mergal eds. *Spiritual and Anabaptist Writers.* Documents Illustrative of the Radical Reformation. Philadelphia: Westminster Press, 1957.

Wilson, Derek. *Out of the Storm: The Life and Legacy of Martin Luther.* London: Hutchinson, 2007.

Wiswedel, Wilhelm. *Bilder und Führergestalten aus dem Täufertum.* Kassel, 1952.

———. "The Inner and the Outer Word: A Study in the Anabaptist Doctrine of the Scriptures." *MQR,* XXVI (July 1952): 171–91.

Wolf, Gustav. *Quellenkunde der deutschen Reformationszeit.* 3 vols. Gotha, 1914.

Wood, Diana, ed. *Christianity and Judaism.* Oxford: Blackwell, 1992.

Wray, Frank J. "The Anabaptist Doctrine of the Restitution of the Church." *MQR,* XXVIII (July 1954): 186–96.

Wriedt, Markus. "Luther's Theology." *The Cambridge Companion to Martin Luther.* Edited by Donald K. McKim. Cambridge: Cambridge University Press, 2003.

Wright, D.F. ed. *Martin Bucer: Reforming Church and Community.* Cambridge: Cambridge University Press, 1994.

Zahrnt, Heinz. *Martin Luther. Reformator Wider Willen.* Leipzig: Evangelische Verlagsanstalt, 2000.

Zeeden, Ernst Walter. *The Legacy of Luther.* Translated from the German by Ruth M. Bethell. Westminster, MD: Newman Press, 1954.

Zschäbitz, Gerhard. *Zur Mitteldeutschen Wiedertäuferbewegung nach dem grossen Bauernkrieg.* Berlin: Rütten & Loening, 1958.

Zimmermann, Moshe. *Wilhelm Marr. The Patriarch of Antisemitism.* New York/Oxford: Oxford University Press, 1986.

Žižek, Slavoj and Boris Gunjevic. *God in Pain. Inversions of Apocalypse.* New York: Seven Stories Press, 2012.

Zschoch, Hellmut. "Luther und seine altgläubigen Gegner." *Luther Handbuch* 2010: 115–21.

———. "Streitschriften." *Luther Handbuch* 2010: 277–94.

Zuck, Lowell H. "Anabaptism: Abortive Counter-Revolt Within the Reformation." *Church History,* XXVI (Sept. 1957).

Index

Abelard, Peter, 131
About the Great Lutheran Fool – and how Doctor Murner exorcised him (Murner), 277
Adler, Clemens, 140–41
Admonition to Pray Against the Turks (Luther), 85–86
Admonition to the Clergy to Preach Against Usury (Luther), 85
Adrian VI, Pope, 97–98
adult baptism, 18–19, 26, 130–32, 151
Against the Antinomians (Luther), 189–91, 196, 199
Against the Celestial Prophets Concerning Images and the Sacrament (Luther), 49–50
Against the Eislebener (Luther), 190
Against Hanswurst (Luther), 261, 262–67; politics of, 267–68
Against the Murderous and Plundering Bands Among the Peasants (Luther), 77–80
Against the Roman Papacy, an Institution of the Devil (Luther), 261
Against the Sabbatarians (Luther), 229, 231
Against the Terrible Errors of the Anabaptists (Agricola), 145
Against the Whole World since the Apostles (Campanus), 196
Agricola, Franz, *Against the Terrible Errors of the Anabaptists*, 145
Agricola, Johannes, 188–89; retraction of, 190–91
Albert of Brandenburg, 278
Albigensian Crusade, 219
Aleander, Hieronimous, *Exsurge Domine*, 95
Allstedt League, 60
Anabaptists: and American Protestantism, 211; apocalyptic visions, 151, 157–58; believers' (adult) baptism, 18–19, 23, 26, 114, 130–32, 135, 136–37, 145, 160;

blasphemous and seditious beliefs of, 207–8; *Christian Baptism*, 213; Christian morality, 141–47; church–state relations, 117, 139–41, 209–10; communalism, 25, 31, 83–84, 139–40; communion, administration of, 115; *Concerning Evil Overseers*, 213; conflicts with Luther, 30–31; conflict with magisterial reformers, 117, 209–10; as "corner preachers," 205; differentiation between groups, 159–61; division within, 23–25, 214–15; expulsion from Zurich, 118, 124; as fellowship of believers, 281; free church concept, 137–41; and free will, 109–12; *German Theology*, 115; hedgepreachers, 118, 119; Luther's view of, 286–87; Melchiorite Anabaptism, 119; missionary activity, 119, 120; and the New Testament, 25, 139–40, 160; origins of, 26–28, 114–15; pacifism, and non-resistance, 140–41, 162, 212; peaceful and revolutionary radicalism, 123–24, 211–14; peasants' defeat, use of as propaganda, 82; persecution of, 117–18, 159, 161–62, 163, 203, 206, 210–11, 219–21, 287–88; polygenesis theory of origins, 114; reconciliation with Lutherans, 294; and religious tolerance, 199, 211–14, 221–22; salvation, and predestination, 104, 110, 111–12; *Schleitheim Confession*, 115; social strata, 117–18; spread of, 118–19, 160; Swiss Brethren, 26–27, 114, 116–18; theological emphases of, 28; variety within, 114–16; vindication of, 280; on war against the the Turks, 244–45; Word of God as weapon against, 122–23. *See also reform movements by name (Münsterite Anabaptists, Mennonites, etc.)*

Anabaptists and the Sword (Stayer), 215

Anfechtungen: of Luther, 4–5, 8, 10, 92; of man, 49

Anna of Oldenburg, 163

Answer to Luther's Malediction (Schwenckfeld), 181–82

Antichrist: destruction of, 157–58; pope as, 55, 261

anticlericalism, 17

anti-Judaism, in Reformation Europe, 225–42

antinomians, 25, 186–89, 284; and Agricola, 188–91; controversy over grace and moral laws, 20, 186; law and gospel, relationship between, 192–93; Loists, 187

anti-Semitism: and anti-Judaism of Luther, 232–33, 236–37; emergence of, 239

anti-Trinitarians, 25, 28, 195–99, 281

apocalyptic visions, 151, 157–58; of Turkish threat, 253–54, 255, 256, 257

Apostolic Creed, 206

Appeal for Prayer Against the Turks (Luther), 245, 256–57

Aquinas, Thomas, 33, 95

Archbishop Albert of Mainz, 11–12, 266; letter from Erasmus, 94–95

Arians, 251

Aristotle, 34, 87–88, 91

Arnoldists, 131

Arnold of Brescia, 131

Assertio septem sacramentorum adversus Martinuum Lutherum (Henry VIII), 99
Athanasian Creed, 193
Augsburg Confession of Lutheran dogma, 262
Augustinian monks, 39–41, 89–90
authority, and the common man: church–state relations, 54–58, 79; oppression of, 81–82; rebellion, crime of, 80
autonomy of local churches, 17
Axiomata Erasmi (Erasmus), 96

Bainton, Roland H., 104, 209, 222, 225, 281–82; *Hunted Heretic*, 281
baptism: controversy over, 18–19, 145, 265, 282; historical perspectives, 130–32; Luther on, 132–37; radical conceptions of, 23–24, 198; sacramental nature of, 136–37; water baptism, 132–34; *Wiedertäufer*, 114
baptismal regeneration, 130–31, 198
Barge, Hermann, 35, 280
Barth, Karl, 282
The Babylonian Captivity of the Church (Luther), 17–19, 48, 90, 93, 202
Bax, Belfort, 54
Beheim, Sebald and Barthel, 170
believers' (adult) baptism, 18–19, 130–32, 135, 136–37, 145, 151, 161
Bender, Harold S., 26, 125–26, 129, 199, 211, 212
Bensing, Manfred, 68
Bertram, Martin, 230
Beruf (calling), 87, 92
Bethke, Eberhard, 241
Beutel, Alfred, 180
Beuys, Barbara, 241

Beza, Theodore, 280
Bible, 5; Acts, 83–84; common sense, use of in reading, 50; Daniel (book of), 63, 65; German translation of, 9, 33; James (book of), 35; New Testament, 9, 137; Old Testament, on circumcision, 135, 136; sovereignty of Scriptures, 6–8; theological differences of Luther and Müntzer, 61–62; Thessalonians, 87
bibliolatry, 61–62
Black Death, 229
blasphemy: defined, 206; Jews as blasphemers, 228, 230
The Blasphemy of John of Leyden (Simons), 162
A Blast Against the Archbishop of Mainz (Luther), 39–40
Blaurock, George, 26, 114, 123–24
Boehmer, Heinrich, 3
Boekebinder, Bartholomaus, 152
Bohemian Brethren, 131, 143
Böhme, Helmut, 84
Bondage of the Will (Luther), 290
Bonhoeffer, Dietrich, 241, 297
Boniface III, 271, 272
Bora, Catherine von, and marriage to Luther, 102
Bornkamm, Heinrich, 49
The Book of the Life of Jesus (*Sefer Toledot Yeshu*), 235
Brady, Thomas, 21, 74
Brant, Sebastian, *The Ship of Fools*, 90
Brecht, Martin, 49, 227, 232, 244, 268, 284, 291; on 1541 revision to Luther Bible, 237–38; *Anfechtungen* of Luther, 4–5
Briessmann, J., 170

Brothers of the Common Life, 2, 4, 27, 150
Brück, George, 46, 66
Brück, Gregory, 6
de Bruys, Peter, 131
Brunner, Emil, 282
Bucer, Martin, 107, 230
Bugenhagen, Johannes, 175, 182, 208
Bullinger, Heinrich, 124, 212–13
Burer, Albert, 43

calling (*Beruf*), 87, 92
Calvin, John, 24, 116, 198; *Conte la secte phantastique et furieuse des Libertines qui se namment Spirituels*, 187; and predestination, 104, 105–6; religious tolerance, 222
Calvinism, and capitalism, 87
Campanus, Johannes, 195–96, 199; *Restitution*, 196; *Against the Whole World since the Apostles*, 196
Campeggio, Cardinal Lorenzo, 96
capitalism, and usury, 85–86, 88
Capito, Wolfgang, 107, 182
cartoons, use of in pamphlets, 21
Castelio, Sebastian, 280
Catechism (Luther), 102
Cathari, 141
Catharine of Aragon, 158
Catholicism. *See* Roman Catholic Church
Cellarius, Martin, 195
Charlemagne, 275, 276
Charles V, 33, 96, 107, 163, 197, 244
Christ, as judge, 4, 5
Christian Baptism (Anabaptist pamphlet), 213
Christian Baptism (Simons), 131–32, 162–63

Christian "fundamentalism," 22
Christian II, King of Denmark, 35
Christians, active involvement of in the church, 29
Chronica (*Bible of History*) (Franck), 216
Church Council of the Evangelical Lutheran Church of America: Lutheran–Jewish relations, 294–95
church–state relations: Anabaptist view of, 117, 160; authority, and the common man, 54–58, 79, 80, 287; free church concept, 137–41; *Fürstenpredigt* ("Princes Sermon," Müntzer), 63–66; sedition, 207–8; separation of, 28, 138–39, 209–10, 246, 297; in time of war, 247–50, 258; treatment of heretics, 206–7
Clasen, Claus-Peter, 219–20
Clement of Alexandria, 101
Clement VII, Pope, 98, 101, 248
clerical marriage, 16
Cochlaeus, Johannes: criticism of Luther, 73, 90; *History of the Acts and Writings of Luther*, 277
Colet, John, 93
Commentary on the Psalms (Luther), 94
common chests, 85, 86–87
common man, 285–86; church–state relations, 54–58, 79; oppression of, 81–82; rebellion, crime of, 80
communalism, 25, 31, 83–84, 139–40
communion. *See* Eucharist (Holy Communion)
Concerning Business and Usury (Luther), 85
Concerning Evil Overseers (Anabaptist pamphlet), 213

Concerning Heretics and those who Burn Them
  (Hubmaier), 212
Concerning Rebaptism, A Letter to Two
  Pastors (Luther), 120, 134–35, 137
Concerning the Abuse of the Mass (Luther), 39
Concerning the Sacrament and Other
  Innovations (Luther), 43–44
confirmation, as Catholic sacrament, 18
Confutation of the Münster Confession
  (Luther), 155
Conrad Grebel Review, 281
conscience: devil as master of, 7; freedom of,
  29, 217; and liberty of worship, 205–6;
  and obedience, 7
Constantine the Great, 26, 139, 218, 275
consubstantiation, 48
Conte la secte phantastique et furieuse des
  Libertines qui se namment Spirituels
  (Calvin), 187
Contra Henricum regem Angliae (Luther), 99
Cornelius, C.A., 280; *Geschichte des*
  Münsterischen Aufruhrs, 149–50
Council of Constance, and Jan Hus, 2–3, 271
Council of Mühlhausen, 66–67
Council of Nicaea, 218
Council of Nürnberg, and Lutheran
  movement, 167–68, 170
Council of Trent, 270, 276, 278; on
  Eucharist, 47–48
Council of Wittenberg, Reformation
  ordinance, 38
Count Bartholomew of Ahlfeld, 163
Counter-Reformation, 270
Coutts, Alfred, 144, 166, 167
Cox, Harvey, 297; *Fire From Heaven*, 297

Cranach, Lucas, 55, 233
Crautwald, Valentine, 173, 176, 178, 182
Creutzinger, Caspar, 208
The Crucified God (Moltmann), 295–96
Cyprian, 130

Daniel (book of), 63, 65
De libero arbitrio diatribe sive collatio (On
  Free Will) (Erasmus), 100–101
Denck, Hans, 24, 26, 28, 67, 159, 166–67;
  and Anabaptism, 114–15, 116, 117; as
  anti-Trinitarian, 195; banishment from
  Nürnberg, 167–68; *The Hearing of False*
  Prophets or Antichrist, 213; influence of
  Müntzer on, 167; inner Word of God,
  166, 167, 168–70; Luther on, 170–71;
  religious tolerance, 215, 281; salvation as
  inward process, 169; *Whether God Is the*
  Cause of Evil, 110, 168–69; *Widderruf*
  (Recantation), 169
Der Judenfeind (Nigrinus), 239
Design for a Dead Peasant (Dürer), 84
the devil: as *Magister conscientiae*, 7;
  and Münsterite Anabaptists, 155–56;
  power of, 10; twenty storms of against
  Luther, 190
Devotio Moderna (Modern Devotion), 27
Die älteste Chronik der Hutterischen Brüder, 30
Diet of Augsburg, 107, 262
Diet of Regensburg, 267
Diet of Speier, 262
Diet of Speyer, 253–54, 269
Diet of Worms, 7, 33, 42, 55, 96, 262
Dillenberger, John, 134
direct speaking, 263–64

dissenters: banishment of, 203–4, 209; and blasphemy, 206; treatment of heretics, 201–3, 206–7
divine righteousness, and grace, 5–6
divine will, 63, 65
Dix, Dom Gregory, 282
Donatist heretics, 131, 141, 219, 251
"Doopsgezinden," 115
Duchess Elizabeth of Saxony, 145
Duke Ernest of Mansfeld, 67–68
Duke George of Saxony, 6, 38, 99
Duke Johann of Saxony, 14
Duke John, 63, 66
Duke Philip of Hesse, 120, 145; bigamy of, 143, 158
Durant, Will, 100
Dürer, Albrecht, 167; *Design for a Dead Peasant*, 84

Eck, Dr. Johann, 35, 138; *Manual Against the Lutherans*, 277
Eck, S., 86
Eckhard, Meister, 27
education, reform in, 91–92
Edwards, Mark U., Jr., 73, 256
Egranus, Sylvius, 58
Einsiedel, Heinrich von, 81
"emergency bishops," 139
Emser, Hieronymus, 99, 277
Emser, Jerome, 73
Epitome of the Doctrine of Luther (Staphylus), 278
Erasmus of Rotterdam, Desiderius, 277; and Adrian VI, 97–98; on the Anabaptists, 145; anti-Judaism, 230; *Axiomata Erasmi*, 96; and Clement VII, 98; criticism of by Catholic theologians, 95–96; *De libero arbitrio diatribe sive collatio (On Free Will)*, 100–101; as father of Anabaptism, 28; free will, 99–102; *Hyperaspistes*, 73, 106, 107–8; and Luther, 90, 92–97, 99, 104–9, 290; on the *Ninety-Five Theses*, 93–94; *Praise of Folly*, 93; *On War Against the Turks*, 244
ethics vs. dogma, 28
Eucharist (Holy Communion), 51; administration of, 18, 19; as sacrament, 133, 198; and transubstantiation, 47–50, 286–87
Eusebeus of Caesarea, 218
Eutyches of Constantinople, 181
Eutychianism, heresy of, 181
evangelical Anabaptists. *See* Anabaptists
excommunication, 212
Exposition of the Magnificat (Luther), 166, 179

Faber, Johann, 96, 277
Fabricius, 236
faith: and divine righteousness, 5–6; as expression of love, 19; and good works, 9–10, 14–15; modern relevance of, 295–96; personal faith, 29; in the "secular city," 297
Fellmann, Walter, 167
Ferdinand, King of Austria, 243
Fire from Heaven (Cox), 297
Fischer, Andreas, 231
Fischer, Hans Georg, 282

Fisher, John, 99
Foundation of Christian Doctrine (Simons), 136
Francis, Pope, 295
Franck, Sebastian, 116; *Chronica* (*Bible of History*), 216; on diversity of reform movements, 24; on growth of Anabaptism, 119; inner vs. outer Word of God, 167; religious tolerance, 215–17
Frederick II, King of Prussia, 293
Frederick the Wise, 12, 33, 35, 38, 39, 42, 76, 94, 95, 247
Free Church movement, 280, 288, 297
free will, 34, 216; in Anabaptism, 28; Erasmus on, 99–102; and salvation, 168–69; vs. un-free will of Luther, 25, 102–6, 108–9, 290
Friedman, Robert, 195
Friesen, Abraham, 28
Friesen, Peter M., 214, 215
The Freedom of a Christian (Luther), 19–20, 73
Fürstenpredigt ("Princes Sermon," Müntzer), 63–66, 128

Garside, Charles, 124
Genesis, on relationship between God and Christ, 196
German Theology, 115
"The German Confession of Faith" (hymn, Luther), 194
Geyer, Florian, 84
God in Pain (Gunjevic, Žižek), 296–97
"God the Father be with us" (hymn, Luther), 194–95
Goertz, Hans-Juergen, 54–55

Goethe, Johann Wolfgang von, "The Sorcerer's Apprentice" (*Der Zauberlehrling*), 185
Goetz von Berlichingen, Gottfried, 84
good works: Catholic Mass as, 18; and faith, 9–10, 14–15, 31; and legalism, 35, 284; and poverty, 86–87; and right relationship with God, 284–85; as substitute for grace, 12
grace: Erasmus' concept of, 101; good works as substitute for, 12, 142; Luther's concept of, 5–6, 102–4; and moral laws, 20
Grebel, Conrad, 26, 114, 117, 159; letter to Luther, 120–21; letter to Müntzer, 125–30, 140, 212; on Müntzer, 69; theological differences with Müntzer, 128–30; on Wittenberg radicals, 127–28
Gregory, Brad S., 220
Gregory IX, Pope, 219
Gregory the Great, Pope, 272
Grisar, Hartmann, *Martin Luther*, 276–77
Gritsch, Eric, 237
Gunjevic, Boris, *God in Pain*, 296–97
Günther, Franz, 58
Gûttel, Dr. Caspar, 189

Habakkuk 2:4, on faith, 5
Hanson, Mark S., 294
Harbison, E. Harris, 211
Hätzer, Ludwig, 124, 155, 158
hedgepreachers, 118, 119
Hegenwald, Erhard, 121
Heine, Heinrich, 288
Henry of Lausanne, 131

Henry the Younger, Duke of Brunswick–
    Wolfenbüttel: as "Hanswurst,"
    262–64; heresy accusation against John
    Frederick, 264; war against, 267–68
Henry VIII, 96, 158; *Assertio septem
    sacramentorum adversus Martinuum
    Lutherum*, 99
hereditary sin, 206
heretics, and heresy: banishment, 203–4,
    209; false prophets, 203; as jurisdiction
    of church, 56; and justification by faith
    (*sola fide*), 8; persecution of, 218–21;
    treatment of heretics, 201–3, 206–7,
    209, 214
Hergot, Hans, 84
Hergot, Kunegunde, 84
The Hearing of False Prophets or Antichrist
    (Denck), 213
History of the Acts and Writings of Luther
    (Cochlaeus), 277
History of Unitarianism (Wilbur), 281
Hoffman, Melchior, 27, 28, 115, 162; as
    Anabaptist missionary, 119, 156;
    apocalyptic visions of, 151
Holl, Karl, 114
Holocaust, historical legacy of Luther,
    239–42
Holy Communion, and transubstantiation,
    47–50, 145
Holy Roman Empire, 275–76
Holy Spirit, 144–45; Anabaptist view of,
    121; importance of, 29; relationship
    between Father and Son, 196
Howart, Robert Glenn, 22, 223

Hubmaier, Balthasar, 26, 27, 28, 110, 120,
    155, 159; and Anabaptism, 114, 116, 117;
    *Concerning Heretics and those who Burn
    Them*, 212; and Denck, 215; expulsion
    of Jews, 229; *On Free Will*, 111–12;
    just war, 140; *On the Sword*, 214–15;
    Wadshut community, 140
Hughes, Philip, 282, 287
Huizinga, Johan, 28
humanism, influence on Luther, 89–90
humanists: criticism of Roman Catholic
    church, 90; objections to Luther, 90–91;
    salvation, and predestination, 103–4
human nature, sinfulness of, 4, 112
Hunted Heretic (Bainton), 281
Hus, Jan, 27, 60; and Council of Constance,
    2–3, 271
Hut, Hans, 27, 114, 116, 159, 160, 214
Hutten, Ulrich von, 244
Hutter, Jacob, 27
Hutterian Brethren/Hutterites, 24, 69, 83,
    112, 119, 161
hymns, 91–92, 194–95
Hyperaspistes (Erasmus), 73, 106, 107–8

Ignatius of Antioch, 130
immorality, 38
indulgences, 11–12, 13, 93, 245, 248, 265
"Indulgences and Grace" (sermon), 13
infant baptism, 18–19, 23, 30, 36, 114, 121,
    130–32, 198, 206, 209; compared to
    circumcision, 135, 136
Inquisition, 187, 197, 198, 219
invisible vs. visible church, 25–26, 139

Irenaeus, 101, 218
Islam: the Koran, Mohammedan beliefs in, 250–51; Luther on, 243–59; religious differences, bridging of, 258–59, 290–91

Japan, theology in postwar world, 296
Jesuits (Society of Jesus), 276
"Jewish sow" motif: city church of Lutherstadt-Wittenberg, 226–28; in depictions of the pope, 21; origin and meaning of, 235–37
Jews, and Judaism: as agents of the devil, 238; cultural-social reasons for hatred of, 228–30; expulsion from Wittenberg, 228, 235; expulsions of, 229, 239; Holocaust, and historical legacy of Luther, 239–42; *On the Jews and their Lies* (Luther), 225; and justification by faith (*sola fide*), 8; Lutheran–Jewish relations, 294–95; Luther's intolerance of, 22, 225–42, 290; Luther's recommendations for treatment of, 234–35; Luther's writings against, 229–38; negative cartoon illustrations, 233; persecution of, 233, 235; and the Sabbatarians, 231–32
Johann Frederick, Elector of Saxony, 206
John Frederick, Elector, 234–35, 263; heresy accusations against, 265–66
John the Baptist, 134, 136
Jonas, Justus, 33, 96–97, 230
Jones, Rufus, 169–70, 171
Josel of Rosheim, Rabbi, 232; petition against *On the Jews and Their Lies*, 234

Journal of Mennonite Studies, 281
Jovinians, 131
Judensau motif. *See* "Jewish sow" motif
Julius II, Pope, 248
justification by faith (*sola fide*), 6, 8, 29, 30, 35, 141, 146, 161, 166, 172, 216, 222–23, 282, 284–85, 293–94
Justinian Code, 198, 206

Karlstadt, Andreas Bodenstein von, 9–10, 28, 33, 106, 116, 120, 121, 280; and the Augustinian monks, 39; communion, administration of, 18, 19; Eucharistic views, recantation of, 50–52; and presence of Christ, 48, 49, 50, 122; religious liberty, 203, 205; sermons against, 42, 44; as Wittenberg radical reformer, 34–36, 45–47, 124, 127, 171, 175, 176, 286; and the Zwickau prophets, 37, 38
Kaufmann, Thomas, 237
Kingdom of Münster. *See* Münsterite Anabaptists
Kirk, Kenneth, 282
Kitamori, Kazoh, *Theology of the Pain of God*, 296
Knipperdolling, Bernhard (Bernt), 151, 153, 154
Knox, Ronald A., 27, 159
Köhler, Walter, 28
Köstlin, Julius, 254
Kramar, Michael, 144, 158
Krechting, Bernhard, 154
Kreider, Robert, 28
de Kuiper, Willem, 152

Lang, Johannes, 17
Lang, John, 55
last rites, as Catholic sacrament, 18
Last Supper, 51; administration of, 35, 121; as *figura* of Christ, 48; spiritual interpretation of, 175–76
The Last Words of David (Luther), 232, 237
Lech, Werner, 294
Lecler, Joseph, 204, 209; on Sebastian Franck, 216–17
legalism, 35, 284
Leo III, Pope, 275
Leo X, Pope, 12, 93, 96, 99, 142, 247; *Exsurge Domine*, 245; letters from Luther, 19; response to *Ninety-Five Theses*, 13
Leppin, Volker, 166
Lessing, Gotthold Ephraim, *Nathan the Wise*, 211
A Letter to the Princes of Saxony Concerning the Seditious Spirit (Luther), 65–66
Leyden, Jan van, 152, 160; execution of, 154; as new King David of Zion, 153; Simon's criticisms of, 162
Liechtenstein, Leonhard von, 214
Lindberg, Carter, 86, 88
Lindsay, Thomas, 27
Link, Wenceslaus, 203
Littell, Franklin, 30, 211, 218
Loci communesi (Melanchthon), 101
Loists, 187
Lollards, 2
Lord's Supper, 124; administration of, 18, 45, 107, 121, 171; interpretation of, 172–73, 174
Lösscher, Thomas, 204
Louis II of Hungary, 96

love, as expression of faith, 19
Luke 9:19–36, on the Trinity, 194
Luther, Martin, 1; on the Anabaptists, 121; *Anfechtungen* of, 4–5, 8, 10, 92; anti-Jewish writings, 229–38; and the antinomians, 189–91; approach to reforms, 43–44; on baptism, 132–37; and capitalism, 85–88; children's hymn, 269; Christian morality, and sinfulness, 141–44, 145–46; church-state relations, 28, 54–58, 79, 80, 138–39; common chests, 85, 86–87; conflicts with radical reformers, 30–31; Diet of Worms, 7, 33, 42, 55, 96; double nature of, 44–45; ecclesiastical visitations, 204–6; on Epistle of James, 9–10; and Erasmus, 92–97, 99, 104–9, 290; exposition of Jeremiah, 179; German translation of the Bible, 9, 33, 87; "God the Father be with us" (hymn), 194–95; on Hans Denck, 170–71; and the Holocaust, 239–42; and humanism, 89–93; influence on Peasants' War, 53–54, 71–73, 74, 76–79; interpretative differences with radical reformers, 29, 289; intolerance against dissenters, 22, 23, 29, 172, 204–6, 209–11, 289; justification by faith (*sola fide*), 6, 8, 29, 30, 35, 141–44, 146, 161, 166, 222–23, 284–85; and Karlstadt, 34–36, 42, 44, 45–47, 50–52; language, coarseness of, 99, 182, 235–36, 262, 263, 269; law and gospel, relationship between, 191–93; marriage of, 102; meeting with Schwenckfeld, 174–76; monastic

life, 3–5, 8, 89–90; and Münsterite Anabaptists, 149, 154–57; opposition to enthusiasts, 122; oversimplification of Luther's theology, 283; predestination doctrine, 4, 100–101; quantity and popularity of writings, 21; and religious tolerance, 201–4, 221, 222–23; return to Wittenberg, 42–44; singing and music as means of worship, 91–92, 194–95; social reforms, 38; *sola scriptura* (by Scriptures only), 6–8, 165–67, 222–23; on the Ten Commandments, 14–15, 55; "The German Confession of Faith" (hymn), 194; theological differences with Müntzer, 60, 61–63; threat of excommunication, 95–96; "tower experience" of grace, 5–6, 10; Trinity, doctrine of, 193–95; on un-free will, 102–6; view of Christ as judge, 4, 5; at Wartburg castle, 33–42; willingness to die, 118–19; and Word of God, 178–80, 184; on the Zwickau prophets, 37–38

Luther, Martin: lectures and sermons: "Admonition against the Jews," 237; *A Brief Sermon on Usury*, 85; exposition of John, 179–80; Galatians, 8, 192; "Indulgences and Grace," 13; "Lectures on Romans," 138, 230; Luke, 194; parable of the weeds and the wheat, 202–3, 208; Psalm 82, 204–6; on the Psalms (Jewish rejection of Christ), 230; against the Wittenberg radicals, 42–44

Luther, Martin: *Table Talks*: on Anabaptists, 141; on Bible study, 8–9; on Erasmus, 92, 108; on Karlstadt, 52; on nature, 92; on the Peasants' War, 81; on Rabbi Josel, 232; self-doubts, 10; the Turkish threat, 243–44, 245–46; Wittenberg radicals, 44

Luther, Martin: works: *A Blast Against the Archbishop of Mainz*, 39–40; *Admonition to Pray Against the Turks*, 85–86; *Admonition to the Clergy to Preach Against Usury*, 85; *Against the Antinomians*, 189–91, 196, 199; *Against the Celestial Prophets Concerning Images and the Sacrament*, 49–50; *Against the Eislebener*, 190; *Against Hanswurst*, 261, 262–67; *Against the Murderous and Plundering Bands Among the Peasants*, 77–80; *Against the Roman Papacy, an Institution of the Devil*, 261, 269, 270–72; *Against the Sabbatarians*, 229, 231; *A Letter to the Princes of Saxony Concerning the Seditious Spirit*, 65–66; *An Open Letter Concerning the Harsh Booklet Against the Peasants*, 79–81; *Appeal for Prayer Against the Turks*, 245, 256–57; *A Sermon Concerning Good Works*, 14–15; *A Terrible Story and Judgement of God Upon Thomas Müntzer*, 69; *A True Admonition to all Christians to Keep from Uproar and Sedition*, 41; *The Babylonian Captivity of the Church*, 17–19, 48, 90, 93, 202; *Bondage of the Will*, 290; *Catechism*, 102; *To the Christian Nobility of the German Nation*, 15–17, 55, 73, 91, 202; *Commentary on the Psalms*, 94;

Concerning Business and Usury, 85; *Concerning Rebaptism, A Letter to Two Pastors*, 120, 134–35, 137; *Concerning the Abuse of the Mass*, 39; *Concerning the Sacrament and Other Innovations*, 43–44; *Confutation of the Münster Confession*, 155; *Contra Henricum regem Angliae*, 99; *Exposition of the Magnificat*, 166, 179; *The Freedom of a Christian*, 19–20, 73; *The Last Words of David*, 232, 237; *News from Münster*, 155–56; *Ninety-Five Theses*, 11–13, 91, 202; *On the Bondage of the Will (De Servio Arbitrio)*, 102–6; *On the Jews and their Lies*, 225, 229, 230, 232–35; *On Monastic Vows*, 39; *On Shem Hamphoras and the Generation of Christ* ("On the Ineffable Name"), 232, 235–37; *On Whether Soldiers Can be Saved*, 82; "Preface to the Epistle of James," 9; *Secular Authority*, 55–57, 202; *Small Catechism*, 133–34, 136, 192; *Temporal Authority*, 245; *That a Christian Congregation has the Right and Power to Judge All Doctrine*, 57; *That Jesus Christ Was Born a Jew*, 228, 230, 231; *That the Words "This is my Body, etc." Still Stand. Against the Enthusiasts*, 122; "to all Christians," 51; *To the Councilmen in Germany that they Establish and Maintain Christian Schools*, 91–92; *To the Elector of Saxony and the Landgrave of Hesse on the Imprisoned Duke of Brunswick*, 268; *War Against the Turks*, 245, 246–48; *Warning Toward Peace Based on the Twelve Articles*, 75–76; *War Sermon Against the Turks*, 245, 255–56; *Whether Soldiers, Too, Can be Saved*, 245

Lutheran Church, and Luther's anti-Judaism, 225–26

Lutherans, commonalities with Münsterites, 164

Lutheran World Federation Assembly, reconciliation ceremony, 294

Magister conscientiae, 7

magisterial reformers vs. radical reformers, 23–25, 31

Manual Against the Lutherans (Eck), 277

Manuel, Niklas, 21

Manz, Felix, 26, 114, 117, 118, 124, 221

Marburg Colloquy, 195–96

Marpeck, Pilgram, 27, 112, 213

marriage: as Catholic sacrament, 18; clerical marriage, 16, 36, 107; divorce and remarriage, 144; polygamy, 153–54, 158, 251

Martin Luther (Grisar), 276–77

Martyr, Justin, 101, 130

martyrdom: of Anabaptists, 220; of Karlstadt, 47; of radical reformers, 29; as sign of God's approval, 220–21

Mass, reform proposal for abolishing, 39–40

Matthew, parable of the weeds and the wheat, 202–3, 208, 219

Matthys, Jan, 152, 153

McNutt, James E., 237

medieval mystics, 27

Melanchthon, Philip, 19, 33, 38, 45, 116, 120, 210, 230, 267, 290; Christian morality, and sinfulness, 143; *Loci communes*, 101; on Luther's writings against the Jews, 236; and Peasants' War, 74; and polygamy, 158; retraction of Agricola, 191; treatment of heretics, 206, 208; on the Zwickau prophets, 36–37; and Zwillig, 39

Melchiorite Anabaptism, 119, 151

Mennonite Anabaptism, 113, 119, 280; baptism, 24, 161; disowning of radicals, 123, 125–26; "Doopsgezinden," 115; excommunication, 212; and Menno Simons, 163; origins of, 115

Mennonite Quarterly Review, 281

Mennonite World Conference, 294

Mennonitische Geschichtsblätter, 281

Metaxas, Eric, 241

Metzsch, Joseph Lewin, 204

Modern Devotion (*Devotio Moderna*), 27

Moltmann, Jürgen, *The Crucified God*, 295–96

monogenesis vs. polygenesis controversy, 27

More, Thomas, 93, 99

Mueller, Hans, 212

Müller, Caspar, 79

Münster, socio-economic reform demands, 150

Münsterite Anabaptists, 26, 113, 286; adult baptism, 151, 160; beginnings, 150–52; commonalities with Lutherans, 164; differentiation between Anabaptists, 159–61; kingdom of, 2, 24; Luther's view of, 149; and the Old Testament, 153, 158, 160; polygamy, introduction of, 153–54; siege against, 153–54

Müntzer, Thomas, 2, 20, 26, 28, 49, 81, 84, 165, 251; Allstedt League, 60; and Anabaptism, 116, 120, 155; battle at Frankenhausen, 68, 69; as corrective of Luther, 280–81; *Fürstenpredigt* ("Princes Sermon"), 63–66, 128; historical views on, 69–70; influence on Denck, 167, 171; influence on Peasants' War, 53–54, 71–73, 74, 83, 285, 286; and Karlstadt, 37; letter from Grebel, 128–30; letter to the Mansfeld miners, 67; "Mystic with the Hammer," 69; origins of Anabaptism, 114; "Prague Manifesto," 59–60; radicalism of, 31, 58–60, 63–70; religious liberty, 203, 205; "spirit of Alstedt," 46–47, 68–69, 121; stages of observance, 62; and the Swiss Brethren, 124–30; theological differences with Luther, 60, 61–63; *Thomas Müntzer's Answer to the Spiritless, Soft-Living Flesh at Wittenberg*, 66; as Wittenberg radical reformer, 137

Murner, Thomas, 21, 90; *About the Great Lutheran Fool – and how Doctor Murner exorcised him*, 277

mysticism, 167; influence on Müntzer, 61, 62; medieval mystics, 27; of Swiss Anabaptists, 115

Nathan the Wise (Lessing), 211

Nazi Germany, and historical legacy of Luther, 239–42

Ndlovu, Danisa, 294

Nebuchadnezzar, 63, 65

News from Münster (Luther), 155–56

Nicene Creed, 193
Nigg, Walter, 44
Nigrinus, G., *Der Judenfeind*, 239
Ninety-Five Theses (Luther), 11–13, 91, 202

Oberman, Heiko, 7, 10, 232, 238
Oecolompadius, Johannes, 98–99, 183
On the Bondage of the Will (De Servio Arbitrio) (Luther), 102–6
On the Errors of the Trinity (Servetus), 197–98, 199
On Free Will (Hubmaier), 111–12
On the Jews and their Lies (Luther), 225, 229, 230, 232–35
On Monastic Vows (Luther), 39
On Shem Hamphoras and the Generation of Christ ("On the Ineffable Name," Luther), 232, 235–37
On the Sword (Hubmaier), 214–15
On War Against the Turks (Erasmus), 244
On Whether Soldiers Can be Saved (Luther), 82
An Open Letter Concerning the Harsh Booklet Against the Peasants (Luther), 79–81
ordination, as Catholic sacrament, 18
Osiander, Andreas, 167, 230
Oswald Glait, 231
Ottoman Turks, 158; advances into Europe, 243–44, 247; as agents of God's punishment, 246, 249, 250, 257; Battle of Mohacs, 245; and justification by faith (*sola fide*), 8; Luther's intolerance of, 22, 290–91

pacifism, and non-resistance, 26, 27, 28, 140–41, 162, 167, 212
pamphlets, quantity and popularity of, 21
pantheism, 198
papacy. *See Popes by name*; Roman Catholic Church
papists, and justification by faith (*sola fide*), 8
parable of the weeds and the wheat, 202–3, 208, 219
Paulicians, 131
Paul III, Pope: letters to Charles V, 269–70; *Against the Roman Papacy, an Institution of the Devil* (Luther), 270–76
Payne, E.A., 281
Peace of Augsburg, 204
peasants, oppression of, 31, 53, 75
peasants' revolts, history of, 71
Peasants' War, 20, 216, 285–86; battle at Frankenhausen, 68, 69; influences on, 53–54, 71–73; Karlstadt's participation in, 51; Luther's charges against the peasants, 77–80; non-peasant participants, 84–85; *Twelve Articles*, 57, 74–76
Pelagius, 100, 219
penance, as Catholic sacrament, 18
Pentecostal movement, growth of, 297
Pentz, G., 170
persecution: of Anabaptists, 117–18, 159, 161–62, 163, 203, 206, 210–11, 219–21, 287–88; differences between Catholics and Protestants, 219–20; of heretics, 218–21; of Jews, 233, 235; of radical reformers, 29, 279–80; and religious tolerance, 201–4

Peter the Venerable, 131
Pfeifer, Heinrich, 67
Philip of Hesse, 207, 210, 218, 230, 235, 246, 247, 263, 265, 266–67
Phocas, Emperor, 271, 272
pluralism, and tolerance of religious faiths, 22
Polycarp of Smyrna, 278
polygamy, 153–54, 158
poverty, as meritorious virtue, 86–87
"Prague Manifesto" (Müntzer), 59–60
Praise of Folly (Erasmus), 93
predestination, 105–6; and free will, 100–101; and human nature, 4; Luther's concept of, 102–4
priesthood of believers, 29, 31
Prince Joachim of Anhalt, 136
Prince Philip of Hesse, 154
princes: duties and responsibilities of, 54, 65, 75, 80–81, 207–8; duties of in time of war, 252–54, 258; feudal obedience to, 56–57
printing press, role of in Luther's writings, 21
Priscillian, 218
Pruystinck, Eloy, 186–87
Psalm 82, exposition of, 204–6
psychopannythism, 198

quietism, 114

radical reformers: communalism, 25; conflicts with Luther, 30–31; interpretative differences with Luther, 29, 289; vs. magisterial reformers, 23–25; medieval origins of, 27–28; misapplication of the gospel, 289; opposition to Luther, 25–26; origins of, 26–29; peaceful and revolutionary radicalism, 123–24; vindication of, 279–82; visible vs. invisible church, 25–26; as *Wiedertäufer*, 114; Wittenberg radicals, 34–36. *See also* Karlstadt, Andreas Bodenstein von; Müntzer, Thomas
rationalism, 20
rationalists: and Renaissance humanism, 25, 28; salvation, and predestination, 103–4
reconciliation, as Catholic sacrament, 18
redemption, through God's grace, 6
Reformation, 2–3, 289–90; and Christian morality, 141–44; consequences of Peasants' War, 82–84; divide with Renaissance humanism, 108–9; law and gospel, relationship between, 191–93; modern relevance of, 295–96; *Ninety-Five Theses* (Luther), 11–13; radical groups as "children" of, 28–29; radical interpretations of, 185–86, 189–90; and religious tolerance, 199, 209, 214–15
religious fundamentalism, birth of, 22
religious tolerance, 289–90, 293, 298; Anabaptists on, 211–14; and bridging of differences, 258–59; dangers of, 207–8; Luther's early views on, 201–4; modification of Luther's views on, 221, 222–23; during Reformation, 199, 209, 214–15; and September 11, 291; of spiritualists, 215–18
Rembert, Karl, 195
Rempel, Gerhard, 241–42

Renaissance humanism: and capitalism, 86; church–state relations, 139; divide with Reformation, 108–9; influence of, 25, 28
Restitution (Campanus), 196
The Restitution (Rothmann), 160
Reuchlin, Johann, 94, 229
Rhegius, Urbanus, 116, 120, 155
Rhenanus, Beatus, 90
Riedemann, Peter, 112
Riegel, Hermann, 182
Roll, Heinrich, 151
Roman Catholic Church: *Against Hanswurst* (Luther), 262–67; *Against the Roman Papacy, an Institution of the Devil*, 269, 270–72; baptism, 130–31, 265; comparison of papacy to Turks, 253; corruption in, 34, 291; crusade taxes, 245; doctrine of grace, 6; as false church, 264–65; indulgences, 11–12, 13, 93, 245, 248, 265; judgement of popes, 274–75; Mass, 39–40, 47–48; modern demands for reform, 295; papacy as the Antichrist, 55, 261; papal authority, 16, 55, 273; papal schism, 271; persecution of heretics, 218–21; pope as head of Christendom, 272–74; questioning of papal authority in *To the Christian Nobility*, 16; reformation as revolution, 2–3; responses to Luther, 21; sacramental controversy, 18–19
Romans: 1:17, on faith, 5; 13, on rebellion, 54, 64–65, 245; 3:28, *allein*, 9; 9:18, on predestination, 111–12
Rose, Paul, 238, 240

Rothmann, Bernhard (Bernt), 28, 152; and Münsterite Anabaptists, 150–51, 154–55; *The Restitution*, 160
Rühel, John, 69, 76, 81
Rupp, Gordon, 124

Sabbatarians, 231–32, 238
Sachs, Hans, 21, 143
sacramentarians, 133, 137
sacraments: Luther's definition of, 134; number and validity of, 17–19, 276
Sailing, Jonathan, 220
salvation: as inward process, 169; and predestination, 101, 102–4; un-baptized children, 132, 134
Sasse, Martin, 240
Sattler, Michael, 25, 117, 244–45, 246
Schaff, Philip, 107
Schelling, F.W.J., 297
Schleitheim Confession, 115
Schmalkaldic League, 262
scholasticism, 34
Schultz, Selina, 174, 180–81, 183
Schurf, Hieronymous, 45
Schwenckfeld, Caspar von, 24, 25, 50; *Answer to Luther's Malediction*, 181–82; Holy Communion, interpretation of, 172–73, 174; inner Word of God, 166–67, 177–78; meeting with Luther, 174–76; oneness of Christ, 181; religious tolerance, 217–18, 221, 281; *Stillstand*, 178; theology of, 172–75, 182, 183–84; twelve propositions, 174; and Word of God, 180–83

Scriptures: interpretation of, 16; law and gospel, relationship between, 191–93; *sola scriptura* (by Scriptures only), 165–67, 222–23; sovereignty of, 6–8
Secular Authority (Luther), 55–57, 202
sedition, 206, 207–8
Sefer Toledot Yeshu (*The Book of the Life of Jesus*), 235
Selnecker, Nikolaus, 239
A Sermon Concerning Good Works (Luther), 14–15
Servetus, Michael, 25, 196, 197–99, 221; *On the Errors of the Trinity*, 197–98, 199
Shachar, Isaiah, 236
Simons, Menno, 27, 28, 112, 115, 117, 195, 215; believers' (adult) baptism, 161; *The Blasphemy of John of Leyden*, 162; *Christian Baptism*, 131–32, 162–63; criticism of justification by faith, 144; *Foundation of Christian Doctrine*, 136; growth of Anabaptism, 119; influence of Hoffman on, 156; influence of Luther on, 161; moralistic legalism, 284; opposition to Münsterism, 162–63; pacifism, and non-resistance, 167; religious tolerance, 213–14; *The True Christian Faith*, 30
sin, and sinfulness: and Christian morality, 141–44, 145–46; freedom from in Christ, 19–20; hereditary sin, 206; of human nature, 4, 5; and the law, 189–90, 284; law and gospel, relationship between, 191–93
Small Catechism (Luther), 133–34, 136, 192
Smith, Henry, 211

Smithson, R.J., 211
social justice, calls for, 31, 53, 71–72
Society of Jesus (Jesuits), 276
Socinians, 28
Socinus, Faustus, 25
sola fide. *See* justification by faith (*sola fide*)
sola scriptura (by Scriptures only), 6–8, 29, 31, 222, 285; inner vs. outer Word of God, 165–67, 168–70, 177–78
"The Sorcerer's Apprentice" (*Der Zauberlehrling*, Goethe), 185
Spalatin, George, 39–40, 41, 42, 62, 121
Spengler, Lazarus, 170
"spirit of Alstedt," 46–47, 68–69, 121
spiritualists, 25, 183–84; Caspar von Schwenckfeld, 172–75; as devil's messengers, 170–71; Hans Denck, 166, 167–70; influence on Luther, 165–67; tolerance among, 215–18, 222; vindication of, 281
Staphylus, Friedrich, *Epitome of the Doctrine of Luther*, 278
St. Augustine, 34, 48, 89; baptism, 136; baptismal regeneration, 130–31; duties of temporal powers, 247; free will, 100; human nature, and predestination, 4, 103–4; persecution of heretics, 219; religious tolerance, 221; Word of God, 177
Staupitz, Johann von, 5, 143, 296
Stayer, James, 74, 83; *Anabaptists and the Sword*, 215
Steinmetz, David C., 50
Stillstand (Schwenckfeld), 178
Storch, Nickolaus, 36–39, 58

Streicher, Julius, 241
Strohl, Jane E., 143
Stübner, Markus, 36–39, 60
Süleyman I, the Magnificent, 243, 247, 254–55, 256
Suso, Heinrich, 27
Swiss Brethren, 26–27, 114, 140, 159, 212, 221, 286; baptism, 132; break with Zwingli, 116–17, 118; contact with Luther, 120–23; and Karlstadt, 122; and modern Mennonites, 123; and Müntzer, 124–30; social strata, 117–18; and Wittenberg radicals, 124

Taborites, 61
Tauler, Johannes, 27, 61, 62, 177
Temporal Authority (Luther), 245
Ten Commandments, 14–15, 55; antinomian view of, 188, 189; law and gospel, relationship between, 191–93
A Terrible Story and Judgement of God Upon Thomas Müntzer (Luther), 69
Tertullian, 48, 101, 130, 218, 221
Tetzel, Johann, 12
That a Christian Congregation has the Right and Power to Judge All Doctrine (Luther), 57
That Christian Princes Must Repress the Anabaptists by Corporal Punishment (Luther), 207–8
That Jesus Christ Was Born a Jew (Luther), 228, 230, 231
That the Words "This is my Body, etc." Still Stand. Against the Enthusiasts (Luther), 122
Theologia Deutsch, 166
Thirty Years' War, and Peace of Westphalia, 2

Thomas Müntzer's Answer to the Spiritless, Soft-Living FLesh at Wittenberg (Müntzer), 66
Tillmanns, Walter G., 162
tithes, 31
To the Christian Nobility of the German Nation (Luther), 15–17, 55, 73, 91, 202
To the Councilmen in Germany that they Establish and Maintain Christian Schools (Luther), 91–92
To the Elector of Saxony and the Landgrave of Hesse on the Imprisoned Duke of Brunswick (Luther), 268
transubstantiation, 47–50, 286–87
Trinity, doctrine of, 193–95
Troeltsch, Ernst, 29
A True Admonition to all Christians to Keep from Uproar and Sedition (Luther), 41
The True Christian Faith (Simons), 30
Turks. *See* Ottoman Turks

Unitarians, 25, 281
University of Wittenberg, 5
usury, 85–86, 88

Vadian, Joachim, 120
Vedder, Henry C., 41, 280
Verduin, Leonard, 113, 288
visible vs. invisible church, 25–26, 139
voluntarism, 211

Wadshut community, 140
Waldeck, Bishop Franz von, 150, 153, 154
Waldensians, 2, 27, 28, 29, 131
Wandscherer, Elisabeth, 153–54

War Against the Turks (Luther), 245, 246–48
Warning Toward Peace Based on the Twelve Articles (Luther), 75–76
War Sermon Against the Turks (Luther), 245, 255–56
water baptism, 132–34
Weber, Max, 86–87
Westerburg, Gerhard, 120
Westphalia, Peace of, 2
Whether God Is the Cause of Evil (Denck), 110, 168–69
Whether Soldiers, Too, Can be Saved (Luther), 245
Whitford, David M., 13
Widderruf (Recantation) (Denck), 169
Wilbur, Earl M., 193, 194, 195; *History of Unitarianism*, 281
Wild, Johann, 278
Williams, George, 187, 198
Wimphling, Jacob, 90
Wittenberg radicals, 34–36, 120, 286–87; influence on Peasants' War, 71–73; sermons against, 42–43; and Swiss Brethren, 124

Witzel, Georg, 278
Word of God: inner vs. outer Word, 133, 165–67, 168–70, 177–78, 184; law and gospel, relationship between, 191–93; Luther's conception of, 178–80; as weapon against Anabaptists, 119, 122–23
Wray, F.J., 112
Wriedt, Markus, 186
Wüst, Michael, 117
Wycliffe, John, 2, 27

Zasius, Ulrich, 73
Zell, Matthew, 182
Žižek, Slavoj, *God in Pain*, 296–97
Zuck, Lowell, 130
Zwickau prophets, 20, 36–39, 49, 60, 114, 137, 195; and Anabaptism, 116, 120, 123, 286; mysticism of, 165
Zwillig, Gabriel, 33, 39, 45
Zwingli, Ulrich, 24, 26, 48, 116, 118, 124, 175, 183, 210; and Müntzer, 124–25

www.ingramcontent.com/pod-product-compliance
Lightning Source LLC
Chambersburg PA
CBHW072143100526
44589CB00015B/2062